The Simplest Game

The Intelligent Fan's Guide to the World of Soccer

Paul Gardner

With a Foreword by Pelé

Macmillan • USA

For the Tahuichi spirit—and the boys who bring it to life

MACMILLAN

A Simon & Schuster Macmillan Company

1633 Broadway

New York, NY 10019

Library of Congress Cataloging-in-Publication Data

Gardner. Paul, 1930–
    The simplest game: the intelligent fan's guide to the world
of soccer/Paul Gardner: with a foreword by Pelé—[3rd ed.]
        p.   cm.
    Includes index.
    ISBN 0-02-860401-6
    1. Soccer.   2. Soccer—History.   I. Title.
GV943. G28   1996
796.334—dc20   96-16777   CIP

Design by Rachael McBrearty

10 9 8 7 6 5 4 3 2 1

Printed in the United States of America

Acknowledgments

Special thanks to Lawrie Mifflin for getting the whole thing moving, to Mike Woitalla for all sorts of crucial help with a whole range of soccer matters, and to editors Jeanine Bucek and Ken Samelson.

Thanks also to Peter Casanas, Keene Curtis, Sergio Di Cesare, Michael Gamarra, Lyn Fairhurst, Alex Fynn, Brian Glanville, Duncan.Irving, Gordon Jago, Paul Kennedy, Andrea Masala, Julio Mazzei, Terry Murphy, José Pekerman, John Sanacore, Graham Turner, George Vecsey, and Eric Weil; and to Keith Cooper and Andreas Herren of FIFA.

Rules of the Simplest Game was the title of one of the earliest sets of soccer rules, drawn up by J. C. Thring of Uppingham School, England, in 1862.

OTHER BOOKS BY PAUL GARDNER

Sports Illustrated Soccer (*with Phil Woosnam*)
Pelé: The Master and His Method
Nice Guys Finish Last: Sport and American Life

Contents

Foreword by Pelé		VII
Introduction to the Third Edition		IX
Introduction to the First Edition		XIII
1	Beginnings	1
2	The World Cup, 1930–1954	18
3	The World Cup, 1958–1974	40
4	The World Cup, 1978–1990	68
5	The World Cup, 1994	107
6	Soccer in the Olympic Games	137
7	Soccer in the Nineties	147
8	Tactics	178
9	The Changing Game	227
10	Soccer Comes to the United States	242
11	American Soccer: The Present and the Future	260
Appendices		
A	Glossary	276
B	The Rules of Soccer	282
C	The Members of FIFA	311
D	Worldwide Winners	314
E	The United States	336
Index		342

⚽ Foreword

The title of my autobiography is *My Life and the Beautiful Game*. Soccer, The Beautiful Game. Paul Gardner calls it The Simplest Game, and perhaps that's the same thing. The simple beauty, the beautiful simplicity that has made soccer the world's favorite sport.

The United States has done things in its own way, in its own time. For decades it resisted the call of soccer. But things have changed over the past thirty years. Soccer has been growing steadily here, and now I believe that its success in this country is inevitable. I see it taking its place, alongside baseball and basketball and football, as a major sport.

In 1975 I came to this country to play for the New York Cosmos. I was excited by the opportunity to bring the joys of soccer to the Americans. Everything pointed to a smooth triumph for pro soccer: the thriving, growing North American Soccer League, large crowds, a national television contract, worldwide interest in what was going on.

Probably I should have been suspicious. One of the beauties, the mysteries, of soccer is that things are never quite what they seem. Certainly, I knew from my playing experience that it is the most unpredictable of sports—that is part of its fascination. Suddenly, things went badly wrong. In 1984, the league collapsed. Soccer, said the pessimists, was finished.

Now, twelve years later, the United States is becoming an important player in the world of soccer. In 1994 it organized the most successful World Cup ever. And this year professional soccer is set to return to the United States.

No, soccer did not die in 1984. The NASL had planted seeds everywhere, and the sport was now delighting kids—boys and girls—all over this huge country. In the twelve years since the death of the league, the sport has gone on growing irresistibly at the youth level.

Today there are millions of kids and millions more parents and relations and friends involved in soccer in the United States. The beautiful game has taken root in this beautiful country. All the time that I and so many others have spent meeting with youth groups and giving instructional clinics over the past twenty years has not been lost.

I'm talking, of course, about the practical side of soccer, what we do on the field. But there is another side to the sport, another whole world of soccer. This is the world that Paul Gardner is writing about in this book. It is the story of the development of the game, of its great events, its great players, the story of all the marvelous things that have happened in the past and are happening today to make soccer the sport that it is. That too is a beautiful world, and from it Paul Gardner has created a vivid picture of the fascination and excitement of the constantly changing world of soccer.

The Simplest Game is not meant to teach you how to play the sport, or how to watch it, or how to coach it. Yet, when you have read all that Paul Gardner has to say, I think you will have a new and deeper understanding of soccer. An understanding of what we need to do to teach our youngsters the true, deep beauty of this game.

Whether you are an interested parent or a player or a coach or a referee or simply a spectator, *The Simplest Game* will help you to get more enjoyment from the sport of soccer.

Pelé

⚽ Introduction to the Third Edition

Introduction to the First Edition

Known simply as The World Cup, the World Championship of soccer has been played every four years (with an interruption for World War II) since 1930.

It has been staged by an impressive array of soccer-loving countries, including Brazil, England, Argentina, Italy, Germany, Uruguay, and Spain.

Now the United States can be added to that list. The USA, a supposedly non-soccer country, hosted World Cup-94 and made a magnificent success of it. Over 3.5 million fans crowded into the stadiums, the largest number since the tournament began in 1930.

The gloom-spreaders who had predicted that no one would turn up were royally routed. So far so good. But the difficult bit was still to come. When FIFA, the international body that runs worldwide soccer, awarded the 1994 World Cup to the United States, it expressed a strong desire, a sort of nonenforceable demand really, that the tournament should serve as the springboard for the launch of a pro league.

The thinking was that if the new league could move in quickly, if it could get going immediately after the World Cup, it could surely capitalize on all the excitement and publicity, it would surely be swept to success . . . well, that ideal scenario didn't work out.

Alan Rothenberg, the architect of the World Cup success, found that putting a pro league together was a much harder nut to crack. The idea of the league starting right after the World Cup was soon abandoned in favor of a spring 1995 debut. Then that was postponed by a year.

Which brings us to 1996. And now it's for real: Major League Soccer (MLS) is here, with ten brand-new teams, a 160-game schedule plus playoffs, and regular televised games on ESPN-2. Is the already crowded American sports calendar ready for this?

There is a school of thought, strong among soccer's most avid advocates, that America must be ready for pro soccer, that it is really years overdue. The confidence is based on the spectacular success of soccer as a youth sport in the United States.

Since the soccer youth explosion began in the 1970s, millions of kids, boys and girls, have grown up playing the sport all over the country. And millions of adults have been drawn into the sport as novice coaches or referees or bus drivers or league organizers.

Those millions are all potential ticket-buyers for a pro league. That is what the pro soccer brigade believes. Some go even further, depicting those millions as hungry pro soccer fans, disenfranchised by the lack of a pro league.

You don't have to go that far to realize that the youth soccer phenomenon is, inevitably, changing the attitude of Americans toward the sport. The traditional knock on soccer—that it is a foreign, virtually un-American sport—now makes no sense at all.

A dwindling number of reactionary baseball and football writers still stick to that myth. It surfaced occasionally during the 1994 World Cup. Sometimes it was mildly humorous, with references to soccer as "the great Albanian game" or a sport "played by 22 tortured souls—Dostoyevsky steals the ball and passes over to Kafka on the wing" (soccer names, it seems, are 'foreign' and therefore to be mocked . . . all this from writers who never had a problem with Csonka or Yastrzemski, Marichal, or Biletnikoff).

At its worst the anti-soccer sentiment came over as offensive xenophobia. In the *Providence Journal* columnist Jim Donaldson asked his readers if they were interested in "Morocco versus Colombia in the Battle of the Lowlifes? I can't wait to see the results of the drug tests after that one."

As it happens, there was no Morocco vs. Colombia game in the 1994 World Cup. But Morocco did play Saudi Arabia. Not by any stretch of the imagination a guaranteed crowd-puller in Giants Stadium, New Jersey. Yet over 76,000 fans, the vast majority of them Americans, turned out. And the drug tests were negative.

The notion of soccer as a foreign sport is in its death throes. Soccer is the world sport, and America, certainly at the youth level, has irrevocably joined that world. The question now is: can the MLS bring America up to strength at the pro level?

Nearly thirty years ago, in 1967, a similar enterprise was started: the NASL, the North American Soccer League. It attracted some of the world's greatest players, including Pelé, Franz Beckenbauer, George Best, and Johann Cruyff. But it folded in 1984.

Which is enough proof for the nay-sayers that the support for pro soccer is just not there. But even the loudest anti-soccer crusader would have to admit that there is a big difference between the 1967 American sports scene, and that of 1996. To wit: all those millions who have been, and are, involved in youth soccer.

The United States Youth Soccer Association (USYSA), and the American Youth Soccer Organization (AYSO) both reported a 25 percent jump in youth registrations over the two-year period 1994–5, which is perceived as a direct result of the interest generated by World Cup-94. SICA—the Soccer Industry Council of America—claims that 18.2 million Americans played soccer "at least once" in 1994.

As a measure of how many Americans play soccer, the figure is undoubtedly a fantasy. It is highly questionable whether anyone who plays soccer only once a year can be counted as being involved in the sport. More meaningful is the SICA figure for "frequent participants": 7.6 million. But the restless advance of the numbers has no time for such niceties.

The significance of the huge numbers is not to be sought in soccer terms. It lies in the fact that nearly 30 percent of the participants come from households with an annual income of over $50,000, or in the fact that 39 percent of the participants are female. That is what interests the sponsors and the marketers, and that is what encourages the money men to invest in a pro league.

The soccer value of these powerful statistics is much more difficult to measure. More interest in soccer, more people playing, has brought better competition and an overall level of play that is noticeably superior to that of 1967.

At that time, the level of American players was nowhere near good enough for a pro league. The reason was clear. The only training ground for young Americans was college soccer. And college soccer, suffering from a laughably short season, eccentric rules, and a general air of being a sport that didn't matter very much to the NCAA, was hopelessly inadequate as a nursery for professional players. The NASL had to be overwhelmingly populated with foreign players.

We are now in a different era. College soccer has gotten a lot better. And bigger. Of 906 NCAA Division I, II, and II schools, 642 have men's soccer programs (582 field football teams). Interest is higher and scholarships are widely available.

The vast youth-club network now provides the colleges with a pipeline of better and better players. While the United States Soccer Federation has been steadily enlarging its national team programs, giving the most promising players—starting at age sixteen—the opportunity to play top-level games against international opposition.

The MLS is banking on the college game now being good enough to produce players who can provide entertaining, pro-level soccer. About 200 such players are needed to make the MLS a predominantly American league, with a strict limit of four foreign players per team.

It is clearly a gamble. But it is a gamble that has to be taken, and it is a gamble that, for the first time in the history of American soccer, has a good chance of succeeding. The MLS has carefully avoided exaggerated claims for its soccer, stating that it will not be up to the level of the first divisions in soccer-power countries like Germany, England, or Brazil. But we are promised an exciting, attack-oriented, goal-scoring brand of soccer.

So American soccer undergoes another beginning. One can quite understand the scorn of the sceptics. But it has to be noticed that, from each of its past failures, soccer has always emerged stronger than before.

New York, February 1996

⚽ Introduction to the First Edition

It has often occurred to me that sport, like sex, is an activity that should be either performed or watched—but not written about. Both lose a great deal in the telling. Such thoughts I chase from my mind as quickly as I can. I do, after all, make my living writing about sports. But there is something to it, I'll admit. Too often we writers are the pornographers of sport: we sensationalize, we titillate, we expose, we try to create again the excitement of a moment. But how often do we come to grips with the real nature, the essence, of sports?

I am wondering, at this moment, about soccer. What is soccer? And I am forced to the conclusion that I am not sure. Not exactly the best way to start a book on the subject, but trying to define soccer is like Mark Twain giving up smoking—easy, he'd done it hundreds of times. And so with soccer, there are dozens of definitions and none of them really works.

It is, we are told, simply twenty-two men kicking a ball around. Yet to the aesthete it is an art form, an athletic ballet. To the spiritually inclined it is a sort of religion. To the sociologist it is an escape from the boredom of everyday life. To the Marxist it is a capitalist trap for holding down revolution. To the cynical it is a big business, to the psychologist it is a catharsis, to the social worker it is a way of keeping kids out of trouble, to the uninterested it is a bore. And so on, and so on.

I suppose each one of these tells us something about soccer, but even the sum of them falls lamentably short of the whole picture. The mind of the novelist does better. Listen to J. B. Priestley describing the game in his mythical northern English city, Bruddersford:

> To say that these men paid their shillings to watch twenty-two hirelings kick a ball is merely to say that a violin is wood and catgut, that *Hamlet* is so much paper and ink. For a shilling the Bruddersford United A.F.C. offered you Conflict and Art; it turned you into a critic, happy in your judgment of fine points, ready in a second to estimate the worth of a well-judged pass, a run down the touch line, a lightning shot, a clearance kick by back or goalkeeper; it turned you into a partisan, holding your breath when the ball came sailing into your own goalmouth, ecstatic when your forwards raced away towards the opposite goal,

elated, downcast, bitter, triumphant by turns at the fortunes of your side, watching the ball shape Iliads and Odysseys for you; and what is more, it turned you into a member of a new community, all brothers together for an hour and a half, for not only had you escaped from the clanking machinery of this lesser life, from work, wages, rent, doles, sick pay, insurance cards, nagging wives, ailing children, bad bosses, idle workmen, but you had escaped with most of your mates and your neighbours, with half the town, and there you were, cheering together, thumping one another on the shoulders, swopping judgments like lords of the earth, having pushed your way through a turnstile into another and altogether more splendid kind of life, hurtling with Conflict and yet passionate and beautiful in its Art. Moreover, it offered you more than a shilling's worth of material for talk during the rest of the week.*

That is getting nearer to the heart of the matter, because there is a suggestion of soccer as a living thing, something that survives after the game is over, something that is vivid enough to brighten the memory for years, so that we can all say of some soccer game "I remember . . ."

*   *   *

Thinking there might be a heavy fog, or an accident, or perhaps a strike—well, so many things can upset railroad timetables—I got up at 5 A.M. to catch a train hours earlier than I really needed. So I got into London around nine o'clock, leaving me some five hours to dispose of before I had to be at the stadium.

This was 1953, and in those days London on Cup final day was like a town under benevolent siege. There always seemed to be at least one northern team represented (that year it was Blackpool and Bolton, both from the north), and the supporters arrived in boisterous little knots, drifting about the streets trying somehow to make a dent in the apathy of the big city. In the narrow streets that used to surround Euston Station these working-class fans—they could have been Priestley's Bruddersfordians—were instantly at home, absorbed without trouble into the cheap boardinghouses and the sleazy little cafes, where their broad Lancashire accents badgered the waitresses endlessly, "Give us anoother coop o' tea, lass," and they talked about soccer. Not intelligently, but with the blind partisanship that had caused them to come all those miles to this heathen city, and to deck themselves out with huge rosettes and scarves and hats and even whole suits in their club colors.

The Good Companions (New York: Harper, 1929).

"It's Stan's year, lads, it's Stan's year, I bloody know it. I bloody told you so when we beat 'Uddersfield, I bloody knew it then, and I'll tell you now, bloody Bolton aren't gonna stop him. Who've they bloody got? Banks? He's a big ox, Stan'll make 'im look bloody daft, he'll wish he'd stayed home with the missus . . . how about anoother coop here, lass?"

Solid agreement from all his Blackpool mates. They had a London newspaper in which one of the writers had picked Bolton—"What the bloody 'ell does 'e know about it?"—the very idea, a London writer daring to give opinions about northern teams.

I sat for a while, a middle-class interloper, listening to them tear Bolton apart until it hardly seemed worthwhile playing the game. As it happened, I agreed with them. I had no ties to either team, but I wanted Blackpool to win. Just because of Stan.

I had first seen Stanley Matthews play maybe ten years earlier, and I had never missed an opportunity to see him again. He had shown me, as he must have shown tens of thousands of others, just how superb a game soccer could be. Any game with Stan in it was likely to be a magical occasion. His nickname, said the papers, was the Wizard of the Dribble. In the papers, maybe, but never on the terraces. There it was always just plain Stan. "Come on, Stan, show 'im. Stan." And Stan, stooping, balding, his face a blank but always slightly drawn—the only thing about him that suggested anything approaching effort—would show them.

At his feet, the ball was at home, comfortably nestling in absolute security, caressed with soft little touches as Stan shuffled his bowed legs toward yet another hapless fullback. Watch the ball, not the man, is considered the defender's golden rule, and you would see them with a mesmerized, almost frightened concentration on the ball as Stan approached. But how could you not watch a man whose seductive body movements seemed to telegraph his every move? Surely no one could lean that far to his left, unless he were actually going to take a step in that direction? And so the fullback would move, had to move, and all was lost. In one smooth burst Stan would straighten up and sail away to his right, leaving the fullback staring at nothing but air, or falling onto his back as he tried to turn while off balance.

Then the roar for Matthews as he headed for the goal line, the ball always just that calculated distance ahead of him where he could get to it but an opponent could not. Matthews was not a speedster, but I doubt whether anyone has ever been faster over those first few yards after he had beaten his man. There was never any hope of the fullback, even if he was still on his feet, catching Matthews. Usually another defender would come running across to cover, but this was just what Stan wanted. A player coming at full speed to tackle a moving Matthews had the most impossible of tasks. He had to get to the ball at once, and as his foot came in, Stan would pull the ball back and cut inside, or he would push it forward, what looked like just a few tantalizing inches beyond the tackler's outstretched foot, which he would step over as though it didn't exist, and complete his enchanted path to the goal line.

There the ball would be pulled sharply back and sent arcing into the penalty area where it would arrive like some gently falling bomb, always out of reach of the goalkeeper, always within reach of the attacking forwards surging in to meet it.

Inevitably, the torment of having to face Matthews invited rough tactics, and Stan was kicked and fouled more than most. The resilient, wiry body bore it all, and the stoic, rather sad face remained as blank as ever. He never had to be cautioned by a referee and, to my knowledge, when he retired aged 50, he had never retaliated, in a 33-year-long career.

What I and most of England—except Bolton—wanted to see was Stan being presented with a Cup Winner's medal, just about the only honor in the game that he had never won. This was Matthews's third final in six years: Twice before, in 1948 and 1951, Blackpool had been beaten and Matthews had walked off the field a loser. Now he was 38 years old and this must surely be his last chance.

The Blackpool fans had it all worked out; it would be 3–1 Blackpool when the final whistle went and I left them happily plotting Bolton's downfall among the empty teacups and the greasy plates. Pick another cafe and you'd have found the same Lancashire accents, wearing the black and white of Bolton, and telling you that Blackpool could put a hundred bloody Matthewses on the field if they liked, it was goals that counted, and "our Nat" scores goals, laddie—how many has Stan scored lately? And there was a lot of truth in that, too.

I walked into the West End, a different world this, of large smart, stores, one where little groups of fans stood out as foreign elements, and defiantly made all the more noise because of it. By one o'clock I was impatient. "You are advised to take up your position by not later than 2:30 p.m.," said my ticket, which left me ninety minutes to make a twenty-minute subway journey. But you never knew, there might be a delay of some sort, an accident. . . . By 1:30 I was at Wembley Stadium, proffering my ticket at the turnstile, holding my breath in case it was rejected as counterfeit (I had no reason to think it was; I had obtained it in the most respectable way, but you never know . . .)

My seat, I decided, was not a good one, too far to one end, giving an excellent view of one goal but a long-range look at the other. The stadium was already a third full, maybe 30,000 people, most of them gathered behind the two goals. Between them the famous Wembley turf, rich, green and glowing like a massive emerald carpet. A treacherous carpet, though, one that did strange things to players' legs. There always seemed to be cramps and pulled muscles and twisted knees at a Wembley final.

Community singing came next. Led by a military band standing in the middle of the field we sang popular songs and music-hall numbers until, with the stadium almost full and only fifteen minutes left, we were ready for sterner stuff, "Land of Hope and Glory," and then the traditional "Abide with Me," a solid working-class hymn sung with a fervor it would never command in any chapel. There is no real ending to "Abide with Me," at Wembley; the last note slides into a sustained cheer as banners wave and rattles rattle, a cheer that turns suddenly to an amorphous deafening roar of relief and expectation from 100,000 throats as the two teams walk sedately side by side onto the field.

More frustrating preliminaries. The new Queen Elizabeth, crowned earlier that same year, came onto the field to meet the teams—"As if she bloody cares, one lot's the same as t'other to her," said a Blackpool neighbor as the pinnacle of Britain's aristocracy and the nobility of its working classes met for a fleeting moment.

Then . . . a whistle, and an ever-changing mosaic of orange shirts and white shirts on the green, all commanded by the movements of a small light brown ball. Within two minutes, tragedy for Blackpool. Nat Lofthouse, our Nat, got the ball some twenty yards out and shot, an unimpressive effort that looked almost like a miskick. The ball spun across in front of the Blackpool goalkeeper, Farm, who went for it much too late . . . and went in.

While the Bolton fans rejoiced, poor Farm stood in dejected agony, engulfed by the noise his error had caused. Wembley nerves, I thought, something everyone knew about but something you didn't talk about for fear of inviting the worst. At least there was plenty of time left for Blackpool to reply. But within minutes the powerful Lofthouse was steaming through again, and this time his shot was hit perfectly, a searing drive that had the Bolton supporters yelling "Goal!" the instant it left his foot. Again, Farm hardly moved as the ball rocketed past him, only to crash against the goal post with a solid smack that seemed to echo around the stadium in a moment of quiet as Blackpool's fans were mutely awaiting the worst and Bolton's were drawing breath for the final triumphant yell. Blackpool were reprieved with their head on the block, but Farm looked anything but happy. "Go easy on 'im, Nat, the poor bugger's shell-shocked!" crowed a Bolton voice.

Then it was Blackpool's turn to roar. Down at the other end, where I couldn't really see what was going on, Stan Mortensen ("the other Stan" on the Blackpool team) got the ball in the net. A mistake by the Bolton goalie, they said, so at least the Wembley nerves were striking impartially. But before halftime, Farm had let through another shot he should have saved, and Bolton went to the locker room leading 2–1, having looked much the better team.

Matthews? He had done little, but then the same could be said of all the other Blackpool forwards. I hoped for better things in the second half, when he would be attacking the goal in front of me. Soon after the restart, Wembley's major jinx struck. Bell, the Bolton left halfback, was injured. In those days there was no such thing as substitution, so Bell, barely able to run, was left on the field as a limping passenger in the rather optimistic hope that he might prove a slight nuisance to the Blackpool defenders.

Within ten minutes he had done the impossible, leaping high to meet a center from the right to head Bolton's third goal. Even now, playing against only ten fit men, Blackpool were floundering. They were getting more of the ball, certainly, but their attacks were halfhearted affairs, quickly snuffed out by the Bolton defense.

With some twenty minutes left and their team apparently home and dry, the Bolton fans were in full voice, shouting cheerfully, "Coom on the ten men!," yelling derisively every time a Blackpool attack broke down.

But it was not the noise of the crowd that was to decide the game that afternoon. It was to be the genius of Stanley Matthews. The pressure on the Bolton defense mounted and always the ball was finding its way to Stan's feet, out on the right wing. I could see him cutting and corkscrewing his way through the left flank of the Bolton defense, stopping, accelerating, twisting to avoid desperate tackles, and now it was the Blackpool fans who roared, grasping feverishly at the hope that Stan was destined to get his medal after all, that he *must* bring off the miracle.

Another incredible Matthews run, going past defender after defender, an early center, beautifully judged to lure the goalkeeper out, and in the race for the ball it was Stan Mortensen who got there first to score. Bolton 3, Blackpool 2—one more goal (and it would be Blackpool's, for Bolton were in deep trouble, burned out as an attacking force) would send the game into overtime. But how many minutes were left? "Plenty of time, lad, plenty," said my Blackpool neighbor, but the minutes ticked away and despite all the Matthews magic, the trail of dazed defenders he was leaving after him every time he got the ball and the terrible tangles he was causing in the Bolton ranks, the crucial goal would not come.

I calculated there couldn't have been more than a minute or two left when Mudie, the Blackpool inside left, was brought down directly in front of the Bolton goal, some twenty yards out. Back came every Bolton player into his own penalty area to defend against the free kick. A wall of white shirts blocked off one side of the goal while goalie Hanson, crouching and rubbing his hands together, guarded the other half. Mortensen, one of the hardest kickers of a dead ball I had ever seen, aimed his shot at the top corner farthest away from Hanson. Either he had spotted a gap in that human wall or he gambled that someone would move out of the way of his ferocious drive.

Whichever, his shot flashed into the top of the goal, straight and unstoppable. All Hanson could do was to turn and watch as the ball bulged the netting and fell to the grass inside the goal. We were all on our feet now, Wembley Stadium nothing but noise as the late afternoon sun seemed to pick out the orange Blackpool shirts with a suggestively triumphant glow.

Time didn't matter now; the game would go into overtime and Blackpool, running riot against a demoralized Bolton, would be the winner. There was less than a minute to go and the ball had found its way back to Matthews, lurking out on the wing, just inside the Bolton half. With the ease of a skater, Matthews was away on another flexuous run, inside one defender, then past his fullback, racing for the goal line. Barrass, the Bolton center-half—and a good one—was drawn out of the middle to cope with the danger. The fatal error. Cutting in, Matthews ran the ball straight at Barrass until, just when it seemed the two must collide, there was that diabolical pivot, that almost ninety-degree turn on the run. The move did not get Matthews past Barrass, but that wasn't the idea; all Stan wanted now, having drawn Barrass out to the edge of the penalty area, was room to get the ball into the middle, and he created the space he needed with that one masterful swerve.

Matthews's center was the final perfect touch. Did he look up to see where he was putting it, or was it just a sixth sense, a soccer sense, that told him what to do? All I was saw the ball flashing low across the face of the Bolton goal, and I remember thinking, maybe saying, "Christ, no, Stan," certain that it must be intercepted by a Bolton defender. But Barrass, the key man, was out of position, and the ball ran through, untouched, until Perry, the Blackpool left winger met it at the far post and hit it, firm and low, into the goal.

With under a minute left, Blackpool were sure winners and from the roar even the Bolton fans must have been cheering, not for the goal, but for the man who had turned the game around, who had treated us all to one of soccer's greatest games. The roar was for Stan.

$$\ast \qquad \ast \qquad \ast$$

I would like to think that a day like that brings together all the things that make soccer what it is, that by describing what I saw and felt I have in some way defined the sport. But have I? Was that the real Cup final that I experienced, or is there another reality, the one explained by Danny Blanchflower, captain of Tottenham Hotspur, winners in the 1962 final:

> In truth we are all brainwashed about the Cup final. A player hears and reads a great deal about it before he ever gets there. He hears about the "Majestic" twin towers of Wembley Stadium ... the "Hallowed" green turf ... the "Royal" greeting ... the crowd singing "Abide with Me" ... it all sounds like some distant religious ceremony that takes place every year in the promised land at the end of the football season. The reality of it can never live up to the dream. The dream is not for the player. It is for the fan, the worshipper without whom there would be no professional game at all. It is for the lover of the game who doesn't really know what it's like out there on the field, and never *will* know. It is as *he* imagines it, a football heaven.

There is more than one way of looking at the Cup final because it is a special event, an occasion in which pageantry and intensely subjective qualities like emotion and excitement figure so prominently.

These are qualities that will vary greatly in intensity from individual to individual, qualities that can apply just as easily to any other sport.

Nevertheless, this idea of different people deriving different satisfactions from the same event brings us closer to the heart of soccer: its fluidity, its freedom of form, a freedom that allows it to be all things to all men. Soccer can be played in a host of different ways, each of them meaning something special to someone, each of them satisfying something different among the myriad sensations that give man pleasure.

Why should it be soccer, more than any other sport, that has this protean ability to take on so many different shapes yet still remain recognizably the same sport, to be molded and reshaped to please the whims and fancies of Italians and Scots and Turks and Brazilians?

Here I have a confession to make. After years of denying that there is anything like a mystique attached to soccer, I have changed my mind. There *is* a unique quality (mystique, though, is too strong a term) to soccer, and it is the obvious one: the fact that it is played without using the hands. This sets it apart from virtually every other sporting activity, and gives soccer its freedom, makes it such a pliable sport. It is free of the overwhelming influence of the hands, which inevitably come to dominate any ballgame in which they are used. In soccer, things are more complicated. The ball cannot be held and manipulated with a few easy, familiar hand movements like catching and throwing. It can only be *controlled*, a technique that may mean using the head or the chest or the thigh or the feet—the whole body comes into play with the feet, so to speak, calling the tune.

If it begins to sound as though I am describing a dance, rather than soccer, this is no coincidence. Are not both among the most widespread of man's physical recreations, both of them formalized yet full of improvisations, both of them showing national and regional variations?

Yes, soccer is a sort of dance, with the ball as a playful, slightly reluctant partner. And knowing that, would one expect the Brazilians with their sambas and their marimbas to play the sport in the same way as, say, the Scots with their reels and bagpipes? British soccer, says the Brazilian anthropologist Gilberto Freyre, is Apollonian, and "whereas the Apollonians have control over themselves, Brazilian football is a dance full of irrational surprises and Dionysiac variations."

It never does to stretch analogies too far, but this one lures to my mind two appropriate examples. I can't resist thinking of the England team that won the 1966 World Cup in Freyre's "Apollonian" terms. Here was a team that seemed to have complete control over itself. For many of us, it had too much control. It was disciplined to play unspectacular soccer, defending methodically and attacking cautiously with the probing patience of a skilled surgeon. Never once did the team lose its self-possession and abandon itself to all-out attack.

Bobby Moore and Jack Charlton, the two cool, unemotional center backs, typified the approach. Their job was to defend and not to put a foot wrong, and they looked capable of doing it for days at a stretch. Charlton with his long neck ("the giraffe," foreign journalists called him) heading away the high balls, Moore using his massive legs to break up ground attacks with superbly timed tackles. In front of them roamed little Nobby

Stiles, his front teeth left safely in the locker room as he played the destroyer's role, attaching himself with grim persistence to the opponent's star forward, yelling gummy abuse at friend and foe alike.

None of these three was required to do much in the way of attacking. That was done in the traditional English way, testing the opposing goal-keeper and fullbacks with long, high balls into the middle, hoping for an error. The mistakes came, and England won the World Cup because they took advantage of them and made so few of their own. Unimaginative they certainly were, and predictable, too—the inevitable price for their Apollonian control?

Four years later in Mexico it was Brazil that won the World Cup, and the contrast between their team and that of England in 1966 could hardly have been greater. The English press, always quick to criticize foreign goal-keepers, decided that the Brazilian Felix was the worst they had ever seen on a World Cup team. An absurd judgment, but even had it been true the Brazilians would not have been too concerned. They readily admitted their weakness in defense. Their strength was in attack. They were there to score goals. If their defense gave one up, well, they would simply score two at the other end. They did it all so beautifully because they had players like Pelé and Jairzinho and Tostão and Rivelino, who could fill the game with "irrational surprises and Dionysiac variations."

Mostly the ball was on the ground, tapped about with bewildering speed and skill between these agile, evasive Brazilians, stopping suddenly, accel-erating again, pushing the ball into gaps between defenders, gaps that only they could espy, all of it accomplished with a wonderful lightfooted, rhythmic grace.

Against England there was Tostão, close-dribbling into the penalty area, turning suddenly to chip the ball into the middle where Pelé paused just long enough to draw two defenders, then flicked the ball casually away with the outside of his right foot, direct to Jairzinho who drove it into the net.

This was the same Jairzinho who had waltzed, jinked, and twisted his way past a line of defenders to score an unforgettable goal against Czechoslovakia four days earlier. The Brazilians had scored four times in that game, but it is the goal they didn't score that hangs in the memory: the ball was at midfield, neither goal in any danger. Viktor, the Czech goal-keeper, did what many goalkeepers do under those circumstances—he wandered out toward the edge of his penalty area.

In a flash all was changed. Pelé had the ball and in one lightning, instinctive motion saw Viktor—some 50 yards away—out of his goal, and released a sort of half shot, half lob. Viktor was slow to see the danger until, at the very last moment he scrambled desperately back toward his goal posts as the ball floated just over his head . . . and wide. Pelé never did accomplish his oft-stated ambition to score a goal from the halfway line, but he never came closer than that. No other player, I am sure, could have sensed that situation so quickly and acted in the flash that it took Pelé to make his move. It was soccer at its most inspired. At its most Dionysiac.

The Cup final, the World Cup, these are the big occasions in soccer, and I am distorting the picture by trying to understand soccer solely in these terms. It is time to take a look at the lower levels of the sport, for one of soccer's greatest strengths has always been that everywhere it has gone it has quickly become a game of the people, the common man's sport.

The strongest of bonds has always existed between the fans and the players, the bond of a common background, a shared view of life. They grew up as next-door neighbors, even with the local club as their neighbor, the stadium nestling awkwardly between rows of working-class houses.

I always felt this intimacy particularly strongly whenever I went to watch the Rangers in what was then my hometown, Stafford. They were not, in those far-off days, very good—pretty awful, really, I suppose—but they were "our lads" and we used to turn out, a few thousand of us on Saturday afternoons, to see them do their worst. They regularly did their worst, but I don't think many of us were really very disappointed. We didn't go looking for heroics; we just wanted two hours of live action, a chance to shout abuse or encouragement and to talk soccer with each other, or even with the players if we could draw their attention away from the game for long enough.

Watching soccer at the Marston Road ground was like that, a social occasion without formalities or pretensions. Considering the surroundings, it could hardly have been otherwise, for Marston Road was not exactly a jewel among soccer grounds. At the beginning of the season there was a rectangle of reasonably healthy-looking grass, marked with spidery white lines, but that never seemed to last too long. The abiding image is of a strip of mud down the middle of the field, flanked by struggling patches of grass. Reading E. M. Forster's *Where Angels Fear to Tread* many years after I had left Stafford, I came across this: "a square piece of ground which, though not quite mud, is at the same time not exactly grass." Forster was describing a decaying Italian villa, but it was the Marston Road ground that suddenly stood before me.

If it rained and we wanted shelter there was, on one side of the field, a dark, brooding shedlike structure with a low roof that leaked, and over which the ball was forever being kicked. Just as regularly, as we waited for it to be reclaimed, would come the cries: "Never mind the ball, get on with the game." That was anybody's line; the first one to shout it got the laugh. It was the same with "Yours are the ones in blue, Alf," whenever a player misdirected a pass.

One afternoon the joke went around that a party of prisoners from Stafford jail was being allowed to watch the game . . . as part of their punishment. That was about as close as we came to original wit at Marston Road, but I still treasure one remark, muttered almost *sotto voce* by an elderly man standing next to me, as a Ranger player, not paying attention to the game, was caught yards offside—"Look at 'im, bloody mushrooming."

Most of the soccer in the world is played in an atmosphere like that. There is a human scale to it that, despite the crudity and the harshness, makes the sport something warm and familiar. It is vibrant and hardy, because it touches people's lives, not just once or twice a year, but every day. It is part of their existence, it is in their blood, and they feel for it as they would feel for a lovable, troublesome, sometimes exasperating member of their own family.

The affection explains the comic: the English player who, when the game ball bounced into the river, jumped into a canoe to retrieve it and was swept a mile downstream. In the meantime they found another ball, and by the time he had made his way back, his ten-man team had lost the game.

The troublesomeness explains the tragicomedy: the Italian who, upset by the things the fans shouted at him, decided he was not tough enough to continue as a referee and quit to become a Franciscan monk.

And the exasperation explains the tragedy: the French fan who could not bear his team's 0–2 loss to another local team and shot a rival fan twice, once for each goal.

Obviously, what lies behind each of these stories is some sort of passion. Love, hate, fear, jealousy, joy—it is impossible to imagine any sport without them. The question is, does soccer generate more passion than other sports? I think it does. Partly because it is so much closer to the lives of its followers than other sports, partly because of its worldwide appeal that makes it a vehicle for nationalistic fervor, and partly because of the nature of the sport itself.

Soccer is a sport in which low scoring is the rule. During a game there is a constant building up and letting down of emotions—expectations are frustrated far more often than they are rewarded. The scoring of a goal, the one goal that could decide the game, means the joyful, explosive release of dammed-up hopes for one group of fans, utter despair for the other.

I have been trying to define soccer, but it remains teasingly beyond definition, as elusive as the soccer ball itself. Yes, yes, I've given the flavor of the ingredients: a free-flowing ball game, a dance, a sport of the people, the passions, the frustration, the grace, the power, the humor . . . but the final mixture, the final proportions, that is something that each must create for himself.

When I want to reduce soccer to a single occasion, I think not of the Matthews Cup final, or indeed of any big game, or even of the lads of Stafford Rangers. I think of a hot, sultry summer's day in Sicily, some ten years ago. I had spent the afternoon among the glories of the cathedral at Monreale, but my mood of satisfaction and enchantment was broken by the bus ride back to Palermo.

The heat, the noise, the crowds, the fumes—as we entered the city, I knew I was going to faint. I brusquely pushed my way to the door, lurched off the bus, and stood for a moment or two watching it roar off in a cloud of gray dust. I had no idea where I was, but I was going to walk for a while until I felt better, then catch another bus.

I remember very little of the street. There were buildings, I suppose, some stores, then, after a few hundred yards, a gap that led to an open space where I could hear and see boys playing soccer. I walked over and sat down against the wall of a little hut, the only shade around. The boys seemed to be about twelve years old and there were, I eventually worked out, sixteen of them—they were difficult to count for the movement was constant. A whirl of sixteen little bodies chasing a battered lopsided ball would rush past me in one direction, then come roaring back in the other, giving off shouts and dust in about equal proportions.

The goals, I remember, were marked by little piles of rocks, except that one of the piles had an upright stick wedged into it, a stick that would periodically topple to the ground, at which the game had to be stopped while it was resurrected. The other important thing about the game was the far touchline, which ran along the top of a railroad cutting. Anyone kicking the ball over that not only had to go down and get it, but had to sit out of the game for five minutes. This I discovered from a boy so banished who came and sat next to me.

"American?"

"No, English."

"Ah . . . you know Bobby Charlton?"

The international language, the names of soccer's stars; we talked about the sport for a couple of minutes, when he jumped up and rushed back into the game, convincing everyone his five minutes were up, turning to me for support, because *l'inglese* had a wristwatch.

His name was Salvatore, and he was the undisputed star of the game; his skinny little legs with their incongruously large black shoes were everywhere, and he was a source of mixed wonderment and amusement to his friends. A hefty swing of his leg sent the ball spinning wildly off the edge of his foot, straight up in the air; never stopping for a moment, he ran around in a tight little circle looking for the ball until it dropped, like a padded thunderbolt, right on top of his head. One of the other boys who had been watching this brief scene suddenly spun around and I could see his face, pulled tightly closed, his eyes wrinkled up, his mouth stretched and compressed into a thin grinning line, his hands dropped helplessly at his side. He made not a sound, but I have never seen such a wonderful portrait of pure joy.

I stayed on to watch that marvelous little game until the shadows grew bigger than the players and it was time for everyone to go home. I was walked to the bus stop and put safely aboard amid promises to return, cries of "Bobby Charlton," and predictions that Italy would win the World Cup. And that was it. Italy did not win the World Cup, and I never did return to that dusty patch of waste ground on the outskirts of Palermo. Or perhaps I did, for I have relived that evening many times, a golden evening spent under the spell of soccer.

New York, 1976

Beginnings

Soccer people like to claim that the word *football* should really be applied only to soccer. What else would you call a game played with the feet and with a ball? Logical enough, but the argument is flawed. The word *football* came into use in England in the mid-fourteenth century to describe a game played not *with* the feet but *on* foot, in order to distinguish it from pastimes that were played on horseback.

In those early forms of football, the participants kicked the ball, handled it, ran with it, and generally moved it about in any way that they could—indeed, the most notable feature of the contests was an absence of rules. It was not until 1863 that a definite division was established between a game played with the feet (soccer) and a game played primarily with the hands (rugby). Until then *football* was neither soccer nor rugby but a brawling mixture of the two.

Trying to work out who first played football, and where, and when, is really rather a fruitless occupation. The basic elements—kicking, throwing, running—have been among man's natural urges since the world began. Games built around these movements have sprung up at different times and in different cultures throughout history. Some of the games we have records of and some, no doubt the vast majority, we do not.

Huang-Ti, a Chinese emperor of 1697 B.C., is supposed to have invented *tsu-chu*, a team game played with the feet and with a leather ball stuffed with cork and hair—possibly an early form of true soccer. A thousand years later the Japanese had a similar game called *kemari*, which may have been their own invention, or may have been their version of *tsu-chu*.

So it could have been the Chinese or the Japanese who started football, except that their games appear to have died out and there is nothing to link them with the modern sport. If the Chinese were not the originators, then perhaps it was the ancient Egyptians, in whose tombs were placed balls that *could* have been used for football. Or perhaps the Berbers of the seventh century B.C. were the first with their *koura*, a game that apparently served as a fertility rite to encourage abundant crops, but again, *koura* seems to have dwindled away to nothing.

The athletic-minded ancient Greeks had a ball game, *episkiros*, which was played on an area marked by boundary lines and involved both kicking and throwing the ball. We think we know what happened to this one: The theory is that the Romans, who were experts at borrowing Greek ideas and debasing them, took it over and turned it into a much rougher affair that they called *harpastum*. It was popular with Roman legionaries, and it is a reasonable assumption that they took it to England during the years of Roman occupation between A.D. 43 and 409. There is a legend that in A.D. 276 the residents of the town of Derby beat a team of legionaries at a *harpastum*/football-type game.

Which, however tenuously, gets us to England, the country that for the next 1,500 years is the scene of all the major developments in the history of soccer. It is more than likely that when the Romans arrived in England the Britons were already playing their own version of football. Something like the *koura* of the Berbers, games associated with fertility rites that were supposed to ensure lavish crops.

In some games the ball represented the sun and was ceremonially kicked across planted fields. In others, the "ball" was the head of a sacrificed animal, with teams from neighboring villages fighting for its possession so that they could bury it in their own fields. The original contests pitted the men and boys of one village—any number to a team—against those of another in a wild cross-country melee. The idea was to move the ball—evidently no longer seen as a prized fertility symbol worth capturing—into the opposing village.

Townsfolk saw no reason why the yokels should have all the fun, and by the twelfth century the ballgame had invaded the cities. In 1175 a London monk named William Fitzstephen described how teams of students and trades apprentices played a ballgame on flat ground just outside the city. Writing in Latin, he describes the game as *ludus pilae*—a game of ball—and his description makes it clear that the event was already a traditional one. Brother Fitzstephen doesn't tell us how the game was played, but he does tell us when: Shrove Tuesday.

A significant day. In the cities, the ballgames had lost their ritual meaning, and were now part of the festivities on Shrove Tuesday (Mardi Gras)—the day that was seen as the last chance for enjoyment before the restrictions of Lent.

Of course things got rowdy. Not everyone was as thoughtful as Brother Fitzstephen's players, who sought out a patch of ground away from the city center. The ballgame took to the streets and became a major menace to life, limb, and property.

Eventually, the authorities took notice and began to express their alarm at this uncontrolled monster that was threatening the law and order of the kingdom. A celebrated proclamation came down from on high in 1314 when King Edward II warned the citizens of London:

> For as much as there is great noise in the city caused by hustling over large balls . . . from which many evils might arise, which God forbid, we command and forbid on behalf of the King, on pain of imprisonment, such game to be used in the city in the future.

Still no mention of football in this, the first of a long series of attempts to put down the game as a public nuisance.

The attempts were invariably unsuccessful, a series of failures that make up the most convincing evidence of the remarkable grip that the sport had on the people. The proclamations themselves give us, at last, some reliable written evidence about the existence of the sport of football.

George Orwell wrote that he could never read the pompous official pronouncements of heads of state or church or whatever without also hearing in the background a resounding collective raspberry from the world's working men. Which was precisely how Edward II's splendid ban was greeted. Nobody paid much attention to it.

Things were no better in 1349, when an exasperated Edward III, needing all the help he could get in his efforts to annex France, took action. He was greatly put out by the thought of all those men who should have been practicing their archery but instead were playing "skittles, quoits, fives, football or other foolish games which are no use." He threatened to imprison them if they didn't get back to their bows and arrows.

So by 1349 the sport was not only a menace to public order, it was foolish and it was unpatriotic as well. It was also important enough to warrant its own name, and the word *football* entered the English language.

Succeeding rulers, Richard II, Henry IV, Henry VIII, and Elizabeth I among them, all slapped bans on the sport. But football flourished—often in unlikely places. Seeking somewhere other than the streets to play, football players found the space they needed in the local churchyard where, disgraceful to say, they were sometimes welcomed—and even joined— by the clergy. As early as 1364 the Synod of Ely had found it necessary to state that *ludus pilae* was not a sport for clergymen.

The church and the government were probably quite right in viewing football, as it was then played, as a menace. Clearly, it was a dangerous, crude affair that—particularly in the cities—could all too easily turn into a general riot with consequent loss of life and damage to property. There is no reason to imagine that writers of the sixteenth century, such as the diplomat Sir Thomas Elyot, were exaggerating:

> Football, wherein is nothing but beastly fury, and extreme violence, whereof procedeth hurt, and consequently rancour and malice do remain with them that be wounded, whereof it is to be put in perpetual silence.

Gory details of football's brutalities were the specialty of the Puritan pamphleteer Phillip Stubbs (though his chief objection seemed to be not so much the dangers of the game but the fact that it was frequently played on Sundays). After defining it as a "bloody and murthering practise," Stubbs wallows in the misfortunes that can befall participants:

> So that by this meanes, sometimes their necks are broken, sometimes their backs, sometimes their legs, sometime their armse, sometime one part thrust out of joynt, sometime their eyes start out; and sometimes hurt in one place, sometimes in another. But whosoever scapeth away the best goeth not scotfree, but is either sore wounded, craised [crushed], and bruseed [sic], so as he dyeth of it or else scapeth very hardly. And no mervaile! for they have the sleights to meet one betwixt two, to dash him against the hart with their elbowes, to hit him under the short ribbes with their griped fists, and with their knees to catch him upon the hip and pick him on his neck, with a hundered such murthering devices: and hereof groweth envie, malice, rancour, cholar, hatred, displeasure, enmitie, and what not els, and sometimes murther, fighting, brawling, contortion, quarrel kicking, homicide, and great effusion of blood, as experience dayly teacheth. Is this murthering play, now, an exercise for the Sabaoth day?*

An extremist Puritan position that even Oliver Cromwell didn't share—he was to be a keen player of football during his college days at Cambridge** in the early 1600s. But advancing years may have moved him closer to the Stubbs view.

Things were relatively quiet on the football front for the hundred years that followed Cromwell's setting up of the Commonwealth in 1649. Quiet, that is, in the sense of any major progress toward acceptance; things were far from quiet in the streets:

> *Here oft my course I bend, when lo! from far*
> *I spy the furies of the foot-ball war:*
> *The 'prentice quits his shop, to join the crew*
> *Increasing crowds the flying game pursue.*
> *Thus, as you roll the ball o'er snowy ground,*
> *The gathering globe augments with ev'ry round.*
> *But whither shall I run?*

---

* *"The Anatomie of Abuses,"* 1583.

** We know very little about that college game, but in all likelihood it was a toned-down version of the street game, with rules notable mainly by their absence. Evidently it had some prestige value. Sir Thomas Overbury, describing college life at Oxford at the end of the sixteenth century, notes that for the student "the excellency of his Colledge (though but for a match at football) is an article of his faith," a sentiment not unknown among contemporary American college students.

Thus John Gay, writing in 1716 on the dangers likely to beset anyone walking the streets of London.*

Football was still not a game for gentlemen, but forces were at work that would soon make it just that. There had always been, even when football was at its wildest, a few voices of reason that saw something other than wanton violence in the sport. Richard Mulcaster, headmaster of Merchant Taylors School from 1561 to 1586, was one who speculated that football must have something going for it, or it would not be so unquenchably popular.

The trouble, as Mulcaster saw it, was that the sport was abused. If only the numbers playing could be limited, if only somebody were appointed to control each game, then surely there would be an end to "the thronging of a rude multitude, with bursting of shinnes and breaking of legges . . ." Instead, football played in an orderly manner

> . . . strengtheneth and brawneth the whole body, and by provoking superfluities downeward, it dischargeth the head and upper parties, it is good for the bowels, and to drive downe the stone and gravell from both the bladder and the kidnies. It helpeth weak hammes, by much moving, beginning at a mean, and simple shankes by thickening of the fleshe no lesse than riding doth. Yet rash running and too much force oftentime breaketh some ineward conduit, and bringith ruptures.

Even if Mulcaster does make it sound like a patent medicine, his message is clear: Football plus discipline keeps you fit. This was the theme that, nearly 250 years later, brought respectability to football.

At the end of the eighteenth century, the public schools** in England were in a state of great turmoil. In many of them the boys themselves were virtually running things, and the masters found it almost impossible to enforce discipline. When they tried, a student revolt was the usual response, and at Winchester and Rugby the army had to be called in to restore order.

Games were a big problem. The boys were greatly addicted, and the masters greatly opposed. Even the gentlemanly game of cricket was frowned upon by the masters, while football was abhorred—a game, said the headmaster of Shrewsbury School "more fit for farm boys and labourers than for young gentlemen."

* Wherever they could, the authorities banished street football, sending it back to where it had begun: open ground outside the towns. Today a number of these "street" football games are still played (in open country, of course), in a tourist-attraction sort of way, notably in Ashbourne, Derbyshire (where it is known as Royal Shrovetide Football), and at Alnwick Castle, in Northumberland.

** A term that, in England, means exactly the opposite of what it logically should mean (and does mean in the United States). English public schools were and to a great extent still are exclusive private schools catering for the sons (and now the daughters) of the aristocracy and the rich.

Football in London's streets, around 1820. A hazardous anything-goes brawl for all ages. The authorities tried, unsuccessfully, to ban it. The first soccer rules did not arrive until forty years later. From an etching by H.Heath.
Courtesy of © FIFA Museum Collection

Credit for restoring peace to the public school scene belongs largely to the formidable Dr. Thomas Arnold, the headmaster at Rugby School from 1828 to 1842. He did it by allowing the boys to retain a considerable amount of self-government, and by making sports a part of the educational process instead of opposing them.

Football had been played at the public schools for many years before Arnold's arrival at Rugby. Although each school had its own way of playing the sport, a division into two main codes was already discernible. One code allowed players to run while holding the ball—this was the "handling game" that was to develop into the sport of rugby.* The other code allowed the use of the hand for stopping the ball, but insisted that the ball be advanced only with the feet—this was the "dribbling game" that was to become soccer.

* The traditional story of the birth of rugby is that one day in 1823 a student at Rugby School, William Webb Ellis, was playing football when he suddenly picked up the ball and ran with it to his opponent's goal, something that caused great consternation as nobody had ever seen the likes of it before. It is a story that should be taken with an enormous pinch of salt. In its early forms, football had always involved some use of the hands, so that the surprise of the onlookers seems somewhat suspect. The likelihood is that the Ellis story contains about as much truth as the legend that Abner Doubleday invented baseball. Precious little.

Arnold's reforms at Rugby were soon copied by other public schools that played a version of the rugby-style handling game. There remained, however, a hard core of influential older schools that stuck to the dribbling game—Eton, Harrow, and Winchester.

For both codes the arrival of respectability was followed by organization, and at long last comprehensive sets of rules were committed to paper. And suddenly the problem was not that there were no sets of rules, but that there were too many. Chaos ruled when students from different schools came together at the universities and tried to form teams.

The first attempt to produce one master game out of the many school versions was made in 1848 by Cambridge University. Those rules have not survived, but we do have a shortened version published in 1862 by J.C. Thring, ten rules for what he called "The Simplest Game." His second rule—hands may be used only to stop the ball and place it on the ground before the feet—makes it clear that Cambridge University wanted to play the dribbling game.

By now there was a deep division between the devotees of rugby and those of the dribbling game. It went beyond the obvious question of handling the ball. Another of Mr. Thring's rules, number three, pinpoints the problem: Kicks must be aimed only at the ball.

This was bound to incense the rugby enthusiasts, who considered kicking an opponent's legs—shinning, or hacking, as it was called—an essential part of the sport. The provocation was increased in 1863 when Cambridge University formulated a new set of rules that confirmed the bans on running with the ball and hacking.

The dispute came to a climax later that same year. The number of football clubs was growing, clubs formed by young men who wanted to continue playing after their college days were finished. A meeting of the leading clubs in the London area was called for October 26, 1863, at the Freemason's Tavern, Great Queen Street, with the idea of forming the Football Association (F.A.), which would regulate the game throughout the country.

One of its first items of business was to lay down an official set of rules, and immediately it was forced to realize that there were now not one, but two, games of football. They tried compromise—the first draft of the new F.A. rules allowed, under rather restricted circumstances, both running with the ball and hacking—but the differences were too fundamental to be papered over.

The final break came over the question of hacking. The majority of the club delegates considered it a barbarous practice and wanted no part of it. Yet a minority considered it vital to the sport—"Hacking is the true football game," said their leader—and, when they were outvoted, withdrew from the association.

If there is a date marking the birthday of soccer, then it is December 8, 1863. The day that the F.A. published its first set of rules—the day that the F.A. banned running with the ball and hacking.

LAWS OF THE LONDON FOOTBALL ASSOCIATION, 1863

1. The maximum length of the ground shall be 200 yards, the maximum breadth shall be 100 yards, the length and breadth shall be marked off with flags; and the goals shall be defined by two upright posts, eight yards apart, without any tape or bar across them.

2. A toss for goals shall take place, and the game shall be commenced by a place kick from the centre of the ground by the side losing the toss for goals; the other side shall not approach within ten yards of the ball until it is kicked off.

3. After a goal is won, the losing side shall kick off, and the two sides shall change goals after each goal is won.

4. A goal shall be won when the ball passes between the goal posts or over the space between the goal posts (at whatever height), not being thrown, knocked on, or carried.

5. When the ball is in touch, the first player who touches it shall throw it from the point on the boundary line where it left the ground in a direction at right angles with the boundary line, and the ball shall not be in play until it has touched the ground.

6. When a player has kicked the ball, any one of the same side who is nearer to the opponent's goal line is out of play, and may not touch the ball himself, nor in any way whatever prevent any other player from doing so, until he is in play; but no player is out of play when the ball is kicked from behind the goal line.

7. In case the ball goes behind the goal line, if a player on the side to whom the goal belongs first touches the ball, one of his side shall be entitled to a free kick from the goal line at the point opposite the place where the ball shall be touched. If a player of the opposite side first touches the ball, one of his side shall be entitled to a free kick at the goal where the ball is touched, the opposing side standing within their goal line until he has had his kick.

8. If a player makes a fair catch, he shall be entitled to a free kick, providing he claims it by making a mark with his heel at once; and in order to take such a kick he may go back as far as he pleases, and no player on the opposite side shall advance beyond his mark until he has kicked.

9. No player shall run with the ball.

10. Neither tripping nor hacking shall be allowed, and no player shall use his hands to hold or push his adversary.

11. A player shall not be allowed to throw the ball or pass it to another with his hands.

12. No player shall be allowed to take the ball from the ground with his hands under any pretext whatever while it is in play.

13. A player shall be allowed to throw the ball or pass it to another if he made a fair catch, or catches the ball on the first bounce.

14. No player shall be allowed to wear projecting nails, iron plates, or gutta percha on the soles or heels of his boots.

The split was finally official, and from now on the two sports went their own separate ways:

 • The dribbling game was now called Association Football—that is, football played according to the rules of the Football Association, without hacking.

 • The handling game was rugby football—it was to get its own organizing body, the Rugby Union, in 1871.

It was student slang, fond of dropping the end of a word and replacing it with "er" or "ers" (e.g., "brekkers" for breakfast) that coined the two words "rugger" from rugby, and "soccer," evidently based on the abbreviation Assoc.

Most of the Football Association's new rules, which were grandiosely called laws, were close to, if not identical with, those for rugger. Just four rules, numbers nine through twelve, were to give soccer its unique nature.

It was inevitable that the two codes would separate, but that the separation should have been caused by the question of hacking rather than by the use of the hands, is surprising and is worth studying for a moment.

Reduced to its essentials, the argument was between those who wanted soccer to be a game of skill and those who wanted it to include a hefty dose of sheer brute force. Those in favor of brute force disguised their intentions by talking of "pluck" and accusing their opponents of being rather sissified, and of liking "their pipes and grog or schnapps more than the manly game of football."

But the vote went against the self-styled defendants of manliness. The pioneers who founded the modern game of soccer were determined that it should be a sport in which skill was the foremost factor. It is a point of crucial importance in the development of the game.

Within twenty years, the London-based F.A. had its rules accepted throughout England and Scotland.

What really put the F.A. on the map—and, it could be argued, started the soccer explosion that was soon to envelop the world—was its decision, taken in 1871, to organize a cup tournament. The competition was to be conducted on a knockout basis, and was open to any team caring to enter.

A silver cup was purchased for £20 and inscribed with the words "The Football Association Challenge Cup." A modest enough trophy, but it immediately drew criticism from those who felt that the competition was a bad thing, and would encourage excessive rivalry among clubs. Soccer, it has to be remembered, was, at this stage, very much an amateur game for *gentlemen* amateurs.

The top teams of the day were composed exclusively of ex–public school and university players, all highly educated men who gave their teams names like Wanderers, Old Etonians (alumni of Eton College), and Old Carthusians (alumni of Charterhouse School).

As things turned out, C. W. Alcock, the president of the F.A. and the prime mover in organizing the cup competition, was the first person to receive the silver cup when the team of which he was captain—the Wanderers—beat the Royal Engineers in the final in 1872. (The Engineers was also a highly exclusive team, composed of nine lieutenants and two captains.)

Amateurs and gentlemen continued to rule the roost, both in administration and on the field, for another ten years, while the popularity of the F.A. Cup spread rapidly. In 1872 the competition had attracted fifteen teams, all from the south of England, and its final game had been watched by "nearly 2,000" spectators.

Ten years later the number of teams was seventy-three, and now they came from the midlands and the north of England, too. For the first time, one of the northern teams, Blackburn Rovers, reached the final where, before a record crowd of 7,000, they went down 0–1 to the Old Etonians. That 1882 final was, unknown to all concerned, the swan song of the southern amateur clubs.

The following year another Blackburn team, the Olympic, beat the Old Etonians in the final and for the first time the trophy was taken north where, it is recorded, they thought it looked like a tea kettle.

Behind the success of Blackburn lay two factors that were to revolutionize soccer in England: The game was no longer solely the province of the upper classes, and professional players (or "professors," as they were called) were beginning to appear. The Blackburn team was composed mainly of artisans—weavers, iron-foundry workers, plumbers, and a picture framer—plus two "professors." Immediately before the final the entire Blackburn team spent several days at the seaside, the nearest soccer had yet come to organizing a training camp.

Given the growing popularity of soccer, it seems certain that nothing could have prevented the rise of professionalism. It began in the industrial cities of the midlands and the north in a covert way, and many of the earliest "professors" were Scots who had come south in search of work and found that their soccer talents were much in demand. Soon clubs in Blackburn and Preston were deliberately importing such players, providing them with jobs, and paying them secretly after each game—a sort of soccer Santa Claus would go round the locker room while the players were bathing, placing money in their boots.

The very idea of professionalism was anathema to the gentlemen of the F.A. and, predictably enough, they bitterly opposed it. Their power was considerable. Any club that wanted to take part in the prestigious F.A. Cup competition—and what club did not?—had to be a member of the F.A. In 1883 the F.A. expelled Accrington for "offering inducements" to a player, and the following year Preston, a team that was heavily populated with Scots, was banned from the competition.

But professionalism was by now too widespread, too obviously successful, for the F.A. to stop it. When the northern clubs threatened to withdraw *en masse* to set up their own competition, the F.A. capitulated. At a special meeting in 1885, it accepted the inevitable. The situation was not after all exactly unprecedented, for there had been professionals in cricket since at least the early 1800s. Now there would be soccer professionals, too. They had to be registered annually with the F.A., which was adamant on one point: The professionals would not be allowed to serve on any committees or attend any meetings of the F.A. The gentlemen-amateurs, having given way to professionals on the field, were determined to retain the administrative control of soccer.

Popularity and professionalism brought their own problems, not least the chaotic state into which most clubs' schedules had fallen. Attempts were made to play a regular schedule of games, but they were continually being interrupted by the attractions of the various local and regional cup competitions, not to mention the F.A.Cup itself.

The Athletic News and Cyclists' Journal, a sporting daily published in Manchester, suggested a way out. Why not do what professional baseball had been doing since 1871 across the water in the United States, and form a league of the top professional teams? The suggestion was taken up by William McGregor, chairman of the Aston Villa club in Birmingham, who had been active in the fight to legalize professionalism.* Within six months he had organized the Football League, composed of twelve clubs, all from the north and the midlands. The first league games were played in the fall of 1888.

The men who ran the Football League were the same men who ran the clubs, mostly successful middle-class businessmen, a very different set from the aristocrats of the F.A. Yet there was no split between the two. The F.A. remained the overall supervisor of the game, the authority on the rules, and the organizer of international games—something that was to become, if not its most important, then certainly its most glamorous, function.

The first international game was played in 1872 between England and Scotland, the idea being that each country should be represented by its eleven best native-born players. The selection of the English team was made by the F.A. and included players from ten different clubs, only Oxford University being represented by more than one player. This is still the

---

* McGregor was a Scot, an example of the important role that Scots have always played in the development of soccer in England. Ironically, at this time the Scottish F.A. was still strongly opposed to professionalism, and had banned the 68 professionals registered in England from ever playing in Scotland.

method of selecting a national team, which is, in effect, an all-star team assembled only for international games.

The players selected obviously have to have the permission of their clubs to play, but because of the great honor involved, this was never withheld—at least not in the early days of soccer. In England, from 1886 on, the honor was, and still is, marked by the presentation to each player of a velvet cap, complete with long tassel.*

Wales played its first international game in 1876, against Scotland, and in 1882 Ireland joined in and was beaten 0–13 by England. The scope of international soccer at the end of the nineteenth century was not really international at all, for all four "nations" were simply different parts of the same country: Great Britain. It was the World Series of its time, the best not because the whole world took part, but because it represented all there was.**

Things were not to remain that way for very much longer. Soccer, so long an exclusively British obsession, was about to become a truly international sport.

But before we follow soccer's global spread, a look at the state of the game in England at the end of the nineteenth century is in order, for it was the English experience of that period that provided the model for the organization of soccer in other countries.

The most important characteristics of the structure of English soccer in the year 1900 were as follows:

1. The various quarrels over what the rules should say had been settled. In 1882, the Football Associations of the four British "soccer nations" (England, Scotland, Wales, and Ireland) had formed an International Board that was now accepted as the supreme authority on the rules of the game. Among other changes agreed by the Board, the use of the hands (except by the goalkeeper) had been completely banned, the goals themselves were now equipped with a crossbar and with nets, and the system of officiating had been changed from two umpires to one referee aided by two linesmen.

2. The sport was now professional at its top level, with a well-organized national league of thirty-six teams (eighteen in the first division and eighteen in the second division) playing throughout the fall and winter. Within each division, each team played all the others twice, on a home-and-home basis, receiving two points for a win, one for a tie, and none for a loss. At the end of each season the bottom two clubs in

* In England, the phrase "to be capped" means to be chosen for the national team.

** Well, nearly all. Teams representing the United States and Canada played each other twice, in 1885 and 1886. The games are not well documented. The United States Soccer Federation lists these games as the first appearance of the U.S. national team, but there is doubt about the representative nature of the teams.

Division I were relegated to Division II, to be replaced by the top two clubs from Division II.

3. Despite the strength of the professional Football League, the overall control of the game was firmly in the hands of the Football Association, an amateur body. The F.A. had, through the International Board, the last word on rule interpretation; all professional players had to be registered with it; and it was the organizer of the annual F.A. Cup competition.

4. The F.A. Cup competition was conducted simultaneously with the professional season, and was open to all clubs, amateur and professional. The names of all the clubs entered (by 1900 there were 242) were placed in a hat and drawn out in pairs—the two to play each other at the field of the first-drawn. The losers were out, while the winners went forward to another draw, and so on, until just the two finalists were left.

The Cup competition was immensely popular for a number of reasons. It provided an opportunity for small clubs to meet, and perhaps beat, the famous clubs. Each game was played in an exciting winner-takes-all atmosphere. Above all, there was the deciding game, the Cup final, a wonderful occasion of pomp and pageantry that was—despite the professional league championship—still viewed as the climax of the English soccer season. From the "nearly 2,000" who had watched the first Cup final in 1872, attendance rose to over 110,000 for the 1901 final.

5. The concepts of national teams and of international play were well established; from 1884 the national teams of England, Scotland, Wales, and Ireland competed regularly for the British International Championship.

That is the way it was over ninety years ago, and it is remarkable how little has changed since then. Maybe, just as in baseball, there is nothing new in soccer either. There was, in 1878, a soccer match played under floodlights in Sheffield. And by 1898 the professional players had formed themselves into a players' union.

At the turn of the century, soccer conquered Europe and South America with all the irresistibility of an idea whose time had come. Its spread was not a slow country-by-country crawl, but a sudden explosion. Within a decade, the game had sprung up all over the two continents.

Soccer had gained widespread popularity in England at the very moment when England was at the height of its maritime and commercial strength. English sailors were regular visitors to foreign ports, and English businessmen, engineers, and artisans often spent long periods living in foreign countries. They took their sports with them, and a pattern emerged that was repeated in country after country.

The sailors or the British residents would play cricket or soccer or rugby among themselves; if there weren't enough resident Brits, then they would invite some of the locals to join in. Cricket never really made it (it needed a lot of space, a well-tended grass wicket, and a fair amount of equipment, and the games could last up to three days), while rugby caught on only in one or two places like France and Argentina. But soccer—that was a different story.

In no time at all, the clubs that the British had founded for their own amusement were flooded with local residents who liked what they saw, started to play, and eventually took over the running of the sport.

What happened in Italy was typical of events in the rest of Europe. In 1887, Edoardo Bosio, an Italian businessman, returned from a trip to London, bringing with him to Turin a soccer ball and a vibrant enthusiasm for the F. A. Cup games that he had seen in England. His attempts to get other Italians interested in the sport were unsuccessful, until events in nearby Genoa changed the scene dramatically.

There, in 1892, a group of Brits founded a sports club that they called the Genoa Cricket and Football Club, but there was to be very little cricket in its future activities. At first there wasn't too much soccer either, for opponents were difficult to find. But whenever a game was played, crowds of Italians turned out to watch. For the moment, watching was all they could do, for the membership of the club was limited to Brits—until 1896 when James Spensley, a ship's doctor who was also a star goalkeeper, proposed that the club accept Italians as members, just fifty of them for a start.

The following year, the citizens of Turin at last took up soccer in a big way, and the most famous of all Italian clubs, the Juventus Football Club, was founded. In Sicily, at the southern tip of the country, English expatriates founded the Palermo Football and Cricket Club, another club that was to produce little cricket and a good deal of soccer. In 1898 came the Federazione Italiana di Football, the Italian equivalent of England's F.A. A championship was organized the same year, and was won by the Genoa Cricket and Football Club with a team that already included seven Italians.

The first decade of the twentieth century saw clubs springing up all over Italy—Lazio (Rome) 1900, Verona 1903, Naples 1904, Inter-Milan 1908, Bologna 1909—and in 1910 an Italian national team took the field for the first time, to score a 6–2 victory over France. Just two more stages—a Cup competition, which was started in 1922, and the arrival of professionalism in 1929—brought Italy level with England, at least in organizational terms.

Professionalism was introduced to Europe in 1924 by the Austrians; the Czechs had followed in 1925, the Hungarians in 1926, and the Spaniards in 1929, along with Italy. But in all these countries, exactly as in England, the game was under the control of amateur organizations, the local equivalents of the Football Association.

Soccer found its way to South America almost as quickly as it did to Europe; it was being played in Argentina in 1889 at clubs organized by British employees of the railroads, which were at that time British owned.

It was an Englishman, Alexander Hutton, who founded the Argentine F.A. in 1893 and who is thought of as the father of soccer in Argentina.

The founding of Uruguayan soccer is virtually told in the title of the first club, formed in 1891: Central Uruguay Railway Cricket Club. English railroad workers wanted to play cricket, but ended up as soccer players and the prime movers in the formation of the Uruguayan F.A. in 1900. Their club, which changed its name to Peñarol in 1913, is today one of the most famous in the world.

Football, in its original sense of a wild soccer/rugby melee, made its appearance in Brazil sometime in the early nineteenth century, in the streets of São Paulo. The usual riots ensued and the authorities clamped down, apparently with more success than those in England, for the game survived only as the name of a street—Rua da Jogo da Bola (which has also disappeared, renamed for Republican hero Benjamin Constant).

But soccer was brought back to São Paulo by Charles Miller, born in the city in 1874, of English parents. They packed him off to be educated in England, where he took up the sport. He returned to Brazil in 1894 with two soccer balls in his suitcase. These he took along to the São Paulo Athletic Club, a cricket club run by Englishmen. Yet again, soccer killed off the cricket, and by 1902 enough clubs were operating for the formation of a São Paulo League.

The events in São Paulo were being duplicated in Rio de Janeiro, where the first soccer was played in 1897 by the Rio Cricket Club. But the lack of good communications between the two cities made a joint league out of the question, and a separate Rio League was formed in 1906.

There was absolutely nothing democratic about the Brazilian game in those early days. The clubs were for high society; the players were composed of wealthy Europeans or the sons of well-to-do Brazilians. The game was described as a "refined and fashionable spectacle."

A foreign team—made up of Englishmen from South Africa—arrived in 1906 and beat the São Paulo All-Stars 6–0, showing that the Brazilian game was a little too refined and exclusive. The lesson was driven home four years later by the famous English amateur club Corinthians, which played teams in both Rio de Janeiro and São Paulo, and made a huge impression, winning all of its games comfortably—the Rio All-Stars went down 1–8!

A direct result of this tour by an elite team of ex-university students was, perversely enough, that soccer became a game for the whole Brazilian people. The Corinthians had barely left São Paulo when a new club was formed in the city and named after them—Corinthians Paulista, a club that included lowly clerks and factory workers among its members. Then came a few mulattoes, who were accepted as whites. The mulattoes were to be followed by a tidal wave of brilliant black players. The Brazilian national team played its first game in 1914, traveling to Buenos Aires and losing 0–3 to Argentina, and the cycle of soccer progress was completed in 1933 with the introduction of professionalism.

The widening popularity of soccer found the English only vaguely interested in what was happening. Foreigners could play the game, by all means, but they would never be as good as the English. Regularly, English teams traveled overseas to show the Brazilians or the Austrians or whomever just how the game should be played, and regularly they won all their games with ease. Thus confirmed in the correctness of their judgment the English stuck to their insularity—though arrogance more accurately describes their attitude.

When a meeting was held in Paris in 1904 to discuss the founding of an international organization to oversee soccer throughout the world, the English did not bother to attend, though they had been invited to do so. They were actually rather put out by the whole business, as they considered their own International Board (see page 12) all that was needed.

The English no-show was disappointing but hardly unexpected. The representatives of Belgium, Holland, Denmark, Switzerland, Spain, Sweden, and France went ahead anyway, and FIFA was formed. The acronym FIFA comes from the official French title of the organization: Fédération Internationale de Football Association. In English it is the International Federation of Association Football.*

Within two years England was a member of FIFA. One of her conditions for joining was that the British International Board would remain responsible for the rules of the game. By the time World War I broke out in 1914, FIFA had twenty-three members, including four non-European countries—Argentina, Chile, Canada, and the USA.

From the very beginning FIFA was unashamedly democratic in structure. Each country was represented by its football association, which had one vote. Except Great Britain, which was represented by the English, Scottish, Welsh, and Irish F.A.s and thus had four votes—but this was considered a price worth paying for the soccer experience and knowledge that these F.A.s brought with them.

Passing on that experience to developing countries was one of the functions of FIFA. But its main aim was to do on an international scale what the F.A. had done within England: to standardize the rules and to make sure that everyone was playing the same game. By 1913 things were going so well that the British even allowed FIFA two votes on the International Board. Just two votes, compared with Britain's four, but the move represented an enormous change in attitude by the British.

World War I temporarily put an end to the friendly atmosphere within FIFA. When the war was over the British wanted Germany, and its former allies Austria and Hungary, banned from FIFA. It was not a popular stand and the four British F.A.s, unable to gain any support, resigned from FIFA in 1920 and, for good measure, took away FIFA's two votes on the International Board.

---

* And not, as it is frequently mistitled, the International Federation of Football Associations.

In 1924, with the war over for six years, the British position was looking a trifle ridiculous. They backed down, and the four British F.A.s came trooping back into FIFA. But not for long. In 1928 FIFA—which was now running the Olympic soccer tournament—ruled that "broken time" payments (i.e. money to make up for loss of earnings) were permissible in that tournament. Britain saw this as a breach of the true spirit of amateurism, and once again the four British F.A.s marched out. This time, though, FIFA was allowed to keep its seats on the International Board, and reasonably cordial relations were maintained.

The British did not return to FIFA until after World War II, a period of almost twenty years during which the rest of the world not only caught up with, but surpassed, them in playing standards.

Not that anyone realized at the time what was going on. Throughout the 1930s England was quite sure that it was the best and, strangely, everybody else agreed. At first, there was reason enough. Up to 1929, England had played foreign teams twenty-four times, winning twenty-three of the games and tying one (this did not include games against Scotland, Wales, and Ireland, who were not considered foreigners).

Then, in 1929, Spain beat them 4–3 in Madrid, a result that the English shrugged off as a fluke. The Spaniards were invited to play in England in 1931 and were thrashed 7–1, and that showed just who was who when it came to soccer.

The crucial test came the following year with the arrival in London of the Austrian national team, the so-called *Wunderteam*, at that time the undisputed kings of continental Europe. England won the game 4–3, but there were many who thought the better team had lost. The English, having gained the expected result, paid no attention to the inventiveness of the Austrians' soccer and made no allowance for their nervousness. "What the English could not know," wrote Willy Meisl, an Austrian journalist who later lived in England, "was the incredible inferiority complex under which these early continental sides labored when they stepped onto a British football field. For them it was sacred soil. They were so overawed they hardly dared to put a foot down."

And so the English went on believing they had nothing to learn, and in so doing they missed out on the birth in 1930 of the greatest of all international sports tournaments, the World Cup.

–2–
The World Cup, 1930–1954*

One of the first things that FIFA had done at its inaugural meeting in 1904 was to proclaim that it alone had the right to organize a world championship of soccer. There was no talk of actually *starting* such a championship. The English, disdainfully following the proceedings from across the Channel, could dismiss the proclamation as mere words.

The English had tried to ignore FIFA. They had to admit their error within a couple of years. But they had learned nothing, and now they got things wrong again. The idea of a world championship was not to be ridiculed out of existence.

The desire for international competition had been growing rapidly throughout the early 1900s. The British should certainly have known that, for their club teams, both amateur and professional, had been playing exhibition games in Europe since the turn of the century. In 1904—the very year of FIFA's formation—Nottingham Forest had completed a triumphal tour of Argentina. The idea of national teams was spreading, too. Five countries were represented in the first Olympic soccer tournament in 1908, rising to eleven in 1912, and fourteen in 1920 when, for the first time, a non-European country (Egypt) took part.

In the 1924 Olympics, the Western Hemisphere joined in with Uruguay (the eventual winner) and the U.S., and the number of countries competing had risen to twenty-two. South American teams dominated the soccer tournament in 1928, with Uruguay defeating Argentina in the all-Latin final.

On the face of it, there was now a true *world* championship of soccer. It looked as though FIFA's grandiose assertion of twenty years earlier—that it alone had the right to organize such a tournament—had been swept aside by the International Olympic Committee.

Things were not what they seemed. In fact, the moment was tailor-made for FIFA. It now knew that soccer in the Americas had reached, if not surpassed, the European level, and that international games were crowd-pulling attractions. Both points had been conveniently demonstrated in 1924

* For tabulated scores of all tournament games, see pages 314–324. For tactical analyses of the World Cups, see chapter 8, pages 178–226.

when 51,000 fans had turned up to watch Uruguay beat Switzerland 3–0 in the Olympic final.

FIFA's trump card was the fact that soccer was now becoming a professional sport. The Olympics, with its strict insistence on amateurism, was forbidden territory for many of the world's best players, particularly those from Britain, Austria, Hungary, and Czechoslovakia, where professionalism had been legalized. The FIFA tournament would have the immense advantage of not having to worry about the impossibly fine distinctions between amateurs and professionals. It would be open to everyone.

Behind FIFA's determination to get its world championship started were two remarkable Frenchmen: Jules Rimet, who had been elected president of FIFA in 1921, and Henri Delaunay, its secretary since 1919. Between them, building on their experience in organizing soccer within France, these two provided exactly the right combination of vision, coaxing, arm-twisting, and ruthlessness necessary to transmute their dream into reality.

Delaunay set his proposal before FIFA's 1928 Congress: Preparation for the world championship should start at once. It was passed by twenty-five votes to five. The championship was to be held every four years, between the Olympic years, starting in 1930, a mere two years away.

Logically—because FIFA membership was at this time overwhelmingly European—it should have been one of the European nations that received the honor of being host.

But Uruguay, which had impressed everyone with its Olympic victories, wanted to stage the tournament to coincide with the hundredth anniversary of its independence. The Uruguayans backed up their bid with an astonishing offer: They would pay all the expenses for visiting teams, including travel to and from Europe, and they would construct a new 100,000-capacity stadium in Montevideo to stage the games. This was sweet music to Rimet's ears, for he had been worrying about FIFA's ability to finance the tournament. Bids from Holland, Italy, Spain, and Sweden were turned down. Uruguay it would be.

URUGUAY, 1930

The decision to hold the first tournament in Uruguay immediately raised almost as many problems as it solved. The four disappointed European candidates went into a sulk and decided not to participate at all. Their lack of enthusiasm spread throughout Europe. With the British nations ineligible (they had walked out of FIFA in 1928), January 1930 arrived with not one European team committed to playing in Uruguay.

One of the problems was that the boat trip to Uruguay took nearly three weeks, so that teams

WORLD CUP FINAL 1930
Montevideo, Uruguay: Uruguay 4 Argentina 2
Captains José Nasazzi of Uruguay (left) and Manuel Ferreira of Argentina
give the pre-game handshake in the Estadio Centenario, Montevideo. Belgian
referee John Langenus (center), nattily clad in plus-fours, looks on.
© Peter Robinson: The Football Archive

would be away for over two months. Neither the club management of the professional players nor the employers of the amateurs found that to their liking. The situation was particularly embarrassing to Rimet and he set to work to make sure that France, at least, was represented in Montevideo. The Uruguayans, after all, had made the trip to Paris for the 1924 Olympics.

In Romania, it took the royal intervention of King Carol, who personally selected the team. The European contingent eventually reached the grand total of four when Belgium and Yugoslavia agreed to compete, but not one of the major soccer powers—such as England, Hungary, Austria, or Italy—was represented and the Uruguayans were understandably piqued.

Uruguay, along with Argentina, Bolivia, Brazil, Chile, Mexico, Paraguay, Peru, and the United States, represented the Americas. The teams were divided into three groups of three and one of four, each team playing the others in its group once, and the four group winners advancing to the semifinals.

The United States was grouped with Paraguay and Belgium. The "Americans," who included a number of ex-English and Scottish professionals, received no praise for their soccer, but everyone was impressed with their powerful physique. "Shot-putters" the French called them. But the shot-putters beat both Paraguay and Belgium by 3–0 scorelines and found themselves, along with Argentina, Yugoslavia and Uruguay in the semifinals.

The lopsided results of those games—Argentina 6 USA 1, and Uruguay 6 Yugoslavia 1—confirmed that Argentina and Uruguay were a considerable cut above the other teams. The final would be a repeat of the 1928 Olympic final in which Uruguay and Argentina had drawn 1–1, with Uruguay winning the replay 2–1.

The new stadium, which had not been ready when the tournament started, was in use, but the crowd for the final was limited to 90,000. Thousands of Argentine supporters made the short boat trip across the Rio de la Plata from Buenos Aires, to be met by highly suspicious Uruguayan police who searched them thoroughly for weapons before admitting them to the stadium.

Before play could begin there was the matter of the ball to settle. The Argentines wanted to play with one of theirs, the Uruguayans insisted on one manufactured in Uruguay. Both balls were used, the Argentine in the first half, the Uruguayan in the second.

And perhaps, after all, the ball did make a difference. The Argentines had the better of the first half, scoring twice after Uruguay had taken the lead, while the Uruguayans dominated the second and, with three goals in the last half hour, became the first official FIFA world champions. The absence of the strongest European countries rendered the title slightly suspect, but the victory celebrations demonstrated that the Uruguayans were not bothered by such doubts.

As Jules Rimet handed over the trophy to José Nasazzi, the Uruguayan captain, the huge crowd sang the national anthem at full voice, then flooded out into the streets of Montevideo for a night of singing, drinking, and dancing. The following day was declared a public holiday, and each of the victorious players was given a house to mark the nation's appreciation.*

The tournament had not been without its dramatic and its farcical episodes, and most of them centered around referees. Before the games started, there had been a meeting of the fifteen referees at which all agreed on the importance of a uniform application of the rules and of dealing harshly with any rough play. Agreements, alas, so much more easily arrived at than put into practice. When Argentina met Mexico, the Bolivian referee clamped down on fouls so furiously that he awarded no fewer than five penalty kicks. At the other end of the scale, John Langenus, the Belgian who refereed the Argentina vs. Chile game, seemed blind to rough play until a general fist-swinging brawl broke out between the two teams and the police had to be called to the field to calm everyone down.

In yet a third game involving the Argentines, this time against France, the Brazilian referee reduced the game to a joke and the French to tears

---

*Meanwhile, back in Buenos Aires, Argentines were bombarding the Uruguayan embassy with stones and rocks.

by whistling for the end of the game at the very moment when a French forward was perfectly placed to score a goal that would have tied the score.

As the triumphant Argentines celebrated on the field and the disconsolate French trudged to the showers, a linesman rushed to the referee to bring him the bad news that he had ended the game six minutes early. Clapping his hand to head, the referee finally admitted that, yes, by golly, he *had* made a mistake. The police cleared the fans off the field, the French were recalled from the locker rooms, and the Argentines were persuaded that the game was not yet over. The missing six minutes were duly played, but the French had had their opportunity stolen from them, and there was no further addition to the score.

Despite the eccentric refereeing—something that remains a problem for international soccer today—the first World Championship of football was a success. Admittedly, the European press had cold-shouldered it, but it had aroused enormous interest in South America. It had produced a vividly exciting final, full of good soccer. It had even made a modest profit.

ITALY, 1934

Perhaps the most important achievement of that first tournament was simply to demonstrate that it could be done. Clearly, the tournament was here to stay, and almost immediately it was recognized by the Italian Fascists as a useful means to political ends. By 1932 Mussolini had been in power for ten years, during which time his regime had assiduously cultivated the idea of a return to the glorious days of the Roman Empire.

A rash of grandiose buildings, mostly post offices and town halls, was breaking out all over Italy as a sign of the new Italian greatness. Modern stadiums* were being built, too.

Sport was particularly suitable as a vehicle for the blend of pageantry and pomp and inflated nationalism with which Fascism sought to inspire the masses.**

What better political ploy than to stage and, of course, to win the World Football Championship? The Italians, whose bid to hold the 1930

---

*Many were of advanced design. They included Pier Luigi Nervi's Stadio Berta in Florence, an elegant example of the use of reinforced concrete.

** Fascism had, in fact, already applied its Italianization process to soccer, decreeing that the sport was not of English origin, but was derived directly from a medieval Florentine game called *calcio*. The word *calcio* is the Italian word for soccer.

One of the country's most famous clubs had been formed in 1899 by Englishmen and called Milan. The Fascists changed it to the Italian *Milano*. After the fall of Mussolini it was changed back to Milan.

tournament had been turned down, started lobbying as soon as it was over, and in 1932 FIFA granted them the right to stage the 1934 competition.

Since 1929, the task of selecting and coaching the Italian national team (the *azzurri*, or "blues," after the color of their shirts) had been in the hands of Vittorio Pozzo, a native of Turin who had become enamored with the sport while studying languages in England. Pozzo had been appointed after a disastrous 0–4 defeat by Austria. Until then the selection and management of the *azzurri* had been the work of an ever-changing succession of committees, but a look at the victorious Austrian team, which was virtually the personal creation of their manager, Hugo Meisl, convinced the Italians that they, too, should make their team the responsibility of one man.

Although he had never played the game competitively, Pozzo had a deep understanding of its strategy and tactics, and perhaps equally important, he possessed an uncanny ability to select the right players and to make them play the way he wanted. By 1932 he had already built Italy into one of the strongest teams in Europe.

The strongest, by general consent, were the Austrians of Hugo Meisl. The son of a wealthy banker, Meisl, like Pozzo, had been intended for a career in business, but, again like Pozzo, he developed an unquenchable devotion to soccer. His desk at his father's bank, where he spent as little time as possible, was invariably piled with letters and documents relating to soccer.

As early as 1905, Meisl was organizing tours of British teams in Austria, but it was not until 1927 that he finally extricated himself from the family bank and devoted his attentions full-time to soccer. Hugo Meisl's passion for soccer also infected his younger brother Willy, who was to become one of Europe's most respected soccer journalists.

Although Austria, in 1924, was the first continental European country to recognize professionalism, most of the players on Hugo Meisl's national team had outside jobs and were in effect only semipros. The best known were goalkeeper Rudi Hiden (who, appropriately enough for a Viennese, worked in a bakery) and center forward Matthias Sindelar. Known as *der Papierene* (the paper man) because of his slim build, Sindelar was the living expression of Austrian soccer, an artist who used his brain rather than his muscles, skill rather than force.

The Austrian style was modeled on the classic Scottish short-passing game that had been introduced into Central Europe by an English coach, Jimmy Hogan. Meisl, a great admirer of Hogan's methods, brought him to Vienna in 1912. Between them, they laid the groundwork for the growth of Austrian soccer, which reached its climax in 1931–32 with a team that beat Scotland 5–0, Germany 6–0, Switzerland 8–1, and—in a personal triumph for Sindelar, who scored three of the goals—routed Hungary 8–2.

The Austrian *Wunderteam*, unbeaten in eighteen games, was certainly one of the best the world had ever known. Even mighty England had struggled to beat them 4–3, in London in 1932. A scoreline that showed there was no longer a yawning chasm between England and the rest.

As far as the 1934 World Cup was concerned, the strength of the England team was of no interest. The British nations were still not members of FIFA, and would not be competing. The reigning champions, Uruguay, were also absent. They had pulled out partly as a snub to Italy, which had refused to go to Uruguay in 1930, and partly out of fear that their team had lost its edge and would not be able to retain the trophy.

Not that there was any shortage of countries wishing to compete; quite the contrary, there were thirty-two, and preliminary games had to be played to reduce the number to the required sixteen.

On the eve of the competition, the Italians got a nasty shock from the Austrians, losing 2–4 to the *Wunderteam* in, of all places, the new Stadio Mussolini in Turin. Pozzo was not perturbed; he had built his team with great care and was confident they could win the championship.

He had made full use of the Fascist theory according to which children born of Italian parents living abroad were Italian citizens. This convenient doctrine enabled him to recruit to his team four Argentines who were playing for Italian clubs.

These foreign-born Italians were known as *oriundi*. One of them— the rugged center half Luisito Monti, around whom the defense was built—had actually played on the Argentine team in the 1930 final. In the forward line was another Argentine, Raimondo Orsi,* the classic winger of the period, speedy, with magnificent ball control and a strong shot.

The star of the *azzurri* was nonetheless a native Italian, the Milan-born Giuseppe Meazza. Originally a center forward, but now converted into an inside forward who became the brains of the team, Meazza was the schemer who excelled in feeding his teammates with defense-splitting passes.

Right up to the last moment, it had not been decided whether Mexico or the United States had qualified for the finals. The two countries should have played each other in an elimination series, but couldn't agree on the travel arrangements between Mexico City and New York. The impasse ended with both teams traveling all the way to Italy. They played each other in Turin, the Americans winning 4–2. Once again, the Americans' soccer skill was considered negligible. The Italian press praised only their competitive spirit.

The Mexicans went home, while the Americans went to Rome for the alleged honor of opening the tournament against the hosts, Italy. The Italians, who had spent the previous six weeks in a secluded camp near Lake Maggiore, romped 7–1, and the *azzurri* were off to a flying start.

The knockout rules of the 1934 tournament meant that a team had only to lose one game and it was out. It was a particularly unhappy

* Orsi had played for Independiente in Buenos Aires. His acquisition by the Turin club Juventus in 1928 greatly upset the Argentines, who did not take kindly to their teams being plundered by the Italians. The Argentine F.A. made him sit out a year, without playing, before he was allowed to leave the country in 1929. The soccer drain to Italy continues today. Over 100 top Argentine players have moved there since the 1930s, including Diego Maradona, who played for Napoli between 1984 and 1991.

arrangement for Brazil and Argentina, both of which lost in the first round and had thus, like Mexico, traveled several thousand miles to play only one game.

Italy's next game, the quarterfinal against Spain, proved to be the tournament's hardest in every sense of the word. This was the Spain of the legendary Ricardo Zamora, the acrobatic and fearless goalkeeper who has remained to this day one of the great heroes of Spanish soccer, indeed of Spanish life. It was Zamora's superb agility that kept the Italians out and very nearly won the day for Spain.

Tied 1–1 after the regulation 90 minutes, the game went into an extra half hour. But after 120 bruising minutes it was still 1–1. There would have to be a replay the very next day, to keep to the tournament's tight schedule. Exhausted and battered, both teams were forced to make changes. The Italians brought in four new players, while the Spaniards had lost no fewer than seven of their team, including Zamora. Even so, it was not easy for the *azzurri*, who eventually scraped through on a lone goal from Meazza.

Next came the semifinal against the Austrians in Milan. The *Wunderteam* was two years past its peak, and Hugo Meisl, who knew that many of his players were not fully fit, was as usual pessimistic before the game. "We have no chance," he said. But most observers felt that these were the two strongest teams and that whoever won would take the trophy.

For the Austrians, little went right. Johann Horvath, one of their key players, was out of the lineup with an injury, and heavy rain had turned the field to mud, the surface least suited to their on-the-ground passing style. In the nineteenth minute of play, the Austrians fell behind on a goal that neutral observers felt should have been disallowed for a foul on the goalkeeper by Meazza; the ball had run loose, and there was Enrico Guaita (another of Pozzo's Argentine *oriundi*) to slam it home.

The lone goal was all the Italians needed, and 40,000 partisan fans, crowding right up to the touchlines, roared their team through to the final where they would meet Czechoslovakia, conquerors of Germany in the other semifinal.

Not among the favorites when the tournament started, the Czechs had impressed everyone with their skillful soccer. They played in the Austrian style, but with considerably more flair and stamina. They had had a comparatively easy passage to the final, but they were clearly a force to be reckoned with. Just before the tournament, they had beaten England 2–1 in Prague.

Rome, capital of the ancient and the new Italian empires, was the scene for the final, which was staged with a curious lack of Fascist ceremony. In their determination to make a profit on the tournament,* the Italians replaced pomp with parsimony and did without bands and parades. A Fascist salute from both teams, a handshake between the two captains,

---

* They were strikingly successful, to the tune of 1,440,000 lire.

Gianpiero Combi for Italy and Frantisek Planicka for the Czechs (a unique moment in World Cup history, for both were goalkeepers), and the game started under the glowering gaze of Benito Mussolini himself.

Both teams were nervous, but the Italians seemed to be more affected. The Czechs gradually took control of the game but could not score until twenty-six minutes into the second half, when their left winger Antonin Puc at last drove the ball into the Italian net. Czechoslovakia piled on the pressure and Svoboda crashed the ball past Combi, only to see it hit the post. The Italians were in deep trouble, and it took a moment of incredible luck to get them back in the game. With less than ten minutes to go, Orsi tried a rather hopeful right-footed shot from his left-wing position. Spinning and swerving, the ball escaped Planicka's lunge, and the Italians had tied the score.

Thirty minutes of overtime was something that the Italians—who had played one more game than the Czechs, that grueling replay against Spain—could have done without. But they got a quick goal—after only five minutes, Angelo Schiavio took a pass from Guaita and drove the ball past Planicka. In the test of stamina and will that followed, it was the Italians, sustained by the roar of the crowd, who proved slightly the stronger of two exhausted teams. They held on for a 2–1 victory.

Mussolini, who was never known to show the slightest interest in soccer, changed his glower to a smile, and applauded. Obviously, the Fascist way had triumphed. Jules Rimet, who had been trying unsuccessfully throughout the game to engage Mussolini in conversation, went down to the field and presented the cup to Combi. For the second time, the host nation had won the championship.

FRANCE, 1938

Jules Rimet brought the World Football Championship to his homeland, France, in 1938. A brave move, because soccer was but one of three major sports in France (rugby and cycling were the others). It was not a national passion as it was for the Uruguayans and the Italians.

There was no longer any doubt about the popularity of the championship itself. Thirteen countries had entered in 1930, thirty-two in 1934, and now thirty-six for the 1938 edition. Preliminary games were again required to whittle the number down to the required sixteen.

But there was another force at work reducing the entrants. Fascism, an irritating shadow during the 1934 games, was now a threatening black cloud. Spain, on the rack of civil war, was a nonstarter. Then, two months before the tournament was due to start, the Austrians, who had already qualified for the final sixteen, informed FIFA that their country—and hence their soccer team—no longer existed. *Anschluss* had made them part of Nazi Germany.

The tournament was played with only fifteen countries,* the missing Austrian team an ominous reminder that sport and politics were inextricably mixed. There were, however, four Austrian players present who had been drafted into the German team. What the Italians could do with "their" Argentines, the Germans could do with "their" Austrians, and, for that matter, the French, who included an Algerian, could do with "their" colonials.

Of the Italian team that had won in 1934, only two players remained, Giovanni Ferrari and Meazza, now the captain. Pozzo was still in charge. In the 1936 Berlin Olympic soccer tournament he had led Italy to victory with a team of questionable (to say the least) amateurs, and he now included three of those players in his World Cup team. All the Italian–Argentines had gone, and the only *oriundo* was now center half Michele Andreolo, a Uruguayan. Silvio Piola, the tall and powerfully athletic young center forward from the Rome club Lazio, was a new star.

The championship opened sensationally in Paris when Germany, Austrian stars and all, was held to a draw by little Switzerland. An embarrassing result for the Third Reich, which was quickly made worse when Switzerland won the replay easily, 4–2. The Germans went home in disgrace, but their coach Sepp Herberger (who had opposed the addition of Austrians to his team) survived. We shall meet him again in this story.

Sensation in Paris . . . and very nearly in Marseilles, where Italy met Norway. Before the kickoff the *azzurri* lined up to give their Fascist salute and were enthusiastically booed by a large contingent of political exiles from Mussolini's Italy. From then on it was the Norwegians who caused all the trouble. After Italy had scored first, the Norwegians piled on the pressure. They hit the goalposts three times and had a goal disallowed for offside, before tying the game with seven minutes left. Two minutes from the end it needed a near-miraculous save from the Italian goalkeeper, Aldo Olivieri, to keep them out. In extra time, the wily Piola snatched a goal, and the Italians staggered through to the next round to play France.

It was obvious to all that there was something wrong with the Italian team, but Pozzo knew immediately what that something was. He made three changes in the lineup and suddenly the *azzurri* looked irresistible, sweeping aside the French hosts 3–1 with nonchalant ease.

In the semifinal, the Italians would be up against Brazil, a team that bristled with individual talent but that had made heavy going of its first two games. First Brazil had beaten Poland, but only after extra time, by the extraordinary score of 6–5. Four of the Brazilian goals had come from their brilliant center forward Leônidas, the Black Diamond, famed for his

---

* England, still not a member of FIFA, was invited to fill Austria's place, but predictably declined.

WORLD CUP FINAL 1938
Paris, France: Italy 4 Hungary 2
Coach Vittorio Pozzo, surrounded by his victorious Italian team, raises the
World Cup trophy. Pozzo was also the coach when Italy won the 1934 World
Cup—making him the only coach ever to have won the trophy twice.
© Peter Robinson: The Football Archive

acrobatic bicycle kick. The next game, against Czechoslovakia, quickly
degenerated into a brawl; one Czech and two Brazilians were sent off,
extra time was played, but the score remained tied at 1–1. The Brazilians
won the replay with a team containing nine new players.

But the price was high. Leônidas was exhausted and could not play
against Italy. Coach Ademar Pimenta then shocked everyone by omitting
another star forward—Tim—from his team.

The story that both were being rested for the final was no doubt an
exaggeration, but Brazilian confidence was certainly at a high level, as the
celebrated incident of the flight reservations demonstrated.

Due to play Italy in Marseilles, the Brazilians had booked all the seats
on the only subsequent flight available to Paris, where the final would be
played. When Pozzo went to see them, suggesting it would be better if the
seats were made available to whoever should win the semifinal, the Brazilians professed amazement. Such an arrangement would be quite unneces-
sary, as they would win. "Then I'm sorry to have troubled you," said Pozzo.
Ever looking for psychological advantages, Pozzo used the story to fire up
his team.

Piola was singled out by the Brazilians as the Italian danger man.
Throughout a scoreless first half he was closely marked by the splendid
black defender Domingos da Guia. The second half was a different story.

Piola began to wander, to draw Domingos da Guia out of position, and winger Colaussi raced in to score. Four minutes later Domingos da Guia and Piola exchanged kicks inside the Brazilian penalty area. Play was going on downfield, but the referee saw the exasperated Domingos da Guia bring Piola crashing to the ground. He awarded the penalty kick, from which Meazza scored the winning goal. Although they scored a consolation goal late in the game, the Brazilians did not need their plane reservations.

It was the Italians who traveled to Paris for the final against Hungary. A clash of styles: the older, more methodical, more artistic play of the Hungarians against the swifter, more direct Italians, noted for the deadly efficiency of their sudden counterattacks. The final score, 4–2 to Italy, was a fair reflection of the way the Italians had dominated the game. The perfect understanding of the Italian trio of inside forwards—Meazza, Piola, and Ferrari—was too much for the Hungarians. Piola scored twice, while Meazza had one of the finest games of his career. Fittingly, he was the man to receive the trophy from French President Albert Lebrun.

Pondering on his two World Cup–winning teams, Pozzo later said that the 1938 team could have beaten England if the game were to be played anywhere but in England. The chance to test his boast was never there. In September 1939 Europe went to war, and World Cup soccer disappeared for twelve years.

BRAZIL, 1950

Devastated by six years of war, Europe in 1950 was busy rebuilding its cities and industries; soccer stadiums were not high on the priority list. Not so in Brazil, where the Fourth World Football Championship was to be staged. An enormous 175,000-capacity stadium, Maracaná, was being frantically erected in Rio de Janeiro, to be ready in time for the opening game on June 24.

Despite FIFA's record membership of 65 nations, it wasn't easy finding sixteen finalists. The war had left political and economic casualties in its wake. The Soviet Union, which had joined FIFA for the first time in 1946, snubbed the tournament and all the Eastern European countries followed suit, except Yugoslavia.

In a satisfying reversal of the 1938 situation, Germany was suspended by FIFA, while Austria was free to enter; but the Austrians dropped out with the excuse that their team was too inexperienced. When Scotland and Turkey, which had both qualified, decided not to compete, Portugal and France were invited to replace them. The Portuguese said no. The French said yes, until they discovered how much traveling they would have to do within Brazil. Then they, too, declined.

The result of all the jockeying was that the tournament got under way with only thirteen teams. Instead of four groups of four, there were now two groups of four, one of three, and one with only two teams—Uruguay and Bolivia. This last coupling was a concession by the Brazilian organizers to the Uruguayan F.A., which was having financial problems. Uruguay had to play only one, absurdly easy, game in the first round—they beat Bolivia 8–0—a piece of generosity that the Brazilians were later to regret bitterly.

The big story of the 1950 World Cup was not the teams that were absent, but the one that was present: England. Having rejoined FIFA in 1945, the English—*i maestri*, the masters, as the Italians called them—decided at last to test themselves in World Cup competition. Just before the tournament, the team lost key defender Neil Franklin. He joined Independiente-Santa Fe in the Colombian outlaw league,* a move that made him ineligible for international games. But the team was still a powerful one. It included two of the most renowned names in the history of English soccer: Stanley Matthews, dribbler *extraordinaire,* still, at the age of 35, one of the most dangerous forwards in the game; and Tom Finney, perhaps the most complete all-around player ever to wear an England shirt.

Italy, the Cup holder, was rebuilding its team after the Superga air disaster of 1949,** and the new team had been playing surprisingly well. Coach Pozzo had retired, but because it was playing in a relatively weak group along with Sweden and Paraguay, Italy was expected to go through to the final round without too much trouble.

Brazil was the joint favorite with England, partly because it was playing on its home turf, but mostly because of the impression its immensely talented if somewhat undisciplined players had made in the 1938 World Cup. The 1950 Brazilian team was considered the best ever, with a blend at last of individualism and teamwork.

Upsets were not exactly unknown in World Cup play, but the 1950 competition outdid itself in shock results. In its first game, Italy went down 2–3 to Sweden. When they went on to tie Paraguay, the Swedes, unfancied to say the least, became the group winners and Italy was out of the tournament.

Nobody was paying much attention to the Americans, a team of part-timers, that included an undertaker, a carpenter, a teacher, two

---

*See chapter 7, page 173.

** Between 1945 and 1949, when the Italian national team had a 7–2–1 record, it was composed mainly of members of the Torino club team. It once included ten Torino players, never fewer than five. On May 4, 1949, Torino was returning from a game against Benfica in Lisbon when, in thick fog, its plane crashed into a hill at Superga, on the outskirts of Turin. There were no survivors. The entire team, the manager, trainer, and coach were killed. The Italian Soccer Federation awarded the 1949 championship to Torino, and the victims were given a state funeral. The memory of the tragedy was still very much alive in 1950, and the Italian team traveled to Brazil by boat.

mailmen, a machinist, an interior decorator, and a factory worker. In 1930 the Americans had stood out for their massive physique: the shot-putters. In 1934 they had been praised for their competitive spirit. The 1950 team had no distinguishing feature. They were just a nondescript bunch of Americans who had played only two games together before arriving in Brazil. The classic no-hopers.

One thing, though. Where the 1930 squad had relied on key foreign-born players, all but three of the 1950 players were born in America. Playing in Belo Horizonte in a group that included Chile, Spain, and England, their chances of scoring a goal, never mind winning a game, could charitably be described as slim.

In their first game the Americans did score a solitary goal in response to Spain's three. Then they went into one of the great mismatches of all time, against England, which had comfortably beaten Chile, 2–0.

The scoreline that came over the wires on June 29, 1950, was England 0 USA 1. It caused worldwide disbelief, but the score was correct. Mighty England, the masters, had been humbled by the Yankee part-timers.*

The hero of the day, scorer of the historic goal, was the Haitian-born Joe Gaetjens. Nobody seems too clear about what really happened. Right halfback Walter Bahr remembers taking a cross-shot from some twenty-five yards out, a well-hit shot that the English goalie, Bert Williams, was moving across his goal to cover.

Enter Gaetjens. The English press claimed that the goal was a farcical accident, that Gaetjens was trying to duck out of the way when the ball hit him in the ear and deflected past Williams. All nonsense, said U.S. fullback Harry Keough: "Joe dove headlong for the ball to head it past Williams."

"Those were the sort of goals Gaetjens scored," said Bahr. "If it had been anyone else I'd say it was probably an accident. But not Joe—he always went for the ball."

England now had to beat Spain to remain in the competition, something that proved beyond them. They went down 0–1 and returned home, their first World Cup adventure an ignominious failure.

Yet another shock occurred in São Paulo: pesky little Switzerland, conquerors of Germany in 1938, now held Brazil to a 2–2 tie. Suddenly it was panic time. Brazil was now in danger. They would have to beat Yugoslavia in their next game. A loss, or even a tie, would let the Slavs through, and Brazil would be eliminated. Unthinkable.

A "Save Brazil" campaign sprang up, with the whole country being urged to support their team. The stars of the 1938 team, Domingos da Guia

---

* Said the Italian referee: "If I hadn't refereed the game myself, I would not have believed the result, no matter who had told me." When the competition was over, the journalists in Belo Horizonte voted this performance of the English team the most perfect of 1950 . . . except that they omitted to score any goals.

and Leônidas, were heard continually on the radio, inciting their colleagues of the 1950 team to supreme effort.

Inevitably, the game was an anticlimax, with Brazil winning 2–0 comfortably enough. It might have been a different story but for an absurd accident to Rajko Mitic, one of the Yugoslavian midfielders, immediately before the game. Leaving the locker room to go out on the field, Mitic walked into a protruding metal beam (Maracaná was still not completed) and cut his forehead open. Heavily bandaged, he ran onto the field four minutes late—just in time to see Brazil score its first goal.

For the first time, the final round of the tournament was not played on a knockout basis. The four surviving teams—Brazil, Uruguay, Spain, and Sweden—would play each other once in a mini-league, and whichever topped the table was the champion. There would be no single game that could be called the final. But things didn't work out that way. With one game left to play, the position of the top two teams was:

	Played	Won	Drawn	Lost	Points
Brazil	2	2	—	—	4
Uruguay	2	1	1	—	3

The one remaining game was between Uruguay and Brazil. It would be the World Cup final, the game that would decide the championship. For Brazil a win or even a tie would do it. Uruguay had to win.

Brazil was the overwhelming favorite. It had annihilated the other two teams in the final round: Sweden was beaten 7–1, Spain 6–1. By contrast Uruguay had edged Sweden 3–2, and had been held 2–2 by Spain. Realistically, the Uruguayans hadn't a prayer. One of the top directors of the Uruguayan Soccer Federation told his players: "We'll be lucky if they don't drown us in goals. Do your best, but even if you lose 4–0 it will be a victory of sorts."

For the Brazilians the question was not whether they would win, but how many goals they would put past the hapless Uruguayans. An enormous crowd, estimated at 200,000, packed the barely finished Maracaná to see the slaughter. On an afternoon of high emotion, the national anthem was sung as it had never been sung before, and the governor of Rio de Janeiro delivered a final, impassioned plea to the team: "Fifty million Brazilians await your victory!" before the referee's whistle started the most important game in Brazil's history.

The Brazilian onslaught began immediately, and the Uruguayan goal was under siege for the entire first half. The brilliant Ademir, who had already scored seven goals in the tournament, supported by the wiles and skills of Zizinho and Jair, worked his magic for 45 minutes, but the expected avalanche of goals would not come. In the Uruguayan defense, the 33-year-old veteran and captain, Obdulio Varela, found a tireless partner in

Victor Andrade*, eleven years his junior. A series of spectacular saves from goalkeeper Roque Maspoli (another 33-year-old) helped to shut out the Brazilians in the first half.

Two minutes after the interval, Maracaná exploded as Brazil at last broke through and Friaça drove the ball past Maspoli. What should have been the beginning of the end for Uruguay turned out to be the signal for their awakening. Varela, absolutely tireless, forsook his defensive duties and moved into the attack, getting the ball more and more to right winger Alcide Ghiggia who, in the first half, had shown that he could beat the Brazilian defense. After twenty minutes he threaded his way through yet again, drawing defenders away from the middle; his pass found Juan Schiaffino just outside the penalty area. The slender Schiaffino coolly controlled the ball and beat Barbosa in the Brazilian goal with an unstoppable shot: 1–1.

Even with the score tied, Brazil would still be World Champions, but the Brazilian players—and the fans—knew that something was awfully wrong. The roar of the crowd was hushed as the nervousness of their team could no longer be ignored. Schiaffino was knocked down in the area, surely a penalty . . . but Brazil survived the moment of suspense as the referee waved play on. The Brazilian defense was once more a shambles as Omar Miguez raced through and hit the post with Barbosa beaten.

Then, the death blow for Brazil. This time their defense was caught with too many men in the middle; the ball was pushed out to the right, where the inevitable Ghiggia ran on to it and slammed the ball between Barbosa and the near post. The goal—the most important of the tournament—was received in stunned silence. "That was when I knew we were going to win," said Schiaffino, "when I heard that silence."

What was to have been an afternoon of national rejoicing was fifteen minutes away from being a total catastrophe. Those minutes slipped away, so impossibly quickly for Brazil, so agonizingly slowly for Uruguay, until there was nothing left to hope for. Uruguay 2 Brazil 1. The 1950 World Cup, so full of upsets, had saved the most astonishing for the final game.

Twenty years after it had won the first-ever tournament, Uruguay was world champion again. In 1930, as Jules Rimet had presented the trophy, the crowd was on its feet, singing and cheering. Now, in 1950, the vast terraces of Maracana were half deserted as the disillusioned Brazilians filed sadly out, ashamed to watch as Varela and Rimet shook hands on the field.

Said Jules Rimet: "There were no guards of honor, no national anthem, no speeches in front of the microphone, no magnificent victory celebrations." By the time the Uruguayans made their traditional lap of honor, the stadium was virtually a hollow shell.

Brazil, confident of success in 1938, certain in 1950, had failed again.

---

* Victor Andrade was the nephew of José Andrade, star of the great Uruguayan Olympic teams of 1924 and 1928, and a member of the 1930 World Cup winning team.

SWITZERLAND, 1954

An unlikely choice as host, tiny Switzerland got the nod because FIFA—headquartered in Zurich and 50 years old in 1954—wanted to celebrate the anniversary in its own backyard.

It turned into a very wet celebration that will always be remembered as a tournament of rain, of mud . . . and of goals, 140 of them in twenty-six games for an extraordinary average of 5.3 per game.*

Hungary, riding the crest of a twenty-eight-game unbeaten string that stretched back over four years, was a clear favorite. They had beaten all the top teams in Europe. They had humiliated England by a resounding 6–3 score—in Wembley Stadium no less, the first foreign team ever to win there. Three weeks before the World Cup began, England had journeyed to Budapest seeking revenge, but found only further humiliation, losing 7–1.

The victories of the Magic Magyars, as the English press had dubbed them, had further damaged the already tottering reputation of England as a world soccer power. Neither England nor Scotland—in the World Cup for the first time—was rated very highly.

Italy was another of the Hungarians' victims. The Italians had made the mistake of inviting the Magyars to play them at the ceremonial opening of the *Stadio Olimpico* in Rome in May 1953. The Hungarians repaid the compliment by trouncing the *azzurri* 3–0 with almost insulting ease. The Italians promptly fired their coach and, for the first time ever, appointed a foreigner: Lajos Czeizler, a Hungarian.

Germany, or at least West Germany, was back, coached by the same man who had suffered defeat at the hands of Switzerland in 1938, the remarkably durable Sepp Herberger. The South American challenge came from the two countries that had played in the 1950 final. Uruguay, the Cup holders, still had five members of their winning team, including Andrade, Schiaffino, and the thirty-six-year-old Varela. Brazil had what was virtually a new team—only Bauer remained from 1950—yet such was the strength of Brazilian soccer that this new team was installed as one of the favorites.

There were also the weak teams that made their way into the final sixteen because of the regional arrangement of the elimination games. In the whole of Asia there was not a national team that was in the same class as even the poorest of those in Europe or South America. But there *was* an Asian qualifying group of Japan, South Korea, and Nationalist China. The Koreans beat Japan, China dropped out, and South Korea, the best of a very

---

* In 1950 it had been 4.0 per game, and in 1958 it was to go back down to 3.6.

weak lot, found itself a finalist. Really a ludicrous state of affairs, considering that countries like Sweden and Spain had been eliminated in the much tougher European qualifying groups.

Sweden's elimination, at the hands of Belgium, was something of a surprise for the team that had finished in third place in 1950. But Sweden's failure in 1954 was a direct result of its success in 1950, when its players had caught the eyes of Italian clubs. No fewer than nine of that 1950 team had been lured to play as professionals in Italy.* Thus Sweden lost most of its best players because the Swedish F.A., a rigorously amateur body, would not allow professionals to represent Sweden.

Television made its World Cup debut on June 16, 1954, with the transmission of the game between Yugoslavia and France. A move that at once brought millions of new fans to the sport and began the move (some would call it the slide) to rampant commercialism that has marked the most recent tournaments.

Not that money had ever been far from the thoughts of the organizers. Their arrangement of the groupings proved that. There would be the usual four groups of four teams each, but this time each group would contain two seeded teams who would not play each other. The seeded teams—that is, the ones that were expected to attract the fans—played two games each, against the two weaker teams in their group. It was an arrangement that made it almost certain that all the seeded teams would have an easy passage.

It was left to the hapless but seeded Italians to demonstrate that the best-laid plans do, indeed, gang aft a-gley. In their first game they were beaten 1–2 by the hosts Switzerland (robbed, they would ever after maintain, by the biased decisions of the Brazilian referee). A play-off game—also against Switzerland—was necessary, and this time the Italians went down 1–4.

The Germans got involved in a play-off game, but this was the result of a deliberate gamble by their coach, Sepp Herberger. Playing in an absurdly unbalanced group, along with the favorites Hungary and the no-hopers Turkey and Korea, Germany was, incredibly, unseeded.

This was because when the groupings had been arranged, it was assumed that Spain would qualify. All it had to do was to beat the minnows Turkey in an elimination game. The result was a foregone conclusion—Spain was one of the strongest teams in Europe. So the seeded place was given to the as yet unknown winner of the Turkey–Spain game. The game was tied and had to be decided by drawing lots; to the embarrassment of all, it was Turkey's name that came out of the hat.

With Turkey seeded, Germany would have to play Hungary in the first round. Looking far ahead, Sepp Herberger reasoned that if Germany were

---

* Signing Swedish players was a profitable exercise for the Italians. As the players were all amateurs, no payment was necessary to their former Swedish clubs.

WORLD CUP 1954
Basle, Switzerland: Hungary 8 West Germany 3
*West Germany's Werner Liebrich (left) clashes with Hungary's Ferenc Puskas
in a first round game. It was a heavy tackle from Liebrich in this game that
seriously injured Puskas. Although not fully recovered, he played in the final—
in which Hungary lost to Liebrich's Germany.*
© Peter Robinson: The Football Archive

to reach the final its most likely opponent there would be Hungary. And so
he decided to hide his first team. By fielding six reserves against the
Hungarians, he virtually threw the game away. Hungary 8, Germany 3 was
the score. The loss made a play-off game against Turkey necessary, but
Herberger was confident that his team, having easily beaten the Turks
4–1, could beat them again in a playoff game, which they did, 7–2. Herberger
now felt that he knew a lot more about the Hungarian team than they knew
about his team.

Scotland's baptism in the World Cup was a dismal affair: beaten 0–1 by
Austria, then absolutely outclassed by Uruguay, who scored seven goals
without reply.

The goal riot went on in the quarterfinals. Switzerland scored 5, but
lost to Austria, who scored 7! Uruguay, with a fine display of the open,
quick-moving soccer that was making it the most admired team in the
tournament, took care of England, whose baggy shorts and heavy shoes
seemed to symbolize its outdated style, by a score of 4–2.

Between Germany and Yugoslavia there was little to choose, unless it
was the increasingly obvious physical aspects of the Germans' game. Two

Yugoslavs were badly injured, so that for much of the game Yugoslavia had to play with only nine men.* The Germans were 2–0 winners.

The remaining quarter-final, between Brazil and Hungary, was theoretically the most attractive. But, alas for theory, it turned out to be one of the ugliest games in the history of the World Cup, remembered as the Battle of Bern. Two penalty kicks were awarded and three players were sent off, two Brazilians and one Hungarian.** As the game finished, with Hungary 4–2 victors, there was the unedifying spectacle of a general punch-up among players, police, photographers, and others (who were they? some thought they were spectators, some said they were members of the Hungarian and Brazilian delegations). The brawl went into overtime outside the locker rooms, long enough for the Hungarian coach Gustav Sebes to be punched in the face, and for the Brazilian captain Pinheiro to collect a three-inch gash in his head.

From the disgraceful to the sublime. Hungary's semifinal against Uruguay is remembered as one of the greatest games of all time. Those who felt that the two teams should have been kept apart in the semifinals viewed their meeting as the "true final" of the 1954 tournament. It was a great game despite both teams being without their number one stars— Ferenc Puskas of Hungary and Obdulio Varela of Uruguay were both injured—and the rain that fell incessantly throughout the match.

Hungary was one up within fifteen minutes, using the sort of rapid, first-time passing movement and brilliant finishing that is so difficult to defend against. A long, probing pass from Nandor Hidegkuti was headed perfectly down by Sandor Kocsis toward the onrushing Zoltan Czibor, a spectacular volley—goal for Hungary. Throughout the first half, the Hungarians dominated without being able to add to their score.

Victor Andrade, captaining Uruguay in place of Varela, was everywhere, an agile muscular obstacle to the inventiveness of the Hungarian attack. Behind him, hardly putting a foot wrong, was the young fair-haired center back Jose Santamaria.

The second half had barely begun when Hungary scored again—a powerful diving header by Hidegkuti that was in the net before Maspoli had a chance to move. Well on top now, the Hungarians showed signs of overconfidence—or were they lulled into it by the clever Uruguayans? Exactly as they had done in the 1950 final against Brazil, almost as though it were the result of a signal from the touchline, Uruguay suddenly raised the level of its game.

Schiaffino, always dangerous, became positively deadly; he and inside forward Juan Hohberg, urged on by the indefatigable Andrade, now totally committed to attack, began to systematically maul the Hungarian defense.

* Substitution was not allowed in World Cup soccer until the 1970 tournament.

** The Hungarian was their captain Jozsef Bozsik, who also happened to be a deputy in the Hungarian National Assembly.

Twice Schiaffino was just wide with rasping shots. Then, with only fifteen minutes to go, his perfect pass put Hohberg through to score. There were just four minutes remaining when Hohberg scored again. Emotionally and physically exhausted, Hohberg collapsed and had to be dragged off the field for a whiff of smelling salts.

Tied 2–2, the game went into overtime, and almost immediately the revived Hohberg was through again. This time his shot hit the post; Schiaffino pounced on the rebound, only to be thwarted by a prodigious save from Gyula Grosics. An injury to Andrade spelled the end for Uruguay. While he was off the field receiving treatment, Kocsis headed Hungary into the lead. Five minutes later he scored again, and Uruguay was beaten for the first time ever in a World Cup game. As the final whistle blew, the two teams saluted each other with smiles, handshakes, and embraces as the crowd rose to cheer them. After the sordid Battle of Bern, Hungary and Uruguay had provided a magnificent affirmation of the sport.

In the other semifinal Germany made surprisingly short work of Austria, to the tune of six goals to one. The Germans had been helped by a number of banal errors by the Austrian goalkeeper, Walter Zeman, but the pace and rhythm of their athletic game had impressed previously skeptical observers.

Hungary vs. Germany in the final—exactly as Sepp Herberger had foreseen three weeks earlier. This time, of course, he would field his full team. But the Hungarians had a problem with Puskas, who had not played since he was kicked—significantly, in that first game against Germany. The injury was the result of a bad foul by the German defender Werner Liebrich, a foul that Puskas later claimed was intentional. Italian journalists, looking at film of the incident, said there could be no doubt that the kick was deliberate.

The Hungarian coach, Gustav Sebes, was concerned about Puskas's fitness. But Puskas, a major in the army, was a commanding personality. He said he was fit. So Sebes played him. After eight minutes of play the decision looked like the masterstroke. Hungary scored twice (one goal to Puskas himself) and was toying with the Germans almost as easily as if Herberger had again put out his reserve team. Professors Puskas, Hidegkuti, and Bozsik seemed set to give another of their celebrated soccer academies.

It was not, however, to be skill that won the day. It was to be stamina. The Germans had played two comparatively easy games in the quarter- and semifinals. The Hungarians had struggled through the Battle of Bern, and then suffered the tension of the emotionally supercharged overtime victory against Uruguay. As the rain poured down, the heavy going began to tell against Hungarians. On top of that, the longer the game went on the clearer it became that Puskas was not really fit.

Three minutes after Hungary's second goal the Germans scored when Max Morlock jabbed the ball home after a mixup in the Hungarian penalty area. Seven minutes later Germany was level on a ferocious shot by right winger Helmut Rahn. At the other end, Hidegkuti hit the post, and Anton Turek saved Kocsis's header when it looked almost too late.

Hungary opened the second half with almost frantic energy, hitting the bar, having a shot kicked off the goal line and forcing Turek to make two more fine saves. But nothing came of it and when the fury died down, Germany took over again, finally going ahead on another goal by Rahn with seven minutes left. Hungary, desperate now, threw everything into attack, and Puskas scored—only to have the goal disallowed for offside. It was a desperately close call and for the Hungarians, certain the goal was legitimate (as were many neutral observers), it was the final blow.

Exactly as in Rio four years earlier, the favorites, the "better" team, had gone down. The Magic Magyars, beaten for the first time in four years, had succumbed to a team out of the classic German mold: high on fitness, discipline, and morale, uncomplicated in tactics.

Standing on a small podium, with an umbrella held over his head against the relentless rain, Jules Rimet presented the trophy to the mud-spattered German captain, Fritz Walter. It was his last official act before retiring after thirty-three years as president of FIFA.

−3−
The World Cup, 1958−1974*

Before 1958, the World Cup had always been won by a nation from the continent where it was played: Uruguay had won both times that the championship was held in South America, while of the three played in Europe, two had been won by Italy and one by Germany. The 1958 competition changed all that when the Brazilians came through in sparkling fashion to win in Sweden. The result satisfied everyone, for, after the upsets of 1950 and 1954, justice was done and the best team had won.

SWEDEN, 1958

A tournament without a clear favorite: both 1954 finalists, Hungary and West Germany, were present, but neither was in sparkling form. Politics had played a cruel trick on Hungary. At the time of the 1956 uprising in Hungary, Honved (the army team for which most of the national team members played) was touring in South America. Three key players—Puskas, Czibor, and Kocsis—decided not to return home, and the Hungarians lost the nucleus of their great team. Hidegkuti was still there, but his thirty-six years were beginning to tell. To the sorrow of all, the Hungarians quickly demonstrated that there was very little left of the Magic Magyars.

Immediately after winning the 1954 championship, the Germans had gone downhill with a vengeance. They won only four of their next seventeen games, amply confirming the views of those critics who felt their win had been a fluke. But Sepp Herberger—and who was willing to ridicule him

---

* For tabulated scores of all tournament games, see pages 314–324. For tactical analyses of the World Cups, see chapter 8, pages 178–226.

any more?—was supposed to have a four-year plan that would ensure maximum strength when it mattered: to wit, during the 1958 finals.

The captain, Fritz Walter, was still playing, aged 38 but wily as ever. Helmut Rahn, the goal-scoring hero of the 1954 final, had been recalled and had vowed he would get in shape by cutting out his remarkable beer-drinking activities. The new players included a twenty-two-year-old center-forward, Uwe Seeler, destined to become the most popular player in the history of German soccer.

An unknown quantity among the finalists was the Soviet Union, which had at last decided to come out of hiding and put its talents on the line. It had won the 1956 Olympic title, it had a formidable goalkeeper in the giant Lev Yashin, and everyone was raving about the skill of the captain, Igor Netto. But were they ready for the pressures of World Cup play?

For the first and so far only time, all four of the British soccer nations were represented. England was still rebuilding after suffering the same sort of blow that befell the Italians in 1949. On February 6, 1958, a plane carrying England's champion club, Manchester United, had crashed on takeoff at Munich Airport. Eight of United's players were killed, including three who were regular members of England's team. A month before the finals, England had been swamped 0–5 by Yugoslavia in Belgrade.

The Welsh were present only because of political problems. Israel, drawn in the same preliminary group as Turkey, Indonesia, Egypt, and the Sudan, found itself, apparently, with a free passage into the finals when all four opponents refused to play it. FIFA was having none of that and decreed that Israel would have to play off against Wales, which had finished second in one of the European qualifying groups. And so Wales, which had already been eliminated by Czechoslovakia, got another chance and, by beating Israel twice, went to Sweden as one of the final sixteen.

Northern Ireland qualified on merit by eliminating Italy. This was the first time the Italians had failed to qualify for the finals. Their disappointment was particularly intense because their team included two brilliant *oriundi,* the Uruguayans Ghiggia and Schiaffino, who were now playing for Italian clubs.

Also playing for Italian clubs were most of the top Swedish players. George Raynor, the Englishman who was Sweden's coach, recalled five of them to make up the nucleus of his team. Among the returning exiles was the thirty-six-year-old veteran Nils Liedholm, who had played so brilliantly for the great Swedish 1948 Olympic team, before being snapped up by Milan.

The Argentine squad had once again been ravaged by the wealthy Italian clubs. One year earlier Argentina had won the South American championship with what many rated as their best team ever. In six games they had scored twenty-five goals, thanks to their dazzling young forwards, Omar Sivori (twenty two years old), Antonio Angellilo (twenty) and Humberto Maschio (twenty-four)—a sassy, skill-laden trio that had toyed with opposing defenses.

The Angels with Dirty Faces they called them, but within the year the angelic threesome was no more. The angels took wing for Europe, lured away by Italian clubs, and Argentina refused to have anything further to do with them, though all three did later return to international soccer, playing for Italy.

As far as most Europeans were concerned, Brazil had been written off as a serious World Cup threat. The team had shown a frightening lack of discipline in the 1954 Battle of Bern. The same thing had happened during Brazil's 1956 tour of Europe, when players and officials had tried to attack the referee after a game in Vienna.

But 1958 was to be the year in which Brazil redeemed itself. The Brazilian Soccer Federation had produced a secret, and brutally honest report on the failings of their players. At last attention would be given to the psychological needs of players—many of them from humble homes—asked to live for long periods thousands of miles from Brazil. The team traveled with its own psychologist.

The new coach was Vicente Feola, a large, easygoing man who hid his sad, slow-moving eyes behind tinted spectacles. He confessed uncertainty about the team he would select, bemused, perhaps, by the wealth of talent at his disposal. In fact, during the 1958 series he never did field the same team twice running. In Brazil's first game, against Austria, only the cool, unflappable Didi and the cultured fullback Nilton Santos remained from the 1954 team. Brazil won the game 3–0, but Feola felt the score should have been higher.

Against England he brought in Vavá, a fast-moving aggressive forward, for more scoring punch. The move was not a success and England held the Brazilians to a 0–0 tie. While Feola pondered what further changes to make, a deputation of his players arrived. They wanted the devastating right winger Garrincha—the Little Bird—in the starting lineup. Feola had the good sense to listen. He also brought in two players from the Santos club—halfback Zito and the seventeen-year-old forward . . . Pelé.

It was the Soviets who were unlucky enough to get the first taste of this new Brazil. In the first minute Garrincha hit the post, two minutes later Vavá scored on a pass from Didi, and the Soviets spent the rest of the afternoon defending grimly, particularly against the Little Bird's dizzying dribbles. The Brazilians were limited to just one more goal by Vavá, but it seemed absurd to measure the margin of their victory in goals. The Brazilian soccer was on a different plane than that of the Soviets.

At long last, here was the team that the whole country of Brazil had been dreaming about. All the natural individual brilliance was there, now allied not with arrogance but with a cool confidence. Brazil swept through to the quarterfinals, joined by France, Yugoslavia, Sweden, Wales, Germany, Northern Ireland, and the Soviet Union, which had beaten England in a playoff game.

Against Wales, Feola left out Vavá and brought back Mazzola, a move that didn't work, for the Brazilians struggled to gain a 1–0 victory. The lone goal was scored by Pelé. It was his first in World Cup play, and one he would later rate as one of the most important of his career. Elsewhere, the inevitable Rahn had scored for West Germany to give them a 1–0 win over Yugoslavia, while Sweden, to the delight and somewhat to the surprise of its supporters, had been well worth its 2–0 victory over a stolid Soviet side, in which only goalkeeper Yashin had enhanced his reputation.

The fourth semifinalist was France, 4–0 conquerors of Northern Ireland. The French, never among the world's soccer powers, had caught everyone off guard with their spirited and skillful attacking soccer. They had scored fifteen goals in four games, eight of them coming from Just Fontaine, the fruits of a wonderful understanding with inside forward Raymond Kopa. They were the tournament's highest scorers, and in the semifinal they would face Brazil, whose defense had not yet conceded a goal.

For the game, Feola brought back Vavá to play at center forward, and it was Vavá who got Brazil off to a roaring start with a goal in the second minute, only to have Fontaine equalize at the nine-minute mark. The outcome of the game was sealed in the thirty-fifth minute when the French defender Robert Jonquet collided heavily with Vavá. Jonquet was carried off with a badly injured right knee, and though he returned later he was merely a passenger. With substitution not permitted, France had to soldier on with only ten fit men.

While Jonquet was off the field, Didi put Brazil ahead with one of his rare goals. In the second half Pelé shone with dazzling brilliance, eclipsing even Garrincha, and scored a hat trick against the disorganized French defense. After the game, the French goalkeeper Claude Abbes said, with considerable feeling: "I would rather play against ten Germans than one Brazilian."

At Gothenburg, in the other semifinal, Sweden took on West Germany, and the authorities decided they had to do something to fire up the Swedish fans, still strangely lethargic when it came to rooting for their team. Cheerleaders, familiar enough to college football fans but almost unheard of in soccer, were the answer.

Thus encouraged with cheers, chants, and flags, the Swedes perversely allowed the Germans to score first, but quickly equalized through Lennart Skoglund, an Italian repatriate. Kurt Hamrin, also back from Italy, then set about picking the German defense apart until, after fifteen minutes of the second half, fullback Erich Juskowiak despairingly kicked him, and was ejected from the game. Against ten men, Sweden's Gunnar Gren scored the go-ahead goal, and Hamrin crowned his afternoon by waltzing the ball past three defenders before beating the German keeper with a violent cross-shot.

Before turning to the final, a quick look at the game for third place. What is traditionally an uninspired affair between two disappointed teams

WORLD CUP FINAL 1958
Stockholm, Sweden: Brazil 5 Sweden 2
The seventeen-year-old Pelé (No. 10), the new sensation of the soccer world, challenges Swedish goalkeeper Karl Svensson. Pelé scored twice as Brazil took the World Cup for the first time.
© Peter Robinson: The Football Archive

turned into a festival of goals: final score, France 6, West Germany 3. Fontaine scored four of the French goals, bringing his total for the tournament to thirteen, a record that still stands.

To say that Brazil was the favorite in the final is to state the obvious. Sweden's own coach admitted that his was the oldest and the slowest team in the tournament. Brazil was younger and faster, and infinitely more talented. All that Sweden seemed to have going for it was the fact that it was playing at home and the hope that Brazil, as so often in the past, would self-destruct when the big moment arrived.

The European coaches still believed that the Brazilian temperament was suspect, that if the team gave away an early goal, the players would not fight back—a theory that was shattered within ten minutes of the start of the final. The Swedes went ahead after only four minutes on a goal by Liedholm. The ball was calmly picked out of the net by Didi almost as though nothing had happened, and the Brazilians set about playing soccer.

It took them six minutes to level the score, and the goal was a beauty. Garrincha took the ball down the right touchline, beat two Swedish defenders with impish ease, raced almost to the goal line, and drove the ball, hard and low, across the middle, where Vavá, running in at full speed, darted between two opponents and turned it into the net.

Garrincha was to be a tantalizing thorn in the Swedish left side all afternoon. Twenty minutes later he broke through yet again and created another goal for Vavá. As if Garrincha were not enough, Zito and Didi were now controlling midfield at will, while up front Vavá and Pelé were throwing the Swedish defense into chaos with their constant interchanging of positions. Every so often Djalma Santos (playing his first game of the tournament—that was Feola's "change of the day") would come racing up from fullback to join in the attack. In the second half Pelé volleyed the ball past goalkeeper Karl Svensson for number three, then Mario Zagalo (in 1970 he would be Brazil's coach) scored the fourth. Sweden got one back through Agne Simonsson, but Pelé had the last word. To make the final score 5–2, he leaped high to head the ball in a perfect arc over Svensson's grasping hands. Sweden, never disgraced, had been outclassed. But could any of the other finalists have done better?

CHILE, 1962

CAMPEONATO MUNDIAL DE FUTBOL   CHILE
WORLD FOOTBALL CHAMPIONSHIP
CHAMPIONNAT MONDIAL DE FOOTBALL   1962
COUPE JULES RIMET

FIFA now began a policy of alternating the World Cup sites between Europe and the Americas. The 1958 competition had been in Sweden, so it would be South America in 1962, and the country chosen was Chile.

A controversial choice given the disastrous earthquake and drought of 1960 that had all but wrecked the country's economy. But the Chileans were insistent, and they were willing to build new stadiums.

In World Cup history, 1962 will not go down as a vintage year. Where 1954 had featured the Magic Magyars, and 1958 the Brilliant Brazilians, 1962 had very little to excite the imagination.

It was thought the Yugoslavs might spring a surprise, because almost anything seemed possible when their mercurial inside forward, Dragan

Sekularac, was in form. England, of course, would go on being steady and unimaginative—gone was the day when anything exceptional was expected from the English.

The Soviets had made a successful tour of South America at the end of 1961, playing Argentina, Uruguay, and Chile and beating all three. Yashin was now being talked about as the greatest goalkeeper of all time. Based mainly on players from Dukla-Prague (the Czech army team), Czechoslovakia had a well-knit side that would be difficult to beat, but they had lost their young goal-scoring star, Rudi Kucera, to a serious head injury. And West Germany . . . well, the Germans still had Herberger, though this was to be his last World Cup.

Of the European teams, the most talented was surely Spain, which was able to profit from the strength of the Real Madrid team that was dominating European club soccer. Real had brought together a galaxy of world stars—Ferenc Puskas (whom we last saw playing for Hungary in the 1954 final), José Santamaria from Uruguay and, perhaps the greatest of them all, Alfredo di Stéfano from Argentina. As naturalized Spaniards, they were now playing for Spain alongside two brilliant native-born Spaniards, inside forward Luis Suarez and winger Francisco Gento.

The favorite had to be Brazil, if only because they had so many of their 1958 team back again. All four years older of course (the fullbacks Djalma and Nilton Santos were thirty-three and thirty-seven), but who could forget how superb the team had been in Sweden? Anyway, there was always Pelé, who was fast becoming a legend, and he was still only twenty-one years old. Ill health had forced Vicente Feola to resign as coach, to be replaced by Aimoré Moreira, brother of Zezé Moreira, who had coached the 1954 team in Switzerland.

The Chileans themselves were an unknown quantity. Never rated as a particularly strong soccer nation, they nevertheless had the psychological advantage of being hosts. National fervor was there to be harnessed—the Swedes had pointed the way with their flag-waving cheerleaders—but no one was ready for what happened when Chile played Italy.

The Italians, always fragile and unpredictable when playing away from home, had nonetheless arrived with high hopes. They had a young team, average age twenty-four, including five members of their 1960 Olympic team, which had been eliminated—on the toss of a coin!—after holding the eventual winners, Yugoslavia, to an overtime tie. The team also included four *oriundi:* the Brazilians José Altafini (who had played for Brazil in the 1958 World Cup under the name Mazzola) and Angelo Sormani, and the Argentines Sivori and Maschio.

The Italian downfall was the result of events that happened off the field—in particular, the bad luck of being drawn in the same group as Chile. Shortly before the competition was due to start, an Italian journalist wrote a series of highly critical articles about the living conditions in Chile. A Chilean living in Italy read them and, scandalized, sent them to the Chilean ambassador in Rome who sped them back to Santiago.

The articles alleged widespread illiteracy, alcoholism, and prostitution and compared Chile unfavorably with underdeveloped nations in Africa and Asia. At once there began a campaign in the Chilean press, radio, and television systematically denigrating the Italian players. They were accused of being Fascists, members of the Mafia, sex maniacs, and, because there had recently been a doping scandal involving the top Italian club Inter-Milan, drug addicts.

By the time the Chile–Italy game came around, the atmosphere in Santiago was so dangerously charged that the Italians selected their team more on the basis of players who would control themselves under provocation than out of any tactical soccer considerations. Before the game, the *azzurri* tried to calm the crowd of 66,000 by waving greetings and throwing roses to them. The Chilean fans replied with insults and threats, and threw the roses back—a suitable start for the carnage that was to follow: kicking, spitting, punching, one Italian with a broken nose, two Italians sent off.

The Italians have never forgiven the English referee Ken Aston, accusing him of at best incompetence, at worst overt hostility. He seemed to see only Italian reaction, and not Chilean provocation, of which there was plenty. Notably the sensational haymaking punch with which left winger Leonel Sanchez broke Maschio's nose—unpunished, and apparently unseen, by Aston.

Later, Aston confessed that he had wanted to call the game off at half-time, but was afraid the crowd would riot if he did so. Reduced to nine men, the Italians went down 0–2, and Chile had fought—in the most literal sense—its way to a quarterfinal game against the Soviet Union, 1,000 miles to the north in Arica. A game that to the astonishment of all they won 2–1, mostly because Yashin had a woeful afternoon and let in two simple shots that he should have saved.

From Viña del Mar came the sensational news that Pelé was out of the World Cup, the victim of a badly pulled muscle during Brazil's 0–0 tie with Czechoslovakia. His loss clearly affected Brazil in their next game against Spain, who were without the injured Di Stéfano. After many an anxious moment, Brazil won 2–1 on two late goals by Amarildo, Pelé's replacement. The Spanish camp also had some disappointing news: Di Stéfano, too, was out of the tournament with a muscle injury. It meant that one of the world's greatest players was never to play in the World Cup.

In the quarterfinal the Brazilians recovered their poise and beat England 3–1 with consummate ease. Amarildo was now fitting in well, but the victory belonged to Garrincha, who scored two of the goals. On one of them, Garrincha—a mere 5' 7"—outleaped the towering English defenders to head the ball home.

Chile vs. Brazil in the semifinals: a game guaranteed to bring to the boiling point the already simmering Santiago fans, who were beginning to suffer the delusion that their team was good enough to win the championship. The fears of those who foresaw a repetition of the Italy game were eventually confounded—but only just—by the self-discipline of the Brazilians and the infinitely superior quality of their soccer.

Had the game been played anywhere else, the Chileans would certainly have been swamped, but they hung on grimly throughout the game. After two early goals by the irrepressible Garrincha, Chile narrowed the gap when Jorge Toro scored direct from a free kick. Vavá, deadly as ever with the half chance, headed a third for Brazil two minutes into the second half. Chile scored again from a penalty, after Zózimo handled in the area, only to have Vavá head his second goal.

WORLD CUP 1962
Viña del Mar, Chile: Brazil 2 Mexico 0
Brazilian winger Garrincha (light shirt) draws a crowd of Mexican defenders—eight of them, plus the goalkeeper! With Pelé injured and out of the tournament after only one game, it was the superb skills of Garrincha that won the 1962 World Cup for Brazil.
© Peter Robinson: The Football Archive

The score was to remain 4–2 in Brazil's favor, but in the closing minutes of the game the Brazilians' sorely tried patience began to wear thin. Garrincha, who had been kicked methodically throughout the game ("at least fifty times," he later claimed), at last returned the blows and was ejected. As he walked to the locker room, he was hit on the back of the head by a bottle.

The organizers, probably not imagining for one moment that Chile would get that far, had made the mistake of scheduling both semifinals for the same hour on the same day. While Chileans throughout the country were gathered around television sets watching Chile lose to Brazil, the game between Czechoslovakia and Yugoslavia in Viña del Mar drew a pathetic 5,000 spectators.

Against the run of the play, the Czechs beat the Yugoslavs 3–1, exactly as, in the quarter-finals, they had been outplayed by—but had eventually beaten—the Hungarians. The difference in both games was the Czech goalkeeper Wilhelm Schroiff, who made save after incredible save.

To universal relief the Chileans won the third-place game against Yugoslavia, giving their fans something to cheer about. Steam was duly let off in the streets of Santiago, leaving Brazil and Czechoslovakia to play the final in the cordial atmosphere of the afterglow.

For Brazil there was the unwelcome possibility that Garrincha might be suspended for the final. FIFA's disciplinary committee was busy deciding whether his ejection in the game against Chile should be followed by a one-game ban. Possibly their deliberations were swayed by the telegram that arrived from Tancredo Neves, the president of Brazil; possibly not. The decision was announced by Sir Stanley Rous, the Englishman who had replaced Jules Rimet as president of FIFA: Garrincha was cautioned, not suspended.

Except for Schroiff and the winghalf, Josef Masopust, the Czechs had no outstanding players. Their game had a deliberate, almost plodding, air to it, mired in a defensive mentality that seemed to find attacking a tedious but necessary chore.

How surprising, then, when the Czechs opened the final with a series of enterprising attacking moves and went ahead on a well-taken goal by Masopust. Amarildo had the Brazilians level within two minutes, shooting violently from the narrowest of angles and squeezing the ball between the badly positioned Schroiff and his near post. Half an hour into the second half, Amarildo crossed from the left and there was Zito, unchallenged, to head home.

For poor Schroiff, who was not having the happiest of afternoons, there was worse to come. From the touchline, a good 40 yards out, the Brazilian fullback Djalma Santos got his foot under the ball and booted it high into the air. Schroiff, looking into the sun, was dazzled as the ball fell toward his goal. He lost it, found it again, caught it—then dropped it, right at the feet of Vavá, who tapped it in for Brazil's third goal.

Brazil thus joined Uruguay and Italy as two-time winners of the Jules Rimet trophy. With an average age of just over 30, it was the oldest team ever to win the World Cup. But the veterans, without Pelé, and without dazzling as the 1958 team had done, had been clearly the best in an off year for soccer.

ENGLAND, 1966

One hundred and three years after the London Football Association had drawn up the rules that laid the foundations of the sport, the World Football Championship arrived in England. Back where the game began, where the first professionals had played, and where the idea of international competition had been born in 1872.

The organizers could be certain that there would no problems with unfinished stadiums. The English had not built a new stadium since Wembley was opened in 1923, and they were not about to start now. What was good enough every Saturday afternoon for the English League clubs was certainly good enough for foreigners, and the games would be played on six club grounds.* England, as it turned out, would play all its games at Wembley.

No new stadiums then, but for the first time the World Cup would have a mascot: the traditional English lion was turned into a cuddly, boylike creature, complete with soccer shoes, and dubbed World Cup Willie. He would grin out from thousands of posters and advertisements, the first of a line of increasingly commercialized World Cup symbols.**

The World Cup trophy was brought to England and put on display at the National Stamp Exhibition, from which, to the horror of all, it disappeared. The chances of its ever turning up again were evidently not good. The Cup, after all, was solid gold, worth 50,000 francs in 1930. Incredibly, it did turn up. A spotted dog called Pickles, out for a walk with his master in South London, rummaged about in a garbage heap and unearthed . . . the World Cup.

England's embarrassment was relieved, and they could now set about acquiring the trophy in a more orthodox manner. They were the favorites, if only because it was still a rare occurrence for a foreign team to beat England on its home soil. But there were other reasons for believing that

---

* There is a story of an American who visited an English first division ground soon after the war—a ground that had emerged unscathed from the blitz—and remarked: "Gee, this must have been quite a place before it was bombed." The story is, no doubt, apocryphal, but it does give a fair idea of the haphazard, ramshackle appearance of most English soccer grounds. It appears the English have something against stadiums; Wembley itself, built for the 1924 Empire Exhibition, narrowly escaped demolition in 1927.

** Another innovation, and a clear sign of the times, was the drug-testing scheme. After each game, urine samples were taken from four randomly selected players (two from each team) and under conditions of great security dispatched to a London laboratory for analysis. In this way, 128 samples were tested—all proved negative.

the English would do well. In 1963 they had appointed a new manager, Alf Ramsey, who had said confidently and had gone on saying, "We shall win." Ramsey, who had played for England thirty-two times in the early 1950s as a fullback,* had built up a solid England team that was going to be difficult to beat. In defense there were the supremely safe goalkeeper Gordon Banks and center back Bobby Moore, the captain, cool and solid as a rock. In attack the team could rely upon the balding Bobby Charlton, a survivor of the Munich air crash of 1958, a world-class forward with a bewildering body swerve and ferocious shot. The quicksilver Jimmy Greaves, the most dangerous goal scorer in the English game, was something of an individualist, and was dropped after the first round. Ramsey's taste was more for hardworking team players.

Looking for its third successive win, Brazil was once again being coached by Vicente Feola. From the 1962 team there were Gilmar, Djalma Santos, Garrincha, and Pelé. Plus, astoundingly, Bellini and Orlando, two players from the 1958 team who had not been selected in 1962.

Portugal was a new name in the World Cup finals, its team built around players from the Lisbon club Benfica, at that time one of the strongest in Europe. Their stars were two black players from Mozambique: Mario Coluna, a strong, intelligent midfield player, and the explosive Eusebio, whose thunderous shooting was to be one of the highlights of the competition.

Sepp Herberger had retired at last. The new coach of West Germany was one of his disciples, Helmut Schön. The team included Uwe Seeler, playing better than ever at center forward, and two young midfielders, the left-footed Wolfgang Overath and the very right-footed Franz Beckenbauer, only twenty-one years old but already playing with the confidence and poise of a veteran.

Italy, too, had a new coach, Edmondo Fabbri, who had enjoyed great success as a club coach, guiding Mantova from the fourth to the first division in seven years. In Giacinto Facchetti, the tall attacking fullback, Sandro Mazzola, an inside forward of superb quickness and ball control, and the twenty-two-year-old Gianni Rivera, the Golden Boy of Italian soccer, Fabbri had some of the most talented players in Europe. But his lack of experience in international soccer was to be a fatal flaw.

North Korea qualified from the Asian–African group. The Koreans had beaten Australia, and were then to have played the winner of the African group. That never happened because all fourteen African countries withdrew. They were miffed because they felt the winner of their group should go straight through to the finals, and not have to play off against the Asian

---

* He was a member of the English team on both of its blackest days: the 0–1 defeat by the USA in the 1950 World Cup, and the 3–6 drubbing by the Hungarians at Wembley in 1953.

winner. And so North Korea came to the finals, a country with no soccer tradition, about which almost nothing was known. Had the team dropped from Mars it could hardly have been more mysterious.

England opened the Eighth World Championship at Wembley Stadium with a game against Uruguay, and a pretty dreadful game it was. The Uruguayans packed their defense and made little attempt to score, clearly and cynically playing for a tie. England was made to look pedestrian, without the skill to cut through the Uruguayans' massed defenders. The result, a tedious 0–0 tie, was unhappily a portent of the defensive nature of much of the soccer that was to come.

Brazil got off to a winning start, 2–0 over Bulgaria, but it was a wretched, physical game from the start, with the Bulgarians providing another example of negative, defensive soccer. Pelé was treated mercilessly, kicked repeatedly by his marker Dobromir Zhechev, who was not even cautioned by the German referee.

Then came Hungary vs. Brazil, their first meeting since the infamous Battle of Bern twelve years earlier. So far neither team had looked particularly impressive, but Hungary (beaten 1–3 in its first game by Portugal) and Brazil (without Pelé, who was still recovering from the mauling the Bulgarians had given him) produced the most memorable game of the 1966 tournament. Not that Brazil had much to do with it; the glorious soccer came almost exclusively from Hungary.

In Florian Albert, Hungary had a worthy successor to the great Hidegkuti. Gracefully body-swerving and accelerating his way through the Brazilian defense, passing with accuracy and almost supernatural insight, Albert had the English crowd chanting his name long before the game was over.

Hungary went ahead after two minutes on a goal by Ferenc Bene, another of their dazzling young forwards. Pelé's substitute Tostão tied the score, but after the interval Hungary was irresistible, sweeping forward time after time with the superb Albert always the catalyst. It was his powerful run through the middle and pinpoint pass to Bene on the right wing that led to Hungary's second goal. Bene raced on to the ball, took it to the goal line and centered hard and low. The ball was met first-time by Janos Farkas with a crushing right-foot volley that sent it flashing into the net. It was soccer perfection—for many the finest goal they had ever seen. The Brazilians' tattered defense held on for another ten minutes of torture until Bene, dancing through for yet another shot, was pulled down in the area. Kalman Meszoly scored from the penalty.

Brazil, beaten 1–3, was now in danger of being eliminated. It would have to beat Portugal in its remaining game. Panic set in, the team was purged, and nine changes were made including the return of the questionably fit Pelé. The result was a disjointed, ineffective team that was no match for the confident Portuguese. Eusebio scored two goals in a clearcut 3–1 win for Portugal. Once again Pelé was liberally kicked and once again the referee (another European, this time from England) did little to protect him. Brazil, the champions, were out. Pelé, bitterly disillusioned by the thuggery and the permissive refereeing, vowed that he would never play in the World Cup again.

The shock of Brazil's elimination was to some extent tempered by the brilliance of Hungary and Portugal, the two teams that had survived. A much larger shock was on its way from Group IV. Italy had won its first game, unconvincingly, over Chile, and had then lost 0–1 to the Soviet Union. To advance, it would have to beat North Korea. Not exactly a tall order. But, just as the Brazilians had done, the Italians panicked.

Fabbri announced his tactical plan to deal with the speedy little Koreans and then proceeded to select players who seemed least capable of putting it into practice. And he persisted with Giacomo Bulgarelli, who had been injured in the game against Chile, and who had a massive question mark hanging over his fitness. Half an hour into the game Fabbri's gamble backfired. Bulgarelli twisted his injured knee, collapsed in agony, and was carried off.

Already finding the Koreans something of a handful, Italy struggled on with ten men. Just before halftime, disaster struck. Gianni Rivera, like most of his teammates having a melancholy afternoon, failed to control a pass. The ball was whipped away from him by Pak Doo Ik, who slammed it into the goal past the vainly diving Enrico Albertosi, the Italian 'keeper. The Italians fought back, created enough chances in the second half to win the game, but seemed fated to miss them all.

The dejected Italians flew home to Genoa airport, where they were greeted by 600 fans who had waited all night to scream abuse at them and pelt them with rotten fruit. It was rumored that Pak Doo Ik, a corporal in the Korean army, had been made a sergeant.

On to the quarterfinals went the extraordinary Koreans, there to meet and scare the life out of the Portuguese. Playing with almost boyish enthusiasm the Koreans scored three times in the first twenty minutes, an avalanche of goals that stunned the Portuguese. The image persists of Portugal's goalkeeper, José Pereira, standing on his line, hands on hips after the third goal had gone in, looking blankly about him, trying to make sense of it all.

For a few precious minutes the idea flared that the Koreans had discovered the secret of perfect soccer, and that they were going to beat everybody. Then Eusebio took over to score twice in the first half, adding two more in the second, leading a remarkable Portuguese comeback that saw them safely through, 5–3.

Had the Koreans been more worldly-wise in soccer tactics, they would have known how to protect a 3–0 lead. But had they been that tactically sophisticated, they would almost certainly never have played with the carefree abandon that gave them those three goals. They disappeared back to Korea as suddenly and as mysteriously as they had arrived, never to excite the soccer world again.

Another sad note for soccer was the quarterfinal elimination of the artistic Hungarians by the ponderous Soviets. Even the skills of Albert and Bene could not compensate for two dreadful errors by the Hungarian goalkeeper Jozsef Gelei.

The other two quarterfinals caused no end of trouble, both on and off the field. Both were Europe vs. South America matches: England vs. Argentina and West Germany vs. Uruguay, and both were refereed by Europeans. Worse, an Englishman refereed the German game, while a German refereed the English game. It was not a sensible arrangement.

This is what happened: The English referee sent off two Uruguayans, and the Germans won easily, 4–0. At Wembley, the German referee ejected the Argentine captain Antonio Rattin, and the English won, though not so easily, 1–0. At first Rattin, professing bewilderment, refused to leave the field. What had he done, he wanted to know? At one point it even looked as though the entire Argentine team was going to walk off.

After ten minutes of discussions, arguments, and gesticulations, Rattin slowly departed. Referee Rudolf Kreitlein was later quoted as saying he dismissed Rattin for misconduct: "I do not speak Spanish, but the look on his face was enough."

The elimination of Argentina and Uruguay brought immediate and passionate protests from the South American camp. The Brazilians were already complaining, with substantial justification, about the lax European refereeing standards that had allowed Pelé to be so maltreated. Now the Argentines and Uruguayans descried an Anglo-German plot that had maneuvered both South American teams out of the tournament.

The English coach, Alf Ramsey, did not help matters when he characterized as "animals" the Argentines who had tried to attack the referee after the game. The South Americans threatened to withdraw from FIFA and demanded an apology from Ramsey. They did not get their apology, did not withdraw, and the World Cup continued with four European teams in the semifinals.

England and Portugal delighted a huge crowd at Wembley with a pulsating game of rare soccer and sportsmanship. England won because Bobby Charlton, at his incomparable best, scored twice, while Eusebio, kept comparatively quiet by England's defense, scored only once. England, in the World Cup final for the first time ever, at last looked as though it had a team capable of winning the trophy. Only West Germany, victors over the USSR in the other semifinal, now stood in the way. Since 1936, England had played Germany seven times: the balance sheet read England six wins, the remaining game tied.

Thousands of German supporters made the trip to Wembley, and after only thirteen minutes they were waving their red, gold, and black flags in ecstasy. Pouncing on a poor clearance by the English defense, Helmut Haller shot. Banks was screened, dived too late, and Germany was one up—the first time in the tournament that England had been behind.

The reaction was swift and devastating. A long free kick by Bobby Moore seemed to be dropping harmlessly ahead of the English forwards when suddenly Geoff Hurst, who had sprinted from the other side of the field, was there to head the ball powerfully past Hans Tilkowski in the German goal.

The game swayed one way, then the other, with both teams playing fast, attacking soccer. Banks saved superbly from Overath and Seeler. Tilkowski was lucky to scramble away another header from Hurst. It was England who appeared to be gaining strength and with twelve minutes to go, when the German defense failed to clear properly, Martin Peters slammed home a loose ball. With the deafening roar of the triumphant English fans ringing in their ears, the Germans pushed everyone up for a final assault, and it was fullback Wolfgang Weber who prodded the ball home for the dramatic last-minute equalizer.

WORLD CUP FINAL 1966
London, England: England 4 West Germany 2
With only seconds remaining in regular time, Wolfgang Weber (on ground at left) scores the equalizer for West Germany as Uwe Seeler and Helmut Haller rejoice. The England players are George Cohen (rear, on ground), Bobby Moore (arm raised), Ray Wilson, goalkeeper Gordon Banks, and Jacky Charlton.
© Peter Robinson: The Football Archive

For the first time since 1934, the final would go into extra time. A cruel test for already exhausted limbs, but one that little Alan Ball, the English midfielder, seemed to revel in. Karl-Heinz Schnellinger, whose task was to mark him, was outpaced time and time again. It was from one of Ball's centers that Hurst drove the ball viciously past Tilkowski. The ball smashed against the underside of the crossbar, bounced down to the ground, and back into play. England appealed for a goal, claiming that the ball was over the goal line before it bounced out. Referee Gottfried Dienst, from Switzerland, was not sure. With 95,000 fans holding their breath, biting their fingernails, and watching his every move, Dienst walked over to his Soviet linesman, who confirmed the goal with a sharp nod of his head and an imperious sweep of his flag.

It seemed unlikely that the ball could have been over the goal line* but the sporting Germans did not press their protests. They attacked desperately, but England, boosted by the goal, was clearly the stronger team now. Geoff Hurst scored again right before the end, making him the first, and so far only, player to score a hat trick in the final.

England, 4–2 winners, had earned its victory with a solid, workmanlike side that reflected Ramsey's no-frills approach to the game. It was not a particularly exciting team to watch, but in a tournament that had revealed a depressingly widespread tilt toward defensive play, it was the most efficient.

MEXICO, 1970

IX football world championship
may 31 – June 21

Four years later soccer mascotry marched on, and World Cup Willie gave way to Juanito, a chirpy, chunky little *muchacho* with a soccer ball and a sombrero that had "Mexico 70" on its brim. The Mexicans had worked hard to make the tournament a success, building new stadiums, including the magnificent 114,000-capacity Estadio Azteca in Mexico City. But there were still many who worried about the altitude problem. The 1968 Olympics had shown that there were very real dangers of exhaustion.

When the organizing committee decided to start some weekend games, including the final, in the full heat at twelve noon instead of at 4:00 P.M., apprehension about the location increased. European television, which wanted the noon kickoffs so that it could transmit the games live during prime viewing time back home, was now powerful enough to get its way.

Rough play was something else to worry about. It had been all too evident in 1966, as Pelé, among others, had reason to remember. Fortunately for the sport of soccer, Pelé had revoked his decision not to play in 1970, but if he had been hacked out of the tournament in 1966, it could

---

* The rules state that all of the ball must have crossed the full width of the line.

happen again. He and all the other skillful, creative players had to be protected. Strict instructions were given to the thirty referees to clamp down on foul play. They had a new weapon in the card system. They would show a player the yellow card for a caution, the red card for an ejection—a sign language to clear up communication problems between referees and players who did not speak the same language.

Another novelty for referees would be the waving of substitutes onto the field. Long resisted in soccer as either a gimmick or something that was akin to cheating, substitutes had finally arrived in the World Cup. They were limited to two per team.

The tournament had drawn a record entry of seventy-one nations, and elimination games had started in 1968. The vagaries of regional qualification were even more apparent than usual: Yugoslavia, Hungary, and Portugal were all eliminated in tough European qualifying groups. Israel, Morocco, and El Salvador* had made it as winners of much weaker groups.

The most surprising of the qualifiers was Peru, coached by the former Brazilian star Didi, but it clearly was not to be taken lightly as it had eliminated Argentina. To get themselves used to the climate and the altitude, England arrived in Mexico a month before their first game. The party consisted of twenty-two players, one coach, two trainers, and a doctor. Already in Mexico, waiting at the hotel that was to serve as England's headquarters, were tons of frozen and canned English food ("What happens if foreign food gives our boys a bellyache?" read the advertisement of one of the suppliers). The preparation was nothing if not thorough, and the team looked a strong one, stronger than 1966 according to Alf Ramsey, who was now Sir Alf. Queen Elizabeth had knighted him in 1967 for "services to football."

João Saldanha, a controversial ex-journalist, was in charge of Brazil's squad until March, two months before the tournament. Then he committed the two cardinal sins of Brazilian soccer: His team lost to Argentina, and he threatened to drop Pelé. The pressure began to tell. Criticized by the Flamengo coach Iustrich, Saldanha turned up at a Flamengo training session brandishing a revolver.

Saldanha had to go. He was replaced by Mario Zagalo, who had been the left winger on Brazil's 1958 and 1962 championship teams. In its qualifying group Brazil had scored twenty-three goals in six games, nine of them to Tostão and six to Pelé. Tostão, a member of the disappointing 1966 team, had been playing brilliantly until, in late 1968, he was hit in the eye by the

---

* In the North and Central American qualifying round, El Salvador had to play Honduras, a neighbor with which she had a long-standing quarrel over alleged discrimination against the 300,000 Salvadoran immigrants living in Honduras. The games were played in an atmosphere of mounting tension, culminating in the flight of some 50,000 Salvadoran refugees back to their homeland. After El Salvador had won the playoff game, which was played in Mexico, full-scale war broke out when 12,000 Salvadoran troops invaded Honduras. El Salvador became journalistically famous as "the nation that went to war over soccer," a facile explanation of a much more complicated series of events.

ball and suffered a detached retina. He had undergone surgery at an eye clinic in Houston, Texas, but his fitness was very much in doubt.

Just as it had done in 1966, the tournament opened with a dreary 0–0 tie. This time Mexico and the USSR were the culprits. Things were not helped by the martinet-ish performance of the German referee Kurt Tschenscher, who rushed hither and thither, stopping the game at the slightest suggestion of an infringement. The Soviets, who seemed to be his chief victims, became exasperated, and four of their players, along with one Mexican, received yellow-card cautions.

But Tschenscher's meddlesome refereeing was a hidden blessing. He had obeyed his instructions with commendable Teutonic thoroughness and he had made it unmistakably clear to players and coaches alike: The referees *were* going to be stricter than in 1966.

Pelé & Co. opened in commanding style against Czechoslovakia, winning 4–1 with exuberant, almost carefree attacking soccer. Tostão played brilliantly, as he was to play throughout the tournament. Jairzinho and Rivelino were revelations with their powerful dribbling and shooting. Pelé, twenty-nine years old, less athletic but more cerebral, looked better than ever. The defense was supposed to be weak, but with such attacking strength, did it really matter? The English players, who all watched the game, felt that it did, and that they could exploit the weakness.

Drawn in the same group, the two teams met four days later in one of the most fascinating games of the tournament. Brazil, without Gerson, its left-footed midfield playmaker, was slightly more cautious than usual, its attacks more methodical, slower to develop. But when they did come, as at the tenth minute . . . a sudden burst down the right wing by Jairzinho, a cross on the run to the far post, and there was Pelé leaping high to head the ball powerfully down, just inside the post. But the ball did not go in. Gordon Banks in England's goal, guarding the near post one second, was across the width of the goal the next, flinging himself full length to somehow scoop the ball off the line, up and over the bar as Pelé raised his arms in disbelief. Banks's save, televised all over the world, was hailed as one of the greatest ever.

England had its moments, particularly an overlapping run on the right by fullback Tommy Wright, whose center found Francis Lee, unmarked in front of the goal. Lee headed powerfully, but straight at goalkeeper Felix, who thankfully grasped the ball. After fifteen minutes of the second half, Tostão dribbled into the English penalty area, turned, and chipped the ball to Pelé, who flicked it on for Jairzinho to beat Banks from ten yards.

Late in the game, with England pressing, Everaldo miskicked and teed the ball up for the England center forward, Jeff Astle, standing almost on the penalty spot. His left-foot shot went wide of the goal, an incredible miss, and Brazil were 1–0 winners, the only time in the championship that they scored fewer than three goals in a game. However, England, by winning against Romania and Czechoslovakia, joined Brazil in the quarterfinals.

Mexico made the quarterfinals for the first time ever. After their opening tie with the Soviets, the Mexicans went on to beat El Salvador and then Belgium before 112,000 spectators in the cauldron of Aztec Stadium. This last game had revived memories of Chile in 1962: A huge, bitterly hostile crowd had intimidated the Belgians and—more important—the referee, who awarded the Mexicans a ludicrous penalty from which they scored the only goal of the game.

In the quarterfinals they met Italy, who had accomplished the seemingly impossible feat of topping their qualifying group while scoring only one goal, but 0–0 ties with Israel and Uruguay and a 1–0 win over Sweden had seen them through. Against Mexico, they at last opened up, scoring four times, with two of the goals going to Gigi Riva, the sturdy left winger who was the current idol of Italian soccer.

The Peruvians, who had shown themselves to be a spirited and skillful team during the first-round games, were unlucky to run into Brazil in their quarterfinal. They scored twice, but Brazil got four, with Tostão again in devastating form. West Germany avenged its 1966 final defeat, fighting back to beat England 3–2 after being 0–2 down. Its equalizing goal came from the veteran Uwe Seeler, playing in his fourth World Cup, while the man destined to replace him as Germany's ace goal scorer, Gerd Müller, got the winner in extra time. Uruguay (coached by Juan Hohberg, hero of its epic game against Hungary in 1954) completed the four semifinalists by beating the USSR 1–0.

The Italians scored early in their semifinal against West Germany, and promptly and predictably withdrew into their customary defensive shell. For most of the second half the Germans battered away at the well-marshaled Italian defense. Beckenbauer, gliding about the field with the grace, balance, and power of an Olympic ice-skater, was a constant menace. Late in the game he was on yet another full-speed run when a brutal foul sent him crashing to the ground. The fall dislocated Beckenbauer's shoulder, but he played on with his right arm strapped across his chest.

The score was still 1–0 to Italy when, in the final minute, Schnellinger equalized for Germany. In extra time the goals came thick and fast. Gerd Müller snatched a typical opportunist goal to put Germany ahead. Italy, goaded at last into attacking play, showed they could do it when they tried, equalizing through fullback Tarcisio Burgnich, then going ahead again on a goal from Riva's mighty left foot. Müller, flinging himself full length at the ball like a torpedo, brought Germany level again, only to have Rivera score the winning goal for Italy straight from the restart.

In Guadalajara the Brazilians met their old nemesis Uruguay, the first time the two nations had played each other in a World Cup game since that fateful final of 1950. Brazil gave away an early goal, equalized with a goal from their gifted young midfielder Clodoaldo, then struggled for the winner. When it did come, late in the game, it was a beauty—Jairzinho dribbling irresistibly down the right, cutting in and scoring with a perfectly

WORLD CUP FINAL 1970
Mexico City, Mexico: Brazil 4 Italy 1
Still the master at age 29. Pelé turns in triumph, having outjumped Italian
fullback Tarcisio Burgnich (on ground) to head the opening goal of the final.
For many devotees, the 1970 Brazil team was the sport's best ever.
© Peter Robinson: The Football Archive

placed cross-shot. Rivelino made it 3–1 in the final minute, converting a pass
from Pelé, but it had not been easy. Beating Uruguay has never been easy
for Brazil.

The final would see the attack-minded Brazilians against the defensive
Italians, soccer's version of the Forces of Light against the Forces of Darkness. But there was some hope that the Italians, having scored eight goals
in their last two games, might be tempted to adopt a more offensive style.

It was a hope that was dashed almost as soon as the game started. The
Italians packed their defense at once, giving Brazil a numerical advantage
in midfield, a situation much to the liking of the cunning Gerson, who
became a key figure of the game.

First blood fell to Brazil, and Pelé. A throw-in by Tostão was lofted into
the goalmouth by Rivelino—it looked innocuous enough, but Pelé turned
it into a goal. As the ball dropped, Pelé leaped high over Burgnich, twisted
powerfully in midair, and nodded the ball wide of Albertosi. Twenty
minutes later Roberto Boninsegna equalized for Italy with a goal that sprung
less from Italy's own efforts than from a calamitous mixup in the Brazilian
defense.

The halftime score of 1–1 in no way reflected the reality of the game
or that, as an attacking force, Italy was nonexistent. The goals, surely, would

come from Brazil. And come they did. Gerson, receiving the ball some thirty yards out, brought his devastating left foot into action ("He could stir his tea with it" was the thought of an admiring English player). Two quick, delicate touches got him past an Italian defender; then a scorching 25-yard drive left Albertosi grasping thin air.

Five minutes later Gerson's left foot struck again: His superbly accurate 40-yard pass was headed down by Pelé to Jairzinho, who ran the ball in. The rout was complete with a breathtaking fourth goal by captain Carlos Alberto, who came storming through from his fullback position to joyfully thump home Pelé's exquisitely judged pass.

A wonderful afternoon for positive soccer, and a fitting moment for the retirement of the Jules Rimet trophy. Brazil, having won it for the third time, now took permanent possession. A new trophy would be designed for the 1974 championship. The Brazilians took the old trophy home to a triumphant reception in Brasilia, and a bonus of some $20,000 for each player. The Italians, despite finishing in second place, went home to their by now almost traditional welcome of insults and rotten fruit, this time at Rome's Fiumicino airport.

GERMANY, 1974

Fußball-Weltmeisterschaft 1974
FIFA World Cup 1974
Coupe du Monde de la FIFA 1974
Copa Mundial de la FIFA 1974

The World Cup flame, were there such a thing, would now pass from Juanito to Tip and Tap, two rather ugly little boys with toothy grins whom the Germans had selected as the official mascots for 1974. And the new trophy, now officially called the FIFA World Cup, made its first appearance. The Italian sculptor Silvio Gazzanigga explained his work: "The lines spring out of the base, rising in spirals, stretching out to receive the world. From the remarkable dynamic tensions of the compact body of the sculpture rise the figures of two athletes at the stirring moment of victory. In a flowing and spontaneous language, the work expresses the force and purity of the spirit of sporting competition." It was announced that the cup was solid eighteen-carat gold, and had cost $20,000.

Mention of its cost was not at all out of place in 1974, for suddenly the World Cup seemed to be more about money than soccer. It was estimated that Brazil had spent $4.5 million preparing to defend their title. The Dutch, having qualified, very nearly did not get their team to Germany because of a squabble over bonuses—eventually settled when the players were guaranteed a payment of $24,000 each plus 70 percent of the profits made from the tournament by the Dutch F.A. The Australians, one of the "weak group" qualifiers (the others were Haiti and Zaire), were said to be on a $4,000 bonus per man if they managed to win a game. Gross income to the

German organizing committee would be around $40 million. Tip and Tap were evidently sitting on top of a gold mine; the contribution from companies licensed to use their grinning faces was over $2 million.

Politics, too, made its presence felt. Just before the USSR was due to play Chile in a home-and-home play-off series, the Marxist Chilean government was overthrown on September 11, 1973, by a bloody coup in which the president, Salvador Allende, was killed. The first game, in Moscow, was tied 0–0. When the Chileans announced that the return game would be played in the National Stadium in Santiago, the Russians balked. Not unreasonably, for the stadium was already famous as, at best, a detention center for opponents of the new regime, at worst (as the Soviets claimed) "a concentration camp, place of tortures and executions of Chilean patriots." The Soviets wanted to play in a neutral country; FIFA said no, and so the USSR withdrew.*

Security measures, already substantial with the memory of the 1972 Munich Olympic tragedy strong in everyone's mind, were strengthened for Chile's games in case of demonstrations from German leftists. Trouble was also expected at the other end of the political spectrum from German rightists protesting the presence of the East German team. Scotland, fired by the success of Scottish Nationalist candidates in the recent British election, was casting a jaundiced ear at being introduced with "God Save the Queen" as its national anthem.

England was not present, having been knocked out in the qualifying rounds by Poland, the 1972 Olympic champions. It was the first time they had ever failed to qualify, and the failure was to cost Sir Alf Ramsey his job.

The favorites, in a rather on-and-off sort of way, were the West Germans. Two years earlier they had won the European Nations Cup with a magnificently inventive team, but the departure of midfield star Günter Netzer, who had gone to seek his fortune with Real Madrid in Spain, seemed to have upset the team's rhythm. Its recent results were not convincing, but it did have the superb Beckenbauer as captain, and the master goal scorer Gerd Müller—*Der Bomber* as he was now known.

Brazil had lost its chief star. Pelé had retired from the national team in 1971 and had stuck to his decision despite immense pressures in Brazil. There was even a financial offer from German businessmen who wanted his drawing power in the tournament. For the first time in sixteen years, Brazil would play the World Cup without him. His absence, plus the fact that it was playing in Europe, had dimmed Brazil's chances of retaining the title.

If strength at club level meant anything, then surely the Dutch had a strong chance. Their two leading clubs, Feyenoord and Ajax, had dominated

---

* Chile went through to the finals after a mock "game" in the National Stadium in which their team, unopposed, kicked off, dribbled the ball downfield, and shot it into the empty goal for an official 1–0 victory. Their poor form in the subsequent tournament led to rumors that it had taken them three tries to score the goal.

WORLD CUP 1974
Frankfurt, West Germany: West Germany 1 Poland 0
Closely watched by teammate Wolfgang Overath (No. 12), West German captain Franz Beckenbauer spins away from Polish winger Grzegorz Lato. Beckenbauer's attacking forays were the trademark of the adventurous way in which he played the libero *position.*
© Peter Robinson: The Football Archive

European soccer since 1969, and it was from the players of these two that most of the national team was drawn. One exception was the captain, Johan Cruyff, a former Ajax player whom the Spanish club Barcelona had bought for $2.2 million. It was Cruyff, the new Golden Boy of soccer, who was expected to replace Pelé as the sport's superstar.

The Dutch had arrived explosively on the world soccer scene, and their freewheeling style seemed to reflect the open, liberal nature of Dutch society. Coach Rinus Michels even allowed them to have their wives with them in training camp.*

Because of their strength in defense, the Italians were much fancied. Their goalkeeper, Dino Zoff, had not been beaten in eleven international games. Experience was not a problem—five members of the squad had played in both the 1966 and 1970 World Cups—but advancing age might be.

---

*An innovation that would have appealed to the Brazilian defender Luis Pereira. Trapped in a month-long, isolated Brazilian camp before the tournament, Pereira complained to a journalist: "This is supposed to make us world champions. World champions of what? Masturbation?"

Breaking with the tradition that the host nation opens the tournament, West Germany gave that honor instead to the holders, Brazil. The Germans had realized that the ceremonial importance of the occasion made for nervousness, and had noted that in 1966 and 1970 the games had been played ultracautiously, both finishing in 0–0 ties.

"The poisoned gift," the Brazilians called it, and, in drenching rain, proceeded to play a cautious, dull game against the equally cautious and dull Yugoslavia: result, yet another boring 0–0 tie.

Despite ducking the opening game, West Germany started negatively anyway, laboring to a 1–0 win over Chile while the Berlin crowd booed and shouted rude remarks about the number of Munich players in the team. Scotland recorded its first-ever World Cup victory by beating Zaire, but the narrowness of the win (2–0) suggested either that the Zaireans were a lot better than expected, or the Scots were a lot worse. It turned out to be mostly the latter.

Poland was off to a fine start when its team beat Argentina 3–2 in a vastly entertaining game. Grzegorz Lato and Robert Gadocha, the tricky and admirably direct Polish wingers, did most of the damage, but Kazimierz Deyna stood out as an attacking midfielder of considerable talent. Argentina, which had earned a reputation for callous, rough play during the 1960s, surprised everyone with its sparkling—and clean—soccer.* In Carlos Babington they unveiled one of the most gifted players of the competition.

Once again the first major surprise came at the expense of the Italians. Little Haiti took a 1–0 lead over the *azzurri* when its muscular winger Emmanuel Sanon, with defender Luciano Spinosi tugging desperately at his shirt, powered his way through to score. The Italians recovered quickly to score three times, but Zoff's scoreless record was gone. Worse was to come. Italy were held to a 1–1 tie by the increasingly confident Argentines, and then beaten 1–2 by a rampant Poland, which had by now convinced everyone that its elimination of England was no fluke. The loss to Poland put Italy out of the competition, and as the team bus drew away from the stadium in Stuttgart, it was stoned by angry groups of immigrant Italian workers.

The Haitians, too, were eliminated, though not before one of their team—Ernst Jean-Joseph—had become the first player in World Cup history to record a positive drug test.

Scotland was out, too, but they went home to a hysterical welcome in Glasgow. Their record was two ties (with Brazil and Yugoslavia) and that 2–0 win over lowly Zaire, not good enough to qualify for the second round, but they were unbeaten! All three minnows—Australia, Zaire, and Haiti—were eliminated, and the 9–0 thrashing that Yugoslavia administered to Zaire, to say nothing of Haiti's 0–7 loss to Poland, brought renewed criticism of the regional qualifying system that permitted such feeble teams to reach the final sixteen.

---

* The reason for the Argentines' good behavior was not hard to discern. They had been selected as hosts for the 1978 World Cup and were determined not to do anything that would cause FIFA to think again.

The toast of the first round was unquestionably the Netherlands. In their first game the orange-shirted Dutch demoralized Uruguay with a dizzying display of fast-moving soccer, a merry-go-round of constant position switches by the whole team, with, always at the center of things, the flowing, impudent skills of Johan Cruyff. Held to a 0–0 tie by Sweden in their next game, the Dutch came back with another masterful display to thrash Bulgaria 4–1.

The East Germans, as expected, proved to be the most disciplined team in the competition, making up in fitness what they lacked in originality. Their 1–0 victory over West Germany, while a considerable boost to their political pride, really meant very little, as West Germany had already made sure of its own place in the second round.

The form of the second round was a new one. Instead of the eight teams playing a single quarterfinal each, followed by semifinals, they were grouped into two groups of four teams: Brazil, Netherlands, East Germany, and Argentina in one, West Germany, Poland, Sweden, and Yugoslavia in the other. The winners of each group would meet in the final. It meant, of course, more games—twelve instead of six—which meant, naturally, more gate money.

The Dutch had little difficulty in the first group, beating all three opponents, though their game against Brazil was one of the roughest of the tournament. This was by no means the Brazil of 1970. The defense was certainly one of the strongest and toughest in the competition, but with Pelé and Tostão gone and Jairzinho painfully out of form, nothing could hide the poverty of Brazil's attack. The star of their side was, appropriately enough, a fullback with a flair for attack, the blond Francisco Marinho. Netherlands beat them 2–0, with Cruyff setting up the first goal and scoring the second himself with a gloriously controlled volley on the run.

West Germany struggled against Sweden, eventually beating them 4–2, but not before the Swedes had shown, yet again, what a formidable team they are in World Cup competition. Next, the Germans faced the Poles in Frankfurt. Whichever team won would play in the final against Holland. Sad then, that such a crucial game should have been played under conditions that made good soccer impossible.

A torrential downpour flooded the field and delayed the kickoff for half an hour. The Frankfurt fire brigade arrived with a monster squeegee roller that they trundled up and down the field. Their valiant efforts made little impression. Parts of the field were virtually underwater when play did start.*

Bad news for the Poles, who found one of their major weapons, the speed of Lato and Gadocha, severely blunted by the clinging mud. Even so, they were by far the better team in the first half, and only a number of excellent saves by Sepp Maier in the German goal kept them out. Seven

---

* The German organizers had fed sixty years of German weather statistics into a computer to pinpoint the driest three weeks of summer for the tournament. The computer flunked the test, for it rained almost as much as it did during the sodden 1954 finals.

minutes after the interval, Jan Tomaszewski, the giant Polish goalkeeper, excelled himself by saving a penalty kick.

The save should have inspired the Poles. Instead it seemed to bring the Germans more into the game. With fifteen minutes left, Gerd Müller, inexplicably allowed to lurk unmarked on the edge of the area, snapped up a pass from Rainer Bonhof and beat Tomaszewski with a low shot into the corner for the only goal of the game. A desperately unlucky loss for Poland, the one team in the tournament that was always ready to attack wholeheartedly. By beating the indecisive Brazilians 1–0, Poland claimed third place in the tournament, but few would have begrudged them a place in the final.

After an enormous 1,500-member choir had sung "Tulips from Amsterdam" (for the Dutch) and a jazzed-up version of the Schiller/ Beethoven "Ode to Joy" (for the Germans), after Henry Kissinger had taken his seat, after the playing of the national anthems, and after the referee had noticed that the punctilious German organizers had forgotten to put up the corner flags, the tenth World Cup final got under way.

The Dutch kicked off, and passed the ball methodically among themselves while the Germans held off; Cruyff, bored by such dithering, came back to collect the ball, surged into the German penalty area, and was blatantly tripped by Berti Vogts. Penalty kick to the Netherlands, a mere eighty seconds after the start. The Dutch had made sixteen passes, and not one German had as much as gotten a foot on the ball. Johan Neeskens scored from the penalty (the first ever to be awarded in a World Cup final), and the Dutch were ahead.

The advantage turned out to be another poisoned gift. Two things were now against the Dutch: tradition (in six previous finals the team scoring first had ended up as the loser) and the well-established fact that the Germans were at their best when fighting back.

Throughout the first half the early goal hung like a lead weight around the Dutch players. They failed to press home their advantage. Indeed, they started to play conservatively, protecting their one-goal lead. An approach totally at odds with their normal swashbuckling style. Inevitably, the Germans forced their way back into the game. After half an hour of hard physical play and mounting German pressure, the equalizer arrived through another penalty kick, though this one of much less obvious validity: Bernd Hölzenbein, running the ball into the Dutch penalty area, appeared to drag his foot into Wim Jansen's admittedly late tackle. Paul Breitner scored to tie the game.

The Germans stepped up their attacks. Vogts broke through, shot hard and true, to be thwarted by a lightning-quick one-handed reaction from Dutch goalkeeper Jan Jongbloed. Six minutes later, after Jongbloed had punched an insidious Beckenbauer free kick over the bar, it was the Netherlands that should have scored. Catching the Germans upfield, Cruyff and Johnny Rep broke free. Cruyff drew Beckenbauer and pushed the ball through to Rep with only goalkeeper Maier to beat. Rep hurried his shot and banged the ball against the desperately lunging Maier.

Three minutes before halftime Bonhof raced away on the right, the Dutch defenders were slow to cover, and his center reached Müller in the area. Müller seemed, for a moment, to overrun the ball, then turned quickly to shoot right-footed along the ground past Jongbloed to make the score 2–1. A typical Müller goal, not struck particularly hard, but perfectly timed and placed.

Try as they might—and they swarmed around the German goal for most of the second half—the Dutch could not score again. They came close, but Maier was equal to everything. When he did make a mistake, Breitner was there to head the ball off the line. As time ran out, the Dutch attacks became frenetic and anxious, and Cruyff, strangely, seemed content to hang back in midfield. The second-half statistics, which showed Germany with just one shot at the Dutch goal, bore out Cruyff's bitter lament: "Germany didn't win the World Cup. We lost it." But the Germans had survived everything that the Dutch could throw at them, and they were the new world champions.

– 4 –

The World Cup, 1978-1990*

The 1974 World Cup had marked the end of Sir Stanley Rous's 13-year reign as FIFA President. FIFA's full membership had to vote twice, but on the 2nd ballot he was beaten 66–52 by the Brazilian millionaire João Havelange.

For Havelange, this was the reward for a two-year campaign in which he had assiduously courted the votes of the growing number of African and Asian countries. For the European powers it was a shock to realize how easily they could be outvoted, to know that the vote of Lesotho or Nepal was now equal to that of England or West Germany.

For the first time, a non-European was in charge of FIFA, elected by non-European votes, making the Europeans unhappy. There was talk of Europe seceding from FIFA to set up their own international body.

Havelange's promise to the Third World countries had been that he would increase the number of places available to them in future World Cups. This meant increasing the number of finalists—it was supposed to go up to twenty in 1978, then on to twenty-four in 1982.

Where Rous had been a soccer referee and an administrator, Havelange had played Olympic water polo, and came from a business background. He was to bring some very different attitudes to FIFA.

ARGENTINA, 1978

In 1978 it was back to Latin America for the World Cup road show, but not quite as intended. The tournament had been awarded to Argentina in 1966. The Peronists had assumed power in 1973 and taken over the organization of the World Cup, believing—just as Mussolini and the Italian Fascists had believed in 1934—that it would bolster their popularity.

The theory was never put to the test—at least not by the Peronists. In 1976 the roof fell in on their government. The country was approaching anarchy. Left wing guerrillas, the Montoneros, were operating

---

* For tabulated scores of all tournament games, see pages 314–324. For tactical analyses of World Cups, see chapter 8, pages 178–226.

openly, carrying out daring raids and kidnappings in the streets. The armed forces seized power, and "the generals" took over the country.

A brutal war against the guerrillas followed. Many people—particularly in Europe—felt that the World Cup should be taken away from Argentina, that it should not be staged under a repressive military regime. FIFA turned a blind eye, and the new government was quick to announce that the tournament, Mundial-78, would go on. For the generals, the World Cup filled the same bread-and-circuses role that it would have done for the banished Peronists.

General Omar Actis was appointed to head the preparations. Driving to his first press conference, he was assassinated in a Buenos Aires street by the Montoneros. But within a year, the generals had gained the upper hand.

It was not pretty. In the Plaza de Mayo, a growing group of brave middle-aged mothers started to gather regularly to protest the disappearance of their sons and daughters—the *desaparecidos*, taken away by the government's secret police, most of them never to be seen again.

But the Montoneros were reeling. They issued a famous statement, vowing that they had never intended to disrupt the World Cup, because *estamos hombres y mujeres del pueblo*, we are men and women of the people.

A captain from the navy, Carlos Alberto Lacoste took over the running of the World Cup, complaining that between 1973 and 1976 "the Peronists talked but did nothing. We are replacing their paper with real things, with buildings and stadiums. Under the Peronists you had 3 days of work and 362 days of strikes. Today there are no strikes. We have banned them."

Havelange's vow to increase the number of finalists was not acted on. It remained at sixteen. Three new stadiums were built, three others were renovated. It was claimed that some $200 million was being spent on permanent improvements to roads, railroads, airports, and communications systems. Color television was introduced for the first time in Argentina, but only in the press centers for the 4,500 journalists covering the event.

Beyond the control of the generals were the qualifying round results. Uruguay was ousted by Peru. A big financial blow. The hordes of Uruguayans who had been expected to make the short ferry trip across the Rio de la Plata in search of tickets would not now be coming. England didn't make it either, but the other former World Cup winners did: Italy, West Germany, and Brazil.

World Cup tradition showed that when a major world soccer power staged the tournament, it won: Uruguay in 1930, Italy in 1934, England in 1966, West Germany in 1974. Only Brazil in 1950 had failed. So . . . if Argentina was a world soccer power, as everyone surely believed, then it should win.

But could it? For all the great players it had produced, Argentina had always flopped in the World Cup. Skepticism among Argentine fans was widespread. It increased when the tournament draw—usually so kind to the host team—placed Argentina into an ominously strong first-round group along with Hungary, France, and Italy.

The man appointed to lead Argentina to glory was Cesar Luis Menotti, coach of the national team. Tall, thin, long-haired, a constant smoker, Menotti had been at work since 1973. Immediately, he had to confront the perennial problem: so many of Argentina's best players were with European clubs. Menotti knew he could not build a team on such players, who were rarely available to him. He declared that his team would consist mainly of home-based players.

It was a decision that, incredibly, led to his toughest battle: To convince the administrators of Argentine soccer to take its own national team seriously. This meant getting full cooperation from club teams in releasing players for training camps and games—cooperation that had never been willingly given in the past.

Menotti, a determined man who knew exactly what he wanted, got his way. But he had to fight off continual attacks on the style of his team. He wanted players with exceptional ball skills—the traditional Argentine skills, as he saw them. His critics insisted that a more vigorous, more physical approach was needed for the World Cup, and mocked his style as *fulbito,* little football.

The start of Mundial-78 was not promising. West Germany and Poland, first- and third-place finishers in 1974, produced what was (and hopefully will remain) the worst opening game ever. Two teams unwilling to take the slightest risk, content to play for a massively boring tactical tie.

Much more was expected from Germany, despite the loss of two key players from its 1974 side: goal scorer Gerd Müller, and captain Franz Beckenbauer. In 1977, at the peak of his game—he had just been voted the 1976 European player of the year—Beckenbauer had stunned the soccer world by signing for the New York Cosmos, and then announcing that he would not play in Mundial-78. But coach Helmut Schön had a new crop of promising youngsters, including the smoothly skilled twenty-two-year-old midfielder, Karl-Heinz Rummenigge.

Poland had the look of a spent force, a bland team with only the lively young Zbigniew Boniek promising anything out of the ordinary.

The Scots arrived bursting with totally misplaced confidence. Despite losing their last warm-up game to England, they were given a rousing send-off from Glasgow by delirious crowds lining the route to the airport. Evidently convinced of his team's superiority, coach Ally MacLeod didn't bother to scout his first opponent, Peru. So the Peruvians ran them ragged and beat them 3–1.

MacLeod said he was surprised at the speed of the Peruvians. He got another shock the following day when winger Willy Johnston became the second player in World Cup history to fail a drug test. He was banned and sent home in disgrace, guilty of taking the pep pill fencamfamin before the 3–1 loss to Peru ("the sort of performance that gives pep pills a bad name" remarked a Scottish fan).

The Scots were even worse in their next game. Their goal in a 1–1 tie with a weak Iran team came when Iranian defender Andranik Eskandarian (soon to join Beckenbauer at the New York Cosmos) put through his own goal. But the tie kept Scotland's hopes of a place in the next round alive. Just. It would need to beat the Netherlands—one of the tournament favorites—by a margin of three goals. Could the Scots score three times against the Netherlands? Jan Jongbloed, now the reserve goalkeeper for the Dutch, pondered the matter and replied: "Yes . . . but not in one game."

With all the perverseness that has characterized Scotland's fruitless World Cup adventures over the years, the three goals were duly scored. One of them, a corkscrew dribble and rasping shot from little Archie Gemmill, was rated one of the best goals of the tournament. But the Netherlands scored twice, so Scotland's famous 3–2 victory was to no avail.

The Dutch went on the second round. They, like the Germans, were without their inspirational figure from 1974: Johan Cruyff, like Beckenbauer, had opted not to play. Without Cruyff, Dutch total soccer was a less intelligent style, relying more on sheer athletic ability than soccer artistry. The typical player was now Johan Neeskens, the combative, nonstop midfielder. Neeskens certainly had his share of soccer skills, but he was a totally different type of player than the subtle, inventive Cruyff. Coach Rinus Michels had been replaced by the Austrian Ernst Happel, who liked to pack his midfield with five or even six players.

Brazil had changed its coach, too. New man Claudio Coutinho came from a physical education background. Cultured, multilingual, Coutinho brought an excess of theory to the largely instinctive Brazilian game. When he stressed the need for "polyvalent" players, some of his team members had no idea what he was talking about. More damaging was Coutinho's continuance of a trend that had been seen in 1974: the swing toward a more physical, more "European" approach. A policy that meant only sporadic playing time for two of his more skilled players, Zico and Rivelino.

Playing in the seaside town of Mar del Plata, Brazil cut a sorry figure in the first round. It tied Sweden 1–1 in a game that it might have won but for a moment of absurdly fastidious refereeing from Welshman Clive Thomas. In the game's final seconds, Brazil took a corner kick and Zico leaped to head what looked like the winning goal. No, said Thomas, no goal, the game is over. He had blown the final whistle while the ball was in the air, just before it reached Zico.

If luck was against Brazil in that game, it favored them abundantly against Spain. With the score still tied at 0–0 late in the second half, the Brazilian goalkeeper, Leão, came out of his goal to intercept a cross. He missed the ball, which went through to the Spanish forward Julio Cardenosa, unmarked, some eight yards in front of the now empty goal. As the crowd roared Goal! for this simplest of scoring chances, Cardenosa froze. He delayed his shot for what seemed an eternity, as the Brazilian defenders scrambled back to cover. Cardenosa's shot, when it did finally come, was weak. Defender Amaral cleared the ball off the goal-line, and Brazil escaped with another tie.

An unconvincing 1–0 win over Austria was enough to get Brazil into the second round. But the Brazilian fans were not happy with a team that had scored only two goals in three games. They burned an effigy of coach Coutinho in the streets of Mar del Plata.

Brazil's second-round group would include Poland, and the other two remaining Latin American teams, Peru and Argentina. It had been tough going for Argentina. A 2–1 win over the skilled but violent Hungarians was followed by a questionable win over France. The French had played delightful soccer in their first game before losing 2–1 to Italy. They were to play equally well against Argentina, particularly their new playmaker, Michel Platini, and their sweeper Marius Trésor.

Argentina struggled until, right on halftime, they got a break from the Swiss referee. The sort of break, said the cynics, that the host nation will always get. Leopoldo Luque, Argentina's big, direct center forward, got behind the French defense. As he tried to left-foot the ball low across the area, Trésor slid desperately in. The ball struck Trésor's hand as he was falling. Penalty to Argentina, said the referee.

That Trésor had handled the ball as he fell was not in doubt, nor was the fact that this had stopped the ball going through to Argentina's René Houseman, waiting in front of goal. But the rules said the offense had to be *intentional*. That was very doubtful.

Captain Daniel Passarella scored from the kick. Platini tied the game for France fifteen minutes into the second half, before Luque's screaming 25-yard volley won it for Argentina. The win assured Argentina's passage to the second round. Which was just as well, for the Argentines lost their next game 1–0 to the increasingly confident Italians.

Coach Enzo Bearzot's team looked excitingly capable of accomplishing his aim: a more positive look for Italian soccer, an end to the defensive negativity of the *catenaccio* system* that had dominated Italian soccer since the early 1960s. Italy had fought back to win after the French had scored the quickest goal of the tournament in just thirty-eight seconds. It had outclassed the Hungarians by a 3–1 score. Now the Argentines were dispatched with comparative ease.

Paolo Rossi—Pablito the Argentines called him, a nickname that stuck with Rossi for the rest of his career—may have been lightly built for a center forward, but his quickness and touch were a delight to watch. And he had scored two goals.

Then just as the praise was piling up, the Italians lost their way. In the second round the familiar caution returned. A 0–0 tie with Germany, a 1–0 win over Austria (goal by Rossi) were followed by a 2–1 loss to the

---

* See chapter 8, page 203

Netherlands. Good enough only to get them to the third-place game. It was the Dutch, winners of the group, who went on to the final.

Deservedly so. Without the brilliance of the team that had been dubbed the Clockwork Orange in 1974, the Dutch were nevertheless playing exhilarating soccer. After annihilating Austria 5–1, they moved on to play the Germans, and to seek revenge for defeat in the 1974 final. They had to be satisfied with a 2–2 tie. The Germans were then beaten 3–2 by Austria in coach Schön's last World Cup game. Schön went home an embittered man, claiming he felt let down by his younger players.

The Dutch marched on to victory over Italy in Buenos Aires—an eventful afternoon for the young Dutch fullback Erny Brandts. After eighteen minutes, attempting to clear an Italian attack, he visited a double disaster on his own team. He collided violently with goalkeeper Pieter Schrijvers and, at the same moment, rocketed the ball into his own net to give the Italians a 1–0 lead. Schrijvers was stretchered off and Jongbloed, veteran of the 1974 team, came on.

All was forgiven four minutes into the second half when Brandts, from 25 yards out, thumped an unstoppable drive past Dino Zoff in the Italian goal. The game was decided twenty-five minutes later when Arie Haan ripped another long-range drive past Zoff—this one from 30 yards.

That same evening Argentina crushed Peru 6–0 in Rosario, thus edging out Brazil on goal difference for the right to oppose the Dutch in the final. Brazil and Argentina had both beaten Poland, and had then played each other to a bad-tempered 0–0 stand-off. But Brazil's 3–0 win over Peru put the pressure on Argentina. They had to beat the Peruvians by a margin of four goals.

A tricky situation because Peru, with two losses, was already out of contention. Was it to be expected that they would offer much resistance? The rumors flew in the Argentine press: Brazilian "representatives" had been seen at the Peruvians' hotel with suitcases full of dollars; Brazilian businessmen were offering the Peruvian players plots of land to hold off the Argentines.

The Brazilians certainly did point out that Ramón Quiroga, the Peruvians' erratic goalkeeper, had been born in Argentina. In Rosario, in fact. Would *he* want to go down as the man who kept Argentina out of the final?

As Argentina piled up its 6–0 win, the crowd in Rosario chanted *Llora Brasil, llora!*—weep Brazil, weep! If they didn't weep, the Brazilians certainly raised a howl of protest, accusing the Peruvians of, at best, not trying. Said Coutinho, "This game will go down in soccer history as the Game of Shame."

Brazil partially redeemed itself with a 2–1 win over Italy in the game for third place. Poor Zoff—yet again he was beaten by a long-range shot, but this one bordered on the incredible. Brazilian fullback Nelinho, some 40 yards out on the right flank, started to dribble the ball in toward the goalmouth, then let fly with the outside of his right foot. The ball, hit very hard, appeared to be going harmlessly wide of the left goalpost . . . but as Zoff moved across, the ball seemed to take a sudden vicious curve, hooking past his right shoulder and into the goal, just inside the post. Brazil thus went home unbeaten, with Coutinho claiming that it was the "moral champion," a phrase that didn't interest the Brazilian fans. They wanted to be champion, period. Coutinho lost his job.

By now, the atmosphere throughout Argentina was electric. The progress of Menotti's team to the final had been followed first with disbelief, now with almost feverish passion. Each Argentine victory had brought the crowds pouring onto the streets of Buenos Aires, celebrating long into the night as though they feared this would be the last chance to make merry. But the victories went on and the crowds got larger and larger.

Each time Argentina took the field, the stadium exploded into a cauldron of noise, a sea of waving blue-and-white Argentine flags, a shower of streamers, and a whirling blizzard of *papelitos*, the confetti that every fan brought with him.

The spectacle was awesome, and Menotti's players responded with nonstop attacking soccer. They seemed to be driven forward by the crowd, a risk-taking team that played with three genuine forwards—Luque, Oscar Ortiz, and Daniel Bertoni—a team that was always looking for goals. Only Luis Galván played a determinedly defensive role; the other three fullbacks—Alberto Tarantini, Jorge Olguin, and captain Daniel Passarella—were ever eager to join in attacking moves.

In midfield the neat, tireless little Osvaldo Ardiles kept the ball moving forward with a string of intelligent passes. Alongside him was the left-footed Mario Kempes, the only foreign-based player on the team. Part midfielder, part forward, Kempes had been scoreless in the early games, but exploded for four goals in the second round, and was emerging as the tournament's outstanding player.

The final at Buenos Aires's River Plate stadium got off to a sour start. Blatant gamesmanship by Argentina. The Dutch were on the field at 2:50. Alone. They had to wait four minutes before the storm of *papelitos* signaled the arrival of the Argentines, who promptly objected to a plaster cast worn on his arm by the Dutchman Rene Van der Kerkhof. A further delay of nine minutes while Van der Kerkhof left the field to have the cast wrapped in a bandage.

If the Argentine idea was to unsettle the Dutch, then—rather surprisingly—it worked. In the first minute of play Jan Poortvliet viciously tripped Bertoni from behind, and seconds later Haan clobbered Ardiles. Referee Sergio Gonella from Italy gave the free kicks, but no yellow cards. Gonella's leniency was duly noted by both teams, and a foul-ridden game inevitably followed.

But if there were too many fouls, there was also plenty of pulsating excitement. How could it be otherwise, with two attacking teams, each likely to leave alarming gaps in its defense? At both ends, the goalkeepers found

WORLD CUP FINAL 1978
Buenos Aires, Argentina: Argentina 3 Netherlands 1
*The teams take the field as the capacity crowd of 77,260 in the Estadio Monu-
mental lets loose a storm of confetti. It needed overtime—and two goals from
tournament star Mario Kempes—for Argentina to take their first World title.*
© Paul Gardner

themselves forced to make heroic saves. For Argentina Ubaldo Fillol
saved brilliantly from Johnny Rep then, just before the break, instinctively
used his feet to keep out a shot from Robby Rensenbrink.

Jongbloed had to save twice from Passarella, whose forward incursions
were a serious menace. But it was Kempes who drew first blood with two
telling left-foot touches, darting between two defenders to collect Luque's
pass at the edge of the box, and slipping the ball under Jongbloed as he
came out.

The 1–0 scoreline stood up for most of the second half, though it was
a nail-biting time for the Argentine fans as the Dutch fought desperately
for the equalizing goal. It came with only eight minutes left. The Argentine
offside trap broke down, Rene Van der Kerkhof had space and time for a
precise cross, and Dirk Nanninga headed home. With only seconds left,
the Dutch had their moment. A long ball from Ruud Krol put Rensenbrink
through; his shot beat Fillol, but hit the post.

At 1–1, the game went to overtime, and the Argentines took over.
After fourteen minutes it was Kempes again, with that uncanny ability to
spot an opening in the Dutch defense. This time it took four left-foot touches,
as the ball bounced off Jongbloed, but Kempes got to the rebound first to
put Argentina 2–1 up.

With four minutes left, the rampant Kempes again bamboozled the Dutch defenders with a powerful dribble into the penalty area to set up Bertoni for the final goal.

The host country had won again. The Menotti miracle was complete. The generals, led by President Jorge Videla, were at the game to see Argentina triumph. Of course, they—like the Peronists—had been right. Soccer had brought the country joy. The incredible scenes in Buenos Aires that night proved the point. Streets jammed solid with hundreds of thousands of men, women, children, singing and cheering, dancing if they could find space, as wave after wave of *papelitos* drifted down from the windows of apartment buildings.

A moment of release for an entire people. After decades of frustration— years that had seen their neighbors and rivals Brazil and Uruguay carry off five World Cups between them—Argentina's long awaited ascent to soccer supremacy had arrived. For a short while, soccer was more important than anything. But the shadow of the Plaza mothers, with their simple, anxious faces, was not something that could be forgotten. The full horrors of the *desaparecidos* and the dirty war waged by the junta would emerge later.

SPAIN, 1982

COPA DEL MUNDO DE FUTBOL ESPAÑA 82

España-82 was touted as the biggest and best World Cup ever. The biggest it certainly was, with twenty-four teams in the final tournament instead of sixteen. This was what FIFA president João Havelange had promised during his election campaign in 1974 in return for votes from Third World countries.

Africa now got two slots, instead of one, as did Asia/Oceania and Concacaf (the North and Central America and Caribbean region that includes the United States). South America went up from three to four teams. European opposition to the plan had died down—after all, Europe, with four more places, was the biggest gainer.

The additional slot for Concacaf countries was enticing news for the United States. The region had always been dominated by Mexico, which had repeatedly won the single slot available in the finals. It had been so in 1954, 1958, 1962, 1966, and 1970. Haiti had pulled an upset in 1974, but Mexico were back in 1978.

But the United States failed at the first hurdle, and was quickly eliminated after finishing last in a three-team preliminary group with Canada and Mexico. By the time the qualifiers were over, Mexico was out, too. To the amazement of all, it was Honduras and El Salvador that went to Spain.

Equally shocking was the qualifying-round elimination of the Netherlands, runners-up in the last two tournaments.

Elsewhere, the regional qualifying system operated as erratically and unfairly as ever. Chile booked its place in Spain by playing just 4 games, while New Zealand had to play 15 games. Altogether, between March 1980 and December 1981, 319 games were played, involving 106 countries.

From the start, España-82 was an ill-defined tournament. Spread throughout the length and breadth of Spain—its 52 games were played in fourteen different cities—it lacked an obvious center of attention. It was also a tournament without a clear favorite. Spain found itself rated among the top teams, but this had more to do with its position as host nation than any obvious playing strengths. Coached by former Real Madrid star José Santamaria (a naturalized Uruguayan), Spain had a solid goalkeeper in Luis Arconada, and a powerful defender in José Camacho. But its offense depended too heavily on the occasionally brilliant but invariably inconsistent midfielder, Jesús Zamora.

France looked a more likely champion. The team was now built around Platini, who had matured into Europe's top player. As midfield partners he had Alain Giresse and Jean Tigana, both small but immensely skilled players. Presiding majestically over the defense from his sweeper position was Marius Trésor from the tiny Caribbean island of Guadeloupe—a French *département.*

The French had acquired a nickname—The Brazilians of Europe—a tribute to their skillful, artistic style. Weighing against them was a long tradition of failure. No French team, national or club, had ever won a major title.

The West Germans, as always, had to be taken seriously. Under new coach Jupp Derwall, they had won the European title in 1980. But a knee injury had ruled out the star of that team, Bernd Schuster. Paul Breitner, whose penalty kick goal had helped Germany to win the 1974 World Cup, was back. Rummenigge had just been voted European Player of the Year, and there was an exciting twenty-one-year-old winger, Pierre Littbarski. But it was the huge, surprisingly mobile defender Hans-Peter Briegel who personified the German threat: strength and stamina. For good measure, they were said to be using a new drink called MS-61, based on ginseng and "biocatalysts," that was marvelous for fighting off tiredness.

Defensively, the Italians looked as good as ever. Goalkeeper Dino Zoff, forty years old, was the most experienced in the business. Sweeper Gaetano Scirea was the best in his position; Fulvio Collovati and Antonio Cabrini were talented, intelligent defenders in the best Italian tradition. Giancarlo Antognoni ran the midfield in his elegant, rangy style, but there were problems up front.

Goals were hard to come by. In its final qualifying game, Italy had managed to score only one goal against the feeble Luxembourg! Coach Bearzot recalled Paolo Rossi—a daring and risky move. Things had not gone well for Rossi since he starred as Pablito in Argentina four years earlier. He had not played competitive soccer for nearly two years because of a suspension for his part in a game-fixing scandal. The suspension ended on April 29, less than two months before the start of Espana-82. Could that possibly be enough time for him to return to match fitness?

Brazil's team had undergone a revolution since Coutinho's "moral champions" of 1978. The new coach, Telê Santana, had a philosophy far removed from Coutinho's theories and tactics. For Telê, the players came first. He gathered in the stars of Brazilian soccer and, as one Brazilian newspaper put it, happiness returned to the game. Key players were Zico, who had proved such a problem for Coutinho, and Falcão, whom Coutinho had not even chosen. Add to them two scrawny midfielders—lanky Sócrates, a medical doctor, and the elusive Toninho Cerezo. Plus the powerful Junior with his violently swerving free kicks. Less convincing was the forward line, normally the Brazilians' greatest strength.

Argentina-82 looked very much like Argentina-78. Menotti was still in charge. Only Luque and Ortiz were missing from the championship team, but the average age of the nine returning players, 29, suggested that this was a team in decline.

Among all those veterans there was the precocious, youthful talent of Argentina's new star, the twenty-one-year-old Diego Maradona. A member of Menotti's original 1978 squad, he had been the last player to be cut. "He is strong, he has talent . . . his time will come," Menotti had said. Maradona had left the training camp in tears, a bitterly disappointed seventeen-year-old boy.

His time had arrived. The powerful, stocky little left-footer was being hailed as the new world superstar—evidently an opinion endorsed by the Spanish club Barcelona, which paid a world record $8.8 million to sign him just before the tournament. Despite the record total of twenty four teams, it seemed almost certain that the new winner would be one of the previous champions: Italy, West Germany, Brazil, or Argentina. England, another ex-winner, was not given a chance. Always difficult to beat at Wembley, England had proved time and again that it did not do well on foreign soil.

There was one other team to be considered, one that nobody paid much attention to at the time. The referees. The Men in Black. Forty-one referees from as many different countries, from Hong Kong to Libya, from Australia to Bolivia. They were to have a determining role in España-82.

A new regulation was on the books. If either semifinal was still tied after overtime, the winner would be decided by a penalty-kick shoot-out.*

The Spanish organizers displayed the worst and the best of taste. For a mascot they chose an orange, gave it arms and legs and an idiot grin and

---

* In which five players from each team alternate in taking one-on-one shots from the 12-yard penalty spot against the opposing goalkeeper. If the shoot-out score is still tied after the ten shots, then the shoot-out goes into its sudden-death phase, in which the kicks are taken in pairs. All eleven players from each team who were on the field at the end of the game must take kicks in rotation.

called it *Naranjito*. Laughable *kitsch*, happily balanced by the superb official poster, a boisterous riot of color and excitement, painted by an eighty-two-year-old soccer fan, artist Joan Miró.

The good taste extended to the opening ceremony in Barcelona, where hundreds of white-clad athletes crouched on the rich green grass of the Nou Camp stadium to form a huge, shimmering Picasso dove of peace. A young boy, dressed in the red and blue of Spain's team, walked to the center of the field and released a real dove. The bird opted for safety rather than freedom. It flew into the stands, and perched under the roof, indignantly straightening its feathers.

Nothing even remotely as beautiful as the Picasso dove was seen in the opening game that followed: Argentina vs. Belgium. The Belgians packed their defense and tackled heavily and dangerously. Maradona was hacked down from behind and muscled off the ball, and referee Vojtech Christov smiled benignly on everything. An advance warning. Worse was on its way.

Argentina had no answer to Belgium's cynical tactics. But at least the opening game, for the first time since 1962, featured a goal. Just one. Belgium got it, in the second half. Not a happy World Cup debut for Maradona in the stadium that would be his new home after the tournament.

Six four-team groups was the new format. Down in Sevilla the Brazilians fired things up. They beat the USSR 2-1, and the word went around that the *real* Brazil, the joyful attacking Brazil, was back. The Soviets kept quiet for a couple of days, then bitterly criticized the Spanish referee Augusto Lamo Castillo for denying them two penalty kicks. They had a point.

But the Brazilians were rolling. Poor Scotland was taken apart, outclassed, by a 4-1 score, goals from Zico, Falcão, Eder, and defender Oscar. Zico got two more, along with one each from Falcão and Serginho, in a 4-0 rout of New Zealand, and Brazil had established themselves as the favorites.

Spain started dismally. Little Honduras gave the Spaniards the fright of their lives, leading by 1-0 for much of the game, until Spain leveled matters—on a penalty kick.* The tremendous pressure from their fans and from the press was clearly unsettling the Spanish players. Against Yugoslavia, they again gave up an early goal. They were rescued from further trouble when the Danish referee awarded them a penalty kick, though it was clear (as was amply confirmed by television replays) that the Yugoslav foul had been committed outside the penalty area.

Even so, the Spanish needed more help. Roberto Lopez Ufarte smashed his penalty kick wide of the goal. Retake, said the referee, indicating that the Yugoslav goalkeeper had moved. This time Ufarte made no mistake. A late goal from Enrique Saura gave Spain its only win of the tournament.

---

* Playing at center-forward for Honduras, and playing extremely well, was Armando Betancourt, former Indiana University star, who had won the 1981 Hermann Trophy for college player of the year.

In the last of its first-round games, Spain lost 0–1 to unfancied North-ern Ireland in Valencia. In their lineup, the Irish included Norman Whiteside—at 17 years and 41 days the youngest player ever to appear in the World Cup finals (Pelé had played in the 1958 tournament at 17 years and 235 days).

Spain had done enough to squeak into the next round, but it was glaringly obvious that not much more could be expected from this team.

All in all, the so-called weak teams did quite well. El Salvador was the only one that played like a weak team, going down 10–1 to Hungary and setting a new World Cup record for goals-against in one game. Cameroon tied all three of its first-round games and delighted the Spanish fans with its fast-moving, athletic style. Algeria provided a major shock, with a 2–1 victory over the Germans.

The Kuwaitis arrived with an unusually large mascot: a real, live camel. It was said they had somehow wangled a press accreditation for it—a story that was good for many cynical remarks about the profession of journal-ism, but which turned out not to be true.

In its first game Kuwait, coached by the Brazilian Carlos Alberto Parreira, very nearly beat the Czechs, but had to settle for a 1–1 tie. The Kuwait–France game in Valladolid will long stick in the memory for the extraordinary goings-on in the second half.

The French were totally in command, already leading by 3–0, when Giresse ran through the Kuwaiti defense to score a fourth. Not so fast, there. The Kuwaitis protested vigorously to the Russian referee Miroslav Stupar that they had heard him blow his whistle for offside. He denied it. The Kuwaitis persisted. They had heard a whistle from *somewhere*, so they had stopped playing.

Confusion reigned. The Kuwaitis kept looking up to the stands, where the president of the Kuwaiti Soccer Federation, Sheik Fahed, was sitting. Not sitting for very long, though. He rose to his feet and headed down to the field, his robes billowing majestically behind him.

Even the formidably unbending Spanish police quailed before the with-ering royal gaze, and the prince was allowed to sweep sternly onto the field to confront the referee. Incredibly, Stupar gave way, and the goal was annulled.* The French then protested, to no avail. The field was cleared, the game restarted, and the French scored a fourth goal anyway.

From dark humor in Valladolid, to just plain disgraceful darkness in Gijon. In the final game of their group, which also included the surprising Algerians, West Germany met Austria. Both teams were well aware of the situation. A 1–0 win for Germany would allow the Germans and the Austri-ans to go to the second round, at the expense of Algeria. A bigger win for Germany, a tie, or a win for Austria would let Algeria in.

---

*In August 1990, Sheik Fahed—by then a vice president of FIFA—was one of the first people to be killed during the Iraqi invasion of Kuwait.

The Germans went ahead 1–0 after 10 minutes, and then the farce began. Neither team made any further serious attempt to score, or even to play. As the crowd of over 40,000 whistled and chanted Algeria! Algeria!, Germans and Austrians, cozy Teutonic brothers for an afternoon, disgraced the sport of soccer for eighty minutes.

It was a contemptible performance. Algeria protested, requesting that both Germany and Austria be thrown out for violating the spirit of the tournament. Regrettably, FIFA rejected the protest. It was Algeria that was out.

The new second-round format had the twelve remaining teams divided into four groups of three teams. The group winners would go to the semifinals. West Germany disposed of England and Spain without much trouble. The Germans would meet the French, who were looking better and better. Now, the talk was of a "dream final" between France and Brazil. It looked increasingly likely.

Poland won its group, beating Belgium 3–0, and tying the USSR 0–0. Banners supporting the banned Polish union Solidarity appeared in the crowd during the Poland vs. USSR game, but they were removed by the police. Eliminating the USSR seemed to give the Poles more satisfaction than advancing to the semifinal.

Barcelona got the cream of the second-round action with a group containing Italy, Brazil, and Argentina. The teams were loaded with talent, but the refereeing, alas, was to be quite horrendous.

Italy had scraped into the second round on the strength of three ties with Poland, Cameroon, and Peru. It had scored but two goals. The players, incensed at the vitriolic criticism in the Italian press, were refusing to talk to journalists. They would chat about the weather, or politics, perhaps, but not about soccer. "Speak to the captain," they said. A joke, for captain Dino Zoff was known as the most taciturn of men.

The Italians beat Argentina 2–1, but it was a distorted game. Defender Claudio Gentile's task was to mark Maradona. This he did with sustained ferocity: ninety minutes of holding, tripping, obstructing, shirt-pulling, elbowing, and kicking. Referee Nicolae Rainea from Romania saw nothing wrong. After one particularly brutal foul, Rainea did at last get out the yellow card—but it was Maradona who got it, for protesting! Gentile got a yellow later, but went on fouling anyway. With six minutes left in the game, Rainea finally discovered his red card. It want to Americo Gallego, of Argentina.

After the game, a stony-faced Menotti sardonically asked the press: "I believe there is a rule that a player who fouls repeatedly must be ejected, no?" A rule that Rainea blatantly ignored. There had been ample reason to eject Gentile even before halftime.

Barcelona seemed to be taken over by Brazilian fans, singing and dancing their sambas in the streets, unfurling their vast banners and flags in the stadiums. Their team was playing brilliant soccer, and Argentina was simply swept aside 3–1. Maradona, unable to make any impression on the game, finally gave vent to his frustration and viciously kicked João Batista. He was ordered off, rightly so. But it was a sad moment to watch such a talented young player take his leave of the 1982 World Cup in a slow, solo walk to the bench, his head down, his eyes seeing nothing.

The final game in the group, Brazil vs. Italy, would decide who went through to the semifinal. For Brazil, a tie would be good enough. Italy had to win. Had Gentile been red-carded, as he so thoroughly deserved to be, against Argentina, he would have been under suspension, unable to play. But Gentile would play, and everyone knew that he would mark Zico. The full effects of Rainea's disastrous refereeing were still to be felt.

For Bearzot the problem was this: He had gone with Rossi in every game so far, but Pablito was not playing well and had yet to score a goal. After much agonizing, Bearzot decided to give him one more chance.

The referee was Abraham Klein of Israel who, for all his officious strutting about, was only marginally better than Rainea had been. Gentile was yellow-carded and then allowed to take up against Zico where he had left off against Maradona. At one point, Zico ran up to Klein to show him the huge hole in his shirt, which Gentile had just nearly ripped off his back. Klein was not interested.

Suddenly, miraculously, Rossi regained his scoring touch. His three beautifully taken goals steered Italy to a 3–2 win. The Italians had found their center forward. The Brazilians never did find theirs. With Reinaldo, Roberto, and Careca all ruled out by injury, Serginho was their fourth choice. He had a nightmare game against Italy, squandering three golden chances to see Brazil safely through.

Now the Italian press was full of praise, delighted at a rare win over Brazil. "We are the real Brazilians!" screamed a headline over a story claiming that Italy had outdone Brazil at its own game of skillful soccer.

The Italians played well, no doubt about that. But, more than anything, they could thank the referees Rainea and Klein for their success. Complacent refereeing had destroyed one half of the dream final. Down in Seville, in the France vs. West Germany semifinal, refereeing of almost unimaginable ineptitude finished off the other half.

A game of immense drama. The Germans were playing without their star and captain, Rummenigge—still, apparently, suffering from a mysterious muscle pull that had plagued him since the start of the tournament. Even so, they took an early lead through the dynamic little winger Littbarski. The French began to organize their swift-passing game as Platini took impressive charge of midfield. Within twenty minutes they were level. Dominique Rocheteau was brought down in the penalty area by Bernd Förster, and Platini hit the equalizer from the penalty spot.

In a pulsating, wide-open game both sides created numerous scoring opportunities, but neither could get the decisive goal. Jean-Luc Ettori, in the French goal, made a series of brave saves. But it was Toni Schumacher, Germany's arrogantly confident 'keeper, who struck the key blow. Ten minutes into the second half, the German defense was ripped open by a through ball that put Patrick Battiston in the clear. Schumacher came roaring out of his goal, made no attempt to play the ball, and simply wiped Battiston out—flattened him, with a massive body block and a forearm in the face.

Battiston, concussed and minus two teeth, stayed down. After three minutes he was stretchered off and taken to the hospital. As brutal a foul as one could imagine. Schumacher should have been ejected and France should have had a penalty kick, which would likely have settled the game. Yet referee Charles Corver, from the Netherlands, found everything okay. No foul, no penalty kick to France, no red card to Schumacher. Nothing.

The game went to overtime and France went ahead 3–1, which seemed to mean the end for Germany. But Mr. Corver had not yet finished. Rummenigge was now on the field and scored Germany's vital second goal after Corver had ignored not one, but two, German fouls in the buildup. Klaus Fischer tied it up at 3–3.

For the first time ever, a World Cup game would be decided on penalty kicks. The Germans won the shoot-out because of two saves by Schumacher, a player who should not have been on the field.

Germany were through to their fourth World Cup final. They would face Italy, who disposed of the Poles without any great exertion, by a 2–0 score, both goals coming from the reborn Rossi. Gentile, suspended, sat this one out, but his absence was more than balanced by Poland having to play without their star and goal scorer, Boniek, also suspended.

Italy was the overwhelming favorite in the final. The Germans, after the contrived tie with Austria, after Schumacher's hideous foul, had few friends. "These Cheats Must Not Win It!" was the day's headline in the London *Sun*.

Plus, there were solid soccer reasons for fancying Italy. It had played an easy semifinal, while the Germans had labored into overtime in the heat of Seville. Rummenigge was still in doubt—at the very moment that he was telling German television he was fit, coach Derwall was declaring that he would not start.

If that was a battle of wills, it was won by Rummenigge. He did start. But there was a key player missing from the Italian lineup. Antognoni, who had injured a foot against Poland. More trouble for the Italians after only seven minutes, when Wolfgang Dremmler's clattering tackle sent Francesco Graziani crashing to the ground. Off went Graziani, his collarbone dislocated; on came the lanky Alessandro Altobelli.

A moment of triumph for Italy came in the twenty-fifth minute with the award of a penalty kick after Briegel had pulled down Bruno Conti. But Cabrini made an awful mess of the kick, putting his shot wide of the goal. Yet, through all these setbacks, the Italians kept playing their steady, defensive game, with Scirea the cool, calculating mastermind.

The Germans did most of the attacking, but it was sterile stuff, and Zoff had little to trouble him in the Italian goal. No score at halftime, but it was clear that the German gamble of starting the unfit Rummenigge had failed. They had hoped for an early lead, and they hadn't got it.

Now, that draining semifinal began to take its toll. Rummenigge was substituted, and as the Germans tired, the Italians pushed forward. Rossi—who else?—opened the scoring, heading in a Gentile cross from close range. At the sixty-eighth minute the magnificent Scirea came forward, skillfully held the ball in the German penalty area as though he were a born attacker, then set up Marco Tardelli for goal number two. Altobelli added the third before Breitner scored for the Germans (and in so doing kept alive the tradition that no team has ever been shut out in the World Cup final).

WORLD CUP FINAL 1982
Madrid, Spain: Italy 3 West Germany 1
Paolo Rossi (center, arm outstretched) opens the scoring with a header twelve minutes into the second half. West German goalkeeper Harald Schumacher, caught flatfooted, can only watch as the ball goes into the net. Rossi, with six goals in Italy's final three games, was the tournament's top scorer.
© Peter Robinson: The Football Archive

The Italians were worthy winners. They had played with more spirit and more skill than the Germans, and they had joined Brazil as the only nation to win the trophy three times. But it was a poor, bleak final, full of fouls, short on artistry. As such, it reflected far too much of the soccer that had preceded it in the tournament. Mediocrity reigned. The little that had been outstandingly good had been sabotaged by scandalously bad refereeing.

MEXICO, 1986

In line with its plan of alternating Europe and Latin America as World Cup sites, FIFA had, in 1974, designated Colombia as host country for the 1986 tournament. It seemed a precarious decision. The World Cup was becoming ever more expensive to stage, an event that required not only top-class stadiums, hotels, and airports, but also highly sophisticated television and communications systems.

Possibly Colombia could have handled a sixteen-team World Cup, as the original agreement had envisaged. But FIFA itself undermined that when, in 1982, it increased the number of finalists to twenty-four. The Colombians held out until January of 1983, when they reluctantly admitted that they couldn't handle it.

Suddenly, the 1986 World Cup was looking for a new home. FIFA solicited bids: Brazil, Canada, the United States, and Mexico spoke up. The process looked democratic enough, but it soon became apparent that Mexico was the favorite. The United States was particularly incensed when FIFA—citing "deviations" in the U.S. bid—curtly announced that its stadium inspection committee would not be visiting the U.S.A.

In May 1983 the FIFA Executive Committee, meeting in Stockholm, awarded the tournament to Mexico. The Americans were convinced that FIFA had already struck a deal with the Mexicans, and that the bid process was a charade. There was talk of suing FIFA. Nothing came of it.

FIFA did have a deal. Not with the Mexican Soccer Federation, or the Mexican government, but with the private television company Televisa, and its immensely rich owner, Emilio Azcarraga. One of Azcarraga's top executives was Guillermo Cañedo, who also happened to be a FIFA vice president, and chairman of its World Cup Organizing Committee.

Azcarraga, through Televisa, was able to give FIFA—quickly—the financial guarantees that it had to have. So Mexico, hosts in 1970, became the first country to stage two World Cups. That earlier experience was of immense value, and Mexico already had eleven modern stadiums. It needed to build only one new one, at Queretaro.

Fear of the debilitating effects of heat and altitude was now much less than it had been in 1970. Advances in sports medicine had proved that these could be handled. Then, suddenly and wantonly, another more deadly natural phenomenon struck.

At 7:18 in the morning of September 19, 1985, one of the most powerful earthquakes in recent history (Richter 8.1) devastated large areas of downtown Mexico City. The death toll was over 7,000, with up to 30,000 made homeless.

Could the World Cup continue? Yes, said the Mexicans, in the best show-must-go-on spirit. None of the twelve stadiums had been damaged, and the tournament was now needed more than ever as a morale booster. They would succeed, just as the Chileans, battered by an earthquake in 1960, had persevered to stage the 1962 tournament.

The Mexican team had been under intensive preparation since 1983. Bora Milutinovic, a former Yugoslavian player who had moved to Mexico in 1972, was the coach. Mexico, a soccer-mad country of 82 million people, had always had ambitions far beyond its strength. It had qualified for eight of the twelve World Cup tournaments, but had achieved little beyond that. Usually it was knocked out in the first round. Only in 1970, when it hosted the event, had it advanced to the quarterfinals. Milutinovic was expected to at least repeat that feat.

In 1984 he took his team to Rome for an exhibition game against the world champions, Italy. Before the game, the players had an audience with the pope. "He gave us his blessing," said Milutinovic. "He held up one hand. Five fingers. The next day the Italians scored five goals against us. We were just happy he didn't bless us with both hands."

The heavy defeat, nevertheless, was a blessing. It proved that it was time for the Mexican Soccer Federation to get serious with its clubs, to make them release the players Milutinovic wanted. In 1985, the Mexican clubs were forced to play their championship without national team players; they were all in the permanent camp that Milutinovic had set up. The only major absentee was center forward Hugo Sanchez, Mexico's one world-class player, who was playing in Spain for Real Madrid. For him, Milutinovic was willing to wait, until the end of the Spanish season in the spring of 1986.

Mexico, host nation or not, was simply not strong enough to be ranked among the favorites. That honor was shared by Brazil, Argentina, and France. An interesting and, at first glance, puzzling trio. Three teams that played a game built around artistry and ball skill. Why should they be favored over teams that practiced the athletic, power game that was becoming increasingly prevalent, particularly in Europe?

Call it the positive effect of heat and altitude. It had already been noticed in 1970 that the conditions had slowed down the pace of the game. Teams that relied on a vigorous all-running, all-action, 90-mph game simply couldn't keep it up. Brazil, the supreme artists, had triumphed.

A repeat performance by the Brazilians was definitely on the cards. The creative nucleus of the team that had been so dazzling in Spain four years earlier was still there: Zico, Junior, Sócrates, Falcão. After an interlude in Saudi Arabia, Telê was back as coach. And in the twenty-six-year-old Careca, Brazil had what it had so fatally lacked in Spain: a goal-scoring center forward.

Argentina had a new coach. Carlos Bilardo was now in charge, a man with a philosophy very different from that of Menotti. Bilardo was a more cautious man. Not for him the adventurous extravagance of Menotti's 1978 team, with its three forwards and two attacking midfielders. He favored all-around players and packed his team with midfielders who were expected to do a little of everything.

Qualifying had been a struggle. In the final game, against Peru, Argentina had been staring down the barrel of elimination: 2–1 down with only ten minutes remaining in the game. A typically gritty run from Passarella led to the tying goal and ensured qualification. But the team was anything but convincing.

Criticism rained down on Bilardo. His team was overly cautious, it was dull, it lacked an attacking mentality. Certainly, the team lacked the explosiveness of Menotti's 1978 crew . . . but then, Bilardo had Diego Maradona.

We last saw Maradona in 1982, plodding dejectedly off the field in Barcelona, red-carded for kicking a Brazilian opponent. Since then his career had taken him from Barcelona to the boiling cauldron of soccer fanaticism that is Naples. By now, few doubted that he deserved his title of the world's best player.

With his powerful, twisting dribbles, his superbly clever and accurate passing, his formidable left-foot shooting, Maradona was a match-winning player. Could he also be a tournament-winning player?

If there was one player who could challenge Maradona's supremacy, then it was France's Michel Platini. Now thirty-one years old, Platini knew that this was likely to be his last chance for World Cup glory. Two years earlier France had at long last won a major title, when Platini led it to the 1984 European championship. The team, it was asserted, was more mature and more worldly than it had been in Spain. A lesson had been learned from the harsh elimination in 1982. The artists Tigana, Giresse, and Platini were still there in midfield, but alongside them now was the bulky, uncompromising Luis Fernandez.

West Germany, beaten finalists in 1982, was now coached by its former captain, Franz Beckenbauer. Rummenigge had much in common with Platini: a thirty-one-year-old facing his last big chance. His heir was already on the scene, Lothar Matthäus. Schumacher, the villain of 1982, was still in goal, and a new crop of robust defenders suggested that Germany, at the very least, would be hard to beat.

England posed a rather special sort of threat. Nothing to do with its soccer strength, which was not rated too highly. The menace came from its wild supporters, now internationally famous for their acts of violence and vandalism. When soccer people talked about security, they were worried less about terrorism than about the presence of the English hooligans.

For years these so-called fans had followed English teams as they played in Europe. Their presence always meant drunkenness, wrecked bars and stores, assaults on innocent bystanders, and pitched street battles with local fans or with the police.*

Making its first-ever appearance in the tournament was Denmark. The Danes, rather like the Dutch in the 1970s, had seemingly undergone an

* See chapter 9, page 231.

overnight transformation. Always viewed as a second-rate soccer country, they had suddenly produced a lively, skillful team that was a serious contender for the world title.

What made the achievement even more astounding was that there was no professional soccer in Denmark. The coach was a German, Sepp Piontek. Of his eleven starters, ten were with foreign clubs, in England, Italy, Germany, the Netherlands, Belgium, and France. The stars were two Italian-based players, Michael Laudrup of Juventus and Preben Elkjaer of Verona.

The Italians themselves had shown indifferent form since the 1982 triumph. Of the twenty-nine games played by Bearzot's team since, thirteen had been won, nine lost, and seven tied. They had performed abysmally in the 1984 European championship, failing to qualify for the final tournament. Hardly championship form.

The Dutch again failed to qualify; so too—for the ninth consecutive time since 1950—did the United States. For the Americans this was a major disappointment. Their team was now made up of young American-born players, with plenty of professional experience gained when playing alongside foreign veterans in the North American Soccer League. The failure was made even more galling when neighbor Canada won the qualifying tournament.

Black African soccer, so excitingly represented by Cameroon in 1982, was in eclipse. All four semifinal spots in the African region qualifiers were claimed by countries from Arab North Africa, with Algeria and Morocco the winners.

FIFA, not happy with the way things had gone in España-82, had introduced two format changes. In the first round, the final two games in each group would be played on the same day at the same time—this to avoid another West Germany vs. Austria fiasco. The arrangement of four three-team groups in the second round was scrapped. Looking for more drama, FIFA ruled that direct elimination would apply after the first round. Sixteen teams would advance—the first and second in each first-round group, plus the four best third-place finishers.

The ill luck of the draw had predetermined that the opening game, in the imposing 114,000-capacity Estadio Azteca, should be between Italy, the holders, and Bulgaria. Everyone knew this would be yet another in the long line of inaugural clinkers.

The Italians would be cautious and as meticulously defensive as only they could be. The Bulgarians were as utterly characterless as only the duller Eastern European sides could be. The most interesting discovery about them was that all twenty-two of their players had names that ended with the letter *v*. The Bulgarians had already played twelve times in four previous World Cup tournaments, and had yet to win a game.

After a lively festival of Mexican dances and mariachi music, and after President Miguel de la Madrid's speech had been loudly jeered and whistled (many Mexicans were dissatisfied with his government's efforts to help the earthquake victims), the Italians and the Bulgarians did their best to put everyone to sleep.

In fact the Italians themselves, having taken a 1–0 lead in the first half, nodded off and allowed the Bulgarians, in one of their pitifully few attacks, to tie the game five minutes before the end.

A game to forget, but fortunately much better was to follow. The following day Spain and Brazil played a splendid game in Guadalajara's Group D. Sócrates got the winner for Brazil, but the Spanish had reason to feel hard done by, because five minutes earlier they appeared to have scored. From a slashing drive by Michel, the ball beat the Brazilian goalkeeper Carlos, hit the underside of the bar, bounced to the ground and out of the goal. Had the ball gone over the goal line or not? Déjà vu for those who remembered the 1966 World Cup final. Then, the English rejoiced as the goal was confirmed. This time the Spanish were in despair as the goal was not given.

In the end, both Brazil and Spain would advance to the next round. Brazil climaxed its first round with a resounding 3–0 win over Northern Ireland. They had unveiled a new star in the dynamic Josimar. The twenty-four-year-old fullback was a late addition to the team, and even the Brazilian journalists confessed that they didn't know much about him. His goal against the Irish, a screaming 30-yard drive, made everyone take notice.

One who noticed, but couldn't do much about it, was the veteran Pat Jennings, playing his final game in the Irish goal. It was Jennings's 119th appearance for his country, a world record at the time.

In Group B, Mexico sent its supporters into a frenzy with a 2–1 win over Belgium in the Azteca. Defender Fernando Quirarte, who came forward on a free kick to head the first goal, admitted after the game that he now had a problem: explaining the goal to his mother, who had told him to stick with his defensive duties and not to go forward.

The Mexican fans celebrated all night in Mexico City, to such an extent that the police ordered the boarding up of monuments and the closing of streets.

Argentina topped Group A, with Italy in second place. The Argentines had not been seriously tested, but one thing was very clear. Maradona was in tremendous form, both as a player and as a team leader.

The woeful Bulgarians tied Italy and South Korea, and then lost 2–0 to Argentina. During the postgame press conference coach Yvan Vutzov was in a subdued, apologetic mood as he admitted that Bulgaria had played badly and dismissed the remote chance that his team could be still alive.

Wrong. When all the first-round results were in, it turned out that Bulgaria—with one loss, two ties, and with a 2–4 goals for-and-against record—had scraped into the second round!

The Uruguayans made it out of Group E with an even worse record of a loss, two ties, and a 2–7 goals record. But then, they had known life wasn't going to be easy when the draw gave them Denmark, West Germany, and Scotland as opponents. The Group of Death, they called it.

The group was dominated by the Danes, who scored nine goals (four of them to Elkjaer) in a triumphant path that included a 6–1 dismantling of Uruguay, and a first-ever win over West Germany.

A 1–1 tie with West Germany was not a bad start for Uruguay. But the behavior of the Uruguayan bench during the game, and of the players during the subsequent dope-control tests prompted FIFA to issue a stern warning. The Uruguayans chose to ignore it; one red and two yellow cards in the 6–1 rout by Denmark didn't improve their image.

When Uruguay met Scotland in its final game, a second-round place was at stake. FIFA had primed the French referee, Joel Quiniou, to stand no nonsense. Advice that he took so energetically to heart that he set a new World Cup record by sending off Uruguay's José Batista in the very first minute of the game.

Playing virtually the entire game with only ten men, the Uruguayans still held out for the 0–0 tie that they needed. After the game, coach Omar Borras commented: "The Group of Death? Yes, there was a murderer on the field today. The referee."

So the Scots made their customary early exit, while Uruguay advanced to meet Argentina. Without its coach. FIFA banned Borras from the bench for calling Quiniou a murderer.

In Group C it was France and the USSR that qualified. The Canadians had lost all three of their games. They never looked like winning any of them, and were content to make life difficult for their opponents.

That lesser teams need not be so unambitious was sharply demonstrated in Monterrey, where Morocco topped Group F after ties against England and Poland, and victory over Portugal. It thus became the first African team to reach the second round.

Money was very much on the minds of the Portuguese players. In a dispute over bonuses with their federation, they threatened not to take the field for their first game against England. The Portuguese requested permission from FIFA to fly in a twenty-two-man reserve squad. The dispute was resolved, Portugal beat England 1–0 . . . but lost its other two games and finished at the bottom of the group.

After losing to Portugal and barely surviving a 0–0 tie with Morocco, England was on the brink of elimination. Then Gary Lineker, just as Paolo Rossi had done for Italy in 1982, suddenly found his touch. His hat trick against Poland saw England through.

On the whole, the Mexicans were praised for an excellently organized first round. Except for one thing. Amazingly, in a World Cup that was basically being run by a television company, Televisa, it was the television transmissions that came badly unstuck. The early broadcasts were a nightmare. The Dutch received a picture, but no sound. The Brazilians got the Italian commentary, the Colombians got the Portuguese. The French got neither picture nor sound. Many countries had to use the regular telephone system to get their commentators on the air.

The European Broadcasting Union was furious and went public with its complaints, calling the shambles "the biggest disaster in the history of sports broadcasting." It accused the Mexicans of incompetence, even of sabotage. Pointing out that its member countries had paid some $30 million for the broadcast rights, it handed FIFA an ultimatum: Get it fixed, now, or we sue for return of our rights fees. The problems were corrected very quickly.

The Mexicans opened the second round with a 2–0 win over Bulgaria. An uneventful game that featured one moment of sheer magic, when Manuel Negrete put Mexico ahead with a spectacular flying scissor-kick volley. It was hailed as the goal of the tournament, but Maradona would have the last word on that topic. This time Bulgaria was definitely out; its World Cup record was now sixteen games without a win.

A huge shock in Queretaro, where the Danes' inexperience, to say nothing of their hubris, let them down badly. All along, the Spanish had been saying that they had the Danes' number. So it proved. The Danes, insanely overconfident, quickly went ahead through a Jesper Olsen penalty kick. Spain then picked Denmark apart, most of the damage being done by center forward Emilio Butragueño, who scored four times in a 5–1 romp.

The holders Italy went tamely out to France, which controlled the game from the start and ran out 2–1 winners. West Germany sweated and strained unimaginatively against Morocco. Three minutes from the end, the Moroccans negligently set up a defensive wall that didn't cover the goal. Matthäus saw the gap, and scored the only goal of the game with his free kick.

Goals galore in Leon. Igor Belanov got three for the USSR, but it was not enough. Belgium got four in a 4–3 overtime win. Brazil rolled over Poland by 4–0, with two of the goals coming from defenders—Edinho, and the unstoppable Josimar, who picked his way merrily though the Polish defense before unleashing a cannonball shot from an acute angle.

A chastened Uruguay, without coach Borras, played defensively against Argentina. The game finished 1–0 to the Argentines, but they had dominated throughout. More significantly, Maradona had dominated. Even the experienced and canny Uruguayan defenders had no answer to his wiles.

With its 3–0 win over Paraguay, England set up a quarterfinal against Argentina—a politically sensitive game that FIFA and the Mexican authorities would have preferred to avoid. It was the first meeting between the two countries since the 1982 Malvinas/Falklands war, and both teams had sizable contingents of boisterous fans with them.

A massive army presence, complete with tanks, was on duty in and around the Azteca stadium for the clash. Some minor scuffles between the opposing fans did develop during the second half, but most of the fireworks came on the field. From Maradona.

After a scoreless first half, Maradona took over. His surging dribble into the penalty area had the England defenders in trouble. When Steve Hodge tried to lob the ball back to goalkeeper Peter Shilton, Maradona darted in and leaped high to head the ball away from Shilton's lunging hands and into the net. Or did he head the ball? England protested that Maradona had used his hand. But the Tunisian referee said the goal was legitimate. Nobody was really certain—even the television replays needed careful study before it was clear that Maradona had blatantly cheated, *had* punched the ball into the net.

Three minutes later, Maradona struck again—this time with ten seconds of pure, unimaginable soccer skill, to score one of the greatest goals in the history of the World Cup. Starting inside his own half, he corkscrewed his way past three defenders as he dribbled down the right flank. At the edge of the penalty area, he swerved past Terry Fenwick, then, while holding off a challenge from Terry Butcher, pulled the ball past Shilton and shot into the empty net as he fell.

Late in the game, England fought back. Lineker headed a goal with nine minutes left, then almost tied it up with another header. Only some remarkable goal line acrobatics by José Cuciuffo, who somehow scooped the ball off the line with the back of his head, prevented the goal. So Argentina marched on, and Maradona evaded questions about his first goal. If there was a hand ball, he said, it was the Hand of God that had scored for Argentina.

Another classic unfolded in Guadalajara, where Brazil met France. After an early goal by Careca was canceled out by Platini's equalizer, Brazil had its chance in the second half. Zico, coming on as a substitute, sliced open the French defense with a pass to Branco. As Branco raced to the ball, he was brought down by goalkeeper Joël Bats. Penalty to Brazil. But Zico's kick was weak, Bats saved, and the game finished 1–1 after overtime.

It was settled in France's favor by a penalty kick shoot-out. A patently unfair way to decide any game, made even more farcical when Bruno Bellone's kick came back off the post, hit the Brazilian goalkeeper, Carlos, in the back of the head, and rebounded into the goal. The referee allowed the controversial goal, but many felt it was illegal. FIFA was quick to support the referee's decision, but the regulations that it cited were anything but clear on the point. A year later, FIFA changed the wording of the regulation.

Mexico's success so far had its fans believing that the miracle was possible. If West Germany could be beaten . . . It might have happened, had Mexico not lost its chief playmaker, Thomas Boy, after thirty-two minutes, victim of a clumsy challenge by Andreas Brehme. In a dull game, played in the intense heat of Monterrey, neither side could muster much of an attack. This one also went to penalty kicks. No contest. Klaus Allofs, Brehme, Matthäus, and Littbarski scored for Germany, but only Negrete found the net for Mexico, and the host country's dreams of World Cup glory vanished.

Penalties were also needed to decide the fourth quarterfinal between the evenly matched Belgium and Spain. Victory in the shoot-out put the

WORLD CUP FINAL 1986
Mexico City, Mexico: Argentina 3 West Germany 2
Diego Maradona, on his teammates' shoulders, brandishes the World Cup.
Maradona, the Argentine captain, dominated the 1986 tournament, trans-
forming a rather ordinary Argentine team into World Cup winners. He scored
five goals—four of them brilliant, the fifth the infamous "Hand of God" goal
against England.
© Peter Robinson: The Football Archive

Belgians into a semifinal against Argentina. This was Maradona's chance of revenge for the mauling that the Belgians had given him in 1982 in his first World Cup game. And how he made them pay.

Two more breathtaking individual goals scuttled the Belgians, and Argentina had reached the final for the first time since 1978. Their opponents would be West Germany. The French had succumbed again at the semifinal stage, again to the Germans. This time it was poor goalkeeping that let them down. Brehme's free kick in the eighth minute was far from unstoppable, but Bats moved late, and allowed the ball to slip underneath him.

The French, all-out attack now their only choice, battered away at the disciplined German defense. A frantic final five minutes saw them camped in the German goalmouth. Chances were created, but each the time the Germans got the ball away. Soccer's perversity had the last word when, with less than a minute to go, Rudi Völler scored a late breakaway goal to give the Germans a 2–0 win.

Bilardo's Argentine team was now brimming with midfielders. It contained only one genuine forward, Jorge Valdano, and he was an example of

Bilardo's "ideal" player: an inexhaustible runner who spent a good deal of energy falling back on defense. Arguably, another midfielder.

The lack of front players was not hurting Argentina, for it had scored eleven goals, nearly two per game. The secret, of course, was Maradona. So commanding was his form, so overwhelming his influence on his team, that it seemed natural to think of the final as West Germany vs. Maradona.

German tactics were discussed in terms of one issue: Whom would they put on Maradona? Almost every German defender and midfielder was mentioned, but none of them seemed up to the job. So the job was shared, Matthäus trying to subdue Maradona when he played deep, Karl-Heinz Förster taking over when Maradona went on attack.

Obsessed with the Maradona threat, the Germans played a tentative, disjointed first half. It was that obsession that led to the first goal. Matthäus, quite unnecessarily, fouled Maradona. Jorge Burruchaga curled the free kick into the area, Schumacher came out to grab the ball but never got to it as it swerved away from him, and there was sweeper José Brown to head home.

Strangely, there was no German reaction. The team went on playing its pedestrian game, rarely threatening the Argentine goal. Ten minutes after halftime, the deep-lying Maradona slid the ball to Hector Enrique, who dribbled forward and then pushed a perfect pass out to Valdano on the left wing. No German defender was near him as Valdano cut into the penalty area and stroked the ball past Schumacher.

At 2–0, Argentina, inevitably, relaxed. The Germans began to apply pressure, but it was a disordered sort of pressure, and in the twenty-third minute it needed a terrible call from the linesman to save them from more trouble. Burruchaga's pass to Enrique was right on the money, sending him sprinting yards clear of the German defense . . . only to be called back for a nonexistent offside.

The German attacks continued, formless but with growing insistence. Only determination, the famed German ability to fight back, could save matters now. And it very nearly did. The Argentine defense caved in twice within eight minutes, both times to close-range shots. First Rummenigge prodded the ball home from five yards out, then Völler made it 2–2 with a header from three yards.

Bilardo had boasted of his team that it could "press the accelerator" and move up a gear anytime it chose. Evidently, it was no idle boast. Three minutes after Völler's morale-wrecking equalizer, Argentina was back in the lead, thanks to the genius of Maradona. His pass, through the middle of the German defense, was perfect. Burruchaga raced on to it, outpaced the lumbering Briegel, and calmly rolled the ball past the onrushing Schumacher.

A 3–2 win for Argentina, and vindication for Bilardo, whose style and tactics had been heavily criticized in Argentina. A large banner displayed by Argentine fans at the final read: "FORGIVE US, BILARDO!"

Above all else, Argentina's victory was a personal triumph for Maradona. No player in the history of the World Cup had ever dominated a tournament in the way that Maradona ruled over Mexico-86.

ITALY, 1990

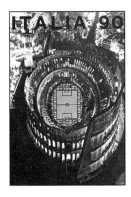

By losing all three of its games in Mexico-86 and failing to score even one goal, Canada ended up as the least successful team. A big flop for the Canadians, right? Not exactly. Their three defeats earned them a check for $966,000.

When the Mexicans had done all the accounting mathematics, they announced a profit of nearly $48 million. FIFA regulations allowed them to keep 30 percent. The other 70 percent ($33.5 million) was distributed among the twenty-four nations that played in the finals on a per-game basis. Each of the fifty-two games was thus worth $644,000, or $322,000 per team. Teams knocked out after the three first-round games took home $966,000. The finalists, Argentina and West Germany, played seven games, worth $2.25 million—clear profit because FIFA paid each team's travel and living expenses during the championship.

Income for Mexico-86 amounted to $96 million, equally divided among three sources: the sale of tickets, television rights, and advertising. Also of vital importance to the running of the show were sponsors. There were twelve of them for Mexico-86, including Coca-Cola, Fuji Film, Gillette, Seiko, Budweiser, Canon, and Opel cars.

There was also Camel cigarettes, which offended many people. When asked whether he felt it advisable for soccer to promote tobacco smoking, FIFA president Dr João Havelange replied that he had been looking at cigarette ads all his life, and *he* had never smoked. It was hardly the sort of response to encourage sponsors who had each paid several million dollars for rights that ranged from using the official logos and mascot, to exclusive promotion of their products and commercials on the game telecasts.

At its birth sixty years earlier, the World Cup had been primarily about soccer. By 1990, as it moved to Italy for its fourteenth edition, it was very much about money, and marketing, and advertising, and sponsorship.

That message came over loud and clear in November 1986, at the first press conference for Italia-90. A gathering of top soccer people, of coaches, and perhaps players? Not at all. Francesco Cossiga, the President of Italy, was there, along with a host of top political, business, and even church figures.

The talk was of marketing contracts and of sponsors, suppliers, products and services, collaborators, and licensees. The official emblem of

Italia-90 was introduced. So was *Ciao*, the official mascot, an imaginative stick figure with a soccer ball for a head.

Almost as an afterthought came the list of twelve cities where the games of Italia-90 would be staged. The money theme was taken up by the Italian government in a big way, which announced the incredible sum of $5 billion in aid to those cities, to allow them to upgrade stadiums, roads, public transport, airport facilities, and the like.

The amount was progressively scaled down, but the message remained: Italia-90 was an event of great national importance. Just as it had been in Mussolini's Italy in 1934. One monument from that earlier World Cup still stood: Nervi's beautiful stadium in Florence. It would be used in 1990, renovated and modernized along with nine other existing stadiums. New stadiums would be built in Bari, and in Turin, where the architecturally futuristic structure dubbed the Spaceship would cost $128 million.

More millions of dollars would have to be spent on security, which was a major concern. Both the Netherlands and West Germany had by now spawned bands of thuggish fans, while the Italians had their home-grown *ultras*. But the English hooligans were still the biggest threat to law and order.*

In November 1989, England clinched a place in the final tournament. Coming to Italy with them would be the hooligans, that was not in doubt. What could be done with them? The thought of drunken hooligans trashing downtown Rome or Turin was too ghastly to contemplate. The answer was to isolate England. The Italian government was consulted, and England was assigned, by a seeding arrangement, to the island of Sardinia. That would keep the hooligans reasonably contained, at least for the first round. It was a cynical arrangement that said a lot about Italian attitudes to Sardinia.

Police work—or detective work—of a rather different sort was required from FIFA during the qualifying rounds. A spectacular scandal erupted in South America, where Brazil and Chile were fighting it out for a place in the final twenty-four. The first leg, in Santiago, had been a violent 1–1 tie in which the Chilean coach, Orlando Aravena, had been ejected. Sebastião Lazaroni, the Brazilian coach, had carried on alarmingly on the sidelines, and had been manhandled by a large contingent of steel-helmeted Chilean police. He had called Aravena "an imbecile," and accused him of inciting the Chileans to play violently.

Accusations and counteraccusations flew to and fro during the three weeks leading up to the second leg. The Chileans said they were afraid of the hostile atmosphere in Brazil. "At the first sign of trouble, we're coming off the field," said Roberto Rojas, their goalkeeper and captain.

Trouble arrived with twenty minutes left in the game, Brazil leading 1–0. From somewhere in the 140,000 crowd packing the Maracaná stadium in Rio de Janeiro, a flare took flight. It dropped softly to earth in front of

* See Chapter 9, page 231.

the Chilean goal. In the drifting smoke, Rojas could be seen flat on his back, holding his head. His teammates carried him off the field, his shirt apparently bathed in blood. Twenty minutes later, with the Chileans refusing to take the field again, the game was called off.

A week later, FIFA acted. The game—and therefore qualification for Italia-90—was awarded to Brazil. Rojas was banned from international games for life. FIFA pressed its investigation, convinced the whole incident had been contrived with the aim of getting Brazil banned or, at the least, a replay of the game at a neutral site. "It is hard to believe," said FIFA, "that the imprudent goalkeeper hatched and enacted that stratagem unaided and unabetted."

Eventually, Rojas admitted that he had not been struck by the flare, and that he had faked his injuries. He was banned from all soccer for life, as was the president of the Chilean Soccer Federation. Aravena got a life ban from international soccer, and the Chilean federation was fined $60,000. Chile was banned from taking part in the 1994 World Cup for "the most ignoble incident of attempted fraud in the history of FIFA."

Another fraud had been attempted by the Mexicans, who fielded overage players during the qualifying round for the 1989 World Youth Championship. The players used false passports, but the scheme was undone by the Mexican federation's own yearbook, which included the correct birth dates of the players.

The wrath of FIFA descended on Mexico, which was banned from the 1990 World Cup, thus giving the United States its best chance ever of qualifying. Coach Bob Gansler's cautious, unimaginative team made hard work of it against Guatemala, El Salvador, Trinidad and Tobago, and Costa Rica, managing to score only six goals in eight games. It all came down to the final game in Port of Spain. Paul Caligiuri's goal gave the Americans a memorable 1–0 win to ensure a place in Italy.

In Europe there were no frauds, but there were a couple of mild shocks when both France and Denmark narrowly failed to qualify, beaten out by Scotland and Romania.

Italy, of course, was the favorite to win its own tournament, just as it had done in 1934. But there were plenty of people around who felt that the pressure to win was precisely what would undo coach Azeglio Vicini's team. If not Italy, then the Netherlands. Defeated finalists in 1974 and 1978, the Dutch had recently struck scintillating form. Led by their tall, elegant, dreadlocked midfielder Ruud Gullit, they had won their first major tournament, the 1988 European championship. And, of course, the Germans. No one would count them out. Brazil or Argentina? Probably not, given how difficult it always was for South American teams to win in Europe.

Italia-90 opened in Milan with the now obligatory pregame extravaganza. Forty minutes of screaming rock music, dancing, fashion models, even a taped segment of grand opera. Argentina against Cameroon followed. In the 1982 opening game in Barcelona, Menotti's Argentina had been roughed up by Belgium, and lost 1–0. The script in Milan was the same. Bilardo's Argentina lost 1–0, this time it was Cameroon dishing it out.

The game highlighted a worrying problem. Michel Vautrot, the French referee, did his best to cope with the violence, giving out three yellow cards to the Cameroons, and ejecting two of their players. Yet they still won the game. Perhaps there was just no way to compensate for the abysmal performance by the Argentines. Their ineptitude was capped in the sixty-fifth minute, when Omam Biyik outjumped the leaden-footed Argentine defense to head the ball straight at goalkeeper Nery Pumpido. It should have been a routine save, but Pumpido fumbled the ball and it rolled into the net.

Only four of Argentina's 1986 team were present, including Maradona. Admittedly, he had taken a beating, but on those occasions when his magic shone, his teammates had not responded. Up front, Abel Balbo was a one-man nonevent. Claudio Caniggia, coming on in the second half, caused some problems with his speed (both Cameroon ejections came when defenders brought him down as he sped away). The irony was that in Ramón Diaz, Argentina had a center forward who would have walked onto any other team. He was not even on Bilardo's squad—because, it was said, Maradona didn't like him. On this form, Argentina would be lucky to survive the first round.

Argentina's next game, against the USSR, started badly. Bilardo had made five changes to the team, and soon was forced to make another. After only ten minutes the misfortunes of goalkeeper Pumpido, whose gaffe had cost Argentina the opening game, took a tragic turn. He was stretchered off with a broken leg after colliding heavily with his own defender, Julio Olarticoechea. Sergio Goycochea came on, and was to prove a splendid deputy.

One minute later, the Hand of God struck again. Oleg Kuznetsov's header was speeding goalward when Maradona popped up, almost on his own goal line. Like a striking snake, his right hand flashed out and knocked the ball down to his feet. Swedish referee Erik Fredricksson, standing no more than five yards from Maradona, staring straight at him, saw nothing.

Argentina won the game 2–0. The Brazilian coach, Lazaroni, remarked: "What a versatile player Maradona is. He can score goals with his left hand, and save them with his right." A 1–1 tie with Romania followed and Argentina did, just, creep into the next round, as the third-place team.

Topping the group were the Cameroons, who had shown that they were capable of some very good-looking soccer. They had also unveiled their secret weapon, the thirty-eight-year-old Roger Milla, who had come on against Romania to score twice within ten minutes. The big question mark against Cameroon was its tackling, some of which was disgraceful. It had already saddled the team with seven yellow and two red cards.

Yugoslavia were supposed to be a good long-shot bet, but the Germans blew them out, 4–1, in their first game. Lothar Matthäus got two of the goals, and the Germans really did look as though they were enjoying things, as though there were plenty more goals to come. After all, with players like Rudi Völler, Jürgen Klinsmann, Thomas Hässler, and Pierre Littbarski in the squad, everything was in place for an attacking festival.

There was, as it happened, a demonstration of German offensive power that same night. It came from hordes of German fans, who went on a rampage in downtown Milan, fighting police and damaging property. Twenty-three injuries were reported. All this despite a day-of-game ban on alcohol sales in Milan.

The hope of a free-scoring Germany seemed to be confirmed by a 5–1 romp over the United Arab Emirates. But the goal flow dried up after a shaky 1–1 tie with Colombia, a game that the Germans were lucky not to lose. After that, they never managed more than two goals in a game.

Even though it was the Germans, and not the expected English, who set the hooligan ball rolling, there was no doubt about which was the big match, as far as fan violence was concerned. England vs. the Netherlands, in Cagliari. Over 1,500 police and *carabinieri* on duty at the stadium, 4,000 more in the town.

Of course, there were ugly scenes. About a thousand English fans chose to march, *en masse*, to the stadium. Mayhem followed. The fans threw rocks and bottles, police in riot gear replied with night sticks and tear gas. The injuries were many, the arrests few—only five. The English issued their now customary statement about "a minority of troublemakers bringing disgrace to English soccer."

On the field, England had slightly the better of the Dutch, but the game ended 0–0. There was a change, almost a revolution, in English tactical thinking. Coach Bobby Robson used Mark Wright as a sweeper; every other country in Europe used a sweeper, had been doing so for two decades. The English had found it difficult to change from their dual-center back system. Wright had a good game against the Dutch, but the innovation was not repeated against Egypt, which was beaten by the minimum 1–0 score.

England topped the group. Next came the Netherlands and Ireland, with identical records: three ties, two goals for and two against. A special draw was necessary to decide which team had finished second, which third. The Irish "won" that, the only thing they were to win in Italy. They were assigned second place, and would play Romania in the next round. The Dutch would have to face West Germany.

The Irish team was a monument to soccer's tangled eligibility requirements. Very few of the players had actually been born in Ireland. Most qualified because they had an Irish parent, or maybe a grandparent. Or, like forward John Aldridge, a great-grandmother. The coach was an Englishman, Jack Charlton, who had been a center back on England's World Cup–winning team in 1966.

Charlton's idea of soccer was to hit the ball long, to get it forward as quickly as possible. The direct approach. His players were workhorses who made life difficult for opponents, and the game boring for spectators.

Spain, Belgium, and Uruguay qualified from the uninspiring Group E. All would fall at the next hurdle.

The United States team of young, inexperienced college players was led by a college coach, Bob Gansler, who had squeaked the Americans into the final round for the first time since 1950. But Gansler's lack of experience of World Cup soccer caught up with him in Italy.

His team bombed calamitously in its first game. Czechoslovakia missed a penalty kick, but it hardly mattered as they slammed in five goals anyway. The Americans were not ready, had not been properly prepared, for this level of soccer. Against Italy they regrouped, packed their defense, and held the Italians to just one goal, though they were lucky when Gianlucca Vialli hit the post with a penalty kick in the first half.

Late in the game the Italian goalkeeper, Walter Zenga, misplayed a stinging free kick from Bruce Murray. The ball ran loose and fullback Riccardo Ferri had to kick Peter Vermes's shot off the goal line. It was the Americans' only chance of the game, but it became the basis of a legend that the United States had given as good as it got and had "nearly tied" Italy. Hardly. The Americans had their backs to the wall for virtually the whole game. But the fact that the young players did not panic in the fever-heat atmosphere of Rome's packed Olympic Stadium was certainly to their credit. A 1–2 loss to Austria then put the United States out of the tournament.

For Italy, the victory over the United States marked its second 1–0 win. Against Austria it had played some of the best soccer of the first round— fast-paced, inventive, attacking soccer—but the goals would not come. The score was still 0–0 when, with fifteen minutes left, coach Vicini brought on Salvatore "Toto" Schillaci. A short, bustling center forward, Schillaci was that rarity in Italian professional soccer, a Sicilian. Three minutes was all he needed. Gianluca Vialli crossed the ball, and Schillaci emphatically headed it in—to detonate the stadium into an explosion of joy . . . and relief.

Vicini again used Schillaci as a substitute against the Americans. But the scrappy little Toto had quickly become an immensely popular hero, the symbol of Italy's hope for the world title. From then on he would start every game. Against Austria he scored again, and Italy marched into the next round with three wins out of three.

Meanwhile, remarkable things were happening in Group C. Costa Rica, probably the least fancied team in the whole tournament, had beaten Scotland and Sweden. Sandwiched between was a 1–0 loss to Brazil. The Costa Ricans could boast just one outstanding player—goalkeeper Gabelo Conejo. For the rest, this was a modest team, coached by Bora Milutinovic to play a modest game. Defensive yes, but always looking for a goal-scoring opening. Their modest skills got the Costa Ricans into the second round.

Brazil made it, too. It managed to win all three of its games and at the same time infuriate its fans. What caused the rumpus was coach Lazaroni's insistence on adopting a European approach. For the first time Brazil would play with a sweeper. That meant reducing the number of forwards from three to two. Pelé, among many others, was aghast: "That is not Brazil. Brazil always plays with three forwards."

Nine of Lazaroni's starting team played for European clubs. They had become used to Europe and European soccer, something that opened up a huge rift between them and the Brazilian press. The journalists, living and working in Brazil, regarded the players almost as foreigners who had forgotten what it was like to be Brazilian, who didn't understand that the Brazilian people would not accept a Europeanized game.

That Brazil should only beat little Costa Rica by 1–0 was an insult to the Brazilian press, which gave Lazaroni a torrid time. They wanted to see goals, they wanted to see the traditional *jogo bonito* (beautiful game) style of Brazil. Instead, here was midfielder Dunga boasting "No more *jogo bonito*, this is the Brazil of sweat and sacrifice."

But the critics, headed by Pelé, turned out to be right: "As soon as we play a good team, we'll lose," he said. The second round brought the old enemy—Argentina. This time Brazil failed to score, and it went down 1–0. A wickedly unfair result, because the Brazilians had dominated the game, had created chance after chance, had hit the goalposts three times. But the old scoring fluency was not there.

It was Maradona who sunk them. He had a quiet game, but just one moment of razzle-dazzle was enough. Ironically, it was the defense, supposedly the strong point of the new-look Brazil, that fouled up. A penetrating Maradona dribble unnerved the defenders. Their soccer instincts, their tactical discipline, vanished as Maradona dominated their vision. Four of them converged on him, leaving Caniggia free.

As the defenders rushed in, Maradona somehow spirited the ball away, through the forest of legs, to the lurking Caniggia. The defenders barely had time to spin around and watch helplessly as Caniggia rounded goalkeeper Claudio Taffarel and scored the game-winning goal. To add insult to the injury, Maradona had made the pass with his rarely used right foot.

For the first time in four attempts, Argentina had beaten Brazil in a World Cup game. "We must try to work out the reasons for this incredible and undeserved defeat," said Lazaroni, but the press didn't want to hear. They already knew the reason: Lazaroni's betrayal of *jogo bonito*.

Brazil went home, and the saddest thing was that no one really cared. When the Brazilians were eliminated in 1982 and 1986, it was as though the heart had been wrenched out of the tournaments. This time, Brazil had been just another team. Said a banner at the Argentina game: "If Lazaroni is a coach, I'm the Pope."

Costa Rica bowed out, heavily beaten 4–1 by Czechoslovakia, though it would surely have been closer had Conejo not been out with an injury. Ireland and Romania, predictably, produced the worst game, a 0–0 tie that had to be resolved by penalty kicks. Ireland took the shoot-out, which put them into the quarter-finals without having won a game. Charlton, dubbed Saint Jack by the Irish press, mused: "We could end up winning the whole tournament without winning a game."

Yugoslavia disposed of Spain 2–1 in overtime, and England also needed the extra thirty minutes before getting past Belgium 1–0. Two of England's younger players teamed up on the only goal of the game. David Platt volleyed a spectacular winner after receiving an inch-perfect free kick from Paul "Gazza" Gascoigne. The twenty-three-year-old Gascoigne was emerging as a new talent, extravagantly gifted, but a player of unpredictable moods whom coach Bobby Robson had once described as "daft as a brush."

Colombia and Cameroon put on a vastly entertaining game in Naples. Attacking soccer, attractively and intelligently played, flowed from both teams. Carlos Valderrama, Colombia's flamboyant midfielder, caught the eye—partly for the explosion of orange-gold hair that enveloped his head, partly for his superb passing and dribbling.

WORLD CUP 1990
Naples, Italy: Cameroon 2 Colombia 1
Cameroon's Cyrille Makanaky (center) forces his way through the Colombian defense in one of the tournament's most attractive games. Cameroon's brilliant soccer convinced FIFA to increase Africa's representation in the World Cup finals from two places to three in 1994.
© Peter Robinson: The Football Archive

Joining in the fun was Colombia's extrovert and adventurous goalkeeper, René Higuita, known for his dribbling forays upfield. Colombia had the better of the first half, and was unlucky when Freddy Rincon's piledriving free kick smashed against a goal post.

Old Man Milla came on for Cameroon in the second half and again proved to be the game winner. In overtime, he blasted a left-footer past

Higuita, and then three minutes later showed that he could still move as quickly as anyone. Higuita, yet again, had come out of his area, the ball at his feet. Milla pounced, stole the ball, and scored. That was the vital goal, for Colombia scored to make it 2–1.

Higuita showed up at the postgame press conference to admit his error: "I have asked my teammates to forgive me. It has never happened to me before, but it was a mistake that a lot of people were waiting for. Well, you all saw it, it was as big as a house."

As always, the Dutch and the Germans threw everything they had into their clash. A little too much, at first. Frank Rijkaard and Rudi Völler got involved in a series of nasty incidents, with Rijkaard clearly seen to spit on Völler. The referee red-carded both of them after twenty minutes. It seemed much too harsh on Völler.

Klinsmann put the Germans ahead in the first half, and Andy Brehme added a second late in the game. With under a minute left, the Netherlands pulled a goal back from a Ron Koeman penalty kick. The Germans had been the better side, and were now solidly established as the second favorites, right behind Italy.

Rome's Olympic Stadium was packed yet again to see the Italians take on Uruguay. Defensive play dominated until the sixty-seventh minute when Toto Schillaci had the Italian fans roaring again with a left-footed rocket from the edge of the penalty area that screamed past goalkeeper Fernando Alvez. Aldo Serena made it 2–0 Italy.

Italy was now the clear favorite to take the trophy. With the home crowds providing frenetic support, the early nervousness had gone, the team was playing well, and had yet to concede a goal.

The Irish came to Rome, duly played their uncompromising, unimaginative game, and were duly beaten, 1–0. Goal by Schillaci. Roberto Donadoni's shot was too strong for goalkeeper Pat Bonner, who could only fend it off. Toto got to the loose ball first and rapped it home.

The Irish, said Vicini, showed "athletic power and strength," but some of their tackling was too vigorous for his liking. He suggested that the Italians needed more protection from the referees. Jack Charlton had little to say about the game: "To tell the truth, I've had it with these press conferences. We're going home. I'll probably be fishing on Monday."

The expected Italy–West Germany final moved a step closer when the Germans also advanced, beating Czechoslovakia 1–0 on Lothar Matthäus's penalty kick.

Argentina played another poor game, and again they came away with a win. This time, Yugoslavia were the victims. The 0–0 overtime tie went to penalty kicks. There had been very little excitement, and no moments of Maradona magic. In fact Maradona, to the crowd's delight, muffed his penalty kick. It didn't matter because Goycochea came up with two saves and Argentina, the same Argentina that had looked so awful in the opening game, was in the semifinal.

Just two goals in the first three quarterfinals. England and Cameroon offset that by coming up with five in their game in Naples. Although England went ahead on a Platt goal, Cameroon came back to take a 2–1 lead in the second half, played some of the best soccer of the tournament, and looked as though they might overrun the English defense.

England was saved by Cameroon's old failing: wild tackling. Twice Lineker was brought crashing down, twice he scrambled up to convert the resulting penalty kicks. A 3–2 overtime win for England, but Cameroon had only itself to blame for not reaching the semifinals.

England, so wobbly against Cameroon, traveled up to Turin to play its best game of the tournament, against West Germany. After dominating the first half, England fell behind on the hour. Brehme's free kick hit Paul Parker's foot, and spun up into the air, heading for the English goal. Veteran goalkeeper Peter Shilton was slow to react, and his last-second backward lunge was too late to stop the ball curling in just under the crossbar. A fluke—but a goal, nonetheless.

Lineker tied it up, and yet another World Cup game had to go to the penalty kick lottery. But not before a touching incident in overtime. Gascoigne fouled Thomas Berthold and was given a yellow, his second of the tournament. It meant a one-game suspension. If England made it to the final, Gascoigne would not play. Television caught it beautifully, Gascoigne staring at the yellow card, realizing what it meant, tears beginning to roll down his cheeks. Gazza's Tears became part of English soccer lore.

But England did not make it. Stuart Pearce, England's top penalty kicker, hit his shot straight at goalkeeper Bodo Illgner, and on the next kick, Chris Waddle missed the goal completely. Germany was through to a record sixth World Cup final.

In the other semifinal, Italy tangled with Maradona's Argentina. The twist was that, for the first time, Italy had to play outside of Rome. In Naples—the city where Maradona played his club soccer, where he was regarded almost as a saint. The street-smart Maradona hinted that the Neapolitans should support Argentina. After all, everyone knew that there was a great deal of prejudice against southerners in the rest of Italy: "Italy wants your support now, but the other 364 days of the year it doesn't even consider you Italians," was Maradona's message.

Whatever, Naples was not Rome, where the stadium had always been jammed, the noise intimidating. In Naples, there were 10,000 empty seats, and an appreciably lower decibel level. Vicini baffled everyone with his lineup. He dropped Roberto Baggio, who had struck up a smooth partnership with Schillaci, and brought back Vialli, so unsuccessful in the early games. The move looked good after only seventeen minutes when a rasping Vialli shot was parried by Goycochea and there was the irrepressible Toto on hand to slam home the rebound from six yards out. The Italians, already assured of a $120,000 bonus per man for reaching the semifinal, looked set to collect the extra $40,000 for a win. For the Argentines, who had been running on empty for so long, the end was surely in sight.

Not yet. The Argentines proceeded to play their best game of the tournament. Slowly they took command. The flow, the pace, even the enthusiasm, seemed to hemorrhage from the Italian game. The defense was a bundle of nerves as Caniggia, Burruchaga, and Maradona piled on the pressure. In the fiftieth minute goalkeeper Walter Zenga had set a new World Cup record, 500 minutes without conceding a goal. But he looked far from comfortable on this day, stretching to make last-second saves, badly bobbling a corner kick.

His record lasted another eighteen minutes, until Caniggia beat him to Olarticoechea's cross, and flicked the ball neatly into the goal. Overtime came and went, though it took much longer than it should have done when referee Michel Vautrot inexplicably allowed the first fifteen-minute period to run for twenty-three minutes. The Italians, spent and dispirited, were beaten on penalty kicks. Goycochea saved splendidly from Donadoni and Serena, and it was Maradona who hit the winning penalty.

Argentina, incredibly, absurdly, was in the final. Italy was in mourning. City streets, so riotously jammed after each Italian victory, were silent and sullen. Third place was all that remained, and the Italians settled that by beating England 2–1. Toto Schillaci got another goal, his sixth, which made him the tournament's top scorer.

But what a price Argentina had paid in beating Italy. Ricardo Giusti had been red-carded. Caniggia, Olarticoechea, and Sergio Batista had received second yellows. All four were suspended, out of the final. Maradona was showing the effects of a badly swollen ankle that he had been nursing for the whole tournament.

If the Italians had a hero in Toto, they now had a villain in Maradona, who was painted as the man who had eliminated Italy. His house in Naples was stoned, and it was clear that—probably for the first time in soccer history—most Italians wanted a German victory.

Before the final in Rome, the Italian fans whistled and jeered all through the Argentine national anthem, just as they did every time Maradona touched the ball. The raucous catcalls provided a fitting background for a truly awful, totally forgettable final.

Any hope that Argentina would play as openly as it had against Italy was ruled out by the suspension of so many key players. In particular, two things demanded defensive tactics: the absence of Caniggia, its one dangerous forward, and the threat (or the hope) of the penalty kick tie-breaker. Argentina knew that if it could defend its way to that stage, it stood a good chance of winning the shoot-out. It had already won two of them on the strength of Goycochea's catlike reflexes.

So the Argentines defended, methodically, dourly . . . and effectively. The Germans could not find a way through. They attacked constantly, but with little in the way of imagination or cunning. Even after Argentina was reduced to ten men when Pedro Monzon distinguished himself by becoming the first player ever ejected from the final, it held on. Until, with only five minutes remaining, a highly questionable call from Mexican referee

Edgar Codesal gave Germany a penalty kick. The Argentines surrounded Codesal, protesting, menacing.

When that was over, Brehme hit the penalty perfectly—hard, low, just inside the post. It had to be perfect, for the diving Goycochea got within inches of saving it. The game was over soon afterward.

Rough soccer justice. Germany, which had lost the 1966 final on a goal that was almost certainly not a goal, had won the 1990 final on a penalty that was almost certainly not a penalty.

Not much comfort in that for Argentina, which had become the first team to be shut out in a World Cup final. Germany, after failing in the finals in 1982 and 1986, was world champion. Beckenbauer, like Brazil's Zagalo, had now gained a winner's medal both as a player and as a coach.

The Argentines again besieged Codesal. Maradona was in tears. When his stricken face appeared on the huge television screen, the fans screamed in delight. Ugliness, ugliness.

Maradona refused to shake the hand of FIFA president João Havelange when he received his loser's medal. For Maradona, it was all a plot by FIFA. Argentina was being punished for dumping Italy, which was the team that FIFA—for unspecified reasons—wanted as winners. "There is a Mafia in the soccer world," accused Maradona. "That penalty did not exist. It was awarded to let the Germans win."

As in 1986, Maradona had left an indelible image on the tournament, but a very different one this time.* Italia-90 had been a sour tournament, lacking in colorful players, lacking in adventurous, entertaining play. Above all, lacking in goals. The average per game sank to an all-time low of 2.2.

But soccer had always survived its dark moments, had always been confident of a bright future, always certain that if today's game was a disappointment, well, tomorrow's, or next week's, or next month's would be sublime. In Rome, even as the curtain came down on that awful final, there was a feeling of exhilaration in the stadium: The fireworks soared noisily into the night, the stadium was bathed in a warm, friendly glow of hundreds of red flares, and the scoreboard flashed "Ciao Italia-90—Hello USA-94."

Soccer was on the move, heading for unconquered territory. The Americans, with all their economic power, their inventiveness, their optimism, were about to discover the World Cup. Surely a reason for excitement.

---

*The career of Maradona, one of soccer's all-time greats, turned tragically to ashes after the 1990 tournament. Playing for Napoli in 1991, he failed a routine blood test when traces of cocaine were found in his blood. FIFA banned him from soccer for 15 months. An attempted comeback with the Spanish club Sevilla in 1992 lasted only one season; the club accused him of being more interested in night life than in training. Returning to Argentina, he signed to play for Newells Old Boys in Rosario. But his struggle to reach game-fitness continued . . . until October 1993, when he was suddenly, and improbably, recalled to the national team. See chapter 5, page 116.

The World Cup, 1994*

The World Cup in the United States? Preposterous! The whole idea of staging soccer's biggest event in a country known to be, at best, lukewarm to the sport aroused opposition and scorn right from the start. Like moving the World Series to India, said an American journalist—who's going to come?

The English, always ready to mock Yankee attempts to get into soccer, thought that hardly anyone would show up. "The United States is under-whelmed about soccer. The World Cup will be played in half empty stadia," wrote Michael Herd in the London *Evening Standard*.

So why had FIFA done this unspeakable thing? What had possessed the normally conservative FIFA biggies to break so violently with tradition and, for the first time in the World Cup's sixty-year history, award it to a non-soccer country?

The critics believed they had the answer: money. Sheer greed, they said, a transparent move to tap the hugely rich American sponsorship scene. World Cup-94 would not be about sport, it would be about piling up huge profits. A one-month circus that pitched its tent in the USA, then took off with the money.

"No, no," said FIFA. The idea was to "promote the game of Association Football," exactly as the FIFA statutes require. And where better to promote it than in the one major country that had so far resisted its call? They were about to turn Americans into soccer fans.

To prove their honorable intentions, FIFA let it be known that they were determined that the 1994 World Cup should leave a lasting impact in the United States. "Soccer in the USA cannot stop with the World Cup," said the FIFA general secretary Sepp Blatter. "It must go on. This is only the first step toward the formation of a professional league."

* For tabulated scores of all tournament games, see pages 314–324. For tactical analyses of the World Cups, see chapter 8, pages 178–226.

More scoffing from the critics—maybe Mr. Blatter meant "yet another professional league"? There had, after all, been a succession of such leagues going back to the 1920s . . . and all of them had flopped.

True enough. Professional soccer had been a definite disaster area in the United States. But the sport kept bouncing back, and it kept getting more ambitious. Back in 1969, the United States Soccer Federation had announced the formation of a National Development Committee whose ultimate aim was "to apply to host the 1978 World Cup finals."

Ambitious, but ill-informed. The 1978 World Cup had already been assigned to Argentina. But as soon as it was over, the Americans tried their luck again. USSF President Gene Edwards sent FIFA an application to host the 1990 World Cup, along with a brochure listing some 48 stadiums, with photographs of 28 of them.

Edwards evidently thought he knew how to get FIFA's ear. He struck the commercial chord: "American business communities have become accustomed to supporting major events, and the staging of the World Cup in the United States would lead to broader participation by these entities in supporting soccer on a worldwide basis."

FIFA showed no interest and awarded the 1990 World Cup to Italy. It looked as though the USA would have to wait at least until 1994. But that all changed in October 1982 when Colombia, the designated host country for 1986, announced that it couldn't afford to stage the tournament. "We have a lot of things to do here," said Colombian President Belisario Betancur, "and there is not time to attend to the extravagances of FIFA and its members."

With under four years to go, FIFA needed a new host country, fast. Canada, Brazil, and the USA applied at once. Mexico put in a bid in January 1983. The USA really worked on this one, even sending Pelé, Franz Beckenbauer, and Henry Kissinger to plead its case before the crucial FIFA meeting in Sweden.

No joy. FIFA, professing annoyance at the USA's high-pressure tactics, gave the tournament to Mexico. There was another reason for the thumbs down. The USSF was in the middle of organizing the soccer tournament for the 1984 Los Angeles Olympics, and FIFA was not impressed. "If they can't manage four stadia for the Olympics," said President João Havelange, "How can they manage twelve for the World Cup?"

The USA persisted. In 1987, along with Chile, Brazil, and Morocco, it sought the 1994 World Cup. Now a very different atmosphere prevailed at FIFA. Because of the 1984 Olympic soccer tournament. Far from screwing it up, as FIFA had feared, the Americans had made a tremendous success of it. The crowds at the Rose Bowl had astonished everyone: 97,451 for France vs. Yugoslavia, 100,374 for Yugoslavia vs. Italy, and 101,799 for the final between Brazil and France.

The new USSF President, Werner Fricker, presented FIFA with two leather-bound volumes—a meticulously prepared bid. There was really no contest. Chile had already dropped out. Brazil's hastily cobbled presentation was panned by Havelange, himself a Brazilian, who said it contained errors and handwritten corrections: "It would have been better to have sent nothing at all."

While the Moroccans, said Blatter, "presented only two stadiums, beyond that only plans . . . . The World Cup is not a development program." On July 4 1988, FIFA voted in favor of the USA.

The Americans now had six years to get the World Cup show on the road. It was to be a rocky road, particularly at the beginning. If there was a honeymoon period, no one noticed it. FIFA was soon locking horns with Fricker, who headed the American organizing committee. Advice flowed freely across the Atlantic from the FIFA office, but Fricker saw it as interference.

Hostilities began in earnest in 1989 with a skirmish over marketing rights. FIFA accused Fricker and the USSF of muscling in on its exclusive territory. That was smoothed over, but not before FIFA had brandished its trump card: if Fricker didn't bend, the World Cup would be taken away.

A major bust-up came in December 1989. Fricker had worked out a deal with NBC to televise the tournament. But after complaints from other networks, including TBS and ABC, FIFA nixed it, saying it had not been arrived at by a competitive bidding process.

Fricker called the FIFA decision "absolutely unconscionable" and accused them of altering the terms under which the USSF was granted the World Cup. By 1990 FIFA had had it with Fricker. It would dearly have loved to set up another organizing committee, but it was trapped by its own constitution, which said that it had to deal with the USSF.

The only answer was to make sure that Fricker did not get returned as USSF President when the summer election came round. FIFA turned to Alan Rothenberg, a Los Angeles lawyer whom they knew and respected as one of the organizers of that 1984 Olympic soccer tournament. Rothenberg was persuaded to oppose Fricker, entering the race only two weeks before the election.

Then FIFA blatantly intervened in the election itself, backing Rothenberg and letting it be known that the World Cup would likely be taken away if Fricker was re-elected.

FIFA was clearly nervous. At 6:20 A.M. on the morning of the election, the USSF treasurer, Paul Stiehl—who was also running against Fricker— received a telephone call in his hotel room. From Zurich, it was FIFA's public relations director, Guido Tognoni, asking him to withdraw so that the anti-Fricker vote would not be split.

Stiehl, appalled, stood anyway. But FIFA need not have worried. Rothenberg swept to victory. The intransigent Fricker was banished. Later Rothenberg said: "People didn't realize how precarious it was. FIFA was prepared to take the World Cup away from us. They told me that. I believed them."

Rothenberg appointed Chuck Cale, who had been his boss at the 1984 Olympics, to run the World Cup. Eventually—it took eight months—Bob Gansler was replaced as national team coach by Bora Milutinovic, the Serbian who had been so successful in getting Costa Rica into the second round in Italia-90. But FIFA's problems with the Americans were not over yet.

In December 1990 came a "major news conference" in New York that was supposed to mark the launching of World Cup-94. A disaster. It was just as the cynics had foreseen. No soccer people were present, all the talk was of money and sponsors, and the big news of the day was the signing of a "historic marketing agreement."

Even that turned out to be a terminological inexactitude. Snags in the negotiations meant that talks were still going on as the press conference got under way. By the time it finished, and the journalists present were wondering just what it was they were supposed to write about, the contract had still not been signed.

Cale lasted just over a year, by which time FIFA was convinced he was not up to the task. Things were getting behind schedule. The rumors started up again, insisting that the Americans couldn't do it, and that Germany was ready to take over. No one knew where these stories started, but there were further rumors suggesting that FIFA itself was using them to put pressure on the USA.

Rothenberg fired Cale in December 1991 and took over the reins for himself. From now on, he was to play a very visible role as the mastermind of World Cup-94.

The sport itself finally put in an appearance at the qualifying-round draw at New York's Madison Square Garden. Pelé and Franz Beckenbauer were up on the platform, while the audience bristled with national team coaches from around the world. Barbara Eden, a television star from the 1960s whom hardly anyone could remember, was the bizarre choice to host the event. The American organizers squirmed in embarrassment as she mispronounced Havelange's name. She called him Dr. Havligang.

On the whole, the draw was judged a success. A low-key production, free of razzmatazz. That was what the Europeans seemed to fear most: that American razzmatazz, whatever that was, would take over and cheapen the sport.

The absence of a specifically American atmosphere could be explained: of the 672 journalists present, only 90 were from the American media. The critics scoffed again. Maybe Americans were still underwhelmed with the sport?

No, that could not be. Rothenberg, a wonderfully optimistic leader, had only to point to the tremendous interest in staging World Cup games. Only nine cities would be chosen, but twenty-four had applied.

When the nine venues were announced, they included two where artificial turf would have to be replaced with grass, a FIFA requirement: New Jersey's Giants Stadium and Detroit's Silverdome. Giants Stadium had the additional problem that the field was narrower than the 68 meters demanded by World Cup regulations. That would be overlooked because Havelange was insisting that New York, under the guise of New Jersey, must be a venue. "Our position," said Tognoni, "is that we should not be arguing over centimeters." Two hundred centimeters to be precise; the Giants Stadium field would be 66m wide.

Havelange had visited the Silverdome and had been suitably impressed, especially by its cleanliness. "Cleaner than a hospital," he said. As for growing grass indoors (something that would normally prompt a visit from the Drug Enforcement Agency, commented the London *Independent*) that was a challenge that would surely be solved by American technology.

The World Cup-94 mascot was introduced in August 1992. On a darkened stage floodlights suddenly revealed a creature with a huge snout. A moose? ventured one onlooker. Rothenberg felt obliged to clarify: "It's a dog." It was wearing a horizontally striped rugby shirt, and holding a soccer ball as though it were a basketball. But the Americans were learning. At its next appearance, the mascot sported a considerably reduced snout, a real soccer shirt, and now had the ball at its feet. It was to be called Striker. A soccer name, but it remained a clumsy, unimaginative sort of creature, far removed in spirit from the grace and elegance of the sport.

Ticket prices were announced in January 1993—anything from $25 for a first round game to $475 for the final. When they went on sale in June, the demand was staggering—especially as fans were buying tickets without any idea which teams they would be seeing. The qualifying games were still going on.

Of vital interest to the World Cup-94 people was Qualifying Group 2 in Europe, the one that included England. If England qualified, it would mean an influx of English fans. Among them, inevitably, would be a core of troublemakers, the so-called hooligans who had caused so much mayhem in European cities, and during Italia-90.

Soccer's detractors in the USA were always quick to seize on examples of crowd riots to show what a violent, crude, un-American sport soccer was. "What's going to happen if all those English soccer fans come here?" asked columnist Steve Jacobson in *Newsday*. "Are they going to want to carry the Washington Monument and the Liberty Bell home with them like tearing down goalposts?"

Television images of marauding bands of drunken hooligans brawling in downtown American cities—a very real possibility—would turn the World Cup into a nightmare and, far from helping to popularize the sport, could inflict a fatal wound.

There was deep concern here. World Cup-94 created a security unit under ex-FBI agent Ed Best, the man who had been in charge of security at the 1984 Los Angeles Olympic Games. "Security will be the single largest item in the budget," said Rothenberg, "If there are serious problems at an early round game and we have to put in high security for subsequent games, it could be incredibly expensive."

No wonder. The 1984 Olympics had used 6,000 police officers, plus 9,000 private security agents. World Cup-94 expected to employ even more. But, said Best, there would be no massive, menacing displays of force; security would be "friendly, efficient, no-nonsense."

That made sense only if the hooligans didn't show up. And they didn't. Rothenberg & Co. got a huge break when, against all expectations, England failed to qualify. The hooligan problem receded into the background.

Nothing but good news on the financial front. Two professors at the University of South Carolina's Economics Department carried out a study that predicted the World Cup would have an "economic impact" of $2.79 billion. Rothenberg said the figure would be nearer $4 billion. He added: "Our mission statement is this: to present the best-ever World Cup and to build a legacy for soccer in the United States."

With ticket money pouring in, with the security budget revised dramatically downward, Rothenberg was now confidently defining that legacy in monetary terms: a profit of $20 million.

By the end of 1993, with the qualifying games over and the 24 finalists known, the world of soccer gathered in the capital of American razzmatazz, Las Vegas, for the final round draw.

Four years earlier, in Italy, the draw had featured Sophia Loren and Luciano Pavarotti. The Americans rolled out Robin Williams, Faye Dunaway, Stevie Wonder, James Brown, Barry Manilow, Willie Nelson, and Evander Holyfield. Plus President Bill Clinton on tape.

Not enough, apparently, to impress ABC television which decided against coverage, and carried live golf instead. Describing the draw as "deathly boring," an ABC spokesman told *The Wall Street Journal* that "It's hard enough bringing in good ratings for soccer when there's action."

Embarrassment all round—after all, ABC was the network that had won the right to televise the World Cup games in the United States.

World Cup year, 1994, began with a major shock. Literally. At 4:30 in the morning of Monday January 17 a massive earthquake (Richter 6.6) hit the Los Angeles area, causing over $30 billion in damage and 57 deaths.

This was positively eerie, a spooky déjà vu that recalled the earthquake that had struck Chile before the 1962 World Cup, and the devastating 1985 shock (Richter 8.1) that caused over 7,000 deaths and had nearly wrecked Mexico's preparations for the 1986 tournament.

According to World Cup managing director Scott LeTellier, the World Cup offices in downtown Los Angeles "looked like a hurricane had blown through here, computers were bounced all over the place, pictures had come off the walls, files were spread all over the floor."

But the big worry was the Rose Bowl in Pasadena, scheduled to be the site of eight games, including the World Cup final. Engineers were called in and soon calmed everyone down by reporting that there was no structural damage.

Damage of another sort was soon to be inflicted by Ed Best and his security department. Possibly finding life a little dull now that the the hooligan threat had been removed, the department sent out a form to all the journalists who had applied for accreditation (over 5,000 were expected) demanding that they sign a waiver allowing the FBI and other law enforcement agencies virtually unlimited access to all their "criminal history and criminal investigative records."

The demand provoked a storm of protest. "We are aghast at the inappropriateness of your request," said *The New York Times* in a letter to Rothenberg, "It strikes us as the grossest invasion of the personal privacy of the journalists." *USA Today* and the *Boston Globe* quickly agreed, while the Associated Press said flatly that it would not cover the event unless the demand was withdrawn.

World Cup-94, trying to cultivate the American press, had shot itself right through the middle of its foot and had managed to antagonize just about everyone who mattered. Even FIFA demurred: "I am truly shocked at this procedure," said Blatter.

Rothenberg, typically, tried to brazen it out. He claimed, in his reply to *The New York Times*, that such a clearance procedure had been used in the 1984 Olympic Games. This was immediately denied by officials from the U.S. Olympic Committee.

As quietly as possible, the waiver demand was dropped. A defeat for the overzealous security department, which soon had to face up to another—this time tragic—mistake.

Terrorists taking hostages and hijacking a train? Nothing even remotely resembling that had ever happened at a World Cup—yet security training in California included the simulation of such an episode. During the exercise, Theodore Brassinga, a thirty-three-year-old police officer playing the role of a terrorist was shot dead by another officer.

Brassinga's was to be the only World Cup–related death in the United States. One policeman shot by another.

Beer then entered the list of possible security threats. Down in Orlando, probably the hottest of the venues, they thought that drunken fans could pose problems. But a suggestion that beer sales should be banned in the stadium was never going to fly. Among the major marketing partners of the tournament was . . . Budweiser. FIFA's Guido Tognoni dismissed the threat: "Beer drinking is only a problem for the toilets. Besides, American beer is light."

So it was OK for the fans in Orlando to drink beer. But what about the players? Would they be allowed to drink anything at all during the games? Ireland had to play a game in Orlando, and coach Jack Charlton believed that FIFA rules prevented the passing of drinks to players during a game. "Players will die out there," he moaned.

He'd got it wrong, drinks were permitted, but his complaint was somehow typical of a European attitude that was determined to find fault with the USA as a venue. In particular, the idea of teams having to fly through different time zones seemed to particularly upset the Europeans. The kickoff times of some of the games was another source of alarm. Ireland's game in Orlando, for instance, kicked off at 12:30, in the full blaze of midday heat.

Ironically, this was a problem caused by European television, which needed early USA kickoff times to ensure evening viewing in Europe.

A different sort of fault-finder was the USA's goalkeeper and captain, Tony Meola. He got paid for complaining. In a television commercial for a new adidas soccer shoe, the Predator, Meola was seen throwing himself all over the place, but being hopelessly beaten by a variety of shots taken by players wearing the new shoe. "This shoe sucks," he said. Then it was the turn of ABC and ESPN to complain. They refused to run the commercial until it was reworded.

Meola and his USA teammates had been training at Mission Viejo in California at a permanent camp set up by the USSF. Their status as host team meant automatic qualification, and their preparation consisted of a diet of exhibition games. Under new coach Bora Milutinovic, last seen guiding little Costa Rica to a second-round berth in Italia-90, the results were patchy. But Bora didn't have to worry. Rothenberg was on record as saying that he didn't care if the USA lost all of its warm-up games—provided they did well in the Cup itself. Translated, that meant simply getting into the second round. No host team had ever failed to do that.

For the rest of the world there was the torture of qualifying games. England's failure to qualify was probably the biggest shock. Going into its final game in Group 2, England still had a slender mathematical chance. For a start, it needed to beat San Marino by a margin of seven goals. Well, how difficult could that be? San Marino, population 24,000, was probably the feeblest team in Europe. And—the difficult part—on the same day, Poland had to beat the Netherlands.

It was not to be. Within nine seconds of the kickoff San Marino scored. England had suffered the indignity of giving up the quickest goal ever scored in World Cup competition—to tiny San Marino! England now needed to score eight; they managed only seven and the Netherlands beat Poland anyway. The inventors of soccer would have to sit this one out.

The Dutch, potentially the strongest team in Europe, made life difficult for themselves. The Dutch Federation worked out an extraordinary agreement with Johan Cruyff: he would coach the team, but only after they had qualified. Dick Advocaat was given the—temporary—job of qualifying the team.

The loss to injury of goal scorer Marco Van Basten—he had been FIFA's World Player of the Year in 1992—was a severe blow. Top star Ruud Gullit soon fell out with Advocaat and walked off the team. After qualification, Cruyff and the Federation disagreed on his terms, and Advocaat became the World Cup coach. Gullit decided to return but walked out again after only a week, unhappy with the team's preparation and with Advocaat's tactics.

Norway finished ahead of the Netherlands in Group 2, qualifying for the first time since 1938. They were a team of big strong athletes and runners and very little by way of soccer skills.

In Group 6 France had pulled the biggest el foldo act in a long time. With two games left—both to be played in Paris—France needed just one tie to qualify. It contrived, somehow, to lose the first game 3–2 to a weak Israeli team. Against Bulgaria, qualification seemed assured with the score at 1–1 and only seconds left in the game. Up popped Emil Kostadinov to score a late winner; Bulgaria would go to the USA, France was out.

Sweden, tall and athletic like Norway, but with more skill and subtlety, was the other qualifier from Group 6.

Russia had qualified from Group 5, but coach Pavel Sadyrin then faced a revolt by seven of his top players, who said they would not go to the USA if he continued as coach. They accused him of antiquated tactics. Others said the real issue was money, and that Sadyrin was blocking higher bonuses. Sadyrin, backed by the Russian Soccer Federation, stayed on. It meant that Russia went to the United States without half a dozen of its top players.

Qualifying ahead of Russia was Greece, a major surprise. It was the first time the Greeks had ever reached the finals.

Italy, as usual among the favorites to win the Cup, had made hard work of qualifying, keeping its supporters in suspense right down to the final game of Group 1, when a 1–0 win over Portugal ensured a place in the USA. Prime Minister Silvio Berlusconi, owner of AC Milan, told the team: "Winning isn't everything. But if you lose, I'll take your passports away and stop you coming home." Of course, he was joking. Wasn't he? Switzerland, absent from the finals since 1966, also qualified from Group 1.

Spain was the strongest of the qualifiers, with eight wins, three ties, and just one loss to Denmark in Group 3. Fellow qualifiers from the group were the Republic of Ireland—coach Jack Charlton and his motley crew of quasi-Irishmen. Just as in Italy, four years earlier, over half of them were born in England or Scotland. All twenty-two of them played for foreign clubs, twenty in England, two in Scotland. They had been the oldest team in Italy, but they had reached the quarter-finals.

This time the average age was again over 29—something that surely explained Charlton's constant sniping at FIFA about the dangers of the heat in Orlando, where they had to play Mexico, qualifiers from the North and Central American zone.

In the USA, Ireland would not be the oldest team. That distinction, or more likely handicap, belonged to Group 4 qualifiers Belgium with an average age of 29 years 5 months.

Only nine of the ten South American countries were involved in qualifying games, Chile being banned as a result of the infamous Rojas incident in 1989.*

Both groups looked cut and dried. Two teams would qualify from the five-team Group B—they would be perennial powers Brazil and Uruguay;

*See chapter 4, page 96.

minnows Bolivia, Venezuela, and Ecuador would be left in their dust. Argentina would win the four-team Group A, Colombia would come in second and go into a play-off with Australia, the winner of the Oceania group. Forget about Paraguay and Peru.

Beaten finalists in 1990, Argentina had been purring along nicely since then under new coach Alfio Basile. They came into the qualifiers with a twenty-nine-game unbeaten streak. They stretched it to thirty one, then lost 1–2 in Colombia. Nothing to panic about: Paraguay had been beaten in Paraguay. Peru would be beaten twice.

After that, the script went awry. Paraguay held Argentina to a 0–0 tie in Buenos Aires. Which meant that Argentina had to beat Colombia in the final game in Buenos Aires to win the group and outright qualification.

Fifty thousand fans massed to cheer the Argentines on, but the afternoon turned into one of the worst ever in the 100-year history of Argentine soccer. A goal down at halftime, Argentina caved in completely in the second half and the Colombians ran riot. Final score: Argentina 0 Colombia 5.

El Grafico, the most respected Argentine sports magazine, put an all-black cover on its issue, with the single word *VERGUENZA!*(Shame!) blazoned across it.

Now came a home-and-home play-off with Australia, a tough team to deal with at any time. But with the morale of the Argentines in their boots . . . what could be done?

Why, this was a job for soccer superman—the man who had led Argentina to World Cup victory in 1986, and had again been the captain in 1990: Diego Maradona. Since that losing 1990 final, Maradona's career had spun downward, thanks largely to a fifteen-month suspension for cocaine use in Italy.

But he was back in Argentina, supposedly getting match fit. Actually his physical condition was hardly important. Such was the public outcry for his return, that Basile would probably have been steamrollered into playing him even if he had been 30 pounds overweight. It wasn't that bad, but Maradona was certainly chubby and slower. He played in Australia and provided a typically skillful assist for the Argentine goal in a 1–1 tie. With Maradona as captain, Argentina won the return 1–0 in Buenos Aires.

Gracias Maradona! Honor was saved. The team was on its way to the United States and coach Basile, whether that's what he wanted or not, would be building it around Maradona.

At least in Group A, though not quite as expected, the two favorites had qualified. Not so in Group B. The alarm sounded in the third game, played in La Paz, over two miles up in the Andes, where the score was Bolivia 2 Brazil 0. The first time that Brazil had ever lost a World Cup qualifying game.

Nor was it a fluke result. Bolivia, under its Spanish coach, Xavier Azkargorta, had been the better team. Its two major stars—Erwin Sanchez and Marco Etcheverry—along with four other players were graduates of the remarkable Santa Cruz youth club, Tahuichi.

Further sensation followed the Bolivia–Brazil game when FIFA announced the suspension of Bolivian defender Miguel Rimba and Brazilian reserve goalkeeper Zetti. Both had been urine-tested after the game, and both had come up positive for cocaine. The suspension was quickly lifted; Zetti and Rimba had done nothing more than drink *Trimate,* a legally available tea that included coca leaves.

Brazil and coach Carlos Alberto Parreira went home to a massive barrage of criticism from the press and the public. Bolivia went on to win all four of its home games in La Paz, including a convincing 3–1 victory over Uruguay. Now the tables were turned. Bolivia looked certain to qualify; Brazil and Uruguay would have to fight it out for the other place.

On the final day of qualifying games, Bolivia ensured its place in the USA with a 1–1 tie in Ecuador. While in Rio de Janeiro, Brazil and Uruguay were having at each other in the huge Maracaná. The venerable stadium had been closed for over a year for much-needed renovations. Now it re-opened with a capacity crowd of 110,000.

Clowns, trapeze artists, bands, helicopters, parachutists, balloons . . . and, finally, football. A tie would send Brazil to the World Cup finals. But if they lost, then Uruguay would qualify and Brazil would, for the first time in history, be missing from a World Cup.

Unthinkable . . . yet a jam-packed Maracaná and the light blue shirts of Uruguay brought back memories of that black afternoon 43 years ago. The 1950 World Cup final, when Brazil needed only a tie to be crowned world champions . . . Uruguay won the game 2–1 and took the crown.

Just as, in Argentina, Basile had been obliged to turn to Maradona for salvation, now it was Parreira's turn to feel the full power of an aroused public. The player they wanted on the team was Romário, the diminutive goalscorer then playing in Spain with Barcelona.

Parreira had cut Romário before the qualifiers began, finding him an undisciplined, disruptive presence on the team. Now, in his moment of urgent need, he welcomed him back.

The parallels with 1950 grew more ominous as the game went on. The score was 0–0 at half time, the Uruguayans were defending well, hoping for a counter-attack goal. With only 20 minutes left in the game, it was still 0–0. Then, within the space of ten minutes, it was 2–0 Brazil. Two superb goals from Romário saw Brazil safely through.

Obrigado Romário! Brazil's record of being the only country to play in every World Cup final round was intact. And, whether that was what Parreira wanted or not, Romário's place on the team was guaranteed.

Out of Africa came Morocco, Nigeria, and the Indomitable Lions of Cameroon, the team that had been so admired in 1990. But behind the smoothness of Cameroon's soccer lay almost total chaos—a bankrupt Federation that could not even afford to pay its electricity bills, pathetic training facilities, a stadium in dangerous disrepair, and the star players having to constantly threaten strike action to collect long-owed wages.

Somehow Cameroon had won its way through to the USA without a recognized coach—its team was selected by a committee before each game! Since qualification, Frenchman Henri Michel had been appointed. He had, no doubt under political pressure, recalled Roger Milla the "old man" who had been such a sensational substitute in Italy. Milla, now 42, would be the oldest player in World Cup-94.

The Super Eagles of Nigeria looked a much better bet to continue the forward march of African soccer. There had been plenty of success at the Under-17 level, with World Cups won in 1985 and 1993, but this was the first appearance in the finals for the senior team.

Eighteen of its twenty-two players were with European clubs. Its coach was Dutchman Clemens Westerhof.It was a European team with African names. Athletic, powerful, and tactically astute like the Europeans, but with often dazzling African skills.

Twenty-nine countries had entered the qualifying tournament in Asia. Saudi Arabia and the Korean Republic (South Korea) were the survivors. Poor Japan had suffered a fate similar to that of France in Europe. Leading Iraq 2–1 with only seconds remaining in the final game, Japan was qualified. But those fatal seconds were enough for Iraq to tie the game, and Japan was out. Korea, with the same number of points, qualified ahead of them on goal difference.

A disaster for Japan, for it was seen as a serious setback to the country's campaign to secure the rights to stage World Cup 2002. A double setback . . . because it was precisely South Korea that was mounting a vigorous challenge to Japan for the 2002 tournament.

A year and a half of qualifying games came to an end on November 17, 1993. A total of 490 games that had featured 1,429 goals for an average of 2.9 per game.

Nearly three goals a game. A considerable improvement over the stingy 2.2 per game that the 1990 World Cup had served up. Could the final round maintain the increased scoring pace?

FIFA had been doing its best, since 1990, to encourage attacking play by means of rule changes. The goalkeeper could no longer use his hands to field a backpass from a team mate, and the offside rule had been altered to favor attacking players.

In the first round of World Cup-94, playing defensively for a tie would be discouraged by the award of three points (instead of two) for a win. But the most far-reaching change was undoubtedly the ban on the tackle from behind. This had long been the most destructive, and dangerous, tackle in a defender's repertoire. FIFA really did sound as though it meant business on this one. Said *FIFA News:* "The dreaded tackle from behind, which rarely results in the attacker gaining the ball but frequently causes injury to the victim will in future be penalized with immediate expulsion."

In case that wasn't clear enough, Havelange weighed in with "Any referee who doesn't show a red card for a tackle from behind will be going home on the first plane the following day."

On the eve of the tournament, *USA Today* published the results of a Harris opinion poll. It said that only 25 percent of all American adults knew the World Cup was about to be be held in the USA, and even when told about it only 15 percent said they were interested in watching any of the games on TV.

But those involved sensed a totally different atmosphere building. For a start they knew, from ticket sales, that all the stadiums would be almost sold out, at around 90 percent of their capacity.

Ladbrokes, the London bookmakers, had Brazil as 3 to 1 favorites to take the Cup. Right behind Brazil were Germany 4 to 1, and Italy 5 to 1. The USA was quoted at 50 to 1.

Chicago, June 17, 1994: Germany vs. Bolivia, the opening game of World Cup USA-94, the fifteenth World Cup. A capacity crowd of 62,000, including President Bill Clinton. And blistering, broiling, heat.

Sweaty security guards shouting "No camcorders, or bottles, or flag-poles, or any stuff like that" tried their best. But while they were struggling to separate one fan's banner from its pole, other fans carrying flagpoles, camcorders, umbrellas, went streaming past.

A security failure? More of a success: the beginning of the realization that this was going to be a friendly tournament.

The spectacular opening ceremonies got things off to a brilliant start. If this was American razzmatazz then the tournament could do with more of it—an excellent combination of color and noise and excitement that admirably captured the international flavor while remaining unmistakably American. Singer Diana Ross did her thing, then tried to shoot a soccer ball into a goal. She missed.

Notably absent from the spectacle was Striker, the gawky mascot. "He's not in the ceremonies because we think he's stupid," said one of the creative types who put the show together.

In charge of the game was Mexican referee Arturo Brizio Carter, recently described by FIFA as the world's best, now chosen to set the pattern for the tournament. After six minutes Germany's Jürgen Kohler clattered into Julio Baldivieso. Not so much from behind as from the side. Kohler was cautioned—an encouraging moment. It did look as though Brizio meant business in dealing with the tackle from behind.

Seven minutes later Brizio wrecked everything. Thomas Hässler went in hard and crudely, from behind, on Luis Cristaldo. Both players went down in an ugly tangle of legs—Hässler got to the ball only after he had demolished Cristaldo. It was surely the perfect example of the type of dangerous foul that FIFA wanted to abolish.

Positioned perfectly, right next to the incident, was Brizio. He called the foul . . . and that was all. No red card to Hässler, not even a yellow. Indeed, Brizio seemed to be more irritated at Cristaldo for not getting up quickly enough.

Just fourteen minutes into the World Cup and FIFA's brave new rule was in tatters. As the tournament progressed, and it quickly became clear that referees were not ejecting the tacklers-from-behind, FIFA changed its tune. It had not meant *all* tackles from behind, only those . . . but the explanation gutted the original, unequivocal orders. A great opportunity to clean up the game had been squandered.

In the opening game, Brizio's refereeing got no better. In the second half he again ignored a Hässler foul. This one was a hand ball that directed the ball into the path of Jürgen Klinsmann for him to score the only goal of the game.

With twelve minutes left, Bolivia brought on Marco Etcheverry. He had been the key player in their qualifying run but then, playing in Chile for Colo-Colo, had suffered a serious knee injury. This marked his return to competitive soccer, after a six-month recuperation. He immediately looked menacing, laying the ball off perfectly to Sanchez, whose shot was blocked for a corner. Two minutes later, victim of a robust tackle from Lothar Matthäus, Etcheverry retaliated.

It looked more like a petulant swing of the leg than a deliberate kick, but suddenly the indulgent Brizio turned implacable. Racing up the field, he brandished the red card. Etcheverry had been in the game for only four minutes.

The Germans—methodical, relentless, uninspired—had won. But this did not look like a team capable of going too far. The better soccer, the stuff that had the crown oohing and aahing, had come from Bolivia.

Etcheverry was hit with a two-game suspension, a severe blow for Bolivia. Without him, Bolivia played Korea to a 0–0 tie. But this was a hyperactive game, crammed with action and chances for both teams. The excitement of the game apparently proved a fatal attraction for referee Leslie Mottram of Scotland. He allowed five minutes of extra time in the first half, then let the second half run over by eight minutes and forty seconds. Bolivia, needing a win in its last game against Spain, went down 1–3, and out of the tournament.

The Koreans had tied Spain 2–2, coming back from 0–2 down to score twice in the last five minutes, showing their by now familiar ability to keep up a high-speed game for 90 minutes. The Germans evidently forgot about that in the 90 degree plus heat of Dallas. Leading comfortably at halftime by 3–0 (two of the goals from Klinsmann), the Germans tried to slow things down.

It takes two to slow a soccer game down, and the Koreans weren't having any. Hwang Sun Hong scored, and ten minutes later Hong Myung Bo made it 3–2. The bewildered Germans were hanging on, and only some superb goalkeeping by Bodo Illgner preserved their victory.

Along with Spain, the Germans advanced to the second round, but they would be without their midfielder Stefan Effenberg. Substituted in the Korean game, Effenberg had flipped his middle finger at the German fans as he left the field. Coach Berti Vogts threw him off the team. Even so, Effenberg profited from the episode: he sold his story ("his lies" said Vogts) to *Sport Bild* for $40,000.

In Group A, USA vs. Switzerland in the Silverdome marked the first game for the Americans, and the first-ever indoor World Cup game. Forgotten in all the hype about the miracle of growing grass indoors was one troublesome fact about the Silverdome. No air-conditioning. With a heat wave raging outside, with 73,000 fans roaring inside, the Silverdome turned into a monster sauna.

At thirty-nine minutes, Georges Bregy took a 25-yard free kick for Switzerland. The ball sailed over the USA's wall and into the net. Bregy had scored the World Cup's first indoor goal. Embarrassment for Tony Meola who should have saved it, but he was caught out, still arranging the wall. Five minutes later Eric Wynalda tied the game for the USA, also on a free kick. But this one was perfection, hit hard, curling over the Swiss wall, and into the top corner.

That was how it finished, a steamy, sweaty 1–1 tie. Satisfactory for both teams, evidently. The USA had shown the usual Bora trademarks. A packed central defense, space on the flanks through which to launch rapid, but controlled, counterattacks. Marcelo Balboa and Alexi Lalas clogged up the middle, helped out by Cle Kooiman, Paul Caligiuri, and Mike Sorber, all of them with primarily defensive duties.

John Harkes played the midfield workhorse. Tab Ramos was the playmaker—though his position out on the right flank made him less influential than he would have been in the center. Ernie Stewart did prodigious amounts of running up front. Wynalda was less mobile but, with his strength on the ball and powerful shooting, was always a threat. Thomas Dooley, by far the most experienced player on the team, did a bit of everything.

Bora's tactics were undoubtedly cautious; not many goals were going to be given up, that was clear. Equally certain, for a team that was never wholly committed to offense, was that not many goals were going to be scored either.

The other Group A game saw the Cup's first upset. Colombia, among the favorites, Pelé's choice to win the Cup, went down 1–3 to Romania. Sure, the Colombians dominated the game—but they persisted in building every attack through Carlos Valderrama, the midfielder with the blond Afro. Everything went through the middle. The Romanians soaked it up and scored three breakaway goals.

Watching the tape, Bora must have rubbed his hands in glee. Romania had beaten Colombia by doing precisely what the USA was good at: block the middle, counter rapidly. If Colombia played that way in its next game against the USA—and it would, there was simply no variation in its game—it would play right into the USA's hands.

So it proved. The Americans got lucky right at the start when Mike Sorber nearly deflected the ball into his own net—it hit the post and came out. Then the game settled into the predictable pattern. Colombia dominated in terms of ball possession. Valderrama made what seemed like a thousand passes, and it seemed that all of them were cut out. The Colombian attack was running into a brick wall, the Americans had acres of space for their counters.

On one of these Harkes, alone on the left, hit the ball low into the center. Hardly a dangerous cross, but defender Andres Escobar stuck out a leg to intercept, wrong-footed goalkeeper Oscar Cordoba, and stabbed the ball into his own net.

The goal the USA had hoped for had been scored for them. Frustrating the Colombians was proving unexpectedly easy. There was time, and confidence, for a more attacking second half. Lalas thumped the ball into the Colombian net, but was declared offside (TV replays showed clearly that he was not offside).

Ramos delivered a perfect pass to Stewart who raced away to score the USA's second goal. Soon afterwards came a sublime moment as Balboa, up on attack, pulled off a perfect bicycle-kick shot at goal. The ball screamed inches wide of the post as the 93,000 Rose Bowl crowd roared in wonder.

Colombia did score a goal, right at the end. But the USA had won its first World Cup game since the famous 1–0 victory of England in 1950 and was now almost certain of a place in the second round. Colombia, with two losses, was the first team to be eliminated.

What had gone wrong? Overconfidence maybe. Something similar had happened to the Colombian Olympic team in 1992. It had qualified brilliantly but had fallen apart in Spain, finishing at the bottom of its group having given up nine goals in three games.

Or something more sinister. The rumor was circulating that the Colombian players had been threatened by drug lords. For what reason? To what end? Not known. It was known that a fax had arrived at the Colombian hotel for midfielder Gabriel Gomez, telling him not to play against the USA or his house would be blown up. Gomez did not play.

After a meaningless 2–0 win over Switzerland, coach Francisco Maturana announced his resignation, and the demoralized Colombians returned home, to find that their agony was not yet over. Andres Escobar, luckless scorer of that own-goal for the United States, went out to a restaurant in Medellin, got into an argument over the team's poor showing, and was shot dead.

The USA needed at least a tie against Romania to be certain of a second-round berth. An uninteresting tussle between two counterattack teams. Romania got the all-important first goal after only eighteen minutes when Dan Petrescu beat Meola with a near-post shot. Seventy-two minutes of stolid Romanian defense and sterile American running followed.

Despite the loss, the USA qualified for the second round as one of the four best third-place teams; they would now have to play the winner of Group B: Brazil.

Group B had quickly turned into a contest for first place between Brazil and Sweden. Brazil took that on goal difference, after the two had played to a 1–1 tie in the sultry Silverdome. Russia and Cameroon were too dispirited to offer a serious challenge. The Russians had not recovered from their player revolt; the Cameroons were still threatening to strike over unpaid wages and bonuses.

WORLD CUP 1994
San Francisco, USA: Brazil 3 Cameroon 0
Close attention from Cameroon defenders Emile Mbouh Mbouh (left) and 17-year-old Rigobert Song fails to stop Brazil's Romário. With five goals and three assists, Romario shared third place—"the Bronze Shoe"—in the goalscoring race. He was voted the tournament's MVP.
© Peter Robinson: The Football Archive

But both teams managed to get into the World Cup record book. At the sixty-third minute of the game against Brazil, Cameroon sent on substitute Roger Milla, at age forty-two the oldest-ever player in World Cup history. In the same game the seventeen-year-old Cameroon defender Rigobert Song became the youngest player ever to get red-carded.

Four days later Milla became the oldest player ever to score a World Cup goal—Cameroon's only goal in a disastrous 1–6 thrashing by Russia. Oleg Salenko set a one-game record that is likely to be around for a long time when he hit five of Russia's goals. And in that one game he rocketed himself into position as the tournament's leading scorer.

Journalists waited to interview Salenko after the game, but he rushed past them, pointing to his crotch and shouting something in Russian. Evidently, it meant "doping control."

Salenko was on his way to urinate . . . if he could. Playing temperatures in the 90s meant dehydrated players, which was not the right formula for a rapid urinary response. It was 1 hour and 45 minutes before Salenko eventually emerged from the control area, which is probably not a record.

The random dope tests—two players per team per game—went smoothly and uneventfully. Except in Group D, up in Boston, where one positive test changed the course of the entire tournament.

The Argentines were looking good. They had brushed the Greeks contemptuously aside, 4–0, on a Gabriel Batistuta hat trick and a goal for Maradona. Greek coach Alkis Panagoulias was embarrassed: "I think my players came to take photographs of the Argentines, they love them very much."

After his goal, Maradona had raced to the sideline and screamed into the lens of a TV camera. The image of Maradona's distorted, wild-looking face went around the world. He had played well, and he was to play even better against Nigeria. Two goals from Claudio Caniggia (his second was the 1,500th goal in World Cup history) gave Argentina a 2–1 win.

After just two games, Argentina was now among the favorites. And why not, with in-form strikers like Caniggia and Batistuta, with Abel Balbo and Diego Simeone, and the elegant Fernando Redondo in midfield? All that and Maradona too.

The Argentine dream crumbled on June 30, the day that rumors of a positive drug test began to circulate. No one knew the player, but the game was revealed as Argentina vs. Nigeria. It was no secret that Maradona had been one of the two Argentines tested. The Argentines had moved to Dallas for their final first-round game against Bulgaria.

A large crowd of journalists gathered at the Cotton Bowl, not knowing, but knowing all the same. It must be Maradona. Many recalled the television image of an almost crazed Maradona screaming into the camera. It had to be Maradona. The Argentine players, including Maradona, arrived, strolled about inspecting the field for half an hour, and departed. Then Julio Grondona, President of the Argentine Soccer Federation, appeared and admitted that Maradona was the culprit.

The test had revealed a range of ephedrine-related drugs in Maradona's urine sample. The drugs are commonly used as weight reducers (Maradona had shed over twenty pounds in preparation for the World Cup), but also have stimulant properties. "Maradona must have taken a cocktail of drugs," said Dr. Michel D'Hooge, head of FIFA's medical committee, "these substances are not found together in one medicine." *

Grondona grumbled "I can't follow every player to the bathroom, they know what they're doing." Fearing that the team, in addition to the player, might be punished, Grondona voluntarily withdrew Maradona from the tournament.

FIFA's fifteen-month, worldwide ban followed at once. It did not meet with universal applause. Most Argentines believed Maradona was the victim of a FIFA plot, that this was the latest move in the ongoing feud

---

*Maradona's personal fitness guru took the blame. He claimed that he had run out of Maradona's special medicine, and had gone into Boston and bought what he thought was the same thing at a health food store.

between the player and Havelange. Unexpected support came from tenor Luciano Pavarotti who revealed that he would be in trouble should they ever start dope-testing for opera stars: "I am upset at FIFA's stupidity. I consider ephedrine a medicine, and I take it every day to be at my best for my public."

The next day, without Maradona, Argentina lost 0–2 to Bulgaria, while up in Boston, Nigeria beat Greece 2–0 to top the group. Bulgaria was second, while Argentina ended up in third place. It meant they would have to travel to Los Angeles to play Romania in the second round.

Nigeria had been expected to do well. The surprise was the Bulgarians, who came into the tournament having played in five previous tournaments without ever winning a game. But that was then, and this was now: what made all the difference was that over half of the Bulgarian players, freed from the restrictions placed on them by the former Communist regime, were now with clubs in Western Europe. In Hristo Stoichkov (he played in Spain, for Barcelona) they had a genuine world-class star, one of the game's most dangerous goal scorers.

Italy began badly. In fact, things could hardly have been worse. Not only did they lose 0–1 to Ireland, but they had played poorly. An early exit looked likely on this form.

A major surprise at the game was that Giants Stadium seemed to have been taken over by Irish fans. The whole idea of having Italy play there was that the local Italian fans would pour in to see them. Yet the stadium was awash with green, white, and orange flags and banners. The fans sang the Irish anthem lustily, but the stadium went quiet when the Italian anthem came on.

Ireland's Ray Houghton scored the goal that sank Italy. The Glasgow-born midfielder hit a looping left-footer over goalkeeper Gianluca Pagliuca, who had wandered too far off his line. Coach Charlton refused to be impressed: "He tries that shot all the time in practice, and I've never seen him make it."

The Irish returned to their camp in Orlando to take on Mexico in the heat that Charlton so dreaded. With reason, it turned out, for Mexico ran out 2–1 winners. Charlton seemed unable to avoid clashes with FIFA. This time, trying to get substitute John Aldridge into the game, he got into a slanging match with sideline officials.

FIFA fined him $15,000 and banned him from the bench for the next game against Norway. But the episode had a glowing sequel. Money to pay the fine poured in from the Irish fans, Jack's Army. Charlton ended up with nearly $100,000, which he gave to the family of murdered Colombian star Andres Escobar.

For the Italians, it was woe upon woe. Twenty minutes into the vital second game against Norway, goalkeeper Pagliuca was ejected for knocking down Øyvind Leonhardsen—the first goalkeeper ever to be sent off in a World Cup game. Coach Arrigo Sacchi had to send on reserve goalie Luca Marchegiani. To make room for him he pulled off Roberto Baggio, the ponytailed forward who had renounced Catholicism to become a practicing Buddhist, the current idol of Italian soccer.

A high-risk move by Sacchi, but all ended well. Dino Baggio (no relation) headed the only goal of the game in the 69th minute. But there was still time for more calamity. Captain Franco Baresi injured a knee and had to be substituted. Pierluigi Casiraghi had to come off, and on went Daniel Massaro, the third—and last—of Italy's permitted substitutions.

Paolo Maldini was the next to be injured—victim of a brutal Norwegian foul—but he had to stay on the field, limping badly, but at least a moving body. Without him, Italy would be down to nine men.

Baresi would need an operation on his knee, and his World Cup appeared to be over. Without him, Italy managed a 1–1 tie with Mexico, while Ireland and Norway tied 0–0 in a predictably awful game between two teams whose idea of soccer was to belt the ball long and chase it.

Mexico, the most enterprising team, topped the group, with Ireland in second place. As a third-place team, the Italians had to wait in suspense for three hours. Then they were assured of a wild card place in the second round by Russia's 6–0 victory over Cameroon.

Norway was on its way home, a relief for lovers of skillful soccer. A team of big athletes, devoid of subtlety or creativity, their monotonous 1–1–1–1–1 record reflected the boredom of their game: one win, one loss, one tie, one goal scored, one goal given up. Coach Egil Olsen claimed: "We are the best team in the world—without the ball." He was trying to emphasize his team's mobility, his players' willingness to run. But his remark led to the counter that, with the ball, Norway was the worst team in the tournament.

Group F featured two European powers, the Netherlands and Belgium, plus two minor countries, Saudi Arabia and Morocco. The Dutch had plenty of support. An estimated 15,000 supporters had traveled from Holland, an orange-clad army, present at every Dutch game, accompanied by the constant oom-pah-pah of their little brass band.

By no means did the Europeans have things all their own way. The Dutch quickly made a mockery of their ranking as Europe's strongest challenger with a shaky 2–1 win over Saudi Arabia. It needed a bad mistake by the Saudi goalkeeper Mohammed Al Deayea to give the Netherlands the win. Belgium, too, were unconvincing winners, 1–0 over Morocco.

Saudi Arabia won the first-ever all-Arab clash in the World Cup, 2–1 over Morocco. The World Cup organizers could smile after this game. It was considered the least attractive tie of the first round—yet it drew 76,000 fans to Giants Stadium.

The Netherlands, despite losing 0–1 to Belgium, won the group. Belgium had to be content with third place, after being upset 1–0 by Saudi Arabia. Saeed Owairan scored the goal, a superb goal, after dribbling half the length of the field, swerving past and hurdling over a succession of Belgian tackles. Owairan's goal ranked alongside Maradona's solo effort against England in 1986 as one of the greatest of World Cup goals. It was confidently dubbed the Goal of the Tournament, on the assumption that nothing better would come along. Nothing did.

The second round, the "round of sixteen" as FIFA called it, went pretty much as expected. Except that Argentina went down, 2–3 to Romania. An enthralling game, probably the most entertaining of the entire tournament. Thanks to Argentina, which did all the attacking, with Romania relying on its usual counterattacks. But Argentina could not overcome the loss of Maradona (disgraced) and Caniggia (injured). The quirks of scheduling didn't help, either. Romania had not had to travel, and took the field having had four days more rest than Argentina.

Germany was the better team against Belgium, and took the game 3–2. The Belgians had cause for complaint, though. Late in the game Josip Weber broke through the German defense and was sent crashing to the ground, in the penalty area, by the German defender Thomas Helmer. A text book penalty kick—but Swiss referee Kurt Röthlisberger didn't give it. This time FIFA acted, and Röthlisberger was sent home.

Jack Charlton was back on the bench for Ireland, and back in the heat of Orlando. The Irish were evidently feeling their age by now. They gave a tired performance, and the Dutch ran out 2–0 winners without any great exertion. Their second goal came courtesy of a banal error by Ireland's veteran goalkeeper, Packie Bonner, who allowed an innocuous shot to slip through his hands. Bonner, refreshingly, offered no excuse: "I don't know what went wrong, but the blame is on me."

Sweden, 3–1 winners over Saudi Arabia, also had a relatively easy game. Of course, Italy did not. Late in the game they were down to ten men (Gianfranco Zola had been ejected) and losing 0–1 to Nigeria. Roberto Baggio saved the day with an 88th-minute equalizer, and then won it with a penalty kick in overtime. It was a foul-ridden game that referee Brizio never properly controlled despite red-carding Zola and dishing out nine yellow cards. FIFA, which only three weeks earlier had hailed Brizio as the world's best, now said he would get no more games.

The Nigeria coach, Clemens Westerhof, quit after the game and lambasted the team's attitude: "They had lost concentration. In the hotel some of them had their wives with them, and some other ladies came . . . team discipline was slipping away."

Brizio's World Cup record of nine yellows lasted only a few hours. Later the same day Jamal Al Sharif of Syria equaled it during the Bulgaria–Mexico game. He also controversially red-carded one player from each team and gave Mexico a dubious penalty kick. Al-Sharif, too, would see no more action in World Cup-94.

Mexico's performance was exasperating. By the time the game went to overtime, tied at 1–1, Mexico was clearly the better team. Yet it never stepped up the pressure. Particularly baffling was coach Miguel Mejia Barón's refusal—in a hot, humid, draining, overtime game—to use any substitutes.

Bulgarian coach Dimitar Penev later admitted that, in overtime, his team was playing defensively, trying to take the game into penalty kicks. They succeeded and duly won the shootout as the Mexicans confirmed their reputation as the world's worst penalty-kick takers. Asked about the negative tactics, Stoichkov replied: "I'm happy that we won—it doesn't matter how."

The Bulgarians did have an unusual problem. Celebrating after the win against Argentina, the players had hit the town in Dallas, and photographs of them posing with female friends had been published back home in Bulgaria. In no time, a charter flight had been organized, and the players' wives arrived in the USA. "Playing the Mexicans didn't worry me," said coach Dimitar Penev, "I was more worried about what the wives would do to us."

Spain, clearly, was hitting form. Their 3–0 win over Switzerland was comprehensive, a convincing answer to those critics who felt that coach Javier Clemente, having included only one genuine forward on his roster, would find goal-scoring a problem.

Even the referee—Dutchman Mario Van der Ende—received praise for his perfect interpretation of the new offside rule. On the Spaniards' first goal, scored by Hierro, midfielder Sergi was clearly in an offside position. But Van der Elde, correctly, judged that he was not involved in the play and allowed the goal to stand.

Two days before the crucial July 4 game against Brazil, President Clinton telephoned the American team from Camp David and told coach Bora: "We're all going to sit here on pins and needles and cheer for you. All of America is." Bora told him: "My English is so bad but my team plays very well."

Presidential pins and needles notwithstanding, the USA's dream of World Cup glory sputtered to an inglorious end. The setting was perfect: a sunny July 4 afternoon at Stanford Stadium, 84,000 spectators, national television on ABC, and Brazil the opponents.

But coach Bora Milutinovic did not respond. He sent his team out to play the usual cautious spoiling game, attempting to frustrate Brazil, hoping the game would drag on at 0–0, through overtime, into the shootout. In the shootout, maybe the USA stood a chance.

It was an approach that virtually guaranteed a tedious game. The USA rarely got anywhere near the Brazilian goal; goalkeeper Taffarel did not have to make a single save during the entire game. The Brazilians did plenty of attacking but were, as Bora planned, frustrated by the densely packed American defense.

Just before halftime, Tab Ramos fouled Leonardo, who retaliated with a vicious elbow to Ramos's head. Ramos left the field on a stetcher, seriously injured with a skull fracture. Leonardo was ejected.

So the Americans would play the rest of the game with a man advantage. Surely they would now attempt to do some attacking? No, the caution continued. If anything, the Brazilian domination was even more pronounced, with Bebeto scoring the winning goal after 72 minutes.

The USA had got as far as they could reasonably expect, and had convinced a lot of doubters. "Nobody is going to take us for granted anymore," said Balboa. True—respect had been earned. But despite that, despite the defiant USA! USA! chant from the fans as the US players waved a final farewell, this was a dull, unexciting way to bow out.

There was even a whiff of discontent out of the normally idyllic American camp. Goalkeeper Meola had told the press that he'd had it with the pressures of soccer. After the World Cup he was going to become a place kicker on a football team. Bora, who had made Meola captain of the team, was furious and seriously considered starting his reserve 'keeper Brad Friedel against Brazil.

In the first of the quarterfinals, in Boston, the Italians gave their fans heart-attacks again. Spain proved quite a handful. Italy controlled the first half and led on Dino Baggio's 25th minute goal. But the second half belonged to Spain. José Caminero tied the game at 58 minutes. Julio Salinas sliced through the Italian defense and bore down on goalkeeper Pagliuca. Salinas shot, Pagliuca stuck out a leg and, without knowing too much about it, deflected the ball wide. Then it was Roberto Baggio time again: the 88th minute. Away he went, to dribble around goalkeeper Andoni Zubizarreta and score the winner.

There was still time for a vigorous Spanish reaction and what became the most controversial incident of the World Cup. Andoni Goikoetxea crossed from the right, into the Italian penalty area. Racing in to meet the ball came Luis Enrique. Matching stride with him was the Italian defender Mauro Tassotti. Luis Enrique, already in the penalty area, crashed to the ground.

The Spanish were enraged. Luis Enrique, blood streaming down his face from a broken nose, charged around trying to get justice, claiming that Tassotti had elbowed him in the face. Strange to tell, neither referee Sandor Puhl of Hungary nor the linesman had seen the incident.

Within a minute the game was over. Spain was out, and Italy once again had Roberto Baggio to thank for surviving yet another crisis.

But, clearly, *something* had happened to Luis Enrique. FIFA's Disciplinary Committee swung into action, and studied television tapes of the game. Their verdict was severe: Tassotti had elbowed Luis Enrique, and was suspended for eight international games, an unusually heavy punishment.

For the first time, FIFA had used televison evidence to decide a disciplinary matter. It was a historic verdict, but it was hardly a consolation for the Spanish to know that they had been right all along. They should have had a penalty kick; Tassotti should have been red-carded.

Down in Dallas, in the Cotton Bowl, the Netherlands took on Brazil. A game of two totally different halves. For the first 45 minutes the Dutch, uncharacteristically, played stolid defense. The plan, surprise, surprise, was to frustrate Brazil.

What the USA had done the Dutch could certainly do, even if it did mean putting everyone to sleep. But the torpid first half was followed by a pulsating second half full of excitement and superb soccer. Thanks to Romário and Bebeto, Brazil's forwards. On an assist from Bebeto, Romário opened the scoring eight minutes after the restart. Bebeto made it 2–0 ten minutes later.

His goal was followed by furious protests from the Dutch, who besieged the linesman, claiming that Romário had been offside. So he had—but he was not involved in the play.

The incident fired up the Dutch. Within a minute Dennis Bergkamp made it 2–1, then Aron Winter powered a header into the net to tie it up at 2–2. Testing time for the Brazilians, who had given up only one goal in their previous four games, and had now been scored on twice in twelve minutes.

Their nerves held, and at the eighty-first minute fullback Branco—who had replaced the suspended Leonardo—settled the game with a mighty left-footed free kick that screamed into the Dutch net from thirty yards out.

The following day came sensational, seismic news from Giants Stadium: The holders, Germany, were out. Beaten 2–1 by Bulgaria. For the first time since 1978 there would be a final without Germany. It was ironic, for in their previous game against Belgium the Germans had, at long last, looked as though they were hitting form. The Germans had taken the lead against Bulgaria in the second half on a Matthäus penalty kick and seemed to be in control. Stoichkov changed all that. He went down under Andy Möller's challenge. "There was no foul," said Möller later. "He just fell down and the referee bought it." Maybe Stoichkov had planned it that way, for the resulting free kick was in his favorite position. The Germans put six of their tallest players in the wall. Up they jumped, but Stoichkov's left foot swept the ball majestically over them and into the goal. Goalkeeper Illgner never moved.

Three minutes later, Nasko Sirakov crossed from the right and the bald head of Iordan Letchkov nodded the ball past Illgner. It was easier than it should have been—there were no tall Germans anywhere near Letchkov, only little Hässler, the shortest player on the team.

A smiling Stoichkov told the postgame press gathering: "Today God is Bulgarian."

Romania and Sweden, predictably, produced one of the worst games of the tournament. Two wary teams waiting for each other to make a move. The supposedly unsophisticated American fans—there were 83,500 of them in Stanford Stadium—had the correct response. They booed. After what seemed an eternity but was actually 78 minutes, there was action: Tomas Brolin scored for Sweden. Romania woke up; Florin Raducioiu equalized. In overtime, Raducioiu scored again. It looked all over for Sweden when their midfielder Stefan Schwarz was ejected.

Despite playing with only ten men, Sweden forced the pace. Kennet Andersson tied the game at 2–2, and it went to a penalty-kick shoot-out.

WORLD CUP 1994
New Jersey, USA: Bulgaria 2 Germany 1
Over 72,000 fans at Giants Stadium saw the biggest upset of the tournament
when Bulgaria beat the holders Germany in a quarterfinal game. A natural
grass field had been installed in the stadium to comply with World Cup regula-
tions, which prohibit artificial turf.
© Peter Robinson: The Football Archive

Thomas Ravelli, a brush salesman and part-time goalkeeper, won the day for Sweden by saving two of the Romanian kicks.

For their semifinal, the Italians traveled to New Jersey's Giants Stadium. They had expected to be playing Germany, about whom they knew a lot. Instead, waiting for them was Stoichkov's Bulgaria, about whom they knew very little.

The Bulgarians had upset a lot of calculations, including those of the marketing crowd. Alan Rothenberg was heard, publicly and unwisely, lamenting the drop-off in T-shirt sales caused by Bulgaria's elimination of Mexico and Germany.

Roberto Baggio was all Italy needed. His two goals within five minutes in the first half saw them through. Bulgaria scored from a penalty at the end of the first half, but that was the end of the goals. Coach Penev was unhappy about that. He felt, with some justification, that Bulgaria should have been awarded two more penalty kicks. Surely that was a bit optimistic—three penalties in one game? Penev agreed: "Yes, one was the most we could expect against Italy."

Stoichkov pointed out that the day's referee, Joel Quiniou, was French. He reminded journalists of the moment in Paris, eight months ago, when with a last-second goal Bulgaria had eliminated France from World Cup-94. "Today God is still Bulgarian," he said, "but the referee was French."

Three thousand miles away, in the Rose Bowl, it was Brazil vs. Sweden in the other semifinal. The same old story. Sweden adopted the "pull-everyone-back" tactics used by the USA and the Netherlands. Inevitably, the game was disappointing. Brazilian goalkeeper Taffarel had almost nothing to do (one Swedish shot in the first half). Brazil did virtually all the attacking, missed many good opportunities to score, or was thwarted by Ravelli's brilliant goalkeeping when they were on target.

So it went on, until the 80th minute, when Romario, the shortest player on Brazil's team, outjumped the towering Swedes to head the winning goal. The Swedish midfielder Brolin simply shrugged and said "They were just too good for us." Coach Tommy Svensson said his team had lost "to the best team in the tournament."

But before Brazil could confirm that title, they had to get past Italy. And before that, there was the matter of third place to be settled. Sweden vs. Bulgaria in the game that nobody wanted. Disappointment Day, two losers trying to make like it mattered. Not even that. The Bulgarians had let things slide after their upset of Germany. After that, said a Bulgarian journalist, "It was whisky, cigars, and fuck." Bulgaria did show up, but the exertion was evidently too much for them.

The final score was 4–0 Sweden, and the Swedes were not exactly putting themselves out. Goalkeeper Ravelli became so bored that he started to boogie in front of his goal, much to the crowd's delight. They cheered him and shouted for Romario.

During the buildup for the following day's final, the Italians, as usual, were in disarray. Defender Alessandro Costacurta was out, suspended after receiving two yellow cards in the second round; Tassotti was also suspended; Baresi was still recovering from arthroscopic surgery on his knee just eighteen days ago. The biggest calamity was that Roberto Baggio was doubtful, nursing a pulled hamstring.

Sacchi seemed to thrive on these problems. He had changed the team lineup for every game, and Italy was in the final. No thanks to Sacchi, thought the Italian fans. A survey by an Italian newspaper found that most fans blamed Sacchi when things went wrong and put his successes down to luck.

Parreira's position in the eyes of Brazilian fans was not much better. They had never forgiven him for his original rejection of Romário, and they found his tactics too defensive—an accusation that Parreira heatedly denied, claiming that he was misunderstood.

He, too, had faced lineup problems. Coming into the World Cup, his back four had been Jorginho, Ricardo Gomes, Ricardo Rocha, and Leonardo. Then Gomes got injured and had to be replaced only days before the tournament. Rocha was injured in the first game against Russia and didn't play again. Leonardo was also out, suspended after his elbow foul on Tab Ramos. Now the back four read: Aldair, Marcio Santos, Branco, and the survivor, Jorginho.

At least Parreira now had the luxury of a stable lineup. His team for the final was the same as it had been in the quarter- and semifinals. Which meant no place for the creative Rai. The Brazilian midfield would be dominated by the power players Dunga, Mauro Silva, and Mazinho.

The Italians, no doubt, smiled when they heard the name of the referee for the final. None other than Sandor Puhl, the Hungarian who had let them off a very uncomfortable hook in the quarterfinal against Spain when he had failed to spot Tassotti's foul on Luis Enrique.

Another brutally hot afternoon for the grand climax of World Cup USA-94. At the last moment, Sacchi announced his team. It included both Baresi and Roberto Baggio. Could they possibly be fit? Giorgio Chinaglia, the former New York Cosmos player now with Italian television, thought not. He shook his head: "They went to Sacchi and demanded to play. You don't say no to those two."

While the two teams got ready in the locker rooms, the 94,000 fans in the Rose Bowl were subjected to an ear-splitting, mega-decibel, pregame show, featuring Whitney Houston, hundreds of kids, thousands of balloons, and the members of the U.S. national team.

When that had subsided, dignity returned and Italy and Brazil walked calmly on to the field, Brazil in their now familiar fashion, the players holding hands to form a chain.

And the excitement of anticipation took over. This had the promise of one of the great finals: so many great players, so much tradition. Whoever won, a new record was sure to be set: the first four-time winner. In four previous World Cup meetings, the record was two wins each. Two games stood out: the 1970 final, when Brazil romped 4–1, and 1982, when Italy eliminated Brazil 3–2.

Ten goals in two games! Was it too much to hope . . . probably it was. Realistically, you had to remember that the Italians were the world's best defenders, and that this Brazil, this 1994 Brazil, had the best defense of World Cup-94. It had been scored on only three times in six games.

A defensive struggle, then? Banish the thought. The World Cup final had always produced goals, with a healthy 4.4 average for the previous 14 finals . . . but then again, the 1990 final had been a meager 1–0.

Sadly, the doubts and the pessimism were justified. It was the defenses that won the day. The first 0–0 final in World Cup history. What had been a lively, eventful, colorful, and—on the whole—offense-minded tournament ended in a disappointing defensive deadlock.

Brazil, unquestionably, was the livelier team, did more attacking. Maybe things would have been different if they hadn't lost Jorginho to injury after only twenty minutes. Despite his nominal fullback position, he was as close to a playmaker as Brazil had.

Maybe if Sacchi had put goal scorer Signori on the field, Italy would have created more chances. Maybe. The reality was that goal-scoring chances were few. Brazil had most of them.

After twenty-five minutes, Branco unleashed one of his free-kick bombs, Pagliuca couldn't hold it, but Mazinho fell over himself in his eagerness to get to the rebound. Then Romário got off a shot, only to see it immediately blocked—the Italians made sure that neither Romário nor Bebeto had any significant space in which to operate.

On one of the rare occasions when Romário did burst through, twenty minutes into the second half, Pagliuca raced out to kick the ball away from his feet. Ten minutes later the game got as close as it was to get to seeing a goal. Mauro Silva whacked a screaming 25-yard shot that surprised Pagliuca; the ball spun off his chest, hit the goalpost . . . and bounced back to Pagliuca, who grabbed it safely this time.

Baggio conjured up a rare chance for Italy with a sudden turn that bamboozled the Brazilian defense, but his shot went sailing high over the bar. In overtime the heat started to slow everyone down, but not Cafu, who twice raced away down the right to deliver dangerous crosses. Both Bebeto and Romário had chances, both missed. Baggio came close for Italy with a 25-yard volley that Taffarel tipped over the bar.

But the question about Baggio's fitness had already been answered. He looked slow and tired. When, with five minutes remaining, he was put clear on the right by Massaro, he could manage only a feeble shot. His legs had gone, but Sacchi had already used both his substitutes. It seemed unlikely that Baggio would be called upon in the now inevitable penalty-kick-shootout.

The other fitness doubt, Baresi, had played a fantastic game, the best defender on the field. Quick, brave, intelligent, skillful—it was well-nigh impossible to believe he had undergone a knee operation less than three weeks earlier.

The first-ever scoreless final turned into the first-ever final to be decided on penalty kicks. Italy to kick first. Up stepped Baresi—"He always takes the first kick," said Sacchi. Taffarel crouched, Baresi swung his right foot . . . and belted the ball a yard over the bar.

Pagliuca quickly restored parity by saving Marcio Santos's kick, and the next two kickers for each team all scored. On Italy's fourth kick, Taffarel saved from Massaro. Dunga scored for Brazil. Then, surprisingly, it was Baggio, with everything at stake. If he missed, Brazil was the champion. He missed, big time, with a labored kick from tired legs. He got under the ball and scooped it way over the goal. Up in the press area, television commentator Pelé leaped up and waved his arms wildly.

The absurd cruelty of the shoot-out was never more starkly obvious. It was the stuff of Greek tragedy. The Italians had fought bravely, but had been bowed by fate, by their own tragic heroes: Baggio, the man whose brilliance had taken Italy to the final, and Baresi, who had played so magnificently on that day.

Al Gore presented Dunga with the World Cup trophy, shoved it at him with a petulant, jerky motion. Romário, wrapped in a huge Brazilian flag, took his medal, and kissed Havelange. He later told the press: "I'm a winner. Wherever I go I win titles." Brazil did their victory lap . . . and the 1994 World Cup was history. Next stop, France 1998.

The best team had won the World Cup, no doubt about that. The team that all the others feared. Bebeto made the point: "Every team changed their style when they played us." But the Cup had been won in the worst possible way. Nobody liked the shootout, but nobody could come up with anything better.

It was not only the shootout that was unsatisfactory about Brazil's win. There were many critics who found Parreira's Brazil too defensive, too prosaic, too European. Not Brazilian enough. Parreira had answered them, had given Brazil its first World Cup since 1970. He told the press: "I did it my way."

Rothenberg and the American organizing committee doubtless felt the same. Those who said it couldn't be done, or that if it were done it would be done badly, or that even if it were done well, nobody would turn up to watch it, or that if people did turn up the whole thing would be drowned in garish American razzmatazz . . . all of the critics, all of the doomsayers had been routed.

It really had been one long party. Fans had arrived from overseas in their thousands and had behaved perfectly—the Irish in green, the Brazilians in yellow, the Dutch in orange, the Colombians in their blond Valderrama wigs, the Argentines throwing their confetti in Foxboro Stadium.

But the vast majority of the spectators had been Americans. They had turned up in unheard-of numbers, a record total of more than 3.5 million, over 1 million more than the previous record, set in Italy in 1990. As omens go, it was a pretty good one for the launching of the professional league that Blatter had ordained as the next step in the development of American soccer.

Television ratings in the USA had quickly outstripped predictions. ABC got egg all over its face early on, when it insisted that the kickoff time for its first televised game, USA vs. Switzerland in Detroit, be put forward to 11:30 local time. It wanted the soccer out of the way so that it could telecast live golf later in the afternoon.

ABC had its way, but the soccer outdrew the golf anyway. The final game was watched by 10 million households. And a Harris poll conducted after the tournament found that 44 percent of all adults had watched at least one World Cup game on television.

Financially, the World Cup was a runaway success. When all the adding and subtracting had been done, each team that had played in the tournament received $685,000 for each game that it had played. Rothenberg's projection of a $20 million profit was a massive underestimate. The final figure was closer to $60 million, to be used for the development of soccer in the USA.

The games themselves, so much more difficult to predict or control, had lived up to the desire for excitement and action. The goal-scoring trend, ever since 1982, had been downward. In Italia-90, it had sunk to only 2.21 a game. USA-94 dramatically reversed the trend, swinging back up to 2.71 per game.

Unchanged, inexplicable almost, was the World Cup's longest-running oddity. Brazil had played in all fifteen World Cups, the only country to do so. Germany had played in thirteen. Yet the two countries still hadn't faced each other in a World Cup game.

Maybe next time, in France in 1998.

–6–
Soccer in the Olympic Games*

To say that soccer was no big deal in the early days of the Olympic Games is putting it mildly. At the first of the revived games, in Athens in 1896, there was no soccer tournament . . . but there are vague memories of a game between a Danish team and a Greek team. Memories only—all records, including the score, of this game have disappeared.

A slight move towards official acceptance came with an exhibition tournament in Paris in 1900, between three club teams from England, Belgium, and France. The English team, Upton Park from London, won the event, but no medals were given.

Soccer was not taken very seriously in St. Louis in 1904. Another unofficial tournament, featuring five club teams from the USA and Canada, was scheduled after the games proper had finished. Only three of the clubs turned up, and the winners were Galt FC from Ontario, who defeated the two American entries, Christian Brothers College and St. Rose Kickers, both from St. Louis. No medals were given. Decades later the International Olympic Committee (IOC) changed its mind, and awarded tardy gold medals to the Canadians, making the 1904 event the first official Olympic soccer tournament.

London 1908 saw, logically enough, a triumph for England. The final score was Great Britain 2 Denmark 0. Correct: Great Britain. The team was totally English, but Olympic regulations recognized only Great Britain.

A more serious political problem arose when Austria prevented teams from Bohemia and Hungary from playing. Each entering country was permitted to send up to four teams. France, with two teams, was the only country to use the rule. Not successfully, alas, for France A was clobbered 17–1 by Denmark in the semi-final, still the highest-ever Olympic score. The humiliated French went home after refusing to play in the third-place game.

Captain of Great Britain, its star and chief goal scorer, "acclaimed" as the best player of the tournament, was Vivian Woodward. A true amateur,

---

* For Olympic tournament winners, see p. 324. For the United States record in Olympic Soccer, see pp 336–337.

Woodward played for the professional club Tottenham Hotspur and was as good as any of the English pros of the era.

England, still under the Great Britain banner, won again in 1912 in Stockholm, again by beating Denmark in the final. The score was 4–2, but the result was in doubt until Woodward sunk the Danes with two second-half goals in four minutes.

Hosts Belgium took the 1920 title in Antwerp amid clear signs that the balance of soccer power was changing. Britain went out in its first game, beaten by Norway. The Danes were out, too, 0–1 losers to Spain, who featured a sensationally fearless and athletic goalkeeper, the nineteen-year-old Ricardo Zamora.

The final, Belgium vs. the newly created Czechoslovakia was an ugly affair. The Czechs were soon two goals down, and when one of their players was ejected towards the end of the first half, they walked off the field and refused to return. The match had to be abandoned, with Belgium declared the winners of the gold medal.

By the time of the 1924 games, staged in Paris, the unsolved, and probably unsolvable, question of just who was an amateur came to a boil. FIFA was now involved in organizing the tournament, and had to face up to the reality that the sport was rapidly being professionalized throughout the world.

To help amateur players keep up with the pros, FIFA and the IOC had authorized payments to athletes who lost wages by taking time off work to train. To the British this was a heinous breach of the true amateur code, and they withdrew from FIFA, and therefore from the Olympic tournament.

But the departure of the British was more than compensated by the arrival of the Uruguayans. The first South American team to enter the tournament, the Uruguayans were a sensation with their skillful, artistic soccer. They were not just better than the Europeans, they were playing a new, more skillful version of the sport. Crowds flocked to see them. Over 18,000 saw their 3–0 win over the United States, also first-time entrants in the Olympics.

When Uruguay played the hosts, France, the crowd was over 30,000. They saw the Uruguayans, in sparkling form, win 5–1. Until then, if soccer had an international superstar it was England's Vivian Woodward. Now all the talk was of Uruguay's midfielder José Andrade: elegant, subtle, quick, he played with a smooth rhythmic grace that Europeans had never seen before. A 3–0 win over Switzerland in the final made it clear that Uruguay was a class above all the other teams.

Uruguay returned in 1928, to Amsterdam. Across the Atlantic with them came Argentina, something of an unknown quantity. Not for long, though. The USA, in its second Olympic Games, had the bad luck to be Argentina's first opponent, and were crushed 11–2. The superiority of Latin soccer was proved when Argentina and Uruguay, having disposed of everyone else, met in the final. Uruguay ran out 2–1 winners in a replay, after the first game was tied 1–1.

But the Europeans, undoubtedly, had an excuse. The British countries had not participated, while the best players of Austria, Italy, Hungary and Czechoslovakia were now professionals and ineligible for the tournament.

In 1930, FIFA solved the problem of the missing pros by inaugurating the World Cup, open to all players, pros and amateurs. The 1932 Olympic Games in Los Angeles featured no soccer, and for a while it looked as though the World Cup had killed off Olympic soccer.

That did not happen, because the IOC needed the income from the soccer tournament. The sport was already the biggest draw in the Games. So soccer returned in 1936 to Berlin, to the Nazi Olympics, where the Germans were confident that they had a team good enough to win the gold medal. Hitler turned up to watch its second game and was mortified to see his team eliminated 2–0 by Norway. Hitler never attended another soccer game.

The British were back. Somehow, the English, Scottish, Irish, and Welsh federations had set aside their differences and come up with a genuine British team, with players from all four nations. Not a successful experiment, the team went out to Poland, 4–5 in the quarterfinals.

The USA was again eliminated after only one game, but gave a good account of itself in a 0–1 loss to Italy.

Neither Argentina nor Uruguay was present, which left Peru to uphold the successes of the Latin game. The Peruvians immediately showed off all their intricate virtuosity in a 7–3 drubbing of Finland. Next came Austria. The Peruvians came back from 0–2 down, to force overtime. When they went ahead 3–2, some supporters raced onto the field and apparently molested the Austrian players. The field was cleared. The Peruvians scored again, and ran out 4–2 winners.

Austria filed a protest, FIFA upheld it and ordered a replay to which spectators would not be admitted. When Peru refused to agree to play again, Austria was declared the winner. A win over Poland followed, and Austria was in the final against Italy.

The Italian coach was Vittorio Pozzo, fresh from his triumph in the 1934 World Cup. His team was made up of students, but there was doubt about their amateur status; all of them were registered with pro clubs. Before an enormous crowd of over 100,000 in Berlin's Olympic Stadium, Italy took the gold with a 2–1 win.

After World War II, it was back to London in 1948. India made its Olympic debut and played barefoot against the French, losing by only 1–2. A FIFA rule change followed: teams would have to wear shoes. The British team, strictly amateur and therefore lacking all of the country's best players, struggled to a fourth-place finish. Sweden and Denmark, countries that did not have a pro league, fielded their best players. Denmark finished third. Sweden won the gold.

But the Olympic amateur regulations were about to be challenged. The country that augured a revolution for Olympic soccer was Yugoslavia, a Communist country that claimed it had no professional athletes, or amateurs either for that matter . . . just athletes. Its best players were on view, good enough to win the silver medal. An era of total Eastern European domination was beginning.

By 1952, when the Games moved to Helsinki, so many countries were entering that preliminary elimination games had to be played throughout the world. Sweden had little chance of repeating—all of the best players from its 1948 team had been bought up by Italian clubs and were now professionals.

Hungary took the 1952 gold, with a 2–0 win over Yugoslavia, in what was possibly the best of all Olympic finals. Small wonder—both countries had their full international teams on the field, and for the Hungarians this meant the Magic Magyars, unbeaten since 1950, the greatest team of the decade.

Captaining them was a short, stocky, very left-footed inside forward with the build and the look of a teenage schoolboy: Ferenc Puskas. His goal in the final, when he dribbled through the entire Yugoslav defense, confirmed his immense talent. He was destined to become one of the great players of all time. The Hungarians, virtually unchanged, stretched their unbeaten record all the way to the 1954 World Cup final in Switzerland, where they went down to the West Germans.

The Hungarians did not play in the 1956 Games in Melbourne, giving the Yugoslavians their best chance yet to take the gold. The USSR was the favorite, and its goalkeeper, Lev Yashin, was already being hailed as one of the greatest ever. He needed to be in top form in the quarterfinal when the Soviets were astonishingly held 0–0 by Indonesia. The USSR took the replay 4–0 and, without further glitches, reached the final. The other finalist was indeed Yugoslavia, which had strolled through with the easiest of schedules. It had played just two games: beating the USA 9–1, then India 4–1.

Yet again, the Yugoslavs had to be satisfied with the silver medal, losing 0–1 to the Soviets. And yet again soccer demonstrated its extraordinary drawing power. In Australia, a country where soccer was certainly a very minor sport, the final drew nearly 100,000 spectators.

In Rome, in 1960, the tournament was for the first time limited to sixteen teams, and modeled on the World Cup format, with a first round of mini-league play before the knockout phase began. Hosts Italy prepared a young team, all the players being members of professional teams but not, apparently, pros. They were unlucky—uniquely unlucky. A 1–1 semifinal tie with Yugoslavia created a problem: there was no time for a replay. For the first time ever in the Olympics, lots were drawn to decide a winner, and the Italians lost out.

Yugoslavia, perhaps, deserved some luck after their string of three consecutive losses in the final. Their opponent in the 1960 final was, surprisingly, Denmark, who had upset Hungary 2–0 in the other semifinal. This time the Yugoslavs got it right and came off the field 3–1 winners, with their much-delayed gold medals.

The suspicions about the amateur status of some of Italy's players in the 1960 tournament surfaced again immediately before the 1964 tournament in Tokyo. Italy had qualified, but when top club Inter refused to release the players Sandro Mazzola and Giacinto Facchetti for the finals, it was obvious that these were not amateurs. Italy had to drop out.

A terrifying disaster hit the South American qualifiers. In the game between Peru and Argentina in Lima, Argentina was leading 1–0 with two minutes remaining. Peru tied the game, but the goal was disallowed. Fans ran onto the field to attack the Uruguayan referee. The stadium police responded with tear gas and rifle fire. In the ensuing panic, spectators trying to flee the stadium found the gates locked and many were trampled to death. The trouble spread onto the streets of Lima, and a night of rioting followed. When it was over, 328 people had been killed, and over 500 injured.

In the finals, Eastern Europe was as dominant as ever. Hungary, Czechoslovakia, and East Germany took three of the semifinal slots. The fourth went to Egypt, which was heavily beaten 6–0 by Hungary. Hungary took the gold with a 2–1 win over the Czechs.

By now, it was unmistakably clear that the Communist bloc's "state amateurs" were too good for the amateurs of the rest of the world. Other countries were beginning to use young professionals in an effort to compete.

Mexico, for example, the host country in 1968, wanted to put on a strong performance in front of its own fans. But a 1–4 loss to France brought everything out in the open. In the post-game press conference, the French coach André Grillon told the press that it was a good result for France "to beat the host team and its professionals." Immediate protests from the Mexican journalists—this was the Olympics, only amateurs were allowed. Grillon silenced them with a huge Gallic shrug and "Come, my friends, everybody knows . . ."

Everybody did know, but nothing was done about it. Mexico finished in fourth place, ironically beaten in the third-place game by Japan, a newcomer on the soccer scene, which very definitely was using amateurs. The 100,000-plus Mexican fans didn't take kindly to losing to Japan, and from all sides of the huge Azteca Stadium, seat cushions rained down onto the field.

The same blizzard occurred during the final, the crowd's reaction to a stormy game between Bulgaria and Hungary. Three Bulgarians and one Hungarian were ejected, and at one point it looked as if the game might have to be abandoned. Hungary took its third Olympic title, 4–1.

In 1972 hosts Germany had the same problem as Mexico in 1968: how to field a competitive team without being seen to use professionals. This time the answer was for certain key players to delay signing pro forms with their clubs. That was OK for the first round; two 3–0 victories over Malaysia and Morocco were followed by a 7–0 pounding of the United States (which was piling up a formidable record of heavy Olympic losses). But the

Germans were ousted in the second round—by a particularly bitter loss to East Germany. East European mastery was complete. All four semifinalists were from the Communist bloc.

Communist fraternity ruled in the third-place game between East Germany and the USSR. With the score tied at 2–2 the game went to overtime, but neither team made any effort to score. Under Olympic regulations, both countries shared the bronze medal. Poland took the gold with a 2–1 win over Hungary.

By 1976 it was widely accepted that the South Americans, for sure, and probably most of the west Europeans, were fielding young pros in the Olympics. Brazil included Junior, France had Michel Platini, both of whom were to go on to stardom in the pros and the World Cup.

Only thirteen teams played in Montreal—the result of a boycott by the African countries, which meant the withdrawal of Ghana, Nigeria, and Zambia. (The boycott was not a soccer matter. Rugby was the culprit. The African nations objected strongly to a New Zealand tour of South Africa.)

Brazil got as far as the semifinal before losing to Poland. That meant another all-Warsaw-Pact final, Poland against East Germany. A 3–1 win for the Germans. Soccer, it seemed could do no wrong at the turnstiles. In Canada, exactly as in that other non-soccer country Australia, soccer was the biggest crowd-puller with a total of nearly 650,000 fans.

The United States qualified for the 1980 Moscow Olympics, but the manner of its doing so was shameful. It was, in fact, eliminated by Mexico. But a USSF official got hold of the Mexican players' passports, which apparently identified them as professional players. This was not exactly a surprise—the Mexicans and many other countries had been getting away with it for years.

But the USA lodged a protest. The Mexicans withdrew their team, and the berth in Moscow was given to the Americans. Had the Mexicans known, they could have lodged an equally effective protest against the Americans. The USA team was made up mostly of young players, already with pro clubs in the North American Soccer League. To safeguard the players' Olympic eligibility, the clubs had signed them on amateur forms and paid them only expenses. Except that all of them then signed "personal service" contracts with their clubs, under which they were rewarded handsomely for things like giving clinics to youngsters. Sometimes they gave the clinics; sometimes they didn't.

The scheme itself—it was rather like tax evasion—was not outrageous, the Germans had used something similar in 1972. But for the Americans to accuse the Mexicans of cheating was hubris of an exceptionally high order. It got its just reward when President Jimmy Carter ordered a boycott, and the Americans didn't go to Moscow anyway.

Logically, in the Soviet Union, the Communist powers had it all their own way, claiming all four semifinal berths yet again. But it wasn't the Soviets who won. They lost to East Germany who in turn lost to Czechoslovakia in the final. The Russians took the bronze.

It was a depressingly poor tournament. The FIFA technical report was damning, talking of "little or no attractive attacking soccer . . . almost total lack of creative thinking and technical finesse . . . the games were monotonous."

There was even a touch of humor, probably unconscious, for technical reports are not known for their jokes. Talking of the third-place game, won 2–0 by the USSR over Yugoslavia, the report said: "The match was a disappointment, with the two halves turning out quite different, one from the other. The first half was poor, and the second was mediocre."

It looked as though the Eastern European domination was producing soccer sterility. Their teams were certainly becoming a bore. Olympic soccer, desperately needing a shot in the arm, got just what it wanted at the 1984 Olympics in Los Angeles.

First the Communist countries boycotted, then the IOC and FIFA at long last bowed to reality and said they would allow professionals to play in the tournament. There was just one restriction: European and South American countries would not be allowed to use anyone who had already played in the World Cup.

The USA, which had been preparing a genuine amateur team, switched to the professionals under national team coach, Alkis Panagoulias. Without luck—the team didn't make it out of the first round. Both semifinals went to extra time. France beat Yugoslavia (which had ignored Moscow's calls to boycott) 4–2, but only after the Yugoslavs had self-destructed by having two players ejected. Brazil, with a 2–1 victory over Italy, was the other finalist. It meant a new name on the champions roster—neither France nor Brazil had ever won Olympic gold.

Both semifinals had been played in the Pasadena Rose Bowl, where the crowds were staggering: 94,000 for the Brazil game, 97,000 for France. France took the final, 2–1 over Brazil, before another huge crowd in the Rose Bowl: 101,799, which still stands as the record for a soccer game in the United States.

The Seoul Olympics, 1988, continued with the same eligibility rules as before, but the Danes had evidently not studied them carefully enough. During the qualifying rounds they used Per Frimann—who had gone to Mexico with Denmark's 1986 World Cup squad, but who had not played at all. The Danes thought that made him eligible. It did not, because he had played in the qualifying rounds. So West Germany, and not Denmark, traveled to South Korea.

The games were only two days old when Italy found themselves on the wrong end of a sensational upset: Zambia 4 Italy 0. The power of black African soccer was beginning to make itself felt. It would be seen again with the splendid Cameroon team in the 1990 World Cup.

The USA once again failed to get out of the first round, after ties with Argentina and hosts South Korea, and a 2–4 loss to the USSR. But traditional powers Brazil, Italy, and West Germany all made it to the semifinals, along with the Soviet Union.

After a 1–1-overtime tie with West Germany, the Brazilians took the game on penalty kicks, with goalkeeper Taffarel making two vital saves—a preview of his performance in the 1994 World Cup final.

The Soviets beat Italy 3–2 in extra time, and went on to take the gold with another overtime win, this time by 2–1 over Brazil, who greatly missed their injured playmaker, Geovani.

That was it for the USSR, a country that would never appear again on the Olympic schedules. The Olympic tournament had already undergone drastic changes from the days when the Soviet Union and her allies ruled the roost. It had become a much more attractive tournament with a greater variety of playing styles. It was also clearly becoming a nursery for future World Cup stars.

The players in Seoul included many who would become familiar to American fans during the 1994 World Cup: Brazil's Taffarel, Jorginho, Bebeto, and Romário; Germany's Thomas Hässler and Jürgen Klinsmann; Italy's Gianluca Pagliuca, Mauro Tassoti, and Alberigo Evani; Sweden's Martin Dahlin and Anders Limpar; Nigeria's Rashidi Yekini; and Paul Caligiuri, Tab Ramos, and John Harkes of the United States.

FIFA and the IOC were still at odds over the eligibility requirements for the tournament. The IOC, more and more delighted at the popularity of the sport—it was invariably the largest crowd-puller at the Olympics—wanted to throw the tournament open to all players. FIFA resisted—such a move would simply make it another World Cup. FIFA's idea was to put an age limit on the players, to make it an under-23 tournament. They made their position very clear: "If the IOC doesn't accept the under-23 rule, then that will effectively remove soccer from the Olympics. It is their choice."

The IOC relented, and the Barcelona-92 tournament was for under-23 players. Yet the tournament, played in one of the most soccer-passionate areas of the world, was not a major success. Crowds were much below the usual levels—only 400 turned up to see Egypt play Ghana.

FIFA accused the Olympic organizers of deliberately not publicizing the soccer games and of scheduling kickoff times that clashed with major track events.

For the USA it was the same old story—elimination in the first round. The team was widely considered to be the best ever, both in terms of preparation and personnel (it included Cobi Jones, Alexi Lalas, Claudio Reyna, Joe-Max Moore, Mike Burns, and Brad Friedel). But a 3–1 win over Kuwait was not enough to offset a 1–2 loss to Italy and a 2–2 tie with Poland.

The Poles made it all the way to the final. So, too, did hosts Spain—a feat that saved the tournament from being a total disaster at the gate (two of the quarterfinals had drawn less than 10,000 fans each).

A crowd of 95,000 was in the Nou Camp stadium to see one of the most sparkling finals for many years. Spain had won its five previous games without giving up a goal. Poland's Wojtech Kowalczyk ruined that record when he scored just before halftime.

OLYMPIC GAMES 1992
Barcelona, Spain: Italy 2 USA 1
Joe-Max Moore (center, arm raised) bends his free kick around the Italian wall and into the top corner of the goal. The 1996 Atlanta Games give the USA its best chance yet to do what it has never been able to do: win its way into the second round.
© Peter Robinson: The Football Archive

Fifteen minutes into the second half the King and Queen of Spain arrived, having rushed over from the track and field stadium. Their appearance seemed to be the cue for fast and furious action. Within five minutes, Abelardo tied the game up, and seven minutes later Quico put Spain ahead.

It only took Poland another four minutes to tie it up at 2–2 with a goal from Ryszard Staniek. A nail-biting final fifteen minutes saw both teams on all-out attack. With seconds remaining, the ball was bobbling around in the Polish penalty area. The Poles couldn't clear it; the Spaniards couldn't put it into the goal until Quico saw his chance and slammed it into the roof of the net from close range.

Spain had won its first gold medal for Olympic soccer, to go alongside the silver that had been won back in 1920, in Zamora's days.

Overall, the tournament had failed to excite the fans, and the IOC continued to press for all restrictions on eligibility to be removed. FIFA compromised: for the 1996 Olympics in Atlanta, the under-23 rule will still be in force, but each team will be allowed to field three overage players.

A much bigger change was the introduction of women's soccer. The Americans were very keen on this idea—and why not, they had one of the strongest women's teams in the world. They had won the first-ever women's World Cup in 1991 and finished third in the second tournament, in 1995. There was a very real chance of a gold medal.

In May 1995 that possibility looked as remote as ever for the men's team after its dreadful showing in the PanAm games in Argentina: three games played, all three lost, no goals scored. The USSF reacted with uncharacteristic vigor. "We were not pleased with the performance," said secretary general Hank Steinbrecher, as he announced that coach Timo Liekoski had been fired.

If the firing of Liekoski was a surprise, the name of his successor was a shock: University of Virginia coach, Bruce Arena. College soccer's most successful coach, Arena had long been one of the USSF's sharpest critics.

But rather than be embarrassed by a poor showing in the Olympics, the USSF swalllowed its pride and gave Arena the job of turning the team around.

Not easy, but at least Arena has the comfort of knowing that he could hardly make things worse. The United States has never played its way out of the first round of an Olympic tournament. Its overall record, in ten tournaments since 1924, is three wins, eleven losses and five ties. The three wins merely add to the embarrassment, for they came against a trio of soccer minnows: Estonia, Costa Rica, and Kuwait.

"No one thinks we should win the gold," said Arena, "the aim is to put a good attractive team on the field that makes American soccer proud. I've always been a proponent of American players. I still feel they're better than they're given credit for. We know we're not going to be the class of the tournament, but if we're smart and move the ball quickly and get involved—we've got a chance."

–7–

Soccer in the Nineties

The traveling circus of the World Cup—now in Brazil, now in Germany, now in the United States—is built on fast, economical airline flights. As long as the only way to get around Europe was by endless train journeys, and a two- to three-week boat voyage was needed to get from Europe to South America, competitive international soccer was going to be a rare occurrence. The 1930 World Cup highlighted the problem: None of the major European teams was willing to make the trip to Uruguay. The four countries that did participate—France, Romania, Yugoslavia, and Belgium—were second-rank teams, and they agreed to go only after a good deal of arm-twisting.

The coming of air travel, and particularly the jet era that began in the late 1950s changed all that. Oceans and continents could now be crossed in a matter of hours. In 1962, every European country entered the World Cup qualifying rounds, and all ten survivors made the trip to Chile.

But the World Cup, the competition for national teams held once every four years, accounts for only a small part of the global comings and goings of soccer teams. The lion's share of the traveling is done by club teams involved in one or another of the international competitions for clubs that are played every year.

The earliest of these tournaments dates back to 1927, when that pioneer of European soccer, Hugo Meisl, started a cup for the champion clubs and runners-up from Austria, Hungary, Czechoslovakia, Yugoslavia, and Italy. The winner, the first club to capture an international trophy, was Sparta of Prague. The Mitropa Cup (a contraction of *mittel Europa,* central Europe) is still played, but it has dwindled to a relatively minor affair, deserted by the champion clubs.

For them a new competition was born in 1955, the brainchild of a Frenchman, Gabriel Hanot, soccer editor of the renowned sports newspaper *L'Equipe.*

In April 1955, *L'Equipe* made its own prediction of which clubs would end up as 1955 champions in eighteen European countries. It sent a letter to each, inviting it to enter the new competition, starting in the fall of that year. Spartak-Prague and Dynamo-Moscow declined to participate, but the other sixteen clubs were enthusiastic.

So quickly and smoothly did things go that FIFA announced it would recognize the tournament, and the Union of European Football Associations (UEFA, a sort of mini-FIFA, formed in 1954, to deal only with matters in Europe) agreed to be the organizer. The official title was the European Champion Clubs Cup, but it was usually called the European Cup.

The games were to be played on a home-and-home basis, and to avoid conflicts with each country's own league games (which are mostly played at weekends), they would take place in midweek under floodlights.

On the whole, *L'Equipe*'s crystal ball worked remarkably well; of the sixteen clubs that went into the draw for the first round, eight were national champions. Among them was Chelsea, which for the first, and so far the only, time in its history had won the English league—a feat that was greeted with universal amazement, for Chelsea was the butt of a thousand jokes about its ineptitude and inability to win anything.

What Chelsea did next was anything but a joke. Under pressure from the English Football League, which feared that its own competition would suffer if clubs started to get involved in Europe, Chelsea withdrew from the European Cup, and was replaced by a Polish club, Gwardia-Warsaw. The English, insular as ever, had once again chosen to miss the international boat.

Unaffected by yet another of Albion's perfidies, the 1956 European Cup forged ahead through a schedule of twenty-nine games to a magnificent 1956 final in Paris, where Spain's Real Madrid beat France's Stade de Reims by four goals to three. Real's blond Argentine, Alfredo Di Stéfano, stamped his authority on the game, causing journalists to roll out all their superlatives. He was a revelation in his inexhaustible ability to be everywhere on the field, scoring a goal one minute, making a crucial defensive play the next, always at the heart of the game.

Twenty-two clubs entered the following year, including the new English champions, Manchester United, who disdainfully ignored the Football League's warnings, but it was Real Madrid, inspired by Di Stéfano, that triumphed again.

These were very much Real's years, for they won the first five editions of the Cup with one of the greatest club teams ever assembled, and *assembled* is surely the word for a process that brought together Di Stéfano from Argentina, Raymond Kopa from France, José Santamaria from Uruguay, Didi from Brazil, and Ferenc Puskas from Hungary. On the backs of these stars the European Cup rode to success, for the whole of Europe wanted to see the dazzling Real Madrid. The 1960 final, in which Real Madrid annihilated Eintracht-Frankfurt 7–3, was watched by 127,600 fans in Glasgow's Hampden Park stadium. The average attendance for all fifty-two games of the competition that year was 53,000.

UEFA was quick to cash in, and by 1961 it was running two more interclub competitions: the Cup Winners' Cup, for each country's cup

Alfredo Di Stéfano (right) scores one of Real Madrid's seven goals against Eintracht Frankfurt in the 1960 European Cup Final. The Argentine star, the greatest all-around player the sport has seen, never played in a World Cup.
© Peter Robinson: The Football Archive

winner (Czechoslovakia, which didn't have a national cup competition, started one so that it could participate); and the Fairs Cup, which began as an invitational tournament between cities that staged trade fairs, but was soon expanded to include most of Europe's top teams other than the champions and the cup winners. This one is now called the UEFA Cup. By 1995 the three competitions involved 167 clubs from forty-eight countries.

European competition, which once meant nothing more than a train journey between London and Glasgow, is now a complicated web of hundreds of jet flights between Moscow and Dublin, Athens and Reykjavik, Madrid and Helsinki.

On the night of September 14, 1995, the schedule of games for the opening round of the Cup Winners' Cup looked like this:

FIRST-ROUND EUROPEAN CUP WINNERS' CUP GAMES—
September 14, 1995

Dynamo Batumi (Georgia) vs. Glasgow Celtic (Scotland)
Dynamo Moscow (Russia) vs. Aravat Yerevan (Armenia)
FC Teuta Durresi (Albania) vs. Parma (Italy)
Hradec Kralove (Czech Rep.) vs. FC Copenhagen (Denmark)
Lokomotiv Sofia (Bulgaria) vs. Halmstads BK (Sweden)

Inter Bratislava (Slovakia) vs. Real Zaragoza (Spain)
Dag Liepaja (Latvia) vs. Feyenoord (Netherlands)
APOEL Nicosia (Cyprus) vs. Deportivo La Coruña (Spain)
AEK Athens (Greece) vs. Sion (Switzerland)
Zalgiris Vilnius (Latvia) vs. Trabzonspor (Turkey)
Club Bruges (Belgium) vs. Shaktyor Donetsk (Ukraine)
Rapid Vienna (Austria) vs. Petrolul Ploiesti (Romania)
Borussia Mönchengladbach (Germany) vs. Sileks Kratovo (Macedonia)
Molde FK (Norway) vs. Paris St. Germain (France)
Sporting Lisboa (Portugal) vs. Maccabi Haifa (Israel)
Reykjavik (Iceland) vs. Everton (England)

That same week there were eight games in the UEFA Champions League (formerly the European Cup), and thirty-two more in the UEFA Cup. And that is just the beginning. Because the other continents now all stage similar club competitions.

The most famous is the South American Copa Libertadores, inaugurated in 1960, which features the two top clubs from each of the continent's ten countries. In 1988 the South Americans started the Super Copa, open to former winners of the Copa Libertadores. To which can be added the African Champions Cup, the Asian Cup Winners' Cup, the Champions Cup of North and Central America, (each with thirty-eight clubs).

In Europe and South America, the vast majority of the clubs involved are professional. The top players are well paid—some of them extravagantly well paid. Just like their football, baseball, and basketball counterparts in America, they are national heroes—their names, their faces, their playing careers, and their private lives familiar to everyone. Except that, with the really top soccer players, it goes further. They are known throughout the world. Television sees to that, with its huge global audiences; witness the 1.2 *billion* who tuned in to the 1994 World Cup final.

How much does a professional soccer player earn? Not an easy question to answer, because the rates of pay differ enormously from country to country. Published figures are often not reliable, suspected of distortion by the "three-contract" factor: one set of figures for the press, one for the tax man, and the real total somewhere in between.

Salaries depend heavily on the number of games played and a system of bonuses that varies according to the importance of the games. For example, a club in the twenty-team English Premiership will play thirty-eight league games. It will be involved in at least two Cup competitions in England. Assuming it is knocked out of the Cups in the first round, and is not involved in any of the European competitions, it will play forty-one games. If, in addition, the club is not in contention for the league championship, there will be no vital games calling for large bonuses.

Compare that with a club that plays in one of the European competitions, that wins its way through to the English Cup final, and is in the race for the league championship. The number of games played will be thirty-eight in the league, six in the Cup (more if replays are necessary), plus anything from two to twelve games in the European competition—say a total of fifty-four games. For players on this club there will not only be thirteen more bonuses, but they will be progressively bigger the nearer the club gets to winning one of the cups or the league.

Keeping these variables in mind, let us take a look at the wage structure of the English Premiership. The average basic wage is around $400,000 a year. Bonuses could add anything up to $100,000 a year. Which is about the same as for German *Bundesliga* (i.e., first-division) players. Top players in England and Germany can earn up to $2 million a year, plus bonuses.

Top players have additional sources of income from personal publicity contracts with sponsors, and from national team games. World Cup games bring the highest bonuses. The English players who won the World Cup in 1966, for instance, received $5,000 each, which was thought to be a staggering figure at the time. Eight years later it was made to look utterly puny when each West German player got $25,000 for winning the 1974 trophy. And so on to 1994 when their World Cup triumph was worth $80,000 to each Brazilian player. That was the "official" bonus from the Brazilian Soccer Federation. Add in the money from team sponsorship deals, and it is believed that the players cleared more than twice that amount.

Affluence has come comparatively recently to soccer. For years the Football League in England enforced a maximum-wage limit that stood at $2,800 a year in 1958, the same year that Ferenc Puskas was signing for Real Madrid for $11,500 a year. A number of top British players left to play for Italian clubs, but it was not until the players threatened to strike that the maximum wage was abolished in 1961.

Neither England nor Germany can claim to be the El Dorado for soccer players. Italy is where the soccer fields are paved with gold, nowhere more so than in the northern city of Milan. There, in 1992, the average annual income of the first-team players of AC Milan was $1.79 million. The figure includes the substantial signing-on fee that each player pockets when signing a contract (it varies according to the contract), and the whopping $365,000 bonus paid to each player for winning the 1992 Italian league.

The early 1990s marked the peak of the Italian spending splurge, when Milan was known as the biggest of the big spenders. At that time Marco Van Basten, Milan's Dutch striker, had a contract that guaranteed him $2.66 million net a year.

Things looked pretty good in nearby Turin, too, where the Juventus players averaged $1.28 million each in 1992. Three years later what passes for economy in the megabuck world of soccer finances arrived.

In 1995 Juventus decided that it couldn't afford to keep paying Roberto Baggio his $2 million yearly salary. It asked him to take a cut, down to $1.8 million. No way, said Roberto. So he moved over to Milan, who paid Juventus $13 million for his contracts, and agreed to the $2 million salary.

Figures like these explain why Western Europe has become a magnet for top players from all over the world. Very few South American players, for instance, can hope to make that sort of money if they stay at home. In Brazil, the average player gets between $50,000 and $100,000 (plus bonuses) with a handful of top players earning between $200,000 and $300,000.

There are now Africans from Ghana, Nigeria, Senegal, Gabon, and Togo, playing in Germany, Belgium, and France. Russians and other Eastern Europeans—formerly barred from joining foreign clubs—are arriving, too. They are an attractive proposition for Western clubs, because they cost less to buy, and accept lower salaries than South Americans. Hardly surprising: a top player in Russia could expect only $1,000 a month, plus apartment and car.

But things are changing rapidly. After a 1992 win against mighty Barcelona, CSKA Moscow players were given a bonus of $25,000 each— "an obscene example of capitalist soccer" said a Russian newspaper, pointing out that it would take the average laborer, earning $20 a month, 100 years to make that amount.

After Rotor-Volgograd had elminated much-fancied Manchester United from the UEFA Cup in 1995, skeptical English journalists asked the Russian coach if his players would receive bonuses. "Oh yes," he replied, though refusing to name a figure, "Russia is not as poor a country as you think it is."

Once big money came to professional soccer, the player's agent was not far behind. FIFA did not at all like the idea of agents, and banned them from getting involved in the transfer of players from one club to another.

The ban was widely ignored, though sometimes attempts to observe it led to farcical situations: a player would negotiate with a club manager, but the proceedings would suffer frequent interruptions as the player left to consult his agent, hovering in the adjoining room.

Pretending that agents didn't exist was not going to work. FIFA abandoned its opposition in the face of the riches that poured into soccer in the '90s. A licensing scheme was drawn up to create a roster of FIFA-approved agents. To receive a license, an agent had to satisfy FIFA that he fully understood the FIFA regulations governing the transfer of players, and also had to put up a bank deposit of $160,000 in favor of FIFA.

The focus of all this money-making and money-spending is the soccer player himself. He may be Dutch or Brazilian or English or Italian or Mexican or, indeed, from almost anywhere in the world. Including the United States: there are now over thirty Americans playing professionally with clubs in Europe and Latin America. To try to paint the picture of a "typical" professional soccer player is like chasing a will-o'-the-wisp, because the game is played by too many cultures and races in too many countries, for a meaningful average to be arrived at.

Not too long ago, there were two characteristics likely to hold good for any randomly selected player: he would be from a working-class background, and he would have finished his formal education in his midteens.

The working-class background should not surprise anyone who has read this far, for one of soccer's greatest strengths has always been that it is everywhere a game of the people. As to the brief period of schooling, it should be remembered that the United States is the only country in the world that uses its colleges as farm teams for professional sports. Everywhere else, professional sport is seen as a trade that needs no academic qualification, a way of making a living that one starts as soon as one is able.

But that traditional pattern is changing, along with a changing society. As the dividing line between working class and middle class becomes increasingly blurred, so the stigma that once attached to soccer is disappearing. Soccer is no longer looked down on as a coarse, unworthy profession. There is now plenty of money to be made, and the idea of a middle-class boy leaving school to pursue a career as a professional player is no longer unthinkable.

This is not to say that soccer is suddenly being flooded with intellectuals. You will not find many university graduates among pro soccer players. During the late 1950s and early 1960s Phil Woosnam—a B.A. from the University of North Wales—played professionally in the English first division. Such was the novelty of a university graduate on the soccer field that in the press Woosnam's name was invariably followed by some such reference as "the footballing B.A." (Woosnam later came to the United States and was a leading figure in the establishment of the North American Soccer League. See chapter 10, page 249.)

Today, more attention is being paid to the whole question of education for young soccer players. There has been a general acceptance of the need for professional clubs to provide alternative training for their youth players. Such training is frequently pretty rudimentary—a day, or a couple of evenings, a week featuring instruction on sports management, for instance. But it does represent a massive change of attitude on the part of the clubs, an admission that they should help prepare boys for an alternative life in case something goes wrong with their soccer careers.*

And those careers stand a pretty high chance of going wrong. In England, it is estimated that three out of every four boys who join pro clubs as youngsters are out of the pro game by the age of twenty-one. Throughout the soccer world it is the same story, because nobody has yet discovered an infallible, or even a reliable, way of developing young players, of detecting which boy will make it and which will not.

A look at three young soccer players from Italy, England, and Argentina, will give an idea of how top clubs go about nurturing talent, and what is involved in becoming a pro soccer player.

---

* Before and immediately after World War II soccer was, by and large, a poorly paid occupation of the working classes. But it had immense glamour, and most of those who made it as professionals gave little thought to what they would do once they stopped playing. The results were seen in many countries—men who were once idols working at menial jobs and living in obscurity, even poverty. A poignant reminder came in 1993. Eighty-year-old Raich Carter, who had partnered the great Stanley Matthews on England teams in the 1930s and 1940s, announced that he was selling all his soccer medals and trophies to pay his medical bills.

ITALY

You take the highway heading northeast out of Milan, heading for Lake Maggiore. About 40km along you get off the *autostrada,* and the narrow roads twist and turn until you reach the little town of Carnago. More twists, more turns, then just when it looks like the road is running out, you see the buildings on your right. A small, red-roofed complex nestling behind a substantial metal gate, it has the quiet, well-ordered air of a prosperous convalescent home.

The gate slides quietly open, you ease your car onto the crunchy gravel of the driveway as the gate moves back into place behind you.

This is Milanello, built in 1963 as a training area for AC Milan soccer club. It has everything—fields, both grass and artificial turf, gymnasiums bulging with modern training equipment, a medical clinic, lecture rooms, recreation areas, and dining facilities. And, as you would expect of Italy's richest club, AC Milan, everything is first class.

There are dormitories, too, where twenty-two young hopefuls live while training to become the Milan stars of the future. Boys from the primavera team (ages 18–20), and the juniors (ages 16–18). Boys from all over Italy, from Tuscany, Sardinia, Calabria, Liguria, Puglia.

Among them is Alessandro Ercolani, born in 1976 in the small central Italian town of Sassocorvara, east of Florence. Soccer life began early for Alessandro, playing with older boys in the local park and—not always happily—in his school yard: "There was this time when I was running backward, watching the ball, and I jumped up to head it . . . but I didn't know there was a tree there, a pine, with a low branch. I hit my head so hard, it knocked me out, right out . . . I was all right, though, just a big bump . . . I don't think there was any blood!"

He has vague memories of Italy winning the 1982 World Cup—"We all watched on television, but after Italy's three ties in the first round, there didn't seem much hope. Then, with Paolo Rossi's goals and a bit of luck, we began to think we could win. After the final, we all went out into the street with flags and banners."

As a boy, Alessandro didn't care much for Milan. He was a Juventus fan. The Milan adventure began in May 1989. A trial game was organized in nearby Montecchio, by Milan, to showcase all the best local boys. Alessandro was invited to play—hardly a surprise, as he had already been contacted by several top clubs, including Torino and his favorite Juventus: "The game was on a Wednesday, after school. I was very nervous all day, right up to the moment when I arrived at the stadium. But once I got on the field, I was all right, and I played like it was a normal game."

Evidently, things went well. Three days after the game, the Milan club telephoned to say they wanted to see more of Alessandro. In June 1989 the fourteen-year-old Alessandro, along with his mother and father, traveled up to Milan, where they stayed in a hotel for three days, at Milan's expense:

"It was a special tournament that Milan had arranged. I really felt exhausted in the end—it was so hot, and I had to play in two games in three days."

Milan was impressed and invited Alessandro to join them. He entered Milanello in August 1990. It seems right to talk of "entering" Milanello, for there is something monastic about the setup. It is known, jokingly, as the Golden Cage, or—perhaps not quite so jokingly—as the Golden Prison.

The typical day for Alessandro and his teammates starts with breakfast at 7:00, then a special bus takes them to the local high school in Cargano. Says Milanello director Antore Peloso: "The education is very important, our president insists on it . . . but there are some clubs that don't."

The boys will attend the school until they leave Milanello at age eighteen. They take the regular classes, but Alessandro found that "at first, the local boys didn't look on us too well, they didn't like us missing classes when we had to be away playing in tournaments. But slowly, we made some friends."

At 1:00 the boys take the bus back to Milanello, where the metal gate closes them in for the rest of the day. A light lunch is followed by training from 3:00 until 5:00 Dinner is at 7:30. The time between 8:00 and 11:00 is for recreation—television, billiards, chess, darts, etc., or studies. Tutors come in the evenings to help boys who have fallen behind because of absence from school.

There is school on Saturday mornings, too, but the afternoon is spent relaxing, getting ready for Sunday morning, when the boys play their games in a regional league. In the afternoon they go into Milan, to attend the Milan first-team games, or—every other Sunday—those of the city's other pro team, Inter-Milan.

The boys are paid a monthly allowance of between $100 and $135, but spending opportunities are very limited. An unnatural life for fifteen-year-olds, this Golden Cage? Alessandro demurs: "I've always wanted to play soccer at the highest level, to become famous. I want to make the most of this opportunity. And here, I think we mature a little earlier. At home there would just be school. Here, we have two schools.

"If there are no girls, well, that's a sacrifice we have to make. We are at work all the time, there are so many things to do. Girls would be a distraction—there's time for that during the summer vacation; we get one and a half months at home then."

Taking young boys away from their homes does sometimes cause problems, as Peloso admits: "We've had cases of homesickness, but we always explain to the boys and the parents that this is part of growing up. We pay for journeys home for the boys, once a year, and, of course, in case of need, maybe illness in the family."

The anxious time for the boys comes each year, in June, when the one-year contracts expire and they find out whether they have been "confirmed" (whether they will be invited back for the following year). Says Peloso: "We have meetings here among the staff, discussions to decide who should be confirmed and who not. We send a letter to the parents telling them, though in most cases we will have telephoned. Probably most of the boys know before they leave here—about fifty percent are not confirmed."

For Alessandro, confirmed every year since his arrival, the big moment arrives with his eighteenth birthday, when he can be signed as a full professional . . . if Milan offers him a contract. He would then leave Milanello and probably be sent on loan to a club in the third division of the Italian league.

He expects to make it, expects to become a top first-division player. "That is my dream. But you don't live in dreams, now is what counts. I must work hard now." And Alessandro Ercolani, 5'10" left-footed midfielder, assesses his play: "I'm not so fast—sometimes when I go up, I can't get back in time, so I have to compensate with my brain, anticipating the play. I've got a strong left foot. . . . I'm not a goal scorer, I'm the one who makes the last pass—the assist" (Alessandro uses the English word, which has become part of the Italian soccer vocabulary). "I'm good at taking free kicks, pretty good with my head. But no one is born the perfect player; you can always learn something.

"If something goes wrong with my soccer career, well, I'm a good student; I would go to university to get a degree. My favorite subjects are math, electronics, computers, but I don't know what I would study, it's too early to say."

ENGLAND

Goal scoring was something that came naturally to young Adrian Clarke. When he was nine years old, he once scored nine in a single game for his team, Haverhill Echo. The following year, 1985, he scored 121 goals in the season, averaging around four a game.

That summer, he was playing in a five-a-side tournament, lots of short games, lots of waiting between games. During one of those pauses: "This tall man came up to me and asked where my dad was. I pointed him out— my dad was the coach of my team. When I was playing the next game, I could see them talking. I thought he was a coach, too, and they were arranging a game. My dad didn't say anything, but at the end, when we were in the car driving home, he showed me the man's card."

The card read "Steve Rowley. Assistant Youth Development Officer. Arsenal FC." Adrian was being scouted by one of most famous clubs in England. "My dad gave him our fixture list, and he came to four or five games next season. I remember he drove a Volvo. My dad never told me when he'd be there, so I suppose I just played naturally, but I could always spot him, in his long trench coat. After the games, he wouldn't say much, just ask me how I was."

Until one day, Rowley popped the question: Would Adrian like to join the Arsenal Centre of Excellence? All the pro clubs in England run these training centers for young players, who could join when they are eleven years old, which Adrian now was. (The admission age has since been lowered to nine.)

By now, other clubs were looking at Adrian. He, in turn, looked at the training facilities at Arsenal, at Southampton, and at Colchester—and chose Arsenal. Attendance at the Arsenal Centre of Excellence in Grays (about one hour's drive from his home), started Adrian thinking seriously about becoming a pro player.

Soccer had always been a part of his life. He was born in Haverhill, a small town some fifteen miles east of the university city of Cambridge. His father, Harry, a chemical analyst, had been a keen player in his youth with the London club Leyton Orient, had encouraged Adrian to play, and coached his son's team.

The usual escapades for Adrian: "They tell me—I don't remember it— that when I was a little kid, in the living room, it must have been a party or something, I tried to head a balloon, and I head-butted the sideboard instead. They had to take me to hospital to put stitches in the cut."

And the trips with Dad to Ipswich, the nearest first-division pro club: "The first game I ever saw was Ipswich against Wolves, I was maybe seven. I was an Ipswich fan, a Junior Blue, that's what they called the kids. I remember that day, because it snowed the whole game, it was settling on the pitch [field]. And Ipswich won 3–1."

In 1982 there was the World Cup in Spain, but Adrian doesn't remember much about that, only that the England captain Brian Robson scored the fastest goal, in twenty seven seconds, against France. Adrian's own goal-scoring exploits were continuing, and the invitation from Arsenal followed.

On his fourteenth birthday in 1988, Adrian signed for Arsenal as an Associated Schoolboy. He had to do some thinking about that, for there were now about a dozen clubs interested in him, including other big names like Chelsea, Manchester United, Southampton, Ipswich, and West Ham United. "I narrowed it down to three in the end—Ipswich, West Ham, and Arsenal. I was still an Ipswich fan, but I was beginning to switch to Arsenal— well, Ipswich were in the second division now. I was the one who made the decision. I'd been coming to Arsenal for two years, I'd got to know everyone. They've got a good youth record and good facilities. But in case Arsenal didn't want me, I visited all the others."

Adrian was now linked contractually to Arsenal. In addition to his training session every week, he played games for Arsenal's under-fifteen team every Sunday.

In 1989 came another invitation, this one from the English Football Association. An offer of a scholarship at Lilleshall. This was the FA's residential School of Excellence to which, each year, the sixteen best fourteen-year-olds in England were admitted.

Clearly, there was a lot of prestige attached to this one, and it was something that Adrian and his family thought about deeply. In the end, Adrian decided it wasn't for him: "I was happy at my school, and anyway I didn't think I needed Lilleshall to improve my football. And wanting to live at home was part of it."

National recognition came to Adrian even without Lilleshall, for he was chosen seven times to play for England Schoolboys during the 1988–89 season, including games in Wembley Stadium against France and the Netherlands.

Another decision day arrived in March 1991 when Arsenal—more than happy with his progress—offered to sign Adrian as a full-time trainee. To stay on at school, or to leave (which, being sixteen, he could now legally do) and start as a trainee with Arsenal in July? "I was a good student, I suppose, I'd taken all ten 'O' levels, and got seven As and three Bs, but it wasn't a difficult decision. I had no doubts; I wanted to be a professional player."

Adrian's decision to quit school and sign as a trainee meant that now he had to leave home. English clubs do not put their young players in dormitories, preferring to place them with families who can provide a cozy "Mum-and-Dad" home-away-from-home atmosphere. Adrian moved into lodgings in North London, where he and another trainee stayed with a family.

Arsenal would pay for that. And Adrian received a weekly wage of $56, paid not by Arsenal, but by the government. He was now part of the Youth Training Scheme, a job-training program that the British government introduced in 1984. He could make a little more from the youth games he played each week for Arsenal, bonuses of $6 for a win, $3 for a tie.

Four days a week, Adrian got up at 7:30 and took a bus to Palmers Green, where he was picked up by a special Arsenal bus taking the trainees to London Colney, Arsenal's training facility at the northern edges of the city.

Once there, he and the other trainees (there were sixteen of them) spent around twenty minutes performing some very menial tasks—pumping up balls, setting out cones, cleaning boots for the first-team players, who arrived for their training around 10:00.

While the first team practiced, the trainees went through their own two-hour session under the Arsenal youth coach. At 12:30, the trainees would clean up after the first team, change and shower, and eat lunch in the canteen. Then it was back home on the team bus.

Wednesdays were different. No training, this was school day, part of the YTS program that requires trainees to study on one day a week. The trainees would come into the Arsenal stadium at Highbury from 9:30 until 4:00 to study for a certificate in recreation and leisure. A two-year course that included field trips to leisure centers to study their management; to swimming pools, where lifesaving could be learned, plus courses on social skills—visiting restaurants, learning how to communicate with the media.

Adrian had a slightly different program, returning home to Haverhill every Tuesday night, and spending Wednesdays at his old high school, studying A-level math. He also studied for the recreation certificate, but in his own time.

Saturdays there were games, at 11:00. In the afternoon, if the Arsenal first team was at home, the trainees would attend that game at Highbury. Sundays were a day off.

The life of a seventeen-year-old learning to become a pro soccer player feels good to Adrian: "I enjoy the life. I can't think of a better way to make a living. It's a very competitive situation here, but that makes you more mentally tough. All the shouting, from the coach and from the other players, it's tough. But after three months, once you get over that, it's much easier."

Adrian Clarke, 5'10", 158 pounds, left-footed forward: "I'm left-footed, but I play left or right wing, sometimes in midfield. I don't really like it right up front; I don't like playing with my back to goal. I quite fancy midfield—I like dribbling, running at people. Those are my strengths, running at defenders, dribbling, getting in shots and crosses. I score goals—they tend to be longer-range goals, from the edge of box—not close-range tap-ins. My favorite players? Pelé and Platini. Nowadays, Chris Waddle and John Barnes, when he's on form."

On his eighteenth birthday, in 1992, Adrian Clarke got the good news: Arsenal wanted him to sign a pro contract. Not a difficult decision for Adrian. He signed on, and in 1995 he made his debut for the Arsenal first team.

ARGENTINA

Rafael Sanchez was born in December 1974 in the small Argentine town of Zapala, an undistinguished place of some 30,000 inhabitants in the foothills of the Andes, just seventy-five miles from the Chilean border.

Buenos Aires, the center of Argentina's soccer activity, lies over 700 miles away to the northeast. There were no top pro games for Rafael to watch as he grew up. He recalls some games on television, which he watched without any great interest. His father, Alberto, originally from Buenos Aires and a passionate Boca Juniors fan, tried to stir Rafael's interest in the sport, but it wasn't easy. Alberto worked long hours as a civil servant for the Neuquen state government, and never had the time to devote to playing soccer with his son.

Enter Uncle Florentino. Rafael recalls: "It's funny how that happened, because my uncle was never a serious player, and he wasn't all that interested in the sport. But when I was about six, we used to play in the street every evening, just the two of us. Just fooling about, you can see that it wasn't really serious, because we never bothered with a ball—we played with those cardboard soft-drink cartons that we used to ball up. We would get through two or three of those every evening. But he knew enough about the sport to teach me how to kick and volley, you know, which part of the foot to use, because I really didn't know anything. It took maybe six months, and then I started to get interested in the sport."

The 1982 World Cup passed by without leaving much impression on Rafael. He watched some of Argentina's games on television but—pressed for a memory—can recall only Daniel Passarella's free-kick goal in Argentina's 1–2 loss to Italy.

By the age of ten, Rafael was a confirmed fan of Boca Juniors. His idol was Diego Maradona, who had once been a Boca player. He joined his first team, Don Bosco, and the coach gave him the #8 shirt. In Argentina, that corresponds to the position of offensive midfielder. His father Alberto now made the time to come and watch Don Bosco's games, and was impressed with his son's play. He promised Rafael that if he wanted to become a professional player, he would take him to Buenos Aires where the big clubs could get a look at him.

Around the time of Rafael's fifteenth birthday, Alberto went to the telephone directory and looked up the number of the Boca Juniors training camp in the suburbs of Buenos Aires—La Candela, as it is called. He gave them a call to sing the praises of his son.

One of hundreds of such calls that Boca Juniors get every year. The man in charge of the youth division, Silvio Marzolini—once a world-class defender with Boca who had played for Argentina in the 1966 World Cup—gave his standard response. Bring the boy along to La Candela, and we'll take a look at him. No promises—and no expenses. Rafael's father would have to pay for everything, the journey and the accommodation in Buenos Aires.

Rafael has no trouble remembering the date: "The trial was to start Monday February 18, 1990. So we left Zapala, me and my father, at six in the evening on Saturday. We got to Buenos Aires around midday on Sunday." An eighteen-hour bus journey, but the fifteen-year-old Rafael found he was too interested in all the new sights to be nervous.

The plan was for Rafael and his father to stay for a week in a hotel near La Candela, which is in the Buenos Aires suburb of San Justo. On Monday and Wednesday Rafael would go to La Candela for training with some twenty-five other young hopefuls from all over Argentina. On Friday the boys would play a regular ninety-minute game.

Things didn't start well. On Wednesday Marzolini spoke with Alberto and told him that Rafael's chances were slight. Rafael admits: "Physically, I wasn't up to it. I couldn't keep up the pace that they wanted." But the coach of the fifteen-year-olds had seen something that he liked in Rafael's play, and said he wanted to see Rafael in Friday's game.

The Friday session decided matters. Boca invited Rafael to stay on at La Candela. Alberto went back to Zapala, and Rafael, at age fifteen, remained to take up the life of a trainee professional.

At La Candela he joined seventeen other boys ranging in age from fifteen to twenty-one. They lived in a dormitory, two to a room, with all their meals provided. Boca paid for two trips home each year. That was it. There was no cash payment from the club. Pocket money for the boys had to come from their families.

A typical day consisted of an 8:30 breakfast, followed by training from 9:30 until 11:30 or midday. Each day the boys living at La Candela were joined by around a hundred boys who traveled in from their homes in the Buenos Aires area for the training sessions. Lunch was taken at 1:00, followed by an afternoon of relaxation, or studying, or maybe some TV-watching—each of the boys' rooms had a television set.

At 6:15 the boys boarded a bus for a short ride to the neighboring suburb of Moron, where they attended regular secondary school classes from 6:30 until 10:30 After that, it was back to La Candela, a meal, and lights out around 11:30.

Saturday afternoons, from April through December, was when the boys played their league games. At age eighteen they played in what is, in effect, the country's fourth division, featuring the youth squads from all the big-name teams like River Plate, Newell's Old Boys, Independiente, etc.

During his three years at La Candela, Rafael was also called up to play for the Argentine under-seventeen national team. He helped the team to qualify for the under-seventeen World Cup in Italy in 1991, but injury kept him off the team in the final tournament.

He continued to play his original position, to wear the #8 shirt of the offensive midfielder, and still felt that he needed to be physically stronger: "I need to work on my stamina. And my heading, I should be better at that, for defensive play. But I prefer attacking; that's where my strengths are. I'm not a dribbler or a goal scorer, but I have good vision of the game, I can find the open man with a pass."

His boyhood idol, Maradona, was replaced by a couple of favorite players: defender Oscar Ruggeri of Velez Sarsfield, and Gerardo Martino, the #8 for that Argentine club with the very English name, Newell's Old Boys.

At age eighteen—not before—the young players can be offered a professional contract. That is what Rafael Sanchez and the other boys at La Candela dream of—the opportunity to make the jump from living on the pocket money provided by their parents, to earning around $25,000 a year plus bonuses, to move from La Candela into an apartment in Buenos Aires.

*   *   *

Despite the geographical and cultural distances that separate them, Adrian, Alessandro, and Rafael have quite a lot in common. All three lead a soccer-centered existence, characterized by an early attachment to a professional club and a meager income. They continue at school until the legal leaving-age—sixteen in England and Argentina, eighteen in Italy. The chances of them going on to college are slim, not because they lack the qualifications, but simply because a college education is not, and never has been, a part of the soccer scene.

Which means that in the traditional soccer countries college soccer teams are rarely of any great caliber—all the best players are already with pro clubs. In Italy and Argentina, as in most European and South American countries, high school soccer barely exists. Rafael did not play soccer at all in high school. Alessandro did, but dismisses it as "not serious." He and Rafael learned to play with their club teams.

The situation is considerably different in England, where the English Schools' Football Association has been in existence since 1904, and schoolboy soccer is a well-organized national sport. Adrian's appearances for the England Schoolboys team at Wembley were organized by the ESFA.

These different frameworks for youth soccer are reflected in the varying methods used for recruiting young players.

In Brazil, for instance, all of the big clubs used to hold regular *dias de peneira* (sieve days) for boys ages twelve and up. Any boy who fancied his chances could come along to the stadium for a trial—and they would come by the score, sometimes as many as one hundred to a session, raw talent, many of them without even a pair of soccer shoes to their name. A haphazard procedure, but it worked because there seemed, in the 1950s and '60s and on into the '70s, to be an endless supply of gifted kids.

Social factors have undermined that system. The breeding grounds that spawned all those kids have been eaten up. The massive migration of people to the cities has meant much less space for kids to play on. Heavy traffic has dealt a mortal wound to street soccer, and even on the famous Rio beaches space and time are now restricted as everything gets more organized. Rising standards of living and better education have meant a significant reduction in the number of boys who see soccer as their only career option.

The search for young stars can no longer be left to chance. Sieve days are held much less often now. Instead, the top Brazilian clubs now operate like the Italians. They employ coaches to scout young players, to cooperate with small second- and third-division clubs to organize trial games featuring all the local hopefuls—exactly the sort of game that Alessandro Ercolani played in when he was fourteen. The coaches are modestly paid, but get bonuses for the players they discover.

Sieve days are regarded as a waste of time in England. "Yes, I was once with a club where we had invitational trials every Sunday," said the manager of a first-division club, "and in one and a half years we must have seen sixty boys a month, and never one that amounted to anything. What would you expect? Schools soccer is so well organized, anyone who's any good will already have been spotted and grabbed by a professional club."

The earliest age at which an English professional club can "grab" a schoolboy is nine, when the boy—or rather his parents—can sign a contract under which he attends the club's Centre of Excellence. This means that the boy goes along to the club several times a week for training and coaching.

The contract lasts for one year, and at the end of that term the boy is free to renew or to sign another one-year contract with a different club.

At age fourteen, the boy can sign for a club as an "associated schoolboy." Each pro club is allowed to sign thirty of these associated schoolboys.

This is a different form of contract, one that gives the club much more control over the boy's future. He cannot now switch to another team without his club's permission; if the move is agreed, the club is entitled to receive a fee from the new team. If the boy continues to impress, a trainee contract will follow at age sixteen, followed by a pro contract at age eighteen.

As there is no such thing as a draft system in England, outstanding schoolboy players are likely to find themselves getting a lot of attention from professional club scouts. Inducements or bonuses—either in cash or in kind—are illegal, say the Football League regulations, but plenty are offered, invariably to the boy's parents. Cash up to $100,000 has been paid to secure a schoolboy player, while in other cases the father has been given a bogus job as a club scout, complete with car and liberal mileage allowance.

Anthony Jackson, unemployed in Manchester, England, got a call from a club "intermediary" in 1994. There was $75,000 for him . . . if he agreed to have his son Kane sign for the club when he reached the age of 16. At the time, Kane was seven years old. Jackson Sr. turned the offer down— but he did hire an agent for Kane.

As we have seen, waste from the ranks of the junior players is considerable. Only one boy in four can expect to make it to the professional level, and three out of four of those survivors will probably have to be satisfied with something less than regular first-team play in the Premiership.

For a boy who does make it all the way to the top, the glamour part consists of million-dollar contracts, fast cars, and national fame. For that he will be expected to play soccer virtually year-round. The old two-month summer break has all but evaporated, taken over by longer seasons, overseas tours, and summer tournaments.

We are talking here of the player in England, but the situation is little different elsewhere. Just as with the junior players, the lives of pro soccer players are remarkable for their similarity throughout the world.

The English season starts in late August, but approximately five weeks before this, say the middle of July, the players report to their club for preseason training, always the toughest part of the schedule. This involves two sessions a day, Monday through Friday, plus a half day on Saturday. The mornings, from 10:30 to 12:00 are devoted to basic fitness and stamina—sprints, jogging, interval running, work with weights, calisthenics. After a light lunch, the afternoon session (90 minutes to 2 hours) begins at 2:00 and centers on ball skills, usually ending with a series of five- or six-a-side games.

The second and possibly the third week of preseason training still occupies five and a half days, but the emphasis now turns away from fitness to individual performance and skills and the development of team tactics, though there will almost certainly be a couple of sessions during the week at the running track, with timed sprints. The remaining two or three weeks will be taken up with a schedule of games against not-too-difficult opponents; many English clubs now spend this period overseas, in Sweden or Holland, for instance, playing against local opposition.

Once the season proper has begun, the players train four days a week, in the mornings only, for two to two and a half hours each session. There is no training on game days, or on the day after. In England and Germany, game day is Saturday, with Sunday off. Other European countries, for example, Italy and Spain, play on Sundays, taking Monday off.

A couple of "typical" weeks—one in England, one in Argentina—might look like this:

**Typical Weekly Training Schedule
for a Player in the English Premiership**

All sessions last from 10:30 until 12:30 or 1:00 and all begin with a light workout: jogging, sprints, calisthenics, etc.

MONDAY Individual skills—ball control, dribbling, tackling, heading, etc.; six- or five-a-side games. Detailed discussion of previous Saturday's game.

TUESDAY Hard day. Either a full-scale game, dealing with specific points (usually weaknesses) of team play, or a morning at the track, including running of timed sprints.

WEDNESDAY Day off (during most of the season, there is a league or cup game on Wednesday evening).

THURSDAY Thorough rundown on the opposing team in the coming Saturday's game. Practice of specific game situations linked to this.

FRIDAY Sharpening up team play, with emphasis on "set-piece" plays such as throw-ins, corner kicks, free kicks.

SATURDAY Game in the afternoon.

SUNDAY Day off.

**Typical Weekly Training Schedule
for a Player in the Argentine First Division**

All sessions begin with a light warming-up and stretching workout lasting 10–15 minutes. Morning sessions last from 9:30 until 11:30 or possibly 12:00. Afternoon sessions are from 4:00 to 6:00 or 6:30.

TUESDAY Morning session only. Recuperation day after game played on Sunday. Five kilometer jog, followed by thirty minutes of 11 v 11 "fun play."

WEDNESDAY Morning: physical workout. Three kilometer run, followed by aerobic and anaerobic exercises involving speed, jumping, changing pace, etc. Afternoon: technique and tactics, with the ball. Small-sided games, reinforcing concepts of play: control, touch, accurate passing, under pressure. Also work on shooting, crosses.

THURSDAY Afternoon session only, at the same hour (usually 4:00) as the upcoming game on Sunday. Sixty or seventy minutes of soccer, 11 v 11. The starting team plays against the substitutes or against a local amateur or semi-pro team.

FRIDAY Morning session only, half devoted to an 11 v 11 game, half to tactics related specifically to Sunday's game—will include shooting, crosses, corner kicks, free kicks. Fifteen minutes of physical workout at end. At night—10:00—the team moves to a quiet hotel ("concentration") where it stays until Sunday's game.

SATURDAY Very light training, 9:30 until 11:00; twenty minutes of warming up, individual work with the ball, then amusement-type games (e.g., football tennis).

SUNDAY Game day.

MONDAY Day off.

This is an attempt to picture typical weeks, if there be any such thing. Some coaches may place their emphasis on different aspects of the game, some may want to include a session of weight training, some may insist on additional afternoon sessions if their team has struck a bad patch. In hot climates training is usually held in the early morning or late afternoon. "Concentration"—moving the team to a hotel for a couple of days before an important game—is also widely practiced in Italy and Brazil.

The man in charge of all this preparation is, of course, the coach. He will be an ex-player, though not necessarily a star. Many of the most brilliant soccer players have been a complete washout as coaches, while many of the most successful coaches were no more than average players. The chances are high that he will have been a defender in his playing days.*

The modern preference is for "track-suit" coaches, those who are young enough and fit enough—and skilled enough—to get out there with the boys and show them how it should be done. Most of today's coaches have attended training courses organized by their national F.A. and possess a coaching certificate or license.

As for the money, in Germany, where all Bundesliga coaches must have attended a six-month, full-time course to attain the German Federation's coaching license, the average salary is around $400,000 per year. About the same as it is in the English Premiership, where they do not require any formal qualification for their coaches.

Brazilians tend to give a monthly figure when talking of coaching salaries—a reflection of the chronic economic instability of the sport in the country. Coaches are hired for a season. If they don't win anything, and obviously most of them do not, they are likely to be looking for another job within a year. Coaches with top clubs like Flamengo and Palmeiras can earn

*See chapter 9, page 230

$20,000 a month ($240,000 a year), but the average is closer to $75,000 yearly.

Not that job insecurity is limited to Brazilian coaches. If a highly paid coach doesn't produce a winning team, he is likely to be shown the door, pronto. During the 1994–95 Premiership season in England, twelve (out of twenty-two) coaches were fired.

Even just one poor result can cause the axe to fall. In early 1993, Gigi Radice had his Fiorentina team purring along nicely in second place in the Italian Serie A. Then it lost a home game to lowly Atalanta. There was a violent locker-room confrontation between Radice and one of the Fiorentina owners, and that night Radice found himself out of a job. An extreme case, but one that forcefully makes the point: big-time soccer is no laughing matter.

The impetuous owner of Fiorentina was Vittorio Cecchi Gori, son of the late Mario Cecchi Gori, rich and famous as a film producer. The powerful business-tycoon-owner has come late to soccer, but he is now beginning to make his mark.

For most of soccer's history, there was no place for that very visible power group, so familiar in American sports: the owners—rich, powerful men running their clubs as profit-making businesses. The reason is to be found in soccer's history, in the insistence with which the English F.A. first spelled out in 1885 that the game be controlled by amateurs.

That sentiment was written into FIFA's regulations (with which all national F.A.s have to comply), which stated that a soccer club "shall not be used as a source of profit to its directors or shareholders."

The English F.A. regulations flatly prohibited a director from receiving any remuneration at all, while the shareholders' dividends were limited to 7.5 percent, a figure that was certainly not going to make anyone very rich. Which was exactly the idea: to keep the profiteers, the smart operators, and the hucksters out of soccer, to ensure that the men who ran soccer clubs had the interests of the sport at heart.

But who would want to be a shareholder or even a director under those conditions? Well, plenty of people did. People who wanted to get close to the game, who wanted to be part of its excitement, who wanted a say, however slight, in its control. These were people who felt the soccer image was good for their business, but all were fans of the game.

The typical owner or director was (and at most levels of soccer still is) a local businessman, with little or no playing experience and certainly none at the professional level. Far from making any money out of soccer, he was expected to come up with an interest-free loan if his club got into debt. If the club did make a profit, the money was expected to go "back into the game"—higher salaries for the players possibly or, less likely, better facilities, but not into the director's pocket.

That the idea worked cannot be denied, but it is a double-edged sword. The get-rich-quick boys were kept out, but so, too, were the wealthy backers that the sport needs. Far too many soccer clubs suffered from a marked lack of skill in administration and personnel management—a lack of professionalism.

Club control by small businessmen is common throughout Europe, at all levels of the game. But the situation has changed dramatically in the past decade. The English F.A. has removed the restrictions on profit making from its regulations. FIFA has modified its ban, and is pressing for soccer clubs to become limited-liability companies.

In Italy, where the game is at its richest and most commercialized, the situation now resembles the American experience. Wealthy individuals or families control most of the big clubs. Italy's most popular club, Juventus of Turin, is owned by the immensely rich Agnelli family, also the owners of the Fiat automobile company.

Wealthiest of all is unquestionably Silvio Berlusconi, the billionaire owner of AC Milan, former Prime Minister of Italy. He is the head of a holding company that grosses over $18 billion a year and has 34,000 employees. It includes the fourth-largest private television network in the world, along with publishing houses, department stores, property, construction companies, and 290 cinemas. Berlusconi has poured money into AC Milan, turning it into the most famous soccer club in the world. In 1992 he paid over $90 million to buy six top foreign players.

Spending at that level is unheard of elsewhere. Jack Walker, owner of the Blackburn Rovers, caused a sensation in England with his 1992 player purchases, by paying out $9 million—one tenth of Berluconi's spending spree.

The Spanish club Real Madrid has a totally different way of running its affairs, a way that is also popular in South America. At Real Madrid they do much more than just play soccer. There are facilities for swimming, athletics, tennis, and gymnastics, and the club has one of the strongest basketball teams in Europe. The financial core of Real Madrid is the money paid by the 62,000 members of the club: an annual fee of $200. Participation in any of the sports activities means further payments, the amount depending on the sport.

So successful has Real's formula been that their original buildings, grouped around the 115,000-seat Santiago Bernabeu stadium near the heart of Madrid, have long since proved too small. Since 1960 the club has developed a Sports City on a forty-acre site two miles from the city center, a complex of tennis courts, four swimming pools, basketball arena, gymnasia, track and field stadium, skating rink, five soccer fields, and two restaurants.

Madrileños who want to join the Real Madrid club face a two-year wait before they can even put their names on the waiting list. The club has had so many cases of fraudulent applications by people trying to jump the queue that it has a special committee that vets all applications.

The 62,000 members elect the president, who in turn appoints a fourteen-member board of directors to run the club which, in 1992–93, had an operating budget of $55.3 million.

Social aspects are even more pronounced in the major Brazilian clubs, particularly those in Rio de Janeiro—like the Fluminense Club, which runs a rather exclusive operation including, in addition to soccer and many other sports, dinners, dances, theater and movie shows, picnics, and parades. In São Paulo, Corinthians have built Corinthians City in the eastern suburb of Penha. It has a thousand-seat cinema and a hundred-room hotel, in addition to the usual swimming pools, gymnasia, stadiums, restaurants, and the like.

But whatever its structure, a soccer club lives or dies according to the number of spectators who pass through its turnstiles. The table below gives an idea of crowd sizes and admission prices in some of the major soccer countries throughout the world.

AVERAGE CROWDS AND ADMISSION PRICES IN FIRST DIVISION SOCCER, 1995

Country	Average Crowd	Admission Prices
Argentina	20,000	$5–$50
England	24,000	$12–$60
Italy	33,000	$20–$145
Spain	30,000	$15–$100
Germany	30,000	$9–$55

Other important sources of income to soccer clubs are sponsors, advertisements displayed at their stadiums, sale of game programs (though these are rare outside England), and radio and television, and sales of club merchandise.

Sponsors include banks, and manufacturers of electronic goods, food, gasoline, and soft drinks. In Italy and Germany, a club may receive from $325,000 to $3.5 million a year from its sponsor. For the sponsor, the most obvious advantage is to have its name prominently displayed on the front of the player's shirts.

Merchandise sales have skyrocketed in the last five years. In 1990, England's Manchester United made only $3 million from them, but by 1995 the total was $35 million. That put merchandise sales ahead of ticket sales as a revenue source.

Soccer has tended to treat television with a great deal of suspicion. Ten years ago live coverage of regular league games was comparatively rare. The fear throughout soccer was that fans would desert minor-league games en masse if they know they could stay at home and see first-division games on the box.

Television coverage was also held back by the fact that most of the major television networks were state-run monopolies that did not carry commercials, which meant a lack of interest from sponsors. The networks

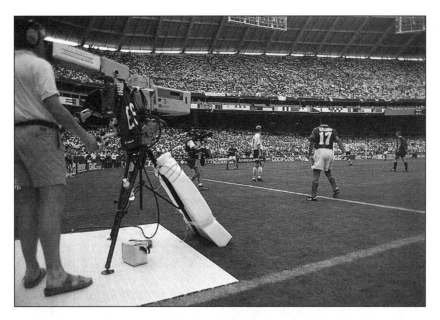

Until recently, live transmission of soccer games was rare. But that has changed dramatically in the 1990s as television has poured money into the sport. FIFA has received an offer of $1 billion for the TV rights to the 2002 World Cup.
© Peter Robinson: The Football Archive

were loath to telecast from stadiums where there were visible advertising signs. Teams that carried a sponsor's name on their shirts had to change to plain shirts for a televised game.

The conservative approach received solid backing from the state networks. They were quite content to pay small rights fees for broadcasting tape-delayed games and highlight shows.

As late as 1974, the money being paid by English television to the Football League was derisory by American standards. That year television offered a three-year contract at $4.7 million, or $1.57 million a year. When that was divided equally among the ninety-two clubs of the Football League's four divisions, it worked out at around $17,000 each. (That same year, National Football League clubs were getting over $1.5 million a year each from network television.)

Deregulation of television in the 1980s and the arrival of cable and satellite broadcasting shattered the old order forever. Competition and open sponsorship arrived, advertising boards proliferated all around the soccer fields, and the fees paid for game rights skyrocketed.

Such was the lure of the millions on offer that the structure of English soccer, unchanged for over one hundred years, was at last altered. The top English first-division clubs had long been fretting that they were held back in making commercial deals by their association with the three lower divisions of the Football League. When it came to television, the top clubs were the attraction; why should they share the money with second-, third-, and fourth-division clubs?

In 1992, the top clubs quit the Football League and formed the Premiership, under the nominal control of the Football Association. The new league's first move—indeed, the very thing that made the Premiership a reality—was to sign a five-year $600 million deal with the BBC and the satellite broadcasting company, BSkyB Television. In Germany, the 18-team Bundesliga club receives $84 million a year from a league deal with state television. In Spain, five national channels pay a combined fee of $40 million to televise soccer.

In 1987 FIFA entered into a long-term contract with a World Consortium of broadcasting unions, selling the rights to the 1990, 1994, and 1998 World Cups for a total of $228 million. A contract covering most of the 1990s, precisely the period when television investment in soccer skyrocketed. In 1995, the bids began to come in for the 2002 World Cup; they started at $1 billion.

But while FIFA pocketed TV money with one hand, the other hand was waving frantically, trying to ward off the flood of televised games being made available around the world.

The old problem—that televised top-class soccer would kill off live soccer of lesser caliber—had taken on an international aspect. Now Brazilian and German and English and Italian and Spanish championship games were available anywhere in the world, via satellite. Highlight packages from the leagues were being aggressively marketed—to say nothing of the ever-growing list of international games between clubs or national teams.

International soccer, which had started its life in leisurely fashion aboard steam trains and transatlantic liners, had now moved on through jumbo jets into the electronic age of instant travel. "The tide must be stemmed," said FIFA, but control of the airwaves, in the face of powerful TV-oriented entrepreneurs like Milan's Berlusconi, and the growing army of viewers equipped with satellite dishes, was not going to be easy.

While American sports have always raised their hands in horror at the very thought of gambling, soccer made peace with it many years ago and takes substantial sums of money from legal betting on its games. The weekly "flutter on the pools" is as much a part of English life as the pot of tea, engaged in by over 12 million English men and women, many of whom have not the slightest knowledge of, or interest in, soccer. Each pool's coupon contains a list of the week's games and the idea is to forecast a certain number of results—simply as a home win, an away win, or a tie.

There is no equivalent of point-spread betting in England. The winnings, tax free, can be enormous: in June 1992 a man from Bournemouth (who did not want to be named) won over $3.3 million for a stake of 80 cents, the sixth time that season that someone had won over $3 million. The pools are based on the Football League's game schedules, and for the rights to use these schedules the pools promoters pay the English soccer authorities over $13 million a year.*

In Italy, the pools—*il totocalcio*—are run by the National Olympic Committee, and 35 percent of the money wagered is used to develop all amateur sports—not just soccer—throughout the country.

One of the biggest items in any soccer club's budget, one that figures under both income and expenses is "transfer fees," the money spent or received for players who are traded. Very few of these deals involve the swapping of players. Usually, they are straight cash deals, which gives everyone the satisfaction of putting a price on a player's head, of knowing exactly how much he is worth.

In 1973 the soccer world was astonished at the sum that Barcelona paid to buy the Dutch superstar Johan Cruyff, who became the first player to be valued at $2 million.

Twenty years on, nobody bats an eyelid at $2 million; you get an ordinary player for that. Now the almighty lira rules. Italian clubs dominate the transfer scene, and the prices have soared. Currently, the most expensive player is the Italian Gianluigi Lentini, bought by Milan from Torino in 1992 for 30 billion lire—$20 million. Right behind him is another Italian, Gianlucca Vialli, who moved from Sampdoria to Juventus for a fee of $19 million.**

The rest of the world is left way behind. The record transfer fee for an English club is the $13 million that Liverpool paid to buy Stan Collymore from Nottingham Forest in 1995. In France it is $7.5 million (the Liberian forward, George Weah, from Monaco to Paris St. Germain, 1992), in Argentina $2.5 million (Claudio Caniggia, from Roma, Italy to Boca Juniors, 1995).

Paying high transfer fees carries tremendous risks. The player may turn out to be not nearly as good as imagined, or the mere fact of knowing that he is so highly valued may upset him. On the other hand, some clubs have paid out small fees and picked up bargains, none greater than Real Madrid's signing of Alfredo Di Stéfano—arguably the greatest player in the history of the game—for whom they paid $70,000 in 1953.

Pelé, another "greatest ever" candidate, never had a price placed on him in this way, for he played all his career for Santos and did not figure in a transfer deal. What we do know is that when, during the 1960s, there were rumors that the Italian club Juventus wanted to buy him, the Brazilian

---

* The only problem with the Football League's schedules is that the season does not last long enough. The insatiable English bettors spend the summer forecasting the results of soccer games played in Australia featuring teams they have never heard of and whose names they cannot pronounce.

**Being the most expensive player evidently does not mean being the best. When FIFA organized a vote among the world's coaches to come up with the World Player of the Year, 1992, Lentini and Vialli came in equal 33rd, with only 2 points each. The winner, Milan's Marco Van Basten, polled 161 points.

government stepped in to declare him a "national resource" and therefore nonexportable.

The explosive escalation of transfer fees draws regular and bitter complaints from the top soccer clubs on how ridiculous and potentially ruinous it all is. But no sooner has the latest broadside been delivered than one of their number forks out a new record sum for another star player.

Menacing as they may seem to the clubs that have to pay them, large transfer fees can be the salvation of the smaller clubs that are lucky enough to receive them. Such clubs frequently live a precarious financial existence, and their continual hope is to discover and develop a young player whose sale will wipe out their overdraft.

Behind the whole system of transfer fees is what, in American sports, is called the reserve clause: the clause in a player's contract that binds him to his club. In soccer, it used to be an unbreakable bond. Unbreakable as far as the player was concerned; the Italians called it the *vincolo a vita*— the bond for life. Once a player had signed for a professional club, he remained the property of that club unless and until they agreed to release him or transfer him to another club.

The arrangement allowed the player very little say in his own career. He could not, when his contract expired, go shopping around, dealing with any club he chose, to see where he could get the best deal. He had to deal only with his current club; it would decide if he was to be traded, and to which club.

Today, the reserve clause has been considerably weakened. Most countries now have tribunals that settle disputes between players and clubs, and that set reasonable fees for player transfers. In some countries, for example, Brazil, players over 30 are permitted to own their contracts.

But it took legal action to really shatter the reserve clause. Jean Marc Bosman applied to the European Court of Justice to have the whole system declared illegal. Bosman was a little-known player in Belgium, one of the few countries where the reserve clause had not been modified. Bosman's claim was that his career had been blighted when his former club, RFC Liege, refused to allow him to leave for another club, even though his contract had expired. Liege cut his salary by three quarters, and asked an absurdly high price for his transfer, thereby effectively blocking any move.

Bosman doggedly pursued his case through the courts for five years, before, in December 1995, the European Court ruled that it was illegal for clubs to receive a transfer fee for players whose contracts had expired.

Immediate reaction to the decision ranged from those who hailed it as a great triumph for players' rights, to those who believed that it would put many small clubs—those that survived by developing and selling players— out of existence.

A player who is in dispute with his club cannot jump his contract and leave the country to play for a foreign team. Soccer's restrictions take in the whole world, and they work like this. All professional players are registered not only with the league that they play in but also with their national

F.A. Whenever they change clubs, the transfer has to be registered with the F.A.; indeed, the player cannot play for his new club until that registration has been made.

If a player moves from one country to another, he must present a certificate of transfer, duly signed by his old F.A., stating that he is a player in good standing and not in violation of any contracts with previous clubs.

A copy of this certificate has to be sent to FIFA because one of the functions of FIFA is to see that its members respect each other's regulations and disciplinary measures: A player under suspension in one country, for example, is automatically under suspension in every other FIFA country. FIFA's power to enforce its decisions is considerable, as it can effectively ostracize a player, or a club, or a league, or even an F.A. from worldwide soccer.

If a player defaults on a contract, his national F.A. suspends him and informs FIFA, which then alerts all its members. The player becomes a pariah, shunned worldwide by any club he may approach. Dealing with single players is easy enough for FIFA, but even whole leagues do not fare much better, as the celebrated Colombia episode demonstrated.

In 1950 a group of wealthy businessmen decided to introduce professional soccer into Colombia. Unable to come up with enough top-class Colombian players to make a go of it, they started to look around for foreign stars. What they didn't particularly like about that arrangement was that it would mean paying hefty transfer fees to the foreign clubs.

Or would it? It occurred to the new league that if it ignored FIFA regulations and broke away from the Colombian F.A., it would then be free to approach directly any player it wanted, and sign him without having to pay a cent to his club. Large salaries and signing-on bonuses were offered to top South American players.

The Colombian promoters were greatly helped by the fact that Argentine soccer was going through one of its recurrent crises, with players striking for more money. Eventually a group of top Argentine players (they included Alfredo Di Stéfano), plus others from Uruguay, Paraguay, Hungary, and England, joined the Colombian pirate league, despite dire warnings from FIFA that any player doing so faced worldwide suspension and fines should he ever want to play again outside the league.

The "millionaires' league," totally cut off from international competition and unable to attract more than a handful of top stars, was brought to its knees, and collapsed in 1952.* The Colombian F.A. resumed control of the sport in Colombia, and the clubs of the league were granted two years to return the players they had poached to their former clubs (one who did not go back was Di Stéfano—he joined Real Madrid instead).

FIFA brings together the national governing bodies of soccer—the F.A.s—from throughout the world, and constitutes an international network

---

* A similar situation involving a pirate league arose in the U.S. in 1967—see chapter 10, page 248.

Like the United Nations, only bigger. The full FIFA Congress—seen here in session in Chicago in 1994—had 191 member countries in 1995, six more than the United Nations. The Congress meets once every two years; between sessions FIFA business is run by the 23-member Executive Committee.
© Peter Robinson: The Football Archive

that is often referred to as "organized soccer." It has more members than the United Nations; at latest count the score was 191–185 in favor of FIFA.

A meeting of the full FIFA Congress is not unlike a UN General Assembly meeting: 191 countries, each identified with printed cards and represented by up to three delegates, many of them using headphones to listen to proceedings in simultaneous translation. The congress meets once every two years, each time in a different city. The detailed running of FIFA is done by the Executive Committee (the members are elected by the congress for a four-year term) and by the full-time secretary and a staff of forty-two at FIFA's headquarters in Zurich, Switzerland. In addition, there are fourteen standing committees, plus a disciplinary and an appeals committee.

The Continental Confederations (see diagram opposite on page 175) are a way of decentralizing some of FIFA's activities, and allowing a degree of home rule. They resolve disputes between national F.A.s within their own continents, and also organize major tournaments—UEFA runs the various European club competitions and the European Championship for national teams, and the South American Federation (CSF) organizes the Copa Libertadores and the Copa America. But in all cases the competitions have to be conducted according to FIFA regulations.

Structure of the Fédération Internationale de Football Association

FIFA CONGRESS

The legislative body and supreme authority • Meets every two years
Composition:
Voting: each of FIFA's 191 national associations has one vote and may be
represented by up to three delegates
Nonvoting: members of the FIFA Executive Committee

FIFA EXECUTIVE COMMITTEE

The executive body • Meets twice
a year
Compositon:
President (elected by Congress)
8 vice-presidents (appointed by the
Continental Confederations)
12 members (appointed by the
Continental Confederations)

CONTINENTAL CONFEDERATIONS*

Africa
Confederation Africaine
de Football (CAF)
**North and Central America
and the Caribbean**
Confederación Norte-
Centroamerican del Caribe
del Fútbol (CONCACAF)
South America
Confederación Sudamericana
de Fútbol (CSF or CONMEBOL)
Asia
Asian Football Confederation (AFC)
Europe
Union of European Football
Associations (UEFA)
Oceania
Oceania Football Confederation (OFC)

GENERAL SECRETARIAT

The administrative body
Full-time Secretary-General, plus
supporting staff, working out of FIFA's
headquarters in Zurich, Switzerland

STANDING COMMITTEES

Emergency • Finance • World Cup
Organizing • Olympic Tournament
Organizing • Youth Competitions •
Futsal (Indoor Soccer) •
Women's Soccer • Referees •
Technical • Sports Medical •
Players' Status • Legal Matters •
Security Matters and Fair Play •
Media • Protocol • Organizing
Intercontinental Championship •
FIFA/Confederations Consultative

Plus two judicial committees:
Disciplinary • Appeal

INTERNATIONAL FOOTBALL ASSOCIATION BOARD

Responsible for the Rules of Soccer
8 members
4 of the members are appointed by FIFA
(they normally include the FIFA president,
the secretary-general, and the chairman
of the Referees' Committee) The other 4
members are one representative
each from the English, Scottish, Welsh,
and Northern Irish Football Associations.
Any proposed change in the Rules must
have at least six votes in favor to pass.

* For full list of all the member nations of each confederation, see Appendix C, pages 311–313.

Soccer Players Registered Throughout the World

Continental Confederation*	Pro	Amateur & Youth	Over 35	Women	Indoor	Totals
Africa	1,436	944,896	160,881	30,475	21,084	1,158,772
Asia	1,211	46,122,761	5,562,755	949,430	713,960	53,350,117
Concacaf**	5,005	4,663,854	146,956	2,174,188	270,980	7,260,983
Europe	20,610	21,310,868	285,567	679,075	264,271	22,560,391
Oceania		609,591	33,032	17,864	18,000	678,487
South America	4,406	2,090,272	871,960	95,500	21,771	3,083,909
	32,668	75,742,242	7,061,151	3,946,532	1,310,066	88,092,659

These figures represent the number of players in so-called organized soccer, i.e., players who are registered with their national associations. The overall total of soccer players throughout the world is considerably larger than the 88.1 million total shown in the table, for there are large numbers of all ages who play casually. Estimates go as high as a total of 120 million players. (Based on figures supplied by FIFA.)

*For full list of all the member nations of each Confederation see Appendix C, pages 311–313.
**North and Central America and the Caribbean.

A glance at the statistics issued by the Players' Status Committee underlines the inescapable fact that in terms of the number of players organized soccer is an overwhelmingly amateur sport. FIFA recognizes two classes of registered players: amateur, and nonamateur. Grouped according to Continental Confederations, the relative numbers in these two classes are shown in the table opposite, on page 176.

FIFA estimates that there are some 150 million registered players in organized soccer. Of these, only 32,000 are professionals, which means that over 99 percent of the world's soccer is played by amateurs. Appropriately, their games are officiated by amateur referees.

Not so appropriate is the use of amateur referees in professional games. It has to be that way, because there are virtually no full-time referees in soccer. Top referees will have taken courses run by their own country's F.A., they will have passed certification tests, they will undoubtedly be devoted men. But they are part-timers.

The fees paid to referees vary from modest ($375 per game in the English Premiership) to pretty good ($1,750 in the *Bundesliga*). In Brazil, referees are paid .005 percent of the gate money from their games; a $50,000 take will give them a $250 fee. In Italy the per game fee is $1,000; expenses are liberal, and referees can receive up to $30,000 a year in compensation for time lost from their jobs.

At best, the leading referees can be classified as semiprofessionals. But in one key respect they remain out-and-out amateurs, because the vast majority of them have never played professional soccer.

This is a disadvantage at the pro level right from the start, for it undermines their authority and induces a defensive (or an overly assertive) frame of mind. Sad but true, the prevailing attitude of pro players to referees ranges from mild scorn to utter contempt. Not that too much should be read into that, for by the very nature of their work referees are hardly likely to find themselves showered with praise from players.

Nobody, not even the most critical of players, suggests that the soccer referee's life is an easy one. He is in sole command of a fast-moving, physical game on a field that is about sixteen times the size of a basketball court. For ninety minutes he has to be everywhere, see everything, and make a constant string of snap judgments—and they had better be the right ones.

But what is undeniable is that under the present system of part-timers, there is a huge variation in the performance of referees, and even in the way in which they interpret the rules. Increasingly, the part-time referee looks like an anachronism in the supercharged, highly commercialized world of pro soccer.

"While football has changed dramatically in terms of pace, competitiveness and anxiety for reward, it is still controlled on the field, where it matters most, from the ranks of the clerks, and shopkeepers and foremen. . . ." That was how an English writer saw things in 1968.*

The clerks and the shopkeepers and the foremen are still in charge, even though the changes in the game have accelerated rapidly.

* Arthur Hopcraft, *The Football Man* (London: Collins, 1968).

–8–
Tactics

Hop into your time-capsule and whoosh yourself back to England in the year 1873. They've been playing soccer under the London Football Association's 1863 rules for ten years now. Head for the nearest soccer field, and ask the players what tactics they employ (don't bother looking for the coach; there won't be one). Note the way the players look at you. They have no idea what you are talking about. Before they start giving each other sidelong glances, before they send for the men in the white suits, retire quickly to your capsule and head back to the present.

There were no tactics in 1873, and even the word itself was unknown in a soccer context. Coaches were not in vogue. For soccer, one of the consequences of being born in England was that nobody really thought about it in depth. It was, after all, only a sport, and all of its early exponents were amateurs who played it simply for enjoyment.

The English have always had a suspicion of analyses and intellectual explanations (something best left to foreigners, the French perhaps), and certainly sport was the very last thing to start getting intellectual about. Soccer was fun, it was healthy, it was manly—why complicate it with thought?

So there is little evidence in soccer's early days of any methodical, thought-out approach to the game. Soccer was, on the whole, a game that was improvised by the players on the field. Things happened during play, perhaps by chance, and if they worked they could be adopted and tried again.

The inspiration of the improvisations, the very lifeblood of those early games, was the skill of dribbling. The sport was often called "the dribbling game." The reason for all this dribbling was built into those 1863 rules, which totally banned the forward pass. Any attacking player who ran ahead of the dribbler was automatically "out of play" as it was then termed, offside as it is now called. Only lateral or backward passes could be used, and evidently they were not considered as much fun as dribbling. Even when the rule was changed, in 1866, to permit an advanced player to receive a pass—providing he had at least *three* opponents between him and the goal-line—it made little difference to the way the game was played.

Heads-down dribbling continued to rule. You got the ball, and you dribbled past as many opponents as you could. If you lost the ball, there would hopefully be one of your teammates nearby to reclaim it and start his own individual dribbling odyssey.

Indeed, the mere fact of a teammate being nearby might be considered a tactical triumph in the 1870s, when C.W. Alcock, an early soccer pundit, was writing of "the grand and essential principle of backing up. By 'backing up' of course I shall be understood to mean the following closely on a fellow-player to assist him, if required, or to take on the ball in case of his being attacked, or otherwise prevented from continuing his onward course." There is no suggestion here that the player with the ball should actually *pass* it to the backer-up.

With this tremendous emphasis on individuality, soccer was not yet a team game and there was no place, indeed no need, for team tactics. The idea of the game was simple enough—to score goals. To this end the early teams swamped their offenses with eight or nine forwards, left two or three defenders to cope as best they could, and got on with the business of dribbling the ball through enemy lines: the goalkeeper, as a specific player who could handle the ball, did not enter the picture until the 1870s.

At about the same time, the Scots—those incorrigible rogues from the north who have never since lost the art of upsetting the staid ways of English soccer—fomented soccer's first revolution. Simply by doing what today seems so utterly obvious: They invented the pass. At last the potential for the forward pass, opened up by the 1866 rule change, began to be realized.

Teamwork based on passing entered the game. The Scotts exhibited their talents during that first 1872 international game against England in Glasgow. The English went home suitably impressed with the new "combination play," as they also were with the Scottish system of using two full-backs rather than one. Both teams were still using seven or eight forwards, and for those who think that such extravagance in attack ought to have produced a deluge of goals, it didn't. The result was a 0–0 tie.

The new Scottish style was based on short passes made along the ground. It radically altered the nature of soccer and the mentality, to say nothing of the skills, of the players. From being a game of individuals in which one skill, dribbling, was paramount and in which players tended to cluster around the ball, it opened out into a team game.

Now, instead of opportunistic backers-up trailing the dribbler like carrion crows in the hope of picking up a loose ball, players had to start thinking about their positional play. They had to take up positions where they could receive the ball. The dribbler was now obliged to get his head up to see what was going on, to decide when to continue dribbling, when to pass, and where to pass. And he had to master the new skill of passing the ball accurately.

Soccer soon found another weapon to add to dribbling and short passing—the long pass. In the light of the subsequent development of the English game, it is entirely appropriate that the English themselves thought up this new development. It was the "secret weapon" of Blackburn Olympic, the team from the north of England that broke the 11-year stranglehold that southern teams had maintained on the famous F.A.Cup. In the 1883 cup final, Blackburn used the long pass to repeatedly bamboozle the Old Etonians with wing-to-wing passing.

More new skills were needed—not only the ability to hit a long ball accurately, but the techniques necessary to receive, or intercept, or clear long passes. As the ball was more frequently in the air, heading, chest-trapping, receiving on the run, and volleying were now much more important parts of the game.

Suddenly soccer was no longer a game where the action was centered around the ball and a few nearby players. Now play might suddenly switch seventy yards from one touchline to the other. The field was getting smaller; no player could now feel that he wasn't involved, wherever the ball might be.

Players had to cover a lot more ground; they needed to be fitter than in the past. Then, in 1885 the English F.A. gave up its losing battle and legalized professionalism. The game was getting serious, was turning into something more than a pastime for amateurs.

With the old individualism being replaced by team play, with professional players now entering the picture, tactics became inevitable. Thus began the slow evolution of the sport, a sort of numbers game that reflects attempts to arrive at formations that ensure an ever more effective distribution of the eleven players on the field.

Depictions of soccer formations always start with the defense, and always include only ten players. It is not considered necessary to include the goalkeeper, as his is the one position in soccer that has remained unchanged over the years.

The fullbacks come first. The formation of those early, offense-laden teams with two fullbacks and eight forwards would thus be 2–8. This was gradually modified to create a balance between defense and offense. First one forward dropped back to become a halfback (2–1–7), then two (2–2–6). By 1900 there were three halfbacks, giving a 2-3-5 formation.

Which is a good moment to pause for some general comments on soccer terminology. As the sport spread throughout the world, it took English words with it, words that were soon "adapted" into foreign languages. The very word football became, phonetically, *fútbol* in Spanish, *futebol* in Portuguese, and for the French *le football* (or simply *le foot*). The cry of "Goal!" was heard all over South America, though they spelled the word *gol*. The Brazilians called the backs *os beques,* the Italians called them *i bec* and shouted *enz!* for "hands" when a player touched the ball.

It wasn't long before each country began to invent its own terms, and an assortment of soccer vocabularies in a variety of languages sprang up all over the world.

But not in the United States, where the English soccer vocabulary came into use. Not only was it authoritative, but it was conveniently in the same language (or one near enough to pass as the same language) as well. The use of English terms has persisted. This is not a particularly satisfactory arrangement. English terminology has failed to move with the times.

Once a simple and acceptable soccer formation had been worked out (the 2-3-5), and the player positions had been given names, the stubborn English resistance to change took over. The game did alter on the field, but the English, in their terminology, did not acknowledge the changes. They went on using (and to some extent still do use) the original but now highly misleading terms for player positions.

Not all the eccentricities of soccer's technical language can be laid at the door of the English. Soccer is the least static of games, in which twenty of the twenty-two players are in almost constant movement, making the concept of "positional play" an extremely elastic one. Playing roles that are so easy to define on paper, or to illustrate in diagrams, tend to become alarmingly vague on the field.

The 2-3-5, for instance. With the team lined up in its own half of the field, waiting to kick off, the 2-3-5 can be represented as in Diagram 1.

Neat—but deceiving. Anyone watching a 2-3-5 team in action and hoping to see a line of five forwards moving smoothly up and down the field, with a line of three halfbacks always just the right distance behind it, and the two fullbacks correctly positioned farther back, would watch in vain. There is altogether too much fluidity about soccer for it to be a game of rigid positional play.

The names given to each player position are shown in the diagram and need no further explanation. The numbers next to each position need a great deal of explaining. First, we are jumping the gun by about thirty years, for numbering was rare in soccer until the 1930s. Second, when it did come, it came more as a means of identifying positions than players. No. 2 was always the right back, No. 3 was always the left back. If right back Joe Smith was switched to left back for a game, then he would swap his No. 2 shirt for the No. 3 shirt.

A pattern was set—and it still exists today—of describing a player by use of his number. "He's a good No. 9" means he's a good center forward. There was never any question of a player being assigned a number that was always his, to wear whatever position he played. That is still the general rule throughout most of the soccer world. In major tournaments such as the World Cup players are required to always wear the same number, and the practice is now used in the English and German leagues.

Because it was the first widely applied team formation and remained the standard for nearly fifty years, the 2-3-5 is often called the classic formation. And for obvious reasons it is also known as the pyramid.

Diagram 1: The 2-3-5 Pyramid Formation

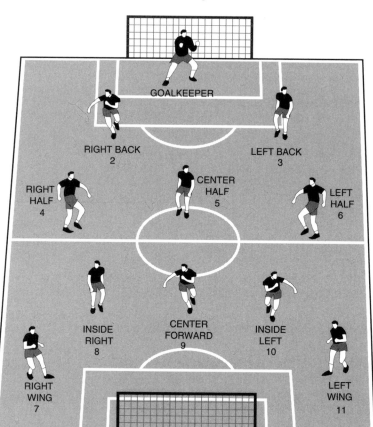

GOALKEEPER

RIGHT BACK
2

LEFT BACK
3

RIGHT
HALF
4

CENTER
HALF
5

LEFT
HALF
6

INSIDE
RIGHT
8

CENTER
FORWARD
9

INSIDE
LEFT
10

RIGHT
WING
7

LEFT
WING
11

"Wing half" was a term applied to either the right or the left half. The right wing and the left wing are known alternatively as the outside right and the outside left, or as the right winger and the left winger.

That was the shape of things in the early 1900s. Rudimentary tactics there undoubtedly were, team-play, too, but the English still did not use either term. In *Association Football and The Men Who Made It,* a four-volume, 850-page encyclopedia of the sport published in London in 1907, you will search in vain for any mention of tactics. Team-play is referred to as *combination-play* and is seen as something desirable that—even at this comparatively late date—is being resisted by the hardy individualists.

Clearly, with five forwards, the 2-3-5 stressed attacking soccer. Only three players, the goalkeeper and the two fullbacks, were out-and-out defenders. The job of the fullbacks was to protect the vital central area in front of the goal. The three halfbacks were expected to be both attackers

Soccer the way it was in England in 1913 . . . still very much the dribbling game. Not much evidence of positional play here, with most of the players keeping close to the ball. From a watercolor by Ernest Prater.
Courtesy of © FIFA Museum Collection

and defenders. The two outside halfbacks (the wing halves) had, as their defensive duties, the job of keeping the opposing wingers quiet.

But it was the center half who was the focal point of the team. Primarily an attacking player, he was the brain of the team, the instigator of attacking moves. From his key position at the center of things, he was the team leader. He could decide whether to pass left or right, long or short, whether to dribble, or whether to surge forward into the opposing penalty area looking for a scoring chance.

Like some brilliantly plumaged bird he strode around the field, glittering in all directions, the multiskilled all-rounder of his day, the glory of the 2-3-5 game. And like many another gaudy-feathered creature, he is now long dead and gone.

What killed him off was a change in the rules in 1925. The complaint in that year (the very same one that was to recur sixty years later) was that not enough goals were being scored. Worse yet, attacking moves were being stifled before they got anywhere near goal by defenses that had become masters of the "offside trap."

At that time a player was offside unless he had three opponents between himself and the goal line when the ball was passed to him. The complaint was that this made life too easy for the fullbacks. What was continually happening was that at the first sign of an opponent's attack, one of the two fullbacks, instead of falling back to cover, would move quickly upfield, away from his goal, leaving only two defenders (the other fullback and the goalkeeper) deep, and invariably trapping the opposing forwards in offside positions. For the spectators—and soccer was now a well-established professional sport—the repeated interruptions of the game as the referee whistled for offside were sheer frustration.

Something had to be done, and the solution was sought in a way that is familiar enough in American sports, but which is rare in soccer: The rules were changed. The offside rule was amended, and from 1925 on, an attacker needed only two opponents between himself and the goal. This made the offside trap a much riskier proposition. Under the old rule if things went wrong, there was still one fullback in a position to challenge. Now both fullbacks would have to move up, and the goalkeeper would be left on his own if they mistimed their move.

Justification for the rule change came immediately. The number of goals in the English first division shot up by over 40 percent, from 1,192 in 1925 to 1,703 in 1926. Now it was the defenders' turn to worry.

Reaction was swift, effective—and tactical. Defenses had to be strengthened, and it was Herbert Chapman who worked out how to do it. Chapman, an example of an average player who turned into a first-class coach, took over the London club Arsenal in 1925, the same year the offside rule was altered. He was then fifty-two years old, and his first step was to sign a veteran player, the thirty-four-year-old Charlie Buchan as his captain.

Arsenal made a poor start under this new regime, and after a disastrous 0–7 defeat by Newcastle, Buchan and Chapman put their heads together to work out a tactical plan to counter the newfound freedom with which forwards were scoring. The player who was doing most of the damage, scoring most of the goals, was the center forward. They decided to put a crimp in his activities by deploying a third fullback, stationed between the other two, whose primary task would be to closely mark the center forward. So was born the first example of the modern-style man-to-man marker. He was soon nicknamed "the stopper," or "the policeman," fair assessments of his negative role.

The change set off a ripple of other changes through the 2-3-5 system. The attacking center half vanished from the English game. His position no longer existed. But the English stubbornly and illogically continued to use the term center half, only now they meant the third fullback. A term that had once (accurately) described an attacking halfback with a glorious repertoire of creative skills, was now applied (inaccurately) to a fullback, who needed to be physically robust, good at heading and tackling, and who never, but never, moved up on attack. (To this day, the English persist in their perversity, even describing the twin centerbacks of the modern game as twin center halves.)

The gaping hole left at the center of the team by the killing off of the old center half was filled by pulling the two inside forwards back to join the two remaining halfbacks. This gave a four-man midfield (the Italians dubbed it the "magic square") and a 3-4-3 configuration, though the formation is usually referred to as the W-M. A look at Diagram 2 will explain why.

Diagram 2: The W-M Formation

*The numbers are inserted to show the relationship between this forma-
tion and the 2-3-5. Thus the center half of the 2-3-5 system, No. 5, has
been withdrawn to become a third fullback. His logical title is center
back, but the English continued to call him the center half.*

Defensive responsibilities were now changed around, with the two outside fullbacks responsible for marking the opposing wingers, and the wing
halves the opposing inside forwards.

The diagram, as always, not only simplifies but also falsifies. In the defensive W, Arsenal would have been horrified to see their three fullbacks playing in a straight line across the field (playing "square," as the English call it).
Horrified, because with such positioning a fullback who is beaten has no teammate behind him to provide what has become known as defensive cover.
To provide this cover, the Arsenal W was always a lopsided one, with the fullback farthest away from the ball retreating to a deep position, and the stopper slightly less deep. Responding to an attack by the opposing left winger,

Diagram 3: Lopsided Shape of the Defensive W

As an attack develops from the opponent's left wing (position X), 2 moves forward to meet the challenge, and 5 and 3 drop deeper so that they are in position to cover 2 should he be beaten.

for instance, the Arsenal right back would move up to challenge, while the stopper, the left back, and the left half fell back as shown in Diagram 3.

Ultimately any system of play stands or falls with the men who put it into practice. Arsenal's W-M prevailed because of the genius of Herbert Chapman in finding just the right players to fill the roles he had worked out. The ideal stopper was Herbie Roberts, not a greatly skilled player, but strong enough and tall enough to beat opponents on the ground and in the air, and with the placid temperament necessary for the unadventurous job he had to do. Roberts became the prototype of all stoppers, the tall, heavy backs who were to dominate defenses in English soccer for so long.

Arsenal's new tactics, though based on reinforcing the defense, were anything but negative in practice. In attack they employed two fast wingers with the ability to cut inside and score goals, while in the middle there was always a burly and brave center forward like Ted Drake, who could score with his head or with either foot.

The key to the success of the Arsenal W-M, though, lay in the function of one of the withdrawn inside forwards. This man now replaced the old attacking center half as the orchestrator of the team, receiving the ball from his own defense and deciding quickly what to do with it—whether to hit it short or long, to the wing or down the middle, or whether to dribble through on his own. The position called not only for a player who had the soccer skills to do all these things, but also for one with the coolness and judgment to read situations quickly and decide which was the correct move to make. That was Charlie Buchan's role until his retirement in 1928. Chapman then brought in Alex James, the wee Scot with the baggy shorts, one of the great geniuses of soccer who was to steer Arsenal to triumph after triumph.

Chapman died in 1934, but between 1927 and 1938 the team that he built won the league championship five times, the F.A. Cup twice, and became known throughout the world as the elite of soccer. Such success did not go unnoticed, and by the late 1930s the W-M, complete with stopper, was the standard formation of every English club.

The defensive tilt was beginning to settle on soccer, for where Chapman had been a true originator, his disciples were content to copy mechanically as far as they could what he had done. And it was much, much easier to copy the third-back defensive alignment than it was to copy the attacking system. After all, finding a big stolid fullback to do Herbie Roberts's job was easy enough, but who could copy Alex James?

The old-style attacking center half may have been banished from the English game, but the breed was not yet extinct. It flourished outside Britain, particularly in Hungary, Austria, and South America, where they still favored the 2-3-5.

In the first World Cup in 1930, both finalists—Argentina and Uruguay—used the 2-3-5 formation. Artistry was the essence of South American soccer, and it was by and large individual talent that decided games. Tactics, evidently, were at a minimum. Asked years later about the role of coaching in those days, the Uruguayan left back Ernesto Mascheroni replied: "What are the coaches for? Only the player can solve problems on the field. What does a player do when he meets another who makes a fool of him? Ask the coach?" Argentina's Carlos Peucelle recalled, "We didn't talk about tactics, we just went out and played, and each of us knew what it was that we had to do."

Maybe, but there are strong suggestions that the Uruguayans were a better-organized team than the Argentines. After the defeat, the Argentine press complained that whereas the Uruguayan halfbacks advanced the ball with passing movements up to their forwards, the Argentine defense was forever kicking long balls that were picked off by the Uruguayans.

The game finished on a note that, over sixty years later, has a familiar ring to it: Argentina, trailing by three goals to two, was doing all the attacking, but it was Uruguay who scored on a breakaway.

In Italy the national team was coached by Vittorio Pozzo, an implacable authoritarian noted for his astute psychological handling of his players. Pozzo had never been much of a player, but he was greatly interested in tactics. For his 1934 World Cup team he devised a scheme based on the classic 2-3-5, as played by the Austrians, Czechs, and Hungarians, the so-called Danubian school of soccer.

Which is where the ubiquitous Scots enter the picture again. For the Danubian school had developed from the Scottish short-passing game, brought to Central Europe by a remarkable Englishman named Jimmy Hogan.

Hogan, like Chapman and Pozzo, had never excelled as a player. But while with the London club Fulham he developed an interest in the theory of the sport. He played alongside and studied and listened to the Scottish professionals on the team. From them he formed his philosophy of the game, one that was never to change: that soccer was a game where the ball belonged on the ground, where it was to be moved around by short, quick passes, to players who moved intelligently into space. "Keep it on the carpet!" was a phrase much used by Hogan.

Arguably the first true coach of any stature in soccer, Hogan was a prophet without honor in his own country. The English weren't interested in his ideas, and his first coaching job came in Holland, in 1910. In 1912, Hogan moved to Austria, where he formed a lifelong friendship with another student of the game, Hugo Meisl. Wherever he went—and he was to coach in Austria, Hungary, and Germany on and off for the next twenty-four years—Hogan preached his "Keep it on the carpet!" gospel.

The Danubian style, based on the 2-3-5, was faithful to Hogan's concept, a neat, thoughtful, almost artistic approach to the game. By 1934 the Austrians had raised the style to its pinnacle. Hugo Meisl was now the national coach, and Austria was considered the strongest team in continental Europe, dubbed the *Wunderteam.*

The Italians at this time had little soccer contact with England (the two countries played each other for the first time in 1933), so it was natural that Pozzo should look to neighboring Austria for inspiration.

Pozzo felt that he could not simply copy the Danubian model—because he did not have a player to fill the vital, playmaking center half role. The player he had in mind for the position was Luis Monti, an *oriundo* who had played for Argentina in the 1930 World Cup final.

Monti, now thirty-three years old, had never been known as a great runner. Pozzo abandoned all thought of using him as an attacking center half, and gave him a more defensive midfield role, where his emphatic tackling and excellent long-passing could be exploited to the fullest.

The role of midfield general and playmaker, formerly filled by the center half, was taken over by two players, the inside forwards Giuseppe Meazza and Giovanni Ferrari, who were withdrawn into midfield.

Thus Pozzo's *metodo,* as it was called, retained elements of the 2-3-5 (particularly the marking assignments under which the fullbacks guarded

Diagram 4: The Italian Metodo

A combination of the 2-fullback, 3-halfback formation of the 2-3-5, plus the attacking M of the W-M. In the Italian metodo *the center half (CH) was still primarily an attacking player.*

the penalty area and the wing halves marked the opposing wingers), but used the M formation for the forward line—a 2-3-M (see Diagram 4).

Monti's role at center half was more defensive than in the classic 2-3-5, but he was far from being the relatively static stopper center back that had become the defensive mainstay of the W-M formation.

The *metodo* proved ideally suited to the Italian player. It stressed methodical defense: As one Italian journalist put it, "The other team does all the attacking, but Italy wins the game." This was the birth of the lightning counterattack, which was to be the basis of the Italian game for so long.

In the 1934 World Cup final, the *metodo* triumphed over the Danubian 2-3-5 of the Czechs. Or did it? The general feeling was that strength and stamina, coupled with more than a hint of ruthlessness, had played a large role in the Italians' 2–1 win.

In the 1938 World Cup final, it was virtually the same match-up: Italian *metodo* against Danubian 2-3-5, this time represented by the Hungarians. An easy 4–2 win for the Italians. The *metodo* had proved itself capable of development, of accommodating a new, faster, more athletic type of game. The 2-3-5 was stagnating, its defensive system no longer adequate. The Hungarians looked slow and just plain old-fashioned.

For the first time in a World Cup final, basic tactics, represented by team formations, and the Italians' more intelligent disposition on the field, were clearly a factor. After a reign of some fifty years, the 2-3-5 was on the way out. It would not be seen again in a World Cup final.

In the years before World War II, then, three main systems of play were in use:

1. The W-M—the standard formation in England.

2. The Italian *metodo*—part W-M, part 2-3-5.

3. The 2-3-5—the pyramid, still favored in South America and Czechoslovakia, Hungary, and Austria.

Within the various systems, soccer had become a game for specialist players, each with certain rather limited functions. Wingers, for instance, invariably stayed wide, waiting out on the touchline for the ball to come to them. It was not their job to retreat into their own half in search of the ball, nor were they often to be seen tackling opponents. Similarly, the center forward stayed upfield as the spearhead of the attack. The stopper had the most limited role of all, rarely if ever getting into his opponents' half of the field. The two wing halfbacks came closest to being all-round players.

There was one system that flew in the face of this trend toward specialization, a system that did not receive at the time the study that it deserved. Partly this was because it was developed in Switzerland, not exactly a mecca for soccer experts, and partly because it was a difficult theory to put into practice.

The *verrou,* or Swiss bolt, system was concocted by Karl Rappan, a former Austrian international player who from 1931 was the coach of Servette–Geneva, and later of Grasshoppers–Zurich. The aim of the bolt system was to create a team that would outnumber opponents in both attack and defense, something that was possible only with players capable of switching rapidly from attacking to defensive roles and vice versa. On attack, the bolt had a 3-3-4 shape, complete with an attacking center half, and with all the players, including the three-man fullback line moving well upfield (see Diagram 5).

When possession of the ball was lost, all ten players retreated. The function of the four forwards was to harass their opponents, to slow down their

Diagram 5: Verrou: Attacking Formation

A 3-3-4 formation, with the center half (CH) playing an attacking roll.
(The verrou *is also called the Swiss bolt formation.)*

attack, while the other six players raced back deep into their own half to take up the formation shown in Diagram 6.

The attacking center half now became the center back, while the former center back retreated to an ultradeep position behind everyone else. From here he could move laterally across the field, covering the other three backs and functioning as the sliding "bolt" to lock out opposing forwards.

The bolt system needed disciplined, highly fit players who could cope with a good deal of high-speed running, who had the skill to operate both as attackers and defenders, and who possessed a well-developed sense of positional play. Small wonder, then, that it was not a system that caught on widely. It did, however, contain two features—the retreating defense and the lone fullback playing deep—that we shall meet up with again.

Diagram 6: Verrou: Defensive Formation

All eleven players are now in their own half. The center back of the attacking formation has retreated deepest of all, to the position marked DCB. The center half of the attacking formation becomes the center back (CB) of the defensive formation.

In South America the game was changing, too, but the demise of the attacking center half was strongly resisted. After World War II, the Uruguayans settled for the *metodo,* which allowed them to keep their center half in midfield. This was the system they took to Brazil, to play in the first of the post–World War II World Cups.

For the Brazilians themselves the overriding consideration at that time was to find a system that allowed as free a rein as possible to their exquisitely skilled forwards. They produced an attack-oriented version of the W-M that they called the diagonal system. With only two full-time defenders, who covered the center and the right flank, the system seemed potentially vulnerable on its left side, where the defensive duties were the responsibility of a withdrawn left halfback who was also expected to move upfield to join in attacking moves. This was also a system that relied on an attacking center half and on two withdrawn inside forwards with the skill to dribble their way forward into the opposing penalty area.

In the 1950 tournament, the formation worked beautifully against Mexico, who were seen off by a 4–0 score, but misfired disastrously against Switzerland, who used their bolt system to hold the Brazilians to a 2–2 tie.

Something near to panic took over in the Brazilian camp, and coach Flavio Costa made six changes for the next game, against Yugoslavia. Brazil switched to a new formation—or at least one that was new to them—an orthodox W-M, with halfbacks Bauer and Danilo and inside forwards Zizinho and Jair forming the "magic square" in midfield.

Desperate measures, but they worked. Brazil dispatched Yugoslavia by a 2–0 score. As the tournament progressed the Brazilian W-M proved ever more successful. In the final round, Sweden and Spain were buried by 7–1 and 6–1 scorelines respectively. The final obstacle to Brazil's first-ever World Cup title was Uruguay, which had been struggling along with its hybrid, and seemingly outmoded, *metodo.*

Except that, when it came to the final, the Uruguayans made all sorts of modifications. The danger to them, of course, came from Brazil's quick-silver forwards and the facility with which they were scoring goals. But the Uruguayans had done their homework. They had seen how the Swiss bolt had contained the danger, and, in particular, they had noted the effective-ness of the deep-lying, covering fullback.

"Don't let them shoot from inside the area" was the advice of the Uru-guayan goalkeeper Roque Maspoli, and coach Juan Lopez worked out a scheme to accomplish just that end.

Fullback Matias Gonzalez became the deep back. When Brazil was on the attack, he was not, under any circumstances, to allow himself to be drawn out of the penalty area. Halfbacks Schubert Gambetta and Victor Andrade (who, under the *metodo,* marked the Brazilian wingers Chico and Friaça) were told to mark tightly and not allow the wingers to get in crosses. Should a cross come in from the opposite flank, they were to leave their man to help cover the center of the penalty area.

Even the center half Obdulio Varela, who was normally the playmaking sparkplug of the team, was given a primarily defensive role (though "there was no need to give him instructions," said Lopez, "he was the captain"), as was inside forward Julio Pérez.

The Uruguayan offense was based on the swift counterattack. Setting off these strikes was the function of the wily Juan Schiaffino, patrolling midfield to pick up balls played out by his defenders. He would then pass long to winger Alcide Ghiggia who, it was thought, could turn what was considered the suspect left side of the Brazilian defense.

Playing according to this scheme, Uruguay bore little resemblance to a *metodo* team. With the deep-lying halfbacks Gambetta and Andrade operating, to all intents and purposes, as extra fullbacks, the Uruguayan formation was much closer to the 4-3-3 that the Brazilians themselves would use so successfully twelve years later in Chile.

For almost the entire first half, intense Brazilian pressure kept the Uruguayans on the defensive. But the Brazilians were held scoreless. They scored early in the second half, but the goal served to increase the intensity of the Uruguayan counterattacks. The fragility of the Brazilian defense was exposed, with right winger Ghiggia racing away to provide the pass for the first Uruguayan goal, then breaking through on his own to score the winner.

Uruguay's 2–1 victory over Brazil in the 1950 final is still the most astonishing upset in World Cup history. Tactics played a large part in that win, and in the words of Juan Lopez, "intelligence, skill, and improvisation did the rest." There was also a suspicion that Brazil, late converts to the W-M, had not really mastered its intricacies.

The 1950 final was, in fact, a tactical mishmash. One undisputed strength of the W-M was the clarity and rigidity of its defensive man-to-man marking assignments. Yet the Brazilians, sweeping headily forward on the attack, failed to assign anyone to mark the lethal Schiaffino. Even more disastrously, they failed either to switch, or provide support for, fullback Bigode, even though it was apparent early in the game that Ghiggia was too quick for him.

On the other hand, tight marking was not supposed to be a feature of the *metodo,* yet here were the Uruguayans, marking tenaciously all over the field. The Uruguayans, said an Italian journalist, had proved themselves the world champions at marking.

By the time of the 1954 World Cup, the attacking center half was on his last legs. The Brazilians had abandoned him along with the diagonal and were now experimenting with a third back. Even the Austrians, who in Ernst Ocwirk possessed one of the greatest attacking center halves of all time, deployed him as a third back. Only the Uruguayans persisted.

It was not the center half that occupied soccer's attention in the early 1950s, however, but rather the center forward, and in particular what the Hungarians had done to him. This was the era of the all-conquering Magic Magyars, and one of the reasons for their success was their use of the so-called "withdrawn center forward."

To understand just what was happening, we must go back to 1925 and Herbert Chapman. His invention of the third back not only killed off the attacking center half, it also meant the end of the old-style center forward. Until then, the center forward had been an all-rounder who needed all the attacking skills—dribbling, shooting, heading, speed. But to cope with the close marking of the rugged third back, a new type of center forward was required. A strong, powerful, battering-ram of a player, typified by Arsenal's fearless Ted Drake. A crucial feature of games involving two W-M teams was always the man-to-man struggle between stopper and center forward.

Brawny center forwards were Hungary's dilemma in the 1950s because . . . they didn't have any. Marton Bukovi, coach of the Budapest club Voros Loboga, got around the problem this way. At "center forward" he put a player, Peter Palotas, who in ball skills and physique was similar to the pre-1925-type center forward. To keep him away from the smothering attentions of the opposing stopper, Bukovi required Palotas to play in midfield, well behind the usual advanced center forward position. This was fine with Palotas, for it meant that he could virtually continue to play in the style of an attacking wing half—his former position.

He was not, in fact, a center forward at all. From his deep position he would be a prompter of attacks, a distributor of passes, rather than a goal scorer. That role now passed to the two inside forwards, who were moved up front into the area vacated by the center forward. The final touch to the reorganization of the forward line was to pull the two wingers back, so that the attacking M had been turned upside down into a W, as Diagram 7 shows.

These changes were the basis for the great Hungarian national team that coach Gustav Sebes formed in the 1950s. The formation that he developed is shown in Diagram 8, along with the names of the players and the numbers they wore.

Unlike American football, soccer is not a game in which a team's offense and defense operate as two discrete units. The two are inseparable, and the radical change represented by the offensive W meant altered roles for the defenders playing behind it.

Midfield was occupied by Nandor Hidegkuti, by Jozsef Bozsik, whose duties were primarily offensive, and by Jozsef Zakarias, who concentrated on defense.

While it is probably true to say that any team that contained four such brilliant players as Hidegkuti, Bozsik, Ferenc Puskas, and Sandor Kocsis would have been successful, it is also true that Sebes's new formation was perfectly tailored to make the maximum use of their talents. The novelty of the style also helped to bemuse opponents, never more so than when Hungary crushed England at Wembley in 1953.

What the English got from the Hungarians was a lesson in the dangers of tactical stagnation. The English took the field with a standard W-M. They had been playing their W-M games for nearly twenty-five years. Week in, week out, in club games all over the country, the stoppers, wearing No. 5, would do battle with the opposing center forwards, who always wore No. 9. The right back No. 2 would mark the left winger No. 11, and the left back No. 3 would mark the right winger No. 7. It seemed as though that was the way God had ordained the game should be played.

If that was the way God wanted it, then the Hungarians were the most dangerous of heretics. The Hungarian attacking W threw the English defenders into total confusion. Incredibly, almost laughably, it seems that the English paid more attention to the numbers on the Hungarian shirts than they did to what the players wearing them were actually doing.

Diagram 7: Hungarian W Attack

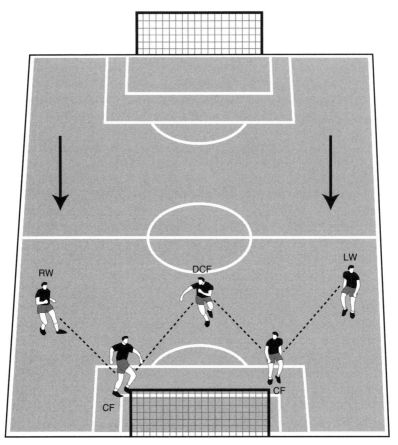

In effect, the old attacking M turned upside down. The wingers (RW and LW) were pulled back, as was the center forward—now playing as a so-called deep center forward (DCF). In his place the two former inside forwards moved up, both playing the role of center forward (CF).

Thus Harry Johnston, the English stopper center half, was quickly confronted with a dilemma. He was accustomed to marking a lone center forward wearing the No. 9 shirt—but he found that the Hungarian No. 9, Hidegkuti, spent most of the time playing behind Puskas and Kocsis, whose numbers, No. 10 and No. 8, suggested that they should have been inside forwards.

If Johnston moved forward to mark Hidegkuti then he left vital, central space unguarded behind him. If he protected the space, then he left Hidegkuti unmarked. The English fullbacks, confronted—or rather not confronted—by the withdrawn Hungarian wingers, faced the same problem. To go or to stay?

Diagram 8: The Hungarian National Team, 1953

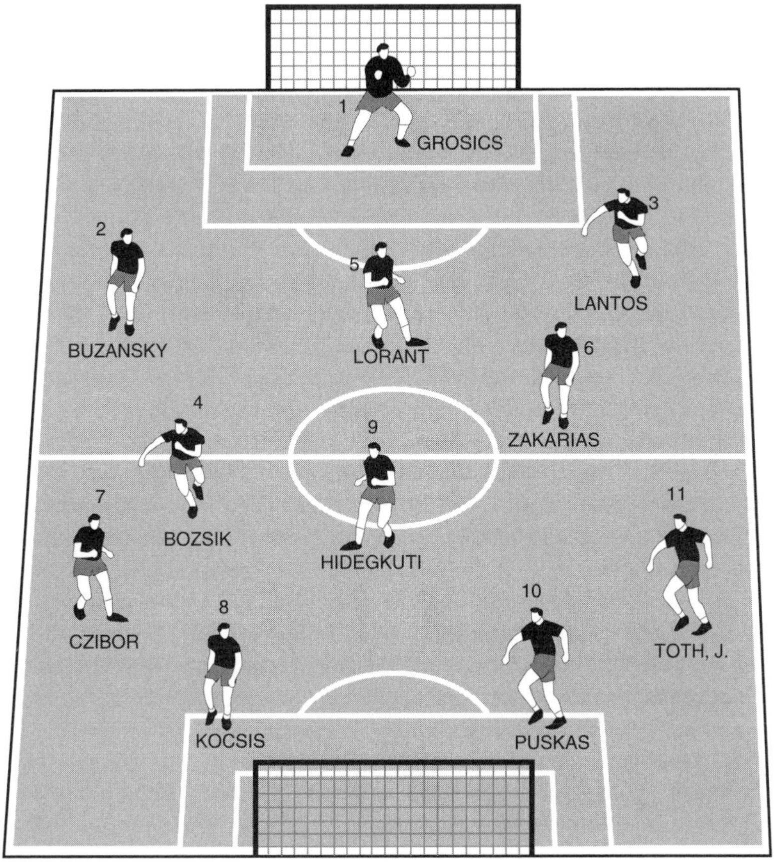

With this basic formation, the Hungarians went undefeated for over four years, from May 1950 until July 1954. They were Olympic champions in 1952. Defeat finally came in the most important game of all, the 1954 World Cup final, when they were beaten 2–3 by West Germany.

There is no need to labor the point: England simply did not know what was going on; they were beaten 3–6 and the score, if anything, flattered them. In retrospect it seems incredible that the basically simple Hungarian idea of reversing the attacking formation could not have been rather quickly countered by altering the defensive alignment. But perhaps that was asking too much of the English, who still retained something of the early amateur attitude that soccer was something to play, not to think about. Tactics were still viewed with at best suspicion, at worst contempt.

The English, so insistent that anyone wearing No. 9 must be a center forward, described Hidegkuti as a "withdrawn center forward." An absurd term, as Hidegkuti was not a center forward at all.

Hungary's dazzling forward play naturally overshadowed everything else about the team, but there was much that was interesting about their defense, too. Diagram 9 shows the Hungarians on the attack, with their forwards deep into enemy territory.

The significant thing about the defense is the extent to which the three fullbacks moved upfield in support of the attack. This left a considerable amount of unguarded space behind them, but the danger of opponents exploiting this by pushing the ball through for their forwards to chase was to some extent mitigated by the adventurous play of the Hungarian goalkeeper Gyula Grosics, who often came out of his area to kick—or even head—the ball away.

The advanced position of the fullbacks also reduced the midfield area (i.e., the space between the forwards and the backs), a desirable effect as the Hungarians had only two players, Hidegkuti and Bozsik, operating there full-time. The other "halfback," Zakarias, was functioning primarily as a fourth fullback.

Way back in the 1860s the English had started playing soccer with one fullback; in 1872 the Scots made it two; in 1925 Arsenal had introduced the third back; and now here were the Hungarians with approximately three and a half fullbacks.

The figure was rounded off to four by, rather surprisingly, the attack-minded Brazilians with the 4-2-4 formation that won them the 1958 World Cup. This is when the numbers game really begins in soccer's vocabulary. The 2-3-5 and 3-4-3 formations that we have been discussing were not talked of in that numerical way at the time; they were the pyramid and the W-M.

But in 1958 all the talk was of the 4-2-4. Methodical coaching was on the rise, and identifying formations with numbers gave them a more modern, a more scientific sound.

The seeds of the 4-2-4 had been sown back in 1950, when the Uruguayans had in effect used four defenders in the final. Certainly the club team Real Madrid—built around the greatest all-round player of them all, the Argentine Alfredo Di Stéfano—also used a 4-2-4 during the 1950s. But it was the Brazilians who brought it to maturity.

The 4-2-4 is a satisfyingly symmetrical formation (see Diagram 10), but once again the simplicity of the diagram belies the sophistication of the reality.

Despite the four fullbacks, the 4-2-4 as played by the 1958 Brazilians was a far from defensive scheme. An exhilarating feature was the attacking role of the two outside backs. This had not been much to coach Vicente Feola's liking in the beginning. Indeed, when Nilton Santos had raced upfield with the ball in the opening game against Austria, Feola had jumped up and yelled at him to pass and go back to his proper position. But Santos raced on, drew the Austrian goalkeeper out, and flicked the ball past him.

Diagram 9: Hungarian Attacking Formation

All players have moved well upfield. Zakarias is functioning virtually as a fourth fullback. The diagram clearly shows the relationship between this formation and the 4-2-4 that the Brazilians were to develop in 1958. (see Diagram 10, p 200).

Feola was quick to applaud the goal, and from then on the overlapping fullback was a regular part of Brazilian play. On attack, the formation became 2-4-4, enabling Brazil to commit as many as eight players to the offense.

The new role called for a new type of fullback, quick moving, with a fair share of the forward's talents, the ability to exchange short passes and to shoot accurately. A far cry from the days of the old W-M fullbacks whose

Diagram 10: The 4-2-4 Formation

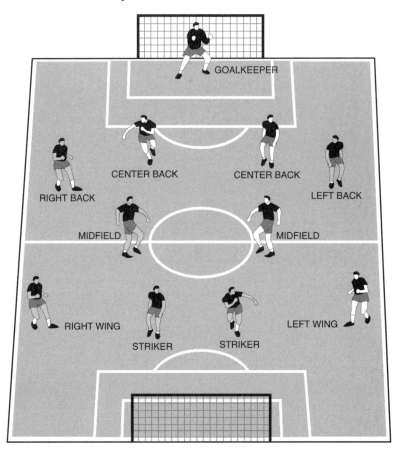

Used by the Brazilians in the 1958 World Cup. The right and left backs were expected to play an adventurous role, even to the extent of joining in attacking moves deep in their opponent's half of the field. The left wing was frequently pulled back to operate as a third midfield player.

main functions were to stay deep, win the ball by hard tackling, then kick it deep downfield.

Up front for Brazil were Vavá and Pelé, absolutely devastating as twin spearheads with their delicate passing, constant position-switching, and thunderous shooting, while on the right wing lurked the bandy-legged Garrincha.

More than Pelé, more than any other single player, it was Garrincha who inspired the Brazilians to their 1958 victory. A fact that is worth underlining, for Garrincha was an uncoached, almost uncoachable player.

Garrincha really had little connection with the 4-2-4. He was just a brilliant ballplayer doing his thing out on the right wing, and his success stands—or should stand—as a warning to those who believe that carefully worked-out tactics and alignment diagrams are what soccer is all about.*

As Brazil spent most of its time on attack, its defensive adjustment excited little comment at the time. When their opponents had the ball, Brazil's left winger, Mario Zagalo, quickly withdrew into midfield to make a 4-3-3 alignment. If the other team's pressure was sustained, he would fall even farther back, into his own penalty area. During the final he was at one point positioned on his own goal line to head away a Swedish shot that had beaten goalkeeper Gylmar.

The 4-2-4 succeeded in 1958 because their extravagant attacking talents allowed the Brazilians to maintain relentless pressure on their opponents. But it contained a serious weakness. When forced into a defensive mode, the 4-2-4 was dangerously underpopulated in midfield.

Whether the Brazilians really needed to worry about this weakness four years later in Chile seemed questionable. But the times were moving against enterprising soccer. Tactics was fast becoming the science of forging cast-iron defenses. Sadly, the Brazilians mirrored this trend by opting for a 4-3-3 formation (see Diagram 11). Zagalo—who, in Sweden, had been a winger who dropped back to help out in midfield—now became a midfielder who occasionally ranged forward to help the offense. Pelé was injured early in the tournament and played no significant part in Brazil's 1962 triumph. The individual star was unquestionably Garrincha, who was, by and large, left alone by coach Aimoré Moreira to use his abundant, unpredictable talent as he wished. It was Garrincha who inspired Brazil's 3–1 quarterfinal win over England and the 4–2 win over hosts Chile in the semifinal.

But, for all his game-winning brilliance, Garrincha was not a representative figure of the soccer of the time. He was an individualist, a freelancer, whose soccer instincts told him where to be and what to do during a game. By the tactical requirements of modern coaching, he was exactly what Feola had called him—undisciplined. Such players, once the game's pride and joy, were becoming problem players.

It was yet another sign of the times, another portent of the defensive clouds that were gathering over the game. Proof of the trend, if proof were needed, could be found in the goal-scoring statistics from the World Cup

---

* One month before the World Cup, during an exhibition game in Italy, Garrincha had dribbled through the entire Fiorentina defense, right to the goal line. There, instead of cutting in and shooting, or crossing the ball, he waited for another defender to challenge, beat him, and then scored the goal. The Italian crowd loved it, but coach Feola was furious: "Garrincha is undisciplined—there's no place for showing off like that in the World Cup." He dropped Garrincha, only restoring him when the other players demanded his return.

Diagram 11: The 4-3-3 Formation

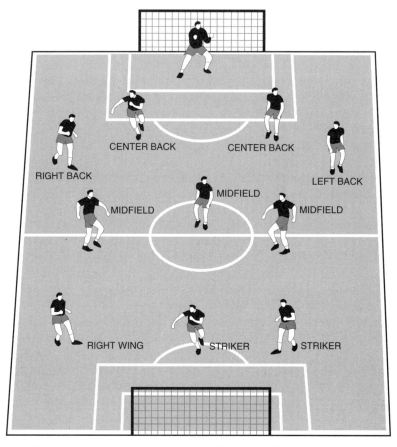

The formation incorporates only one winger—the diagram shows him positioned on the right, but he can equally well be on the left.

tournaments. The high point had been reached in 1954, with an average of 5.38 goals per game. In Sweden, in 1958, the average dropped to 3.60 per game. In Chile it sank to its lowest ever, 2.78.

World Cup	Goals	Games	Average Per Game
1954	140	26	5.38
1958	126	35	3.60
1962	89	32	2.78

It was Italy that provided the most fertile soil for the growth of defensive tactics. The Italians had perfected a system that used the deep-lying

Diagram 12: Catenaccio

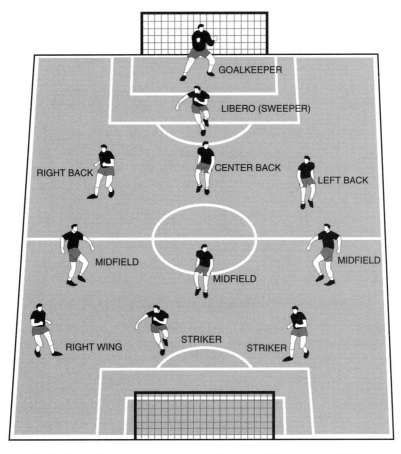

GOALKEEPER

LIBERO (SWEEPER)

RIGHT BACK

CENTER BACK

LEFT BACK

MIDFIELD

MIDFIELD

MIDFIELD

RIGHT WING

STRIKER

STRIKER

In its ultradefensive forms, catenaccio *features a* libero *playing behind a line of four fullbacks (with an extra center back), three midfielders, and only two strikers up front—or even four midfielders, with only one striker.*

fullback seen in Switzerland's 1950 *verrou* formation. *Catenaccio,* literally meaning a great big chain, was the name the Italians gave to their system.

A chain of defenders, that is, designed to strangle the opposing offense. Three of the fullbacks were given strict man-to-man marking duties. Behind them was the deep fullback—the Italians called him the *libero,* or free man, because he had no specific opponent to mark. His job was to patrol the entire center of the defense and to quickly close any gaps that might be opened by other defenders' errors.

The history of *catenaccio* tells much about the development of soccer tactics. There was absolutely nothing positive about its origin. It was not designed to win games, but rather to avoid losing them, or to avoid losing by heavy scores.

The Italian *Serie A* (first division) had long been an unbalanced league, with a few rich clubs regularly carrying off all the honors. In 1947, coach Nereo Rocco took over at Triestina, a small club that was barely surviving in *Serie A*. It was Rocco who loosed *catenaccio* on the soccer world, finding in it the means by which his small club could be competitive. He had immediate and dramatic success: In 1948, Triestina climbed to second place in the league. Other clubs began to copy.

The trend accelerated in the early 1950s when, as we have seen, the rich Italian clubs started to spend large sums of money signing up players from Argentina and Uruguay (the amateur Swedes and Danes could be signed without having to pay big transfer fees, but only the rich clubs could offer them attractive salaries). Almost without exception these imports were brilliant attacking players, and to counter them the smaller clubs sank further and further into the grips of *catenaccio*. Soon it was being played at home games, as well as away, then the defense was even further padded by having the *libero* play behind a line of four fullbacks, rather than three, leaving only two forwards to cope as best they could up front.

There was no denying the success, in terms of results, that *catenaccio* brought. It did make it very difficult for the opponents to score, and there was always the possibility that the defending team, breaking away suddenly, might snatch a goal. It happened far too many times for it to be accidental.

Eventually *catenaccio* became more than a style of play. It became a mentality that dragged Italian soccer down through boring negativity to almost total sterility. For, inevitably, the big clubs joined in. They did so with considerably more flair than the small clubs, but it was still *catenaccio*.

Helenio Herrera perfected the system with Inter-Milan, who won the European Cup twice using their brand of *catenaccio*. And it must be admitted that Herrera's version was by no means a wholly defensive affair, for Inter featured several fine attacking players such as Jair (from Brazil), Luis Suarez (from Spain), and Sandro Mazzola, while at left back there was the tall and rangy Giacinto Facchetti, who had perfected the role of the "over-lapping" fullback, ever ready to race upfield and join in the attack.

When Inter did attack they were an exciting team to see, but it happened too rarely, an occasional firework of brilliance shooting out from the gloomy darkness of the *catenaccio* defense. Watching them was a frustrating experience, for there was always the feeling that the players were under constraint, that their considerable talents were being shackled by the system.

That was Inter, the cream of the *catenaccio* crop. When two so-so teams met and both employed *catenaccio*, both packing their penalty areas and hoping to snatch a sudden goal at the other end, then the game degenerated into a colossal bore.

But *catenaccio* had a special appeal for the Italians because it relied on the sudden counterattack to score goals. The quick break-away, the rapid switch from defense to attack, had long been a feature of the Italian game. Now it had been given an almost scientific basis.

The English, ever averse to foreign influence, were not greatly interested in the development of *catenaccio.* They acknowledged the coming of the *libero,* but coined their own term for the position. They called him the sweeper, the man who moved about at the back of the defense, cleaning up the errors of his teammates.

Having named the position, the English proceeded largely to ignore it. In the 1966 World Cup, their two center backs were Jackie Charlton—the tall, rock-like personification of the stopper—and the captain Bobby Moore. Moore's role certainly allowed him more freedom than Charlton's, but he was not in any sense a deep-lying fullback. To complete the confusion, the English stuck to their traditional nomenclature, and referred to the two center backs as "twin center halves."

Looking at soccer, for the moment, in geometric shapes, *catenaccio* had turned the old pyramid formation upside down. Now, instead of a team having just two fullbacks and fanning out to a profusion of five forwards, it started off with a phalanx of five fullbacks and withered away to two or even just one forward.

In this whittling away of the forward line, the main victim was the old-fashioned winger. The 2-3-5 and the W-M, two systems that between them ruled soccer for nearly seventy-five years, both featured two wingers. To those who remember the "good old days" of soccer, the very word "winger" will always have a magic ring to it. When wingers got the ball, beautiful things used to happen. No matter if it was the electrifying corkscrew runs and deadly shooting of Garrincha, or the subtler, exquisite trickery of Stanley Matthews. Whichever, it was soccer at its best.

Now, those lovely skills were not seen nearly so often. The blame could, perhaps, be laid on the Brazilians, whose 4-2-4 had required a left winger who could also play midfield, leading to the 4-3-3, which required a midfielder who might occasionally play on the left wing. But the Hungarians had really done the same thing in 1953 when two of the players they alternated on the wing—Lazslo Budai and Jozsef Toth—were more midfield players than true wingers. Brazil, of course, had Garrincha on the right wing, more than enough to compensate for the lack of a left wing, but by the time of the 1962 World Cup he was, at the age of 29, one of precious few wingers on view.

Wingers were an endangered species and what looked like their burial took place in 1966 when England won the World Cup using a formation that included no wingers at all. It was dubbed the "penguin" formation. Wingless.

Just as the 4-2-4 formation had lost a forward to midfield and become the 4-3-3, the process of denuding the offense went on, and the 4-3-3 became England's 4-4-2. Or more accurately, a 4-1-3-2 (Diagram 13), because the new four-man midfield included a novelty. This lay in the use of the tiny

Diagram 13: England 1966

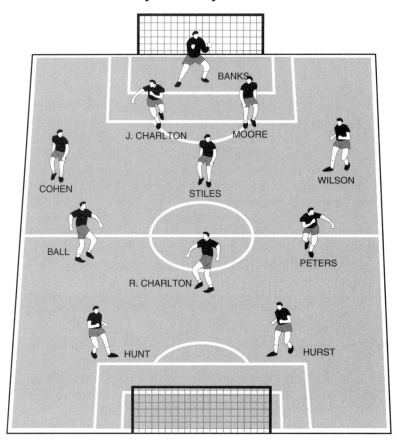

A team without wingers, but with Ball and R. Charlton playing mainly attacking roles. The novelty was the use of Stiles as a sweeper, or defensive screen, playing in front of *the fullback line.*

but combative Nobby Stiles as a sort of sweeper playing in front of the back four. Either he was given a specific marking assignment (as against Portugal, in the semifinal, when he neutralized Eusebio) or he was free to roam, sensing danger and snuffing it out with his ferocious, but usually effective, tackling.

Ramsey's scheme put a premium on what was now, voguishly, called "work-rate." Geoff Hurst and Roger Hunt, the two forwards, had acres of ground to cover. They were expected to be in almost constant movement, not necessarily in expectation of getting the ball, but trying to pull defenders out of position to create gaps that the midfielders—in particular Alan Ball and Bobby Charlton—and even the outside fullbacks, could move into.

Hurst and Hunt were hailed as the epitome of "unselfish" players, prime exponents of the newly discovered arts of "decoy running" and "off-the-ball" movement. Hunt was now a "target man," the tall strong forward at whom his teammates aimed long passes from the back. His job was to win the ball, usually in the air, and either flick it on, or to hold it while his teammates moved up in support. Along with the new role came the newly discovered skill of "playing with your back to goal."

It was a time for tactical terms and buzzwords. The Italians, who were the most deeply involved, called the trend *tatticomania*. But the English, who had for so long derided the science of coaching, were now taking it up with a vengeance and had produced a generation of coaches trained and duly licensed by the F.A. They had introduced a serious methodical approach to the game, which was presumably a good thing, but as they all came from the same "school" they brought with them a new orthodoxy which was not so welcome.

Ramsey wanted players with a high work-rate, players prepared for ninety minutes of constant action (there was, remember, still no substitution permitted in World Cup games), players who would attack and defend, players who, to use another term from the new jargon, were willing to indulge in "positive running."

This was definitely not the sort of job for wingers, traditionally rather temperamental players who waited to be brought into the game by their colleagues' passes, who rarely went looking for the ball, and who never came back to help out on defense.

It was only fitting that England's victory in the final was largely due to the inspired and tireless play of Alan Ball, another player whose appetite for running far outstripped his skill. England's "wingless wonders" took the World Cup because they were the best of a rather substandard crop, a solid no-nonsense team that kept errors down to a minimum.

The nationalistic passion that gripped England during the tournament obscured the fact that, by any objective standards, this was not a very attractive team to watch. "Workmanlike" was the word that seemed to best describe it, a group of highly trained men doing a job of work, rather than enjoying a game.

From George Raynor, the Englishman who had coached Sweden to the 1958 World Cup final, came a cutting comment: "There is, in football, no substitute for skill, but the manager's job is usually to try to find one. Ramsey obviously found one."

During the 1966 World Cup only the tactically unrestrained North Koreans and the irrepressible Eusebio seemed to remember how to smile . . . but it was the North Koreans' lack of tactical know-how that cost them a place in the semifinals, and after Portugal had been beaten by England in the semifinals, Eusebio left the field with his wonderfully boyish, open face wet with tears.

The 1966 World Cup, despite the advent of so much scientific talk and preparation (for the first time, FIFA appointed a group of coaches to write a technical study of the games), was not technically distinguished. Before the tournament, the participating coaches—the very people who would control the type of soccer played—predicted to the FIFA study group that the 1966 World Cup would show a trend toward defensive soccer and aggressive tackling. Hardly surprisingly, that is exactly what happened.

However it is viewed, 1966 cannot be seen as a high point in the development of soccer. The game had become unmistakably harder; much of the enjoyment seemed to have drained away. Replacing it was a mean-spirited atmosphere in which grim-faced players had discovered new "tactical" skills: they argued with the referee, they faked injuries, they snarled at opponents. And they committed cynical fouls which—in keeping with the permissive attitude—were even given an air of justification by being called "tactical" fouls.

The forecasts for the 1970 World Cup in Mexico were, inevitably, gloomy. Attendances were static or falling throughout the world. There had been several disgraceful clashes in the World Club Championship, notably in 1967 when Racing Club of Argentina and Celtic of Scotland indulged in a brawl that saw four Celtic and two Racing players sent off the field, and in 1969 when Milan were so outrageously mauled by Estudiantes de la Plata that three of the Argentine players were slapped with lengthy suspensions—on the insistence of the president of Argentina!

Soccer was going through a dangerously negative period. It badly needed a shot in the arm to restore its tarnished image, and in Mexico fortune smiled radiantly in the form of a wonderful Brazilian team that won all its games by joyously putting the accent on attacking play.

Ostensibly the Brazilians were a 4-4-2 team, with only Tostão and Jairzinho up front. But behind them, in midfield, were Pelé, Gerson, and Rivelino. A total of five magnificent attacking players, three of them (Tostão, Gerson, and Rivelino) superbly, menacingly left-footed, a factor that couldn't be assessed in tactical terms, but one that surely posed massive hidden problems for opposing defenders.

The Brazilian defense, it was said, was weak. Felix was held to be a second-rate goalkeeper ("Weak on crosses," said the English, as they always do of any non-English keeper), center back Brito's temperament was questioned, Carlos Alberto was too attack-minded, and so on.

In particular, the critics derided the Brazilian midfield as being, in defensive terms, hopelessly inadequate. There was something in that. Only the inexperienced twenty-one-year-old Clodoaldo had a defensive role, doing the sort of thing that Stiles had done for England in 1966. Gerson would play deep, but his role was primarily that of all-seeing brain for the attack. His effectiveness as a defender, like that of Pelé and Rivelino, was hardly the toast of Brazil.

Yet it all worked with unmatchable brilliance. None of the criticism mattered at all. Only once in the tournament—during a tight 1–0 victory over England—did the Brazilians score fewer than three goals in a game. Otherwise, such was the irresistible surge of their attacking play that their defenders were rarely put under the sort of pressure that might have exposed the alleged weaknesses.

It was not formations that carried Brazil to the heights, but the surpassing skills of players like Pelé, Tostão, Rivelino, Gerson, Clodoaldo, and Carlos Alberto. The dashing right winger (yes, a winger!) Jairzinho scored in every game, racing away across the field after each goal had gone in, leaping and twisting and laughing as he went, pursued by a stream of yelling and grinning teammates.

Nothing was more appropriate than that this happy band of men should win the final by swamping the Italians, still enmeshed in the slough of *catenaccio.*

A sparkling beginning, then, for the 1970s. The attacking message of the Brazilians was taken up in Europe, notably by the West Germans, who won the 1972 European championship with a team that attacked, if not with the *brio* of the Brazilians, then certainly with a flair that exploded the myth of Teutonic stodginess.

The Dutch arrived out of nowhere. A small country with a long but unremarkable soccer record, that suddenly produced a most extraordinary generation of free-spirited young soccer players who made Feyenoord (Rotterdam) and Ajax (Amsterdam) the strongest club teams in Europe.

What the Germans and the Dutch were doing was what the FIFA technical study group had described in its report on the 1970 World Cup: "The best teams in Europe have freed themselves from rigid patterns of play. Players are capable of varying their functions between defense and attack. . . ."

A new phrase, "total soccer," entered soccer's ever-expanding vocabulary. It was seen as the ultimate marriage of the three Bs of soccer: brawn, brain, and ball skills. The new breed of total soccer players was fit enough and skilled enough to play any position on the field, and intelligent enough to know exactly when to switch roles.

The style reached its zenith with the Dutch national team in the 1974 World Cup under coach Rinus Michels. Made up mostly of players from Ajax and Feyenoord, the Dutch team was, in terms of time spent together, one of the least well-prepared teams in the tournament. Yet such was the ability and the mutual understanding of the players that it was not necessary to work out complicated systems of play.

The Dutch seemed always able to defend *en bloc,* to attack *en masse,* to flood midfield whenever they wished, all their players in constant kaleidoscopic motion, their goalkeeper ever ready to leave his area to clear the ball.

The speed with which the Dutch surrounded the ball with as many as five or six—or was it ten?—players, on both offense and defense, was dizzying. The sudden surge of the whole team on offense left many an opposing forward stranded yards offside.

Off-the-ball movement was constant, all done purposefully. "It's not difficult to get players to move about," Rinus Michels would say, "but to get them to do it intelligently, that is the difference."

Remarkably, the essence of the Dutch style had been foreseen nearly twenty years earlier by journalist Willy Meisl, who wrote in his 1955 book *Soccer Revolution:*

> In my opinion the future belongs to The Whirl. It must rotate on *individuality* rooted in *all-round* capacity. . . . A full-back seeing an opening in front must seize his chance without hesitation. A wing-half or winger will fall back, if necessary, and being an all-rounder, will not feel uncomfortable or out of place. The consciousness that he also is a capable forward will give the back's thrust weight and impetus. The knowledge that whoever has taken over from him (behind his back) will make a good job of it should the occasion arise, will enable him to carry on with his action (raid) without undue hurry or nervousness. He must and will be perfectly sure that he has left no exposed flank behind himself.

Thus Willy Meisl's "whirl." It describes exactly what the Dutch looked like to their opponents, a menacing whirl of orange shirts, with the ubiquitous Johan Cruyff orchestrating everything. The Dutch whirl is too fluid to be given any meaningful expression in diagrams or numerical formations. It was 4-3-3, 4-2-4, 2-3-5, 4-4-2, and all their variations rolled into one. It was all of them, but it was none of them.

In the 1974 final, Dutch total soccer, led by the brilliant Johan Cruyff was opposed—and beaten 2–1—by the German variety, led by the equally brilliant Franz Beckenbauer.

Single-handed, Beckenbauer had revolutionized the role of the *libero* in soccer. In his early career as a midfielder, Beckenbauer had always liked to go forward, to score goals. When he switched to *libero* for his club team Bayern Munich, he reshaped the position so that he could still use his attacking talents.

His inspiration came from the Italian club Inter. As *catenaccio* had become more widespread in Italy, most teams had cut back to only two forwards. This left one of the three fullbacks without any compelling man-to-man marking duties. Inter's left back Giacinto Facchetti took advantage of this freedom, by making attacking runs into the opposing penalty area, where he became a potent scoring threat. In an eighteen-year career with Inter, defender Facchetti scored sixty goals.

What Facchetti could do from the fullback position, Beckenbauer decided could be done from the *libero* position. Beckenbauer's sudden forays into enemy territory caused huge problems for defenders already preoccupied with their own man-to-man assignments.

Beckenbauer and Johan Cruyff were, quite clearly, the outstanding players of the age. Soccer geniuses. Their brilliance raised the questions: How

Johan Cruyff—here, he is about to score against Argentina in the 1974 World Cup—was the key player in the Dutch Total Soccer style of the 1970s. He went on to become an imaginative coach with Barcelona.
© Peter Robinson: The Football Archive

much did total soccer owe to their individual skills? And would it work without them?

The feeling that total soccer was, to some extent, an optical illusion, received support four years later during the 1978 World Cup in Argentina. Both the Netherlands and West Germany were present, both apparently still playing total soccer. But each country now lacked its inspiration, Cruyff and Beckenbauer having announced in advance that they would not play in the tournament.

Without Beckenbauer, the Germans were a mundane team that won only one of the six games it played. The Cruyff-less Dutch had a new coach, the Austrian Ernst Happel, a cautious man who, in the qualifying games, had experimented with a five-man midfield. The team was certainly going through the motions of total soccer—the attacking and defending en masse, the quick passing of the ball to a player in motion—but Cruyff's artistry was sorely missed.

Without it, the less acceptable face of total soccer was now more clearly visible. The light, springy quality that Cruyff had given to the team was gone. Now the Dutch players looked heavier and slower ("rugby players" was an Argentine journalist's scornful dismissal of the powerful van der Kerkhof brothers), and their often brutal tackling was there for all to see. And now the offside trap was being deliberately used as a defensive tactic, rather than as an incidental result of fast, mass attacking play.

Total soccer, it seemed, had owed more to its key individual players than to its tactics. Beckenbauer was later to say: "It owed more to the element of surprise than to any magic formula. I think the Dutch got away with it for so long because the opposition could not work out what tactics they were facing. It never dawned on them, certainly not until it was much too late, that there were no tactics at all . . . just brilliant players with a ball."

Nevertheless, in 1978 enough remained of the total soccer that had so baffled and enchanted four years earlier for the Dutch to reach the final, just as they had done in 1974.

The Argentines, the other finalists, had at last managed to harness the immense individual skill of their players into a functioning team. Coach Cesar Menotti had said from the start that he wanted players who were team players, but that his team would be built around the traditional skills of the Argentine player: "I will always select skill over fitness. You can, with work, take a skillful player and make him fit. But if the player has only fitness, no amount of training will make him skillful."

To allow an Argentine player to use his natural skills is to allow him to attack, and that is what Menotti's team did in every game. Tactically speaking, there was nothing new here. Very much the opposite. Argentina's play was a throwback to earlier times, basically a 4-3-3. Defensively, it was aligned in the way that all Argentine club teams played, with a line of four fullbacks, marking zonally.

But with the tendency of so many players to move forward, the formation was usually closer to a 4-2-4 and there were times when it almost seemed that soccer had returned to the days of the 2-3-5.

The announcement of the death of wingers had evidently been much exaggerated. Menotti used two wingers, Daniel Bertoni and Oscar Ortiz, plus a "big-man," Leopoldo Luque, at center forward. A real forward line, one that any player from the 1930s would have recognized at once. Constantly attacking from midfield was Osvaldo Ardiles, while Mario Kempes varied his role from game to game—sometimes striker, sometimes more midfielder—but he was always Argentina's goal-scoring threat.

How strange, then, that the Dutch, who employed man-to-man markers in front of a sweeper, should fail to do anything about him in the final. Kempes was repeatedly allowed to race forward from midfield into the penalty area, scoring two goals and assisting on the third in Argentina's 3–1 victory.

If Happel failed tactically by not paying attention to Kempes, he had a short-lived success when he brought on his first substitute, Dirk Nanninga, in the fifty-ninth minute. For the first time in a World Cup final, a substitution was made with a clear, tactical aim.

The entry of the tall Nanninga, an excellent header of the ball, signaled a switch to an aerial game as the Dutch, losing 0–1, tried to overcome the effectiveness of the Argentine central defense. The move paid off at the eighty-second minute when it was Nanninga's powerful header that tied the score at 1–1.

In the final analysis, the thing that counted in the 1978 final was—once again—not so much tactics as mentality. The Argentines were a team with

Diagram 14: Argentina 1978

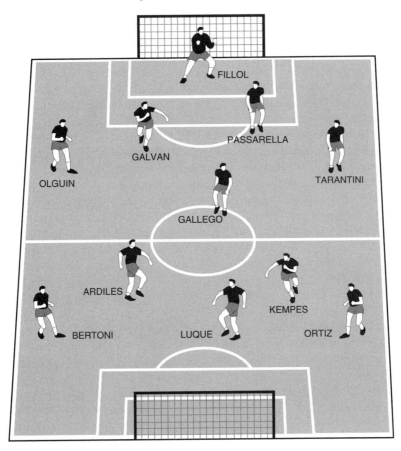

an attacking mentality, a team that seemed incapable of slowing things down, of protecting a lead.

This was nicely demonstrated at the seventy-fifth minute of the game. With his team holding on to a precarious 1–0 lead, and with Holland beginning to dominate the game, Menotti prepared a substitution. The obvious move, the logical and safe one, was to take off an attacker and send on a defender. Menotti did take off an attacking player—winger Ortiz—but he replaced him with René Houseman, another totally offense-minded player.

When Holland tied the game, the move appeared to have misfired. But the feverish support of the fans, never allowing the team to pause, urged Argentina forward to an overtime victory—in which Houseman played a significant part.

The negativity that had been predicted for 1978 was certainly there. Most teams seemed to have as their number one priority the nullifying of their opponents' game. There was almost universal acceptance of the defensive tactic of getting seven or eight men behind the ball as soon as it was lost. The consequently packed defenses led to much sterile lateral and back passing.

Bucking this trend were, surprisingly, the Italians. Under new coach Enzo Bearzot they seemed at last to have cast off the shackles of *catenaccio,* and were one of the more adventurous teams of the tournament. The change in mentality was personified by defender Gaetano Scirea. A *libero,* but not the traditionally Italian defensive *libero.* The immaculately skilled Scirea frequently came forward, in the adventurous Beckenbauer manner, to join in attacks.

In 1978 there was, ultimately, encouragement to be found in that it was Holland and Argentina—the two teams most committed to attacking soccer, most willing to take risks—that reached the final.

But there still seemed to be plenty of coaches and teams around willing to give "attacking soccer" a very different interpretation, one that had been predicted in that 1966 FIFA report that talked of aggressive tackling.

In 1970 the referees had been given clear instructions to penalize rough play by defenders. The result was a clean tournament in which the ball-artists of the game were able to demonstrate their skills and to produce open, attacking soccer.

But by the time of the 1982 World Cup in Spain, all was forgotten. The instructions given out to referees must have been of a totally different order. The opening game, Argentina against Belgium, turned out to be a bleak warning of what was to come. The Czech referee Vojtech Christov consistently turned a blind eye to heavy, clumsy, and dangerous tackling, especially from the overtly physical Belgian midfield.

The recipient of most of this treatment was, inevitably, the man who was being talked of as the "new Pelé," Argentina's twenty-one-year-old Diego Maradona. Repeatedly knocked down, tripped, obstructed, and tackled from behind, and receiving no protection from the referee, Maradona dropped farther and farther back into midfield as the game progressed. And, of course, he lost his effectiveness for Argentina.

No doubt this was what the Belgians wanted. It was, for want of a better word, a tactic. But it was based on repeated fouling, and only pathetically lax refereeing allowed it to succeed. It was precisely the sort of play that has given tactics a bad name. The Belgians won the game, and the message came over loud and clear: Physical play is okay.

The results were catastrophic, for—very directly—they led to the elimination from the tournament of its two best teams: France and Brazil. The French were manhandled out of the competition by West Germany, while Brazil suffered the same fate at the hands of Italy. In both cases, hopelessly permissive refereeing was at fault.

"No spectacular systems were created in 1982," said the official FIFA technical report on the tournament. True enough. France and Brazil were similar teams, both blessed with intelligent players in almost every

Diagram 15: France 1982

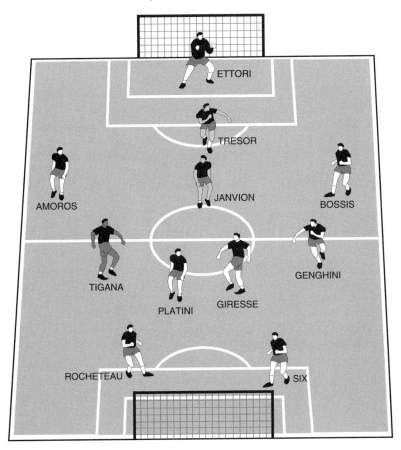

position, and playing magnificent, quick-moving, attacking soccer with an exciting artistic flair.

But they presented nothing new tactically. France used a sweeper behind three fullbacks (two of them man-to-man markers), Brazil played a back four, marking zonally, with the outside backs spending most of their time in midfield. Both teams bristled with midfield talent, both had finishing problems up front.

Italy, the eventual winner, was still a team that defended tightly and based its game on quick counterattacks, but the overly negative caution of *catenaccio* had gone. Now there was a much more dynamic midfield, and four of the five defenders, including the masterful Scirea, were ready to join in offensive moves.

Total soccer, the talk of the tournament just eight years earlier, barely got a look. The Dutch, its chief architects, had failed to qualify, while the

Diagram 16: Brazil 1982

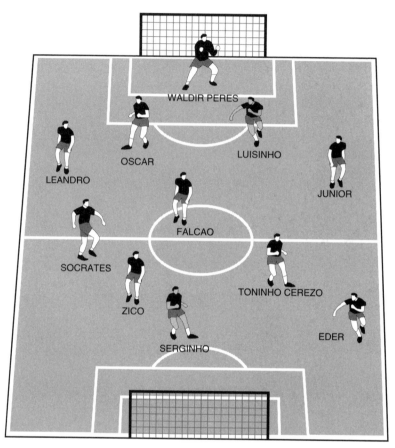

Germans had sunk back into their well-known, well-organized, overly physical mode.

Why the lack of innovation? The FIFA technical report—no doubt unintentionally—offered an important clue. The coaches who authored it seemed always to see the sport through defensive spectacles. Analyzing Brazil's failure, the report criticized the four-defender zonal approach, saying that it lacked depth and cover.

Not mentioned, though it was surely more to the point, was that Brazil had ample opportunity to win or tie the crucial game against Italy, and was thwarted only by center forward Serginho's pitiful inability to put away the simplest of chances. It was left to coach Telê Santana to point out what the report omitted to say: that Italy had scored the winning goal after a corner kick—at a time when virtually the whole Brazilian team was pulled back on defense.

Diagram 17: Italy 1982

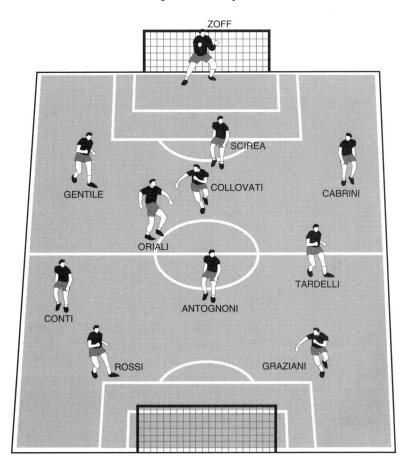

As to the relative benefits of man-to-man or zonal coverage, the Italians, and Gentile in particular, had made a rather twisted contribution to that debate. Who could argue now? If the referees were going to allow Gentile's style, which was really more man-to-man mugging, then who would bother with the intricacies of a zonal defense?

More ominously, if skilled ballplayers like Maradona and Zico could be kicked with impunity, for how long could we expect to see such players gracing the game?

That was not something with which the FIFA coaches concerned themselves. In their report was a fine photograph of Maradona surrounded by four Belgian defenders, being knocked down by one of them. The caption read: "Individual actions getting caught in the funnel formation." Only the defensive tactics, the way that midfielders funneled back to close down space, the way that pressure was immediately applied in midfield, were of any interest to the coaches. The constant fouling had apparently become something not worth commenting on.

But the growing trend toward packing the midfield did call for comment. The report had this to say: "Based on the growing consideration of the players' specific mentality as well as their individual and collective spiritual mobility, a creative dynamism evolved in midfield which made play more positive, diversified and impenetrable."

Impenetrable seemed exactly the right word to describe such verbiage, which was typical of the high-flown, pseudoscientific parlance that coaching had adopted. Even if its language could be fathomed, even if huge allowance were made for the pro-defense slant of its analyses, how could one take seriously a technical report that contained no reference at all to the crucial effect of referees' decisions during the tournament?

The stark truth was that defenders were brazenly flouting soccer's rules, that they were getting away with it, and that nobody seemed inclined to do anything about it. The view of FIFA, and of coaches in general—as reflected in the FIFA technical report—was that everything was fine.

When the 1986 World Cup rolled around, fitness was very much on everyone's mind. Mexico again—Mexico, with its heat and its altitude. Conditions that demanded fitter and better-prepared players—a theme that was constantly stressed by Argentina's new coach, Carlos Bilardo, a medical doctor. Whenever he was asked about the future of the game, Bilardo talked about fitness and speed. Tomorrow's soccer wouldn't be about new tactics, he said, so much as a quickening of the game. Players would have to be more skilled, fitter, and faster.

There was no doubt that modern soccer demanded much more physically from its players than it had done in the past. Total soccer had left its mark. Attacking players now had to come back and help the defense, while defenders were expected to get upfield and join in the attacks. (The use of outside fullbacks as attacking players produced a bizarre situation in the 1986 final, when two such players—Julio Olarticoechea for Argentina and Thomas Berthold for West Germany—found that, rather than marking opposing forwards, they were marking each other.)

The theory behind all-purpose players was fine, but in practice it was yet another system that was heavily skewed toward the defensive part of the game—because there was never, on any team, a shortage of defenders, but there was frequently a massive lack of attacking players. Not a lack of players who attacked . . . a lack of attacking players.

Forwards, real specialist forwards, were hard to find. Argentina, the eventual winners in 1986, exemplified the trend. In the first game, Bilardo fielded only one out-and-out forward, Pablo Pasculli. By the time of the final, Pasculli was on the bench, and the Argentine side was crowded with midfield players.

A state of affairs that led to an anomaly. This was a tournament where attacking soccer was felt to be making a comeback. That was the impression, yet it was contradicted by the statistics, which showed this to be the worst World Cup yet in terms of goal-scoring—just 2.54 per game.

Plenty of attacking then, but poor finishing? Possibly. Scoring chances that, in years gone by, would have been snapped up by a specialist goal scorer, were now likely to fall to a much less expert finisher—a midfielder or a fullback.

The six-man midfield had arrived. Argentina had Diego Maradona, Jorge Burruchaga, Jorge Valdano, Sergio Batista, Ricardo Giusti, and Hector Enrique. One of them, usually Valdano, sometimes Maradona or Burruchaga, might be pushed forward to occupy a forward position. Batista was primarily defensive.

Argentina was never an explosively attacking team. Its play was defensively sound, and it would have been an unspectacular team . . . but for the presence of Diego Maradona. It was the totally unpredictable individual skills of Maradona that made Argentina such a dangerous attacking force.

Ever since the arrival of total soccer, soccer had been blurring the differences between defenders, midfielders, and attackers. Very few people tried now to define a team's formation with a numerical formula. How to describe Argentina, for instance? As a 1-2-6-1, perhaps, or a 1-2-5-2, or sometimes a 1-3-5-1, or maybe a. . . ? There was simply too much movement, too much interchanging of roles, for such descriptions to be meaningful. They had always been approximate, anyway. Now they were almost irrelevant.

The ongoing argument over man-to-man or zonal marking swung decisively toward those of the zonal persuasion. Most teams employed one or two defenders as markers, but the rigidities of the system would not work in the new crowded but fluid midfield. The FIFA technical study group, which again refrained from any comment on the refereeing (it had been much better than in 1982) reported that, in the 1986 World Cup, as in 1982, "no truly new tactics were seen."

It was a verdict that gave rise to the thought that perhaps there simply wasn't anything new to come, that we had seen it all before in one form or another. Certainly, the 1982 report, when it talked of "attacking moves starting with a midfield player who switched over to the offensive immediately after getting the ball" brought back memories of the little Scottish genius Alex James and his role for Arsenal back in the 1930s.

But the 1986 technical study group (as usual, it was overwhelmingly European in composition) seemed to come up with a conclusion that would make a comeback for the James-type player unlikely. Playmakers, said its report, are dying out.

The reason? "Today's soccer, with the overpopulated midfield, limits the room of activity of this zone to a large extent. Little time is left for the control of the ball and the vision of the game. The player who awaits the ball standing or in slow run, is attacked immediately and put under pressure. The midfield stars have the tendency, however, to wait for the ball."

Yes, but . . . what about the decisive influence of Maradona, surely a midfielder, surely a playmaker *extraordinaire,* and surely the outstanding player of the tournament? The FIFA group got neatly around that anomaly by classifying Maradona as a forward.

Which he certainly was, on frequent occasions. Just as he very definitely was a midfielder on others. A point that merely emphasized the decline of the specialist, and the rise of the all-rounder.

Yet, given soccer's long history of anomalous, almost perverse, behavior, it seemed quite absurdly unlikely that the playmakers had gone forever. The betting was that the ghost of wee Alex James would continue to hover over the soccer fields of the world.

By 1988, Bilardo was saying that he had been proved right: "Everyone has copied Argentina." By which he meant that the bloated midfield was the order of the day. He had a point. But the question was, did it matter?

Tactics were beginning to look irrelevant. What mattered was that soccer was losing its attractiveness. Virtually every tactical innovation in the history of soccer has been designed to strengthen defenses. By the time the 1990 World Cup arrived, many teams were playing with just one forward. Goal-scoring was down; soccer as a spectacle was suffering.

The great Argentine player Alfredo Di Stéfano had said: "A soccer game without goals is like an afternoon without sunshine." Just how bleak the lack of goals could make things was revealed in 1989 when Argentina played Italy to an appallingly tedious 0–0 tie. It was an exhibition game with nothing at stake, yet both teams played defensively. Said the Italian coach, Azeglio Vicini: "This is the sort of soccer that we are going to see in the 1990 World Cup. It will be difficult to find spectacular games."

Vicini got it just about right. The 1990 World Cup, by general agreement, rated poor on the entertainment scale. The World Cup of fear: fear of taking risks, fear of attacking, fear of opponents.

No team illustrated the craven attitude more clearly than Brazil. Brazil, the masters of attacking soccer! Heavily criticized because his team scored only twice against Sweden in its first game, coach Sebastião Lazaroni told the press that they could expect more scoring against the next opponent, the minnows Costa Rica. That same night, Lazaroni went to scout Costa Rica, and saw it beat Scotland 1–0.

A scoreline that scared Lazaroni. The following day there was no more talk of scoring a lot of goals. Lazaroni said he'd be satisfied if Brazil won by an own-goal* in the ninety-third minute. And mighty Brazil duly did beat tiny Costa Rica 1–0, on an own-goal.

Echoing its thoughts in 1982 and 1986, the FIFA technical study group declared that the 1990 tournament "did not produce anything startlingly new." Their report admitted that "at present, the defense is dominant," and felt obliged to offer a defense of defenders: "Correct behavior in a

* See Glossary, page 279

defensive role can be an attractive task. There are players who have even turned it into an art."

This, of course, was coaches speaking, and it was not encouraging. In fact it got worse. Not only were defenders praised, but forwards were scorned: "It is not at all decisive just how many forwards a coach includes in his lineup, what is decisive is just how many players can join in the attack. . . ."

Soccer tactics had evidently switched from a numbers game to a words game. But what spoke most loudly and most insistently was the game as seen on the field. Not good enough. Italia-90 produced the worst final in the history of the World Cup. "A disaster," commented Rinus Michels. And it touched a new record low on the scoring chart, with 2.21 goals per game.

World Cup-94 did a lot better. Goal-scoring went up by 23 percent to 2.71 goals per game. Half a goal per game better. The reason? Well, it could have been more accurate shooting, or the new soccer ball that the goalkeepers didn't like, or rotten goalkeepers, or the hot weather, or stricter refereeing . . . or just about anything. Who knew?

No shortage of explanations. But one explanation that was not put forward was that the jump in goal-scoring was the result of new tactics. There weren't any. "On the tactical side there was not a lot that was new," said the FIFA technical committee, repeating itself for the umpteenth time.

One of the more thoughtful English coaches, Frank Clark of Nottingham Forest, suggested: "I don't think there were any outstanding tactical innovations to emerge, probably because there aren't any left."

The death of tactics? If that was stretching things a little, no one could deny that tactical stagnation had set in. Normally, after a World Cup, coaches set to work analyzing the winning team, trying to discern the methods and secrets that had led to success. Carlos Alberto Parreira, coach of Brazil, told them, in effect: Don't bother. "As far as tactics went," he said, "we didn't do anything different. We played with a flat back four, zone marking, the usual Brazilian way."

He could have gone further. There wasn't even anything new from the Brazilians in an area where they had always been so cunning and inventive: free kicks. Only one of the eleven goals scored by Brazil came from a free kick, and there was nothing subtle or artistic about Branco's 30-yard thunderbolt against the Netherlands.

What Parreira did go on about, what he clearly did see as the secret of Brazil's success, was a different type of tactics altogether, what might be called psycho-tactics. The psychology of team play: "I didn't have to teach our players how to play soccer, but I did have to help them play as a unit. Off the field we didn't make the same mistakes as in previous World Cups, when our players were not happy in each other's company."

The Brazilian captain, Dunga, took up the theme: "We were a real team at last," said Dunga. "We had no stars, not even Romário. It was because he knew he was among friends that Romário played so well."

A FIFA rule change had helped here, thought Dunga. Not one of the highly publicized changes to the playing rules, but the change that allowed all the players to sit on the bench during a game (previously only the five named substitutes were permitted). Said Dunga: "It made a tremendous difference to us that all the members of the squad were allowed to be on the bench at this World Cup, and not have some players forced to sit in the stand during their own team's games. It made the group so much stronger to be all together during the games."

The unit. The team. The squad. The group. The theme of all-for-one and one-for-all had come over beautifully at each Brazilian game as the players emerged from the tunnel . . . holding hands, a human chain slowly making its way on to the field.

A chain? We've heard that before, the *catenaccio,* the great big chain, the ugly big chain, that blighted soccer in the 1960s. But this was something very different. Nothing big or ugly about this, simply a chain, a plain *catena,* of soccer players. Perhaps this was the new formation, one that transcended tactics. Brazil-94: 1-1-1-1-1-1-1-1-1-1-1.

Tactics, went the old joke, are what you need when you don't have players. Could it be that the decline of tactics meant that soccer was returning to its roots, to become a game that was about players, rather than about coaches and formations?

An exhilarating thought. One that meshed nicely with a mood that had been growing for several years. There had been signs that the modern, highly trained coaches were having second thoughts about what they were up to.

The awful truth had sunk in that, once upon a time—when there were no coaches—there was no shortage of good players. There was even a hint that the players might have been better in those coachless days.

Where had the players come from? Why, they grew up playing soccer in the streets. But street soccer was dying, killed off by heavy traffic, superhighways, and a whole host of social changes. Not to worry, the coaches would reinvent it.

Street soccer was subjected to serious analysis, and its key was discovered: the teams were small, so that each player got a lot of touches of the ball, and the space was restricted. A new coaching vogue swept in: small-sided games in restricted areas.

In 1993 the United States Youth Soccer Association adopted small-sided games as the official USYSA way to develop young players. The enthusiam was tremendous, and really rather sad.

For the modern, scientific, *organized* approach to street soccer left out, or completely squashed, the key element. Which was that it was never really seen by the participants as anything more than messing about. Sure, plenty of good players started that way—but did they take part with the attitude of "now for another training session that will help make me a better player and get me a job as a pro"? Messing about, and the fact that adults disapproved, was justification enough.

Nothing complicated or glamorous, just boys at play in Mexico City. The free-dom and joys of the fast-disappearing street soccer were praised by coaches in the 1990s. But their attempts to simulate it as a training method missed the crucial point.
© Peter Robinson: The Football Archive

It was a child's world in which the children were free to make all sorts of dreadful mistakes—without the destructive interference of the well-meaning, helpful adult. Bluntly, a world in which a coach was the last thing that was needed.

The worst fault of the modern coach was exposed. Nothing could be left alone; everything had to be organized and, if possible, "corrected."

The meddlesome touch was seen again, at the end of the promising World Cup-94. The soccer played in the tournament was definitely more open, more attack-oriented, than most of that seen in 1990. But the coaches, not the players, had the last word. At the last gasp, when the 1994 tourna-ment had built up to what promised to be a brilliant final, Arrigo Sacchi and Carlos Alberto Parreira took over.

Two coaches who had never played soccer at a high level, two coaches much intrigued by the theory and practice of tactics. Parreira was right; there was nothing new here. Just caution. More of a chess game than a soccer game, ending in stalemate. A dreadful anticlimax to a colorful, dramatic tournament. A tactically imposed 0–0 tie.

We have followed soccer tactics for over one hundred years, from the primi-tive days of the backer-up, to the pyramid and the numbers game, and on to the present where player movement is so fluid that diagrams and num-bers can no longer explain what is going on.

Perhaps they never did. Certainly, they can never be accurate guides to everything that happens on the soccer field. Rather, they are a first step to understanding the action. They should provide the mind with a loose basic structure against which the significance of player movements can be intelligently assessed. They should never be seen as rigid frameworks into which players and action *have* to fit.

The difficulty of analyzing something as unpredictable as soccer is already substantial, and it has not been helped by the problem mentioned at the beginning of this chapter, namely, the disorganized state of the sport's vocabulary, particularly that part of it that deals with player positions.

Terminology has struggled to keep up with changes on the field, with the result that old terms are used for new positions, and no longer describe the function. As the game has become more fluid, the terms have tended to become more general.

Where once there were center forwards or left or right wingers there are now, simply, strikers or forwards. Fullbacks have become defenders, shedding the implication that they stay at the back. Indeed, the outside backs are now often called wingbacks to emphasize that they do go forward into the areas that used to be occupied by wingers.

Function is now more important than position. A back is described as a marking back, or simply as a man-marker. Halfbacks have become midfielders, and they, too, are not about to be positionally tied down by strict definition as left or right midfielder. They are described as right-sided or left-sided players.

Johan Cruyff, the star of Dutch total soccer in the 1970s, was a key figure in this breaking down of the rigidity of soccer positions. When he turned to coaching at Barcelona, he created a team in the modern image, one of rapid movement and position switching, which he found difficult to describe: "When journalists ask me how Barcelona plays, I give them a 3-1-2-2-1-1 formation, so that they have an approximate idea. But that's just for the journalists." All modern formation diagrams bristle with arrows, the nearest they can get to conveying the bustling movement. Diagram 18 is an attempt to capture the player movement on Cruyff's Barcelona.

If the naming of player positions has caused problems, the numbering has added to the confusion. The original idea that each number would represent a position had some merit in days when there was only one team formation, and when there was no substitution. Today it is patently absurd. Positionally, the numbers mean nothing anymore. The sooner that the American system of assigning a number to a player—his to wear whatever the position he plays—is universally adopted the better it will be for soccer.

Before finishing this survey of soccer's tactical history, two important themes that have run through this chapter should be revisited.

First, the relationship between systems and individual players. Many coaches are fond of saying that players must never be forced into a

Diagram 18: Barcelona 1993

ZUBIZARETA

KOEMAN

GOICOCHEA

FERRER

NADAL   AMOR

GUARDIOLA

BEGUIRISTAIN

BAKERO

STOICHKOV

LAUDRUP

system, but that the system must always be adapted to the players. An engaging theory, but at best only a half-truth. For the superstars, yes, the system will more likely than not be adapted. But a merely good player who cannot or will not play the role his coach desires will almost certainly be replaced by a player who will. There is no shortage of good players. What is true is that the more skillful the players, the more flexible and therefore the better a system will be.

Second, the attitude of the players and, above all, of the coach. The growing defensiveness of soccer has been discussed at length. Yet it should be clear that the decisive factor in this negative trend is not so much the positioning of the players, as their state of mind. A team that *wants* to attack, *will* attack, regardless of its formation.

The opposite of course is equally true. A team that is unwilling—read frightened—to attack, will not attack, or will do so without conviction. It was that caution, that fear of taking risks, that lay at the root of soccer's problems at the beginning of the 1990s. The orthodox view—and statistical support for it was not lacking—was that coaches who concentrated on building strong defenses were the ones who won titles, and the ones who kept their jobs.

Immediately after the disastrous 1990 World Cup, FIFA Secretary General Blatter had asked: "What is up with the coaches who, more than anyone else, have the power to change the face of soccer?" It was surely a rhetorical question; no one really expected any move toward more exciting soccer to come from the coaches.

Not even Blatter—because FIFA quickly embarked on a series of rule changes designed to liven the game up, to cut down on the negative things that were dominating the game. Far from relying on the development of new tactics, this approach was, if anything, antitactical. An attempt to counter the fear-ridden, defensive tactics that had the game in their grip.

The challenge for the sport's leaders was to devise new rules that would change that defensive mentality—that would ensure that risk-taking, entertaining soccer could also be winning soccer.

–9–
The Changing Game

Once upon a time, soccer had been a freewheeling, positive game in which the primary aim was to score goals. But as the sport entered the 1990s, negativity ruled, and what mattered most was to prevent the other side from scoring. What had gotten into soccer to so distort its original nature?

In a word: money. Those bewhiskered Victorian English gentlemen who had so stoutly resisted the rise of professionalism in the nineteenth century would have tut-tutted many an "I told you so." The sport moved from recreational activity, on through spreading professionalism, until during the 1970s and 1980s, it became a worldwide industry generating an annual turnover of some $200 billion.

Along the way, it lost its innocence and a great deal of its freedom. Millions of dollars could now be at stake on a single result. At the top, soccer was no longer a game to be played; it was a business venture to be calculated, to be financed—and to be organized.

Organized not only on the business side, but on the field as well. Gone were the days when a team "just went out and played" as Carlos Peucelle's Argentina had done in 1930. No more of that. Organization, which meant tactics, was now required. Enter the coach as the high priest of the modern game.

Suddenly, it was not the players who won games. That was the coach's job. Or was it? Taking the field determined to win, to play attacking soccer, was considered a rash way of going about things. After all, every game started with the score tied—if you didn't give up any goals, you couldn't lose, right?

Rather than Thou Shalt Win, the first commandment of coaching became Thou Shalt Not Lose. And the way not to lose was to concentrate on defense. Well-organized defenses, often manned by average or even mediocre players, were the representative feature of soccer teams in the 1980s.

This was not exactly new: The Italian *catenaccio* system of the 1960s had been built around a strong defense. But *catenaccio* had always had a place for the skilled attacking players who could operate its sudden counter-attacks.

The new defensive mentality of the 1970s and 1980s paid little attention to the attack. Now, the priority was to destroy the opponent's game—"stop them playing" became a much valued phrase—and hope to steal a goal that would settle the game. "In the past," said the former French star Michel Platini, "a team made sure that it built up its own game before destroying that of its opponents. Nowadays, the primary objective is to destroy and only afterward, if at all, to build up."

Packed defenses and tight, overtly physical marking became common-place. The emphasis placed on defense meant that everyone was expected to defend, including the forwards, though there was often only one of these. Everyone was expected to cover an enormous amount of territory. Work-rate became another hallowed term. The sad thing for soccer was that it worked. Heavily populated, hard-tackling defenses could make it almost impossible for the opponents to score.

The loneliness of the modern striker. Romário of Brazil is confronted by the usual massed ranks of Italian defenders. During the 1970s the defensive tactic of getting as many players as possible behind the ball was widely adopted.
© Peter Robinson: The Football Archive

The pendulum started to swing heavily against the skilled players, the ball-artists, the dribblers. Soccer was becoming a game for athletes and for runners; stamina was more important than skill. Irishman George Best, the most talented British player of his generation, had this to say in 1975: "Stamina's all right, you've got to be able to run, but you've also got to be able to do the main thing and the main thing at soccer is to know what to do with the ball. At its simplest level that's what is wrong with British football today. Too many people who can run all day but can't kick a bloody football."

The reliance on physical power was only half the story. As the marking got tighter, the fouling got worse and worse. Defenders seemed to have been given *carte blanche* to rough up forwards, barreling into them from behind, tripping and holding them. Nothing was done about it. The kicking went on; the game deteriorated. George Best quit soccer in 1972 at the ridiculously early age of 26 because he was tired of being close-marked and kicked, because he no longer enjoyed playing the game.

Claudio Gentile, the Italian defender whose roughhouse play helped Italy to win the 1982 World Cup, shrugged off criticism with, "Soccer is not a sport for ballerinas." This was the voice of machismo echoing down the ages, the very same voice that, in 1863, had wanted to make soccer a "manly" game in which hacking, or kicking opponents' legs, was okay. The champions of brute force had lost out then, but they had never really gone away. One hundred and twenty years later they were back, threatening to dominate the sport.

The easy answer to those who complained about the trend was that the referees were to blame for not enforcing the rules. But this was much too simplistic. The fact was that flagrant fouling had become accepted by most players and coaches, who excused even the worst transgressors with a cynical "What else could he do?" plea.

Even when a referee did feel inclined to clamp down, the rules did not really offer punishment harsh enough to discourage offenders. Things got to the point where a defender was *expected* to trip a forward who was heading for goal, and would probably be castigated by his coach if he didn't. The resultant free kick and maybe a yellow card for the defender were worth it to prevent a shot on goal.

That was the so-called professional foul, also known as the tactical foul. The new coach-dominated version of the game was never at a loss for words and terms that would hide the ugliness of what was going on.

As the coach became more important, the discipline of coaching started to dress itself up in academic garb. Suddenly, there was the coaching industry. Coaching courses, licenses and diplomas proliferated all over the world. Coaching seminars, coaching symposia, coaching workshops, and coaching clinics were all the rage. Learned treatises and books and videotapes on coaching were published at an alarming rate. A pseudo-scientific coaching jargon spread across the sport. What J.C. Thring had called The Simplest Game in 1862 was in danger of becoming The Most Complex Sport.

This sport, which had once been improvised by the players on the field, now seemed to be more about charts and diagrams and Xs and Os than about people. There was not much room anymore for the freelance, inventive type of player. The coach had his plans and his tactics, and the players had to fit in, had to play their roles, and not wander off into flights of creative fantasy.

The artists were a problem for the coaches, who recognized their brilliance but didn't know what to do with them, didn't trust them to do what they were told. The coaches were right, of course. The artists couldn't be trusted to play according to instructions. The essence of their game was the sudden burst of unpredictable skill, the genius of the unexpected.

Treated with suspicion by coaches, mercilessly fouled by opponents, the artists began to disappear from the game. Pelé, one of the greatest of them, looked at the game of the 1980s: "It used to be, in the 1960s, even into the 1970s, that every national team had two or three world-class players. Now, it is difficult to find five or six in the whole world."

Soccer's slide into defensive negativity was greatly helped by the curious fact that so many of the modern coaches had been defenders in their playing days. Maybe not so curious. The creative players were the instinctive players, the ones who never had to do much thinking about their game, who were not interested in elaborate theories of how to play. Players like England's Jimmy Greaves, a prolific goal scorer in the 1960s, who said of one coach: "The way he talks about football sometimes, I think it must be easier to split the atom than score a goal."

Greaves was never interested in becoming a coach, nor was Pelé. Johan Cruyff, the Dutch creative genius of the 1970s, did become a coach and nurtured a wonderfully lively attacking team at Barcelona.

The defenders were often no more than average players who had spent a good deal of time thinking about the game in an effort to improve their own performances. They were the perfect raw material for the age of academic coaching.

Functional. That is the kindest word to describe the type of soccer that dominated in the 1970s and 1980s. A no-frills game that eschewed risk taking and that squeezed the inventive ballplayers out of the game. Along with those players went the very lifeblood of the sport: goals. In the English first division, the average was 2.5 per game in the 1980s, the first time it had ever sunk below 3.00. In low-scoring Italy, it went from 2.2 in the 1970s, to 2.0 in the 1980s.

And of course, the game suffered as a spectacle. The stars who produced the oohs and the aahs from the fans were lacking. Players were now complimented—by the coaches—for their commitment rather than their skill; teams were praised for being well-organized, or hard to beat. The fans voted with their feet, and during the 1980s attendances were at best static, more often they were falling.

The eighties were an unhappy decade for soccer, not only because so much of the soccer was barren, but because no one felt the urge to do anything about it. This *laissez-faire* attitude produced its most damaging results off the field.

Throughout the 1970s the menace of crowd violence was growing, particularly in England. Games became the excuse for a weekly orgy of bloodletting between rival gangs of fans. Pitched battles on the terraces, field invasions, and skirmishes with the police outside the stadiums became a Saturday afternoon ritual. Excursion trains were wrecked, stores looted, innocent bystanders were often injured.

The problem was exported to Europe. Whenever England, or an English club team, played on the continent it was bound to be accompanied by an army of mindless thugs, intent on getting drunk and causing mayhem. They seemed to have little interest in soccer, and were constantly described as "a small group of troublemakers who aren't even soccer fans."

Maybe so. But they were a frightening menace wherever they went, and if they were a small group, then there always seemed to be far too many others willing to join in once the violence had started.

English soccer stadiums, once the scene of good-natured fraternization among opposing fans, began to resemble concentration camps, as huge metal fences were erected to separate—and cage—the home fans from the visiting fans, and hundreds of uniformed police were on duty.

The countermeasures were expensive, and not particularly effective. Arrests and prosecutions were rare. And very little was done to prevent the hooligans—as England's fans were now widely known—from traveling to Europe.

By the 1980s, other countries were producing their own groups of violent fans, frequently—as in England—professing extreme right-wing and racist views. There was talk of an international fraternity of hooligans. Could anyone doubt that a major disaster was on its way?

Just as no one wanted to do anything about soccer's on-the-field problems, so no one wanted to think about hooligan problems. The awful climax duly arrived, on May 29, 1985, at the Heysel Stadium, in Brussels. The day of the European Cup final, the climax to the club season, between Liverpool of England and Juventus of Italy.

Crammed into the ancient stadium were tens of thousands of fans from both teams. A dangerous situation, made lethal because at one end of the field they were separated only by a flimsy wire fence. That was where, before the game, the Liverpool supporters began taunting the Italians. Insults flew, then missiles, then the English charged, and broke through the fence. The Italians tried to flee, but there was no escape. Thirty-eight people—mostly Juventus fans—were either suffocated or crushed to death.

This carnage had been produced by a "small group of troublemakers"? The lie to that convenient myth was given when the Belgian authorities decided to go ahead and play the game anyway. It started ninety minutes late, while bodies were still being removed from the stadium. The game had to be played because the organizers were afraid that worse trouble would follow if they canceled it!

At long last some action was taken. UEFA banned English clubs from playing in Europe, though the England national team, always followed by some of the worst of the hooligans, was absurdly exempted. The Belgian authorities were roundly criticized for not adequately separating the opposing fans. But the real culprits were those soccer authorities, particularly in England, who had dozed for so long while the problem grew.

Was there any connection between the violence that was now so common on the soccer field, and the violence of the fans? That was one for the sociologists to fathom. Superficially, it did seem appropriate that the grim-faced, cynical soccer of the 1970s and 1980s, a sport in which kicking opponents was the done thing, should be followed by louts looking for trouble.

It was also appropriate that the Juventus–Liverpool game that was allowed to overlap the killing, was a dull, tedious 1–0 affair that was decided in Juventus's favor when the referee awarded the Italians a penalty kick for a Liverpool offense committed well outside the penalty area.

Heysel had rammed home the message that the gloves had to come off if hooliganism was to be halted. But an unmistakable call for action to clean up the game on the field had yet to be heard. Alarm bells were ringing throughout the 1980s, the tide of violence on the field was rising, but FIFA replied only with exhortation.

Before the 1982 World Cup in Spain, FIFA asked all the participating countries to sign a pledge that read: "Violence distorts and disgraces sport . . . . We are aware of our responsibilities and undertake to play with respect for the rules, the referees, and our opponents." It was during that tournament that Toni Schumacher brutally assaulted Patrick Battiston, and Claudio Gentile fouled his way to a World Cup winner's medal.

A FIFA Fair Play Campaign had been started in 1987, because, said FIFA, "The idea of fair play has been neglected for so long that certain unfortunate excesses have brought discredit to sports." But exhortation was not enough. The "unfortunate excesses" continued, along with all the little defensive tactics that had been developed to stop opponents' playing, or to waste time: defenders refusing to retreat ten yards on free kicks, players feigning injury, goalkeepers freezing the action by holding on to the ball. Players had become so expert at time-wasting that there were games during the 1986 World Cup in which the actual playing time was only forty-three minutes.

Before Italia-90, FIFA general secretary Sepp Blatter had said: "What FIFA wants the sport to do at the beginning of the new decade, is to 'Go For Goal,' so that soccer shall be an enjoyable, attacking game. Scoring goals is the most enjoyable activity on the field."

Italia-90 made a mockery of Blatter's words, by recording the lowest goals-per-game average ever: 2.21. The shortcomings of the soccer played during the tournament could not be ignored. The sport was clearly having problems.

The winds of change began to blow through the hitherto inflexible minds of the FIFA bosses, including the president, João Havelange. FIFA was now looking for ways to make soccer a goal-scoring game, to return it to its attacking roots, if you like. A task force was set up, Football 2000, to evaluate the situation and suggest what needed to be done, including possible rule changes, to "safeguard the game's attraction (motto: more goals)."

This was a spectacular U-turn for FIFA, a body that had always cast a withering eye on anyone brave enough to suggest that the rules be altered. Sepp Blatter, the driving force behind the upheaval, said: "You have to appreciate the change that has occurred in FIFA. Dr. Havelange was for a long time a very conservative man, but now he is very open."

The classic example of FIFA's orthodoxy had come in 1982 when the English—yes, the conservative English—decided that something had to be done to stop the "professional fouls." They ruled that in England such fouls would be punished with a red card.

It was a sensible, long overdue attempt to reverse the "anything goes" attitude that prevailed in the sport. FIFA stepped in and told the English they couldn't do it, they were not entitled to change the rules of the game.

That was FIFA in 1982. But in 1990, FIFA itself introduced precisely the same rule change. By then, it was clear that there had to be rule changes if soccer was to escape from the defensive mire that it had fallen into. The idea that the required change in mentality would come about through the development of new tactics was no longer credible.

Even then, the road to reform was anything but smooth. Rule changes had to be approved by FIFA's own Referees Committee, and then by the rigidly conservative International Board. As if those two obstacles weren't enough, it was soon clear that there was a third barrier—the officials, linesmen as well as referees—themselves.

One of FIFA's changes was to the offside rule: An attacker in line with the last defender was now onside, rather than offside, a move that would help attacking play, and would make the use of the much-disliked offside trap more risky. The benefits were slow to appear—because linesmen could not, or would not, change their habits. It was almost as though the officials were intent on sabotaging the change. Jack McCabe, chairman of the United States Soccer Federation's Referees' Committee, spelled out the attitude: "I think the new rule isn't going to change things very much. Linesmen are still going to call offside pretty much the same. . . ."

That was the view from the United States, but it was an accurate reflection of the worldwide situation. Ironic really, for the world's soccer officials to agree on a question of interpretation. Historically, this had always been the great problem area.

One of the duties of FIFA's Referees' Committee had for years been spelled out as "to establish as far as possible uniformity in methods of refereeing." The very wording—"as far as possible"—revealed a pessimistic view of the possibilities of success.

A more positive note was struck in 1990. The Referees' Committee was to "establish uniformity." Period. No more pussyfooting around with "as far as possible." The referees had obviously been targeted for a shake-up by the increasingly active Sepp Blatter.

Nobody was happy with the referees' performances during the World Cup in Italy. In fact, Blatter was disgruntled ten weeks before the tournament even started, when over 50 percent of the selected referees failed the preliminary fitness test. Blatter openly criticized referee performance during the tournament and announced that, for future World Cups, the maximum age for referees would be reduced from 50 to 45, hinting that he thought it should probably be even lower. For good measure, international referees would also need a basic knowledge of English, and a new class of specialist international linesmen was created.

None of this came easily. "It has taken me five years to get the Referees' Committee to accept the idea of specialist linesmen," said Blatter. "For that we don't even need to change the rules. But they don't want to try anything, they just say no. We have to convince them that they should be part of the spectacle of soccer. They are not messengers sent by God to control the show." The somber image of the referees, dressed in their traditional all-black uniforms, was not much to Blatter's liking. By the time the 1994 World Cup came around, the funereal black had been banished. Referees now had a choice of silver, gold, or pink shirts.

When Blatter said in 1991 that "raising the standards of refereeing is one of the key considerations in our sport" what he had in mind was the introduction of professional referees: "Before the end of the century, the referees in most national leagues will be full-time paid officials."

It had the ring of a worthy, forward-looking idea, but it was an idea that—like so many things involving referees—was to prove difficult to put into practice.

Blatter's own insistence that 45, or maybe even 40, should be the maximum age for international referees did not help. If there was to be a new profession of refereeing, such early exclusion from its top level could not be counted a selling point.

In Italy the plan was to introduce fully professional referees by the 1993–94 season. It didn't happen. What did happen was that the Italian Federation greatly increased payments and allowances for working time lost. The top referees, therefore, tended to be those whose normal work allowed them to devote a fair amount of their time to refereeing matters: games, travelling, training, attending clinics, etc.

FIFA quietly stopped talking about professional referees, and referred instead to the professionalization of refereeing.

Despite its newly progressive attitude, FIFA remained curiously blind on the matter of tiebreakers. The word itself was comparatively new to the sport. But it cropped up constantly during the 1980s as defensive play and coaching caution led to an inexorable increase in the number of tied games.

Not genuine ties, where both teams had tried their darndest to win, but things had finished in a standoff anyway. These were engineered ties, in which one team, or even both teams, had played deliberately for a draw. The scoreless tie was now a common feature of the game.

Frequently reviled, rarely revered, the referee posed all sorts of difficulties for FIFA. Attempts to introduce professional referees ran into problems. And FIFA's rule changes were likely to be sabotaged by referees who did not enforce them.
© Peter Robinson: The Football Archive

FIFA intervened, not because 0–0 ties were boring but because tied games messed up the schedules in tournaments. A winner had to pass on to the next round, and there was no time for replays. So the penalty-kick tiebreaker was introduced, a move that will not go down as one of FIFA's more thoughtful contributions to the game.

The penalty-kick tiebreaker is a gimmick tacked on to the end of a game that has absolutely nothing to do with what has gone before, and that is very likely to reward defensively oriented teams. If a team feels that it cannot beat its opponents by playing soccer during the regular game, the alternative is to play defensively for 120 minutes, get the tie, then trust to the 50-50 toss-up of the tiebreaker.

Anyone who doubted that scenario had his eyes opened by Red Star of Belgrade and its performance in the 1991 European Cup final. Its opponent was Olympique-Marseille. It was a game that many had been savoring, as it brought together two attacking, goal-scoring teams. The morning of the game, the London *Times* rejoiced: "The match has all the ingredients for a marvelous final, especially with such a profusion of skill in midfield . . . both teams are riding a crest, both attack persistently."

A reasonable forecast, but one that was destroyed by Red Star's tactics. Said coach Ljupko Petrovic: "We realized that we could not beat Marseille unless they made a mistake, so I told my players to hold out for penalties."

Hold out they did. Defending with sullen tenacity, making no use at all of their attacking talent (just three shots in the whole game, all off target), Red Star turned the game into a monstrous bore, and a deplorable farce. But they got what they wanted, a 0–0 tie after 120 minutes, and went on to win the penalty-kick tiebreaker.

"We did not invent the present rules, which include penalty kicks and invite the use of tactics to reach the penalty kick shoot-out stage," said Petrovic. In other words, the tiebreaker had encouraged Red Star to play for a tie!

In 1987 the under-17 World Championship was won by the USSR—on penalty kicks. An absurd result, for the USSR had been comprehensively outplayed during the game by Nigeria, which did everything but put the ball in the net.

But FIFA did not take the hint, and persisted with penalty kicks, even when its own Football 2000 Task Force reported that 80 percent of the letters it had received were hostile to the use of the penalty-kick tiebreaker.

It was soccer's familiar pattern of allowing things to slide until the worst was bound to occur. That moment duly arrived at eleven minutes past three in the Rose Bowl on July 17, 1994. Franco Baresi began his run up, and the World Cup final was about to be decided on penalty kicks.

Seven minutes later, as Roberto Baggio ballooned his kick over the bar, Brazil were world champions . . . not because they had won a soccer game, but because they had won the shootout. The Italians, understandably, didn't like it: "A lottery," said defender Luigi Apolloni. But the winning coach, too, was unhappy: "It's not the best way of deciding a championship," said Parreira.

So what was the best way? Before 1986, World Cup rules had stipulated that if the final game was tied after overtime (it had never happened) the game would be replayed three days later. The U.S. organizers had requested a return to that system. FIFA had turned them down.

Should FIFA reconsider? "No," said Parreira, "the players are completely concentrated on the day of the final itself, and it would be impossible to motivate them for a replay three days later. There's only one World Cup final day."

Another possibility was sudden-death overtime (traditionally, the two 15-minute overtime periods have always been played to a finish, regardless of scoring). This was tried out during the 1993 and 1995 under-20 and under-17 World Cups. Only three games (all three, oddly, involved Australia) in the four tournaments were decided by a sudden-death goal, hardly enough to provide any convincing evidence either for or against. "Further tests should be carried out," said FIFA's Technical Committee.

But the outcry against the use of penalty kicks in 1994 had been so great that FIFA felt obliged to move rapidly. In less than a year (that is rapid movement when it comes to changing soccer's rules) the change was made. If there was overtime in the 1998 World Cup in France, the game would end as soon as the first goal went in. Sudden death.

Actually, no. FIFA found negative, possibly even necrophilic, connotations in the phrase "sudden death." They preferred to emphasize the winning goal with the term "golden goal."

The golden goal was supposed to make it less likely that a game would have to be resolved on penalty kicks. But would it? There were those who thought sudden death would make penalty kicks *more* likely. Among them Martin Dahlin, the Swedish forward who had scored four goals during World Cup-94: "It would encourage even more negative play because teams would be frightened of conceding the goal. In 'normal' overtime, a team that goes behind still has a chance of equalizing and winning."

A much more plausible tiebreaker—the counting of corner kicks during a game—remained unexplored. The advantage of corner kicks was that it was something that worked throughout the regular game. To get corner kicks, a team had to attack, it had to get down the other end of the field. If it played defensively, camped in its own half, it would inevitably give up corners and not gain any. The chances were high that with the game opened up, more goals would be scored and it would not be necessary to use the tiebreaker.

Much less controversial was FIFA's amended "back-pass" rule. The sight of a defender playing the ball backward, into the safe hands of his own goalkeeper—who then took anything up to twenty seconds to release it—could almost stand as a symbol of negative play. FIFA put a stop to that by banning the goalkeeper from using his hands on such a pass. That was a worldwide, permanent rule change, approved by the International Board, and generally welcomed within the game.

There were other changes that applied only for the duration of certain FIFA tournaments. Published in memoranda issued to referees and coaches before the tournaments, these were often substantial changes that contradicted the rules of the game. The memorandum put out before Italia-90, for instance, stated: "Coaching of players during a game is permitted only from the team's bench." Yet the FIFA rules clearly stated that a referee "shall not allow coaching from the boundary lines."

The thin end of the sideline-coaching wedge was in place. Three years later FIFA rammed that wedge right into the heart of the game and allowed what it had so long resisted. Capitulation was complete: the rules were altered to allow the coaches to "convey tactical instructions" provided they stayed within a yard of the bench.

Give 'em a yard and they'll take . . . whatever they can get away with. Coaches were to be seen running up and down the sidelines, nowhere near their benches. A further addition to the rules was necessary. In 1993 came the technical area, which stretched out from the bench, stopping 1 yard short of the sideline. It was OK for the coach to yell instructions from within that area.

Some teams apparently had four or five coaches. A lot of people always seemed to be on their feet in the technical area, right out near the touchline. Another addition to the rule was necessary: only one person would be allowed to shout instructions, "after which he would be obliged to return to the substitutes' bench immediately."

Then it was discovered that there were coaches who had so much to say, particularly during critical moments of the game, that there just wasn't time for them to return to the bench between each salvo of vital coaching instructions. What could one do about them? Nowhere did the rules put any limit on the amount of coaching that could be done from the sidelines.

Sideline arguments between coaches, usually in a state of high agitation, and FIFA officials trying to get them to sit down were a regular feature of World Cup-94.

If this was symbolic of a struggle between FIFA and the coaches in general, the next round went to the coaches. FIFA agreed to experiment with another idea that was unheard of in soccer, that had always caused the purists to keel over backwards: time-outs.

Admittedly, there was considerable doubt about who really wanted time-outs. Was it the coaches—or was it television? When he heard about it, Burkhard Weber of the private German television channel RTL told *The European*: "We are very much in favor of this idea. A slot during the game would be much more desirable for our advertisers than one at half time when many fans are no longer paying attention to the screen. We would therefore get proportionately more income for that airtime, and that would help us to cope with the increasing expense of buying rights to matches."

That sounded right. Television money, which began to pour into soccer in the 1990s, could now force changes in the way that the game was played on the field. Not so, apparently. Television moguls denied exerting any pressure. Steve Dixon, in charge of soccer at ISL, the marketing colossus employed by FIFA, said "It took us by surprise . . . of course, it's something we're going to take at look at now."

It was the coaches, after all. "For some time now coaches have been clamoring for the chance to be able to exert more immediate influence on the course of the game," said the February 1995 *FIFA News*. So time-outs would be tested at the under-17 World Cup to be held later that year in Ecuador.

Where FIFA ran into another vocabulary problem. The local press insisted on calling the time-outs *tiempo muerte,* dead time. Blatter asked them to use instead *tiempo fuera,* a more literal translation.

It soon became clear that whoever "the coaches" were who had demanded time-outs, they didn't include most of those in Ecuador. Each team was allowed to call two 90-second time-outs per game, one in each half. Of a total of ninety-six time-outs that could have been called in the tournament's twenty-four games, only thirty-three were actually used. The tournament was won by Ghana, whose coach Samuel Arday did not use any time-outs and said: "The time-out should be abolished, it makes soccer like a basketball game, some other game altogether." Former Scottish international player Dave Mackay, the coach of Qatar said: "I'm all against them.

They just get used for time-wasting, or to stop a team that's putting you under pressure."

Rui Caçador, Portugal's coach, liked the time-out, but only for the boys, he didn't think it belonged in the senior game. Argentina's José Pekerman said: "There are pluses and minuses. It is good for the coaches. But I don't know whether it is good for the fans."

The fans made it pretty clear what they thought. The very first time-out of the tournament, called by Japan, was greeted with a prolonged barrage of derisory whistling. The fans did not appreciate the interruption.

Why would they? There could now be as much as six minutes of dead time during a game—and for the fans it clearly was dead time, whatever FIFA called it. As Dave Mackay had said, it was wasted time.

All very odd, because FIFA was waging a war on time-wasting, and had issued clear instructions to referees: any player who wastes time shall be cautioned. Two of its more successful recent rule changes—the ban on goalkeepers' handling back passes, and the requirement that injured players not be treated on the field but removed at once on a stretcher—were aimed at time-wasters. Yet here it was, experimenting with a change that allowed coaches to interrupt play four times a game.

The other main target for FIFA's flurry of rule changes in the 1990s was rough play. The "professional foul" had been outlawed in 1990. Next came what FIFA defined as "the dreaded tackle from behind." This was another step toward protecting the skillful players, the dribblers, who were always being clobbered from behind. Such tackles invariably resulted in the dribbler's being brought down, and quite often injured. The tackler would plead innocence of any foul, claiming, "But I got the ball, ref!" But rarely, if ever, did he get the ball without also getting the man.

The fate of Dutchman Marco Van Basten was dramatic proof of that. A prolific goal scorer, Van Basten was FIFA's 1992 World Player of the Year, one of the sport's most glittering stars. But years of being kicked by defenders had taken their toll. In 1993, at age 28, Van Basten needed an operation on his right ankle. Then another, and then a third. Comebacks were attempted, but all failed. After three years of suffering, Van Basten announced his retirement in 1995.

The memorandum issued to referees before the World Youth Championship (under-20) in 1993, declared flatly: "The tackle from behind is prohibited."

To see the tackle from behind banned—even if only for the length of a tournament—was a major step forward for attacking soccer. The fact that the rule change had been sneaked in by the back door of a memorandum (the rules themselves contained no mention of such tackles) was soon forgotten.

FIFA was on the warpath over this one, and during the run up to World Cup-94 repeatedly stressed that the ban would again apply. The tackle would be penalized with "immediate expulsion."

It sounded too good to be true, and it was exactly that. Mexican referee Arturo Brizio Carter, in the opening game of World Cup-94, made it clear that either his definition of a tackle from behind was greatly different from FIFA's, or he was simply ignoring the directive.

Other glaring examples of unpunished tackles from behind soon followed in other games, and FIFA backtracked with a much narrower definition of the tackle. "What we want to avoid," said Blatter, "are these no-chance situations of the attacker sprinting away and the defender attempting not to take the ball but to stop the player from behind. If the tackling player does not touch the ball, then he should be sent off."

The rule change was now pretty toothless. During the tournament, thirteen red cards were given, and not one of them was for a tackle from behind. FIFA could argue that the threat of expulsion had banished the tackles, but this was not so; defenders were still clattering into players from behind.

When the 1995 FIFA rules were published, they contained no mention of the tackle from behind. For that you had to turn to the back of the book under "Additional Instructions," where it did say that such a tackle, if "violent with little or no attempt to play the ball," should be punished with a red card.

But ejections were rare. The ban on tackles from behind was being sabotaged by the referees' reluctance to enforce it. "They have to get accustomed to it," said David Will, Chairman of FIFA's Referees' Committee, "You have to allow them time."

Possibly, though a check of the offside rule did not encourage optimism. The change in the rule had been made in 1990, yet five years later linesmen—even the new, specialized international linesmen—were still regularly flagging for offside against players who, being in line with the last defender, were onside under the new rule.

Of one thing there could be no doubt: The aim of FIFA's rule changing was to make life more difficult for defenders, to make them clean up their act. A determined effort was under way to counter the situation pictured by the Football 2000 task force members at its first meeting: "Present-day soccer is not very attractive to watch."

But the rule changes, however well-intentioned, did not please everyone. There were plenty of soccer people around who felt the game was perfectly OK as it was. They resented not only the changes, but the authoritarian way in which FIFA imposed them. In the mid-1990s opposition began to mount to what was seen as the increasingly autocratic rule of João Havelange, who had occupied the President's chair for over twenty years.

When the time came in 1994 for his re-election to what would be his sixth four-year term, there was talk of a candidate running against him, something that had never happened before. But no one could be found to stick his head above the parapet, and the formidable Havelange, at age 78, was elected yet again.

A year later UEFA issued a position paper on the future of soccer, which called for a strengthening of the continental confederations (such as UEFA), and a weakening of FIFA's power. Havelange, no doubt correctly, immediately read it as a threat to his authority: "I do not understand their hostility," he said. "If they want me to leave, they should say so, and I will go."

No one who knew Havelange believed a word of that, and sure enough, the old man who had already said he would not stand again in 1998, was soon saying that he just might run again.

If the sudden flurry of rule changes and a power struggle at the top suggested a sport in crisis, that was certainly not reflected down at the grass roots.

The number of players throughout the world registered with FIFA rose from 18 million in 1976 to 88 million in 1993. There were huge increases in China, which had not been a FIFA member until 1979, and in Africa, where improved organization allowed the counting of previously unregistered players.

Much of the growth was at the youth level. Now there were world championships for players in the under-17 and the under-20 age brackets. In 1989 came the first indoor, or five-a-side, world championship.

Women's soccer was on the rise, too, suggesting that another massive increase in playing numbers was yet to come. Three of FIFA's new realms came together in November 1991 when the first-ever Women's World Cup was staged in China . . . and won by the United States.

The growth of the game in the United States had not gone unnoticed by FIFA. The hugely successful staging of the 1994 World Cup in the USA sent a signal. The anomaly that this huge country, with its immense resources and its fanatic interest in sports, was not a part of the worldwide soccer family seemed to be coming to an end.

–10–

Soccer Comes to the United States

Until the 1990s not even the most chauvinistic American could claim that the United States had any influence on the development of soccer. For 130 years soccer's history was written in Europe and Latin America, rarely in the United States.

Once or twice the Americans were noticed, for relatively modest achievements like reaching the semi-finals of the first World Cup in 1930, or beating England in 1950. Achievements that were remarkable only *because* the United States was regarded as a lightweight in world soccer competition.

The lack of impact on the international scene was a faithful reflection of the sport's minor-league status within the United States. But it does not mean that there was no soccer activity at all. There was plenty.

Football, in its primitive rugby-soccer form, had crossed the Atlantic hard on the heels of the first New England settlers, and was soon giving the doughty Puritans the same sort of problems that it had caused in the home country. The Boston town authorities struck a familiar note in 1657:

> Forasmuch as sundry complaints are made that several persons have received hurt by boyes and young men playing at foot-ball in the streets . . .

and went on to impose a fine of twenty shillings on anyone who should be caught practicing the sport. It was not the first such ban, nor was it to be the last, but it was, like all the others, a waste of words.

Football found its way into schools and colleges, and by the early 1800s games were being played at several Ivy League universities, notably Harvard, Princeton, and Yale. Just as in England, rules were conspicuously absent, and it didn't take the university authorities long to decide that these tumultuous affrays between freshmen and sophomores were a blot on their academic escutcheon. By 1860 both Harvard and the local townsfolk had had enough of Bloody Monday—as the football day was called —and the sport suffered yet another banishment.

By this time "the dribbling game" had also arrived from England and had found a home in two New Jersey colleges, Princeton and Rutgers. When these two played each other for the first time, on November 6, 1869, the rules they used were a modification of those published in 1863 by the London Football Association.* In other words, the great Princeton–Rutgers game that is alleged to mark the beginnings of intercollegiate football was really a soccer game. Not soccer as we know it today, but soccer as it was then played, which included the use of the hands to catch or stop the ball.

Three years later Columbia and Yale had joined in, and it seemed that soccer was on its way as the fall sport of American colleges. Things did not work out that way because Harvard preferred its own version of football, in which players could pick up the ball (a round ball, let it be noted) and run with it. When other American colleges refused to play Harvard under such rules, the college turned to Canada and in 1874 scheduled two games with McGill University of Montreal.

The second of these was played with an egg-shaped ball under rugby-football rules, and proved greatly pleasing to the Harvard players. They adopted rugby, and induced Yale to follow suit. A game between the two in 1875 was watched by two Princeton players who returned to their own campus singing the praises of rugby and called a meeting to propose that Princeton's brand of football should henceforth be rugby, not soccer. By a narrow margin the students voted in favor of rugby, and as far as the colleges were concerned, soccer had to take a backseat.

To speculate a little, one has the feeling that even if the vote had gone in favor of soccer, the sport would not have lasted very long in the colleges. This was a time when America, beginning to assert its own nationality, was anxious to demonstrate that it was not a country built on other people's traditions.

The English, in particular, were a constant irritant, forever going on about the crudities of American life and declaiming that the only good things about it were those that had been imported from England. If there was one thing that American sportsmen wanted to avoid, it was the accusation that their sports, too, were crude imitations of the English originals. Cricket, that most English of games, had been, up until 1850, the most popular sport in the United States, but it was now condemned as effete and slow, and had given way to baseball, which, it was claimed, was of 100 percent American origin.**

---

*See chapter 1, page 8.

** When the English, quite rightly, pointed out that baseball was a form of rounders (an English game, of course), the Americans responded by concocting the rather silly tale that Abner Doubleday had invented baseball, all on his own, in 1839. It was not a very convincing story, but such was the desire of Americans to Americanize their sports that it was accepted uncritically.

In the colleges, rugby was soon swallowed up by the Americanization process. Within ten years a stream of rule changes had produced a new sport—football—that bore only the slightest likeness to rugby. Soccer, surely, would have suffered the same fate, producing heaven knows what kind of hybrid sports monster. Perhaps it is just as well for those who like soccer more or less the way it is that the sport escaped the clutches of the colleges in the 1870s.

By 1900, despite the college setback, amateur soccer was widely played throughout the eastern seaboard area, particularly around New York, New Jersey, and Philadelphia. *The New York Times* of the period covered many more soccer than football games, featuring teams such as Brooklyn Celtics, Anglo-Saxons F.C., Clan McKenzie F.C., Spanish–American F.C., and Over-Seas F.C.

The team names tell the story—teams composed largely of immigrants, jealously guarding the honor of the old country. What might be called the "ethnic factor" established itself very early in American soccer and has been a considerable nuisance ever since.

Actually, to say that soccer flourished "despite" the college setback is probably a non sequitur, for there is no evidence that the goings-on at Harvard and Princeton held any interest whatever for the organizers of amateur soccer. To them, the word "football" meant soccer, and when they got together in 1884 to form a league, they called themselves the American Football Association.

This was a notable first for the Americans: the first Football Association to be formed outside Britain. But within five years it was in trouble, plagued by internal squabbling, an activity that has since become almost the trademark of soccer in the United States.

The New York clubs complained that the league schedule put them at a disadvantage, and threatened to withdraw. Eventually, they did so, to form their own league, the American Amateur Football Association, thus distinguishing it from the AFA, which by the early 1900s had become a semi-professional league.

In 1912 both the AFA and the AAFA turned up at the FIFA congress in Stockholm, each requesting recognition as the controlling body of American soccer. FIFA, unaccustomed to such bickering among its members, sent them both packing with instructions to get together and form one national body. Within a year the AAFA had rounded up support from almost every other soccer group that it could find and formed yet another organization, the United States Football Association. In 1913 this group, USFA, returned to FIFA representing just about everyone except the semipro clubs of the AFA, but they, too, joined when FIFA announced recognition of the new organization.

Although its membership did include soccer leagues in Chicago, Pittsburgh, and St. Louis, the USFA was primarily an East Coast affair. In the soccer tradition it was run by amateurs, most of whom were not

Americans. Men like Randolph Manning, the English-born, German-educated doctor who was elected the association's first president and promptly declared that "the USFA aims to make soccer the national pastime of the winter in this country."

American soccer now had its governing body, but it was not headed for the glory foreseen by Dr. Manning. The birth pains of USFA had exposed some irritating faults in the American soccer community. Faults that, unfortunately, were to recur repeatedly throughout the following fifty years. The USFA was to undergo a series of name changes, but it could never move beyond what it had always been: an amateur organization, controlled in the main by immigrants and hyphenated-Americans. Its attempts to promote soccer as a major league sport, were constantly undermined by its own internal bickering and lack of vision.

Not that there is anything wrong with either immigrants or amateurs. The problem was that over the years the USFA tended to become a gathering place for immigrants whose devotion to soccer was a pretty good measure of their reluctance to become Americans, and for people who were amateurs mainly in the pejorative sense of the word. The very idea of such a group moving soccer into the American major league sports scene is almost hilarious.

There is no need to dwell on USFA's adventures for the next fifty years, for so very little was accomplished. Certainly, the organization slowly expanded its membership throughout the country, but at the same time it was withdrawing farther and farther into an ethnic shell. The colleges and high schools were completely ignored, while attempts to upgrade the professional side of the sport invariably ended in failure.

The most determined push for a pro league came in 1921 with the birth of the American Soccer League, an East Coast loop that included teams backed by major companies such as Bethlehem Steel Mills. A number of top international players, mostly from Scotland, joined the league, and it flourished until the end of the decade. Most of the players on the U.S. team that reached the semifinals of the first World Cup in 1930 were from the ASL.

But the league was greatly weakened—not by competition with baseball or football, but by an ongoing struggle with USFA over whether ASL teams could be forced to play in USFA's Cup competition. For a while, the ASL operated as a pirate league, unsanctioned by the USFA. By the time the dispute was settled, on October 9, 1929, the Wall Street crash was only weeks away. The depression, with its soaring unemployment and factory closings killed off the ASL in 1930.

For fifty years soccer remained an immigrant sport outside the mainstream of American sporting life. Americans had good reason to think of soccer as a foreign sport because, even within the United States, it was practiced mainly by foreigners who seemed to rejoice in giving their leagues and teams foreign titles and names.

Another turn-off was the possibility of trouble at the games. No doubt this was the exception rather than the rule, but it was still far too common. Discipline, exercised ultimately by USFA in the form of club or player suspensions, was simply not enforced, and the newspapers had a field day with stories like these:

From *The New York Times*, April 20, 1927

FOUR HURT IN RIOT AT SOCCER CONTEST
2 Women & 2 Men Injured During Fight in
Uruguay-Boston Game at Malden, Mass.

SOUTH AMERICANS RESCUED
Members of Team Rushed from Scene by Police when Crowd Threatens

TWO PLAYERS UNCONSCIOUS
Boston Athletes Carried Off as 2000 Persons Swarm on Field -
Referee's Decision Starts Melee

From *The New York Times*, February 13, 1928

POLICE IN BATTLE WITH SOCCER FANS
Reserves Called Out When the Spectators at Bayonne
Join Fight Among Players

NIGHTSTICKS SWING FREELY
Melee Starts After Hispano Eleven Beats Rovers
for Northern New Jersey Title

And so on, and so on. American soccer, through its own slackness, was building up an image of riots and referee-bashing rather similar to that which had surrounded baseball at the turn of the century. Baseball, in the person of Ban Johnson, quickly solved its problem by taking firm steps to enforce the rules and protect the umpires. Soccer did nothing, and the image of rampaging fans is one that continues, to this day, to damage soccer's standing in the United States.

But even an institution as insular as American soccer had become could not forever remain untouched by what was going on around it. In 1945 USFA showed that it had, at last, realized that the word football did not mean soccer in the United States and changed its name to the United States Soccer Football Association (USSFA).

It was the slenderest of straws in the slightest of winds, but it was certainly drifting in the right direction. Then the increased efficiency of air travel resulted in more visits from top foreign teams. Liverpool of England

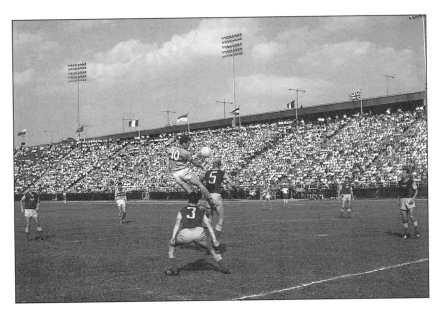

The International Soccer League, Randall's Island Stadium, New York 1963. Geoff Hurst (#10) of England's West Ham United in action against Dukla-Prague of Czechoslovakia. Organized by promoter Bill Cox, ISL games consistently drew five figure attendances.
© Paul Gardner

made two highly successful tours in 1946 and 1948. The climax of the second tour was a game against the Swedish team Djurgaardens, played in the old Brooklyn Dodgers stadium at Ebbets Field. Billed as the first meeting on American soil of two major foreign teams, the game drew over 18,000 spectators.

A point had been made. Top teams, playing in major league stadiums, could draw big crowds. Throughout the 1950s an average of six foreign teams a year came to the United States, including some of the really big names: Real Madrid, Manchester United, Vasco da Gama, Celtic, Rapid-Vienna.

They played exhibition games only, and it occurred to one promoter that the games might be better if there were something at stake. That individual was Bill Cox. Significantly, he was an American, and a baseball rather than a soccer man. At least, he had once been a baseball man, owner of the Philadelphia Phillies. Caught betting on his own team, he had been banished from baseball by Commissioner Judge Landis.

In 1960 Cox organized the International Soccer League in New York, composed of eleven foreign teams, plus the American All-Stars, playing for a championship. They were by no means top teams (though, looking back, one has to admire Cox's talent for selecting young teams—like West Ham United of London and Dukla-Prague—that were on the verge of success), and the organization of the tournament, played at the Polo Grounds, left much to be desired. But it was still incomparably better than anything the local ethnic leagues had to offer.

The International Soccer League broke no box-office records, but its better games consistently drew five-figure crowds. At a time when the major league sports of football, basketball, baseball, and hockey were falling over themselves to expand or start new leagues, it began to occur to franchise-seekers that pro soccer might have some potential. Better yet, because it would be starting virtually from the ground level, it might have the greatest potential of all.

Suddenly, in the fall of 1965, soccer had what it had never had before: wealthy American businessmen and promoters eager to invest in it. In fact, it had rather too many of them. Three distinct groups now wanted to start up nationwide pro soccer leagues, groups that included men like Lamar Hunt, Jack Kent Cooke, Judge Roy Hofheinz, and major corporations such as Madison Square Garden and R.K.O.-General.

The scene was set for the showdown that would drag American soccer into the twentieth century. The catch for all the new soccer investors was this: if they wanted to operate within the structure of FIFA-controlled worldwide soccer, which they assuredly did, they would have to have the approval of the USSFA. Most of them were aware of this, but regarded it as a trifling formality, a bit of meaningless form-filling. All three groups duly sent off letters to USSFA requesting sanction for their proposed leagues.

What happened next could have come straight out of a quaint English comedy movie. On one side big businessmen, wealthy, influential boardroom people, with assistants and secretaries and chauffeured limousines at their beck and call. On the other, USSFA, an organization made up of part-timers, mostly foreign-born, housed in an incredibly dingy and untidy office in midtown Manhattan. Presiding over the office, with his sleeves rolled up and his suspenders in full view, a sharp-tongued Irish-American, Joe Barriskill.*

For soccer, there was to be more tragedy than comedy in the confrontation. Suspicion and mistrust were mutual. USSFA appointed a committee—composed of a Romanian-American, a Scottish-American, and a German-American—to deal with the proposals. The committee was, not without reason, dubious about the motives of the new soccer fanatics: Were they genuinely interested in the sport, or did they simply want to exploit it, to make money out of it?

For the new owners, the situation was downright incredible. In any other American sport, if you wanted to start up a league, you just got the capital together and went ahead and did it—yet here they were, asking for permission from an organization run by amateurs.

---

*Soccer's image was not greatly helped by the fact that Barriskill used to spend his summer evenings working as a ticket usher at New York Yankee baseball games.

Poor USSFA. After dozing for decades, it was suddenly confronted with an insoluble problem, not of its own making. It knew that three competing leagues would rapidly kill each other off, and urged the groups to get together to form one league. Two of them did combine, but that was as far as anyone would go. USSFA would now have to pick one of the leagues, or recognize both.

It chose to sanction the group headed by Jack Kent Cooke, which gave itself the name United Soccer Association—USA, you see. This meant that the other league, the National Professional Soccer League, had either to fold its tents and slink away, or to operate as a pirate league, outside organized soccer.

Still bursting with optimism about the future of soccer (at least, as an investment), the NPSL chose the pirate route. At the same time, it made frequent approaches direct to the FIFA headquarters in Zurich, pleading for recognition. FIFA's advice—shades of 1912!—was that it should return to the United States and make peace with USSFA.

One thing that both leagues had realized very quickly was that they would not be able to stock their leagues with American players. They just weren't good enough. Foreigners it would have to be. The NPSL was quickly off the mark, sending its scouts around the world to sign up players for a 1967 kickoff.

The scouts ran smack into the problems that came with the NPSL's outlaw status. USSFA had informed FIFA that this was an unsanctioned league, FIFA had informed all the other national F.A.s, and they in turn had informed all their players that to join such a league was to court suspension from playing anywhere else. The worldwide soccer monopoly was at work.

Despite the barriers, the NPSL managed to sign enough players to stock its ten teams, though they were mostly players from second- and third-division clubs. This all came as a nasty surprise to the USA, which had not believed that the NPSL would get off the ground, and had been planning to begin its own operations in 1968. Even more alarming, the NPSL had pulled off a two-year game-of-the-week television deal with CBS.

Obviously, the NPSL could not be allowed to have 1967 all to itself. The USA rushed onto the scene by importing whole teams from Europe and South America, one for each of its twelve franchised cities. Again, these were not really top teams.

When 1967 was over, all twenty-two clubs in both leagues had lost money, and the NPSL announced an $18 million restraint-of-trade lawsuit against USSFA, the USA, and FIFA. The suit was settled out of court when USSFA agreed to recognize the NPSL. The two leagues then merged to form the seventeen-club North American Soccer League, and everyone sailed forth to make 1968 the gala year of American soccer.

It was, if anything, even more disastrous than 1967 had been. Everyone lost money again, CBS bowed out, and suddenly there was a rush for the exits. When the 1969 season began, the NASL was down to just five clubs.

Yet another soccer debacle, but one for which the USSFA was only partly to blame. Most of the responsibility lay with the ignorance and the arrogance of the new franchise holders, who blithely assumed that soccer was simply another commodity that could be successfully marketed by public relations puffery. They talked repeatedly of "being in this thing for the long haul," but the moment it became clear that they were not going to be drowned in quick profits, they bolted. USSFA's suspicions had been correct—these men cared not a fig for the good of soccer.

The fiasco had its constructive side. The NASL had taken soccer to parts of America where it had never been seen before—Atlanta, Dallas, Kansas City—and where it had been surprisingly well received. So well, that all three cities were among the five survivors in 1969.

By the skin of its teeth, the NASL survived and slowly rebuilt its strength. It is taking nothing away from the enthusiasm and nonstop industry of the league's commissioner, Phil Woosnam, to say that the key figure in the NASL's survival was Lamar Hunt, owner of the league's Dallas Tornado. As long as he was there, nobody could afford to write off the NASL.

It was not a question of the fabled Hunt millions being poured into soccer—nothing of the sort happened. It was a question of confidence and image. If Lamar Hunt thought that pro soccer had a future, there would always be plenty of other investors willing to lend an ear to what he had to say.

Plenty did. By 1978, the NASL was up to twenty-four clubs; it included the major TV markets and even took in the Canadian cities of Vancouver and Toronto.

The master move came in 1975 when the New York Cosmos—a member of the league since 1971—signed Pelé. But this was something that began back in the dark days of 1969.

Clive Toye and Phil Woosnam, the NASL's only executives, were desperately trying to keep the five-team league alive. For them, a useful exercise for warding off the fear that the league might not last out the week was to leapfrog over the bleak present and to imagine the glittering future.

Soccer would be suffering, both agreed, as long as it did not have its own superstars. Even just one superstar would do. Obviously he could not be American; no American player was good enough or likely to be good enough in the foreseeable future. Whichever way they looked at it, there was really only one man who could fill the role: Pelé.

His popularity had been proved many times when his club, Santos, toured the United States, always drawing crowds far above average. He was a draw, he was a name, known—if not for his soccer brilliance—then for the fact that he was reputed to be the highest-paid athlete in the world. He was the man who could provide the glamour that major-league soccer must have, concluded Toye and Woosnam as they peered presumptuously into their rosy-hued crystal ball.

Slowly, circumstances began to arrange themselves more and more favorably. The NASL rebuilt its strength and began to attract some substantially wealthy backers. Among them was Warner Communications, which owned the New York Cosmos. The Turkish-born brothers Ahmet and Nesuhi Ertegun, recording industry magnates and keen soccer fans, ran the club, and chose Clive Toye to be their general manager. They did not need much convincing on the idea to sign Pelé.

Starting in 1971 hints were dropped to Pelé that, after he retired from playing with his club Santos in 1974, he might think about joining the New York Cosmos. His response was a grin, a nod, and an inscrutability that meant neither yes nor no. Toye, ever the optimist, took it to mean that Pelé was interested. By June 1974 he was talking directly to Pelé about the opportunities that awaited him in the United States if he played with the Cosmos.

Pelé played his last game for Santos in October 1974. Eight months later he was in New York, at the fashionable "21" Club, signing a three-year, $4.5 million contract with the Cosmos.

The arrival of Pelé immediately proved to be everything that Toye and Woosnam had dreamed of in terms of bringing soccer into the limelight. His first game with the Cosmos was nationally televised by CBS.

The Cosmos were still playing at the rundown Randall's Island Stadium in New York (CBS had to paint the muddy patches green), but suddenly the austere press box at Cosmos games was jammed, full of people who could not pronounce Pelé's name, and whose conversation made it painfully clear that they knew nothing of soccer. But well-heeled people who moved with a swagger not seen before in soccer press boxes, and who made a fuss if they didn't get a good seat.

Articles on Pelé began to appear in all the chic magazines; Pelé was on the Johnny Carson show, Pelé was at the White House showing President Ford what a soccer ball looked like. And everywhere the fans poured out: capacity crowds in Boston (where the Boston Minutemen billed their game against the Cosmos as Minutemen vs. Pelé), St. Louis, San Jose, New York, Los Angeles, and Seattle, a league record 35,000 in Washington.

What Lamar Hunt had done for the financial end of the NASL, Pelé now did for the on-the-field side. Other top players began to arrive—Johan Cruyff, George Best, Giorgio Chinaglia, and Franz Beckenbauer.

In 1977 the Cosmos moved from Yankee Stadium to Giants Stadium in New Jersey, and suddenly the crowds poured in, climaxing with nearly 78,000 for the play-off game against Fort Lauderdale. The celebrities, too. The postgame scene in the Cosmos locker room was always likely to be a frantic mixture of half-naked athletes, struggling journalists, hordes of autograph hunters, and the likes of Mick Jagger, Rod Stewart, or Dr. Henry Kissinger.

An ABC TV contract came in 1979. It seemed like the crowning touch, the proof that soccer was now on a level with football and baseball. In reality, it marked the beginning of the end. In 1981, the NASL lost three franchises, and the following year ABC, dissatisfied with soccer's ratings, did not renew its contract. That same year, the NASL lost seven more clubs; one of them was the Dallas Tornado. Lamar Hunt's faith in soccer no longer outweighed the financial losses.

Everyone was losing money—indeed, no one had ever made any money—and panic surfaced. Phil Woosnam, the only commissioner the NASL had ever had, was fired; he was blamed for expanding the NASL too far, too fast. But none of it had been done without the owners' approval. And the Cosmos were accused of bankrupting the league as the other clubs tried to match their spending.

Leadership of the NASL was handed over to Howard Samuels, a New York politician who had successfully launched the state's Off Track Betting program. It was felt that he had the necessary business sense to save the league.

Samuels looked at all the figures, the clubs' income and expenditure, and exclaimed, "These guys are crazy!" The way he figured it, no one could make any money; the income just wasn't there. The maximum roster size was reduced from twenty-eight to nineteen, and a salary-cap agreement was worked out with the NASL Players Association.

Band-Aids for a hemorrhaging league. It was down to twelve clubs in 1983, nine in 1984. When Samuels died suddenly in October 1984, no move was made to replace him. Already there was a feeling that the NASL was without a future.

In March, the NASL, or what was left of it, announced officially that it would not operate in 1985. It also threw the Cosmos out for not posting its letter of credit. Warner Communications had sold out, but the new Cosmos owners—a group put together by former goal-scoring ace Giorgio Chinaglia—put on a brave face and announced a series of exhibition games in the summer.

On Father's Day, the Cosmos played Lazio of Italy in Giants Stadium. No huge crowds now, just 9,000 fans. "The money is nearly zero, the outlook isn't bright," said Chinaglia. "Nobody wants to invest in soccer in this country."

The sad ending to the Lazio game, and to the shining Cosmos adventure, was the spectacle of both teams in an all-out brawl on the field. The Cosmos were finished; they would never play again.

The collapse of the NASL meant the end of professional soccer in the United States—real soccer, the outdoor game, that is. There was always the six-a-side indoor game, as played by the thriving Major Indoor Soccer League (MISL). Spurned by the purists as an unspeakable corruption of their game, indoor soccer had what proved to be a fatal attraction for many of the NASL owners.

Various forms of indoor soccer had been played in Europe and South America since the 1930s. It was not a new sport, but what appealed to the NASL owners was that it enabled them to get more use out of players on twelve-month contracts. To the short twenty-four-game summer season, they could now add a winter season. Indoor soccer also allowed them to do something that FIFA would not permit with the outdoor game. They could tinker with the rules, they could get on with that Americanization process that we have encountered before.

So, in 1975 and 1976 the NASL ran a winter indoor season. It was a divisive experiment. Not all of the clubs joined in. The Cosmos didn't take part because, said Nesuhi Ertegun, "We play *soccer.* That is what our fans want." While the NASL clubs argued and dithered over the merits of the indoor game, a Philadelphia lawyer, Earl Foreman, jumped in and formed the MISL. The MISL said it was playing "a truly American sport, the human pinball game," and suddenly soccer had penalty boxes and massive substitution, to say nothing of laser-beam light shows and screaming announcers and dancing girls. "This is the game Americans want," crowed Foreman.

The NASL had hatched a soccer cuckoo. The MISL gained in strength; the NASL weakened. As the NASL tried to peg back its salaries, the MISL lured away its best players with higher offers. The defection of Rick Davis—captain of the U.S. national team, the leading American player of the day—came as the cruelest blow in the fall of 1983. When the Cosmos offered to renew his contract, but without a raise, Davis jumped to the St. Louis Steamers of the MISL.

Soccer had found yet another internal division—indoor vs. outdoor—with which to wound itself. Neither side triumphed. The NASL had lasted eighteen years, during which one of its biggest problems had been to find stable ownership. Only once in that period did it field the same lineup of clubs in consecutive seasons. It was to be no different for the MISL, which lasted only fourteen years before it withered to five teams and folded in 1992, with Commissioner Earl Foreman declaring that it was "unable to attract new owners."

Luckily, the cuckoo-sport of indoor soccer was not the only legacy of the NASL. It left behind much more positive influences, not least in the way that it acted as a catalyst to growth in other areas of the game. College soccer, for instance.

During the roughly fifty years of USSFA-controlled soccer in the United States, there had always been college soccer. Ironically, it was strongest in those Ivy League schools that had rejected it in the 1870s. Harvard, for instance, had taken up soccer in 1905, and when the Intercollegiate Soccer Association was formed in 1926, it included both Princeton and Yale among its twelve members.

USSFA and the colleges showed little interest in each other's activities. That was fine with the colleges, who went their own way, unburdened by interference from USSFA, which would have obliged it to stick the internationally accepted FIFA rules.

Surprise, surprise, the collegians made some Americanizing changes to the sport. They played the game in four quarters instead of two halves, they used two referees instead of one, they replaced the throw-in with a kick-in. And they permitted liberal use of substitutes, where FIFA rules did not permit any.*

College soccer grew slowly until the 1960s, when it was hit by the same groundswell for the sport that was to give rise to the NASL. There were two special circumstances working in favor of soccer in the colleges: As college basketball and football became increasingly specialized, soccer was recognized as an ideal sport for the average-sized athlete, and it was a cheap team sport to organize, an attraction to budget-conscious colleges.

In 1959 the National Collegiate Athletic Association (NCAA) inaugurated a national championship for college soccer. By 1972 the sport had a national ratings system and a Senior Bowl game, and scholarships were increasingly available, something that further encouraged an already formidable growth in the game at the high school level. Soccer could now offer American boys the same thing as basketball and football, a high school and college career leading to the pros.

It looked that way, but the reality was something different. By 1972 the NASL was coming under criticism for its reliance on foreign players. The Non-American Soccer League, said its critics, who pointed out that there were virtually no ex-college players at all in the league (although a substantial exception must be made in the case of the St. Louis Stars, which drew heavily on graduates from St. Louis University, at that time the strongest team in college soccer).

Phil Woosnam, the NASL's Welsh commissioner, had the answer: a college draft. A baffling experience for the eight NASL coaches, all of them foreign-born, who knew very little of college soccer. The draft was a farce, as the eight clubs picked thirty-five players they knew very little about. Eight of them were signed; only two made it as first-team starters.

All that could be put down to teething problems, and certainly the subsequent drafts were much more meaningful occasions. From 1972 on, NASL coaches were seen regularly at college games, and Phil Woosnam stated that the aim of the NASL was to field all-American teams. As the NASL increased the number of its teams, the number of players drafted went up—forty-four in 1973, seventy-six in 1975—but the signings remained pitifully small, six in 1973, twenty-four in 1975.

Disillusion came quickly. The college players were not good enough. In 1977 the Cosmos signed a promising young forward, Gary Etherington, straight out of high school. The following year they plucked Rick Davis away from his junior year in college. The message was clear: The colleges could not be relied on to develop talent. Indeed, how could they, with a short season of only around twenty games. Worse yet, there was a widespread feeling among NASL coaches that the colleges retarded the growth of players. It was a very awkward message for a league that was trying to Americanize itself.

---

*In its search for positive rule changes in the 1990s, FIFA actually considered, or experimented with, all of these ideas.

A league regulation was introduced requiring a quota for North Americans.* By 1981, over 50 percent of the league's players were Americans, and during the NASL's final 1984 season each team had to have five Americans on the field at all times.

By then, the cost-cutting owners were embracing Americanization with a vengeance. It was cheaper to sign Americans. Money was saved, but the flood of young, inexperienced Americans, many of them straight out of college, brought with it a sharp lowering of the playing standards. The college players were still not good enough.

Strangely, very strangely, the quality of their product did not come up for discussion among the businessmen who were busy trying to bring financial sanity to the league. It was an extraordinary oversight, but one that was to become a hidden, destructive theme of subsequent events in U.S. soccer.

The game on the field was pushed aside, almost forgotten it seemed, as short-term monetary considerations took over. For those with sensitive ears for this sort of thing, the signs had been there for some time that the NASL, having at last brought American methods and American accents into soccer, was placing increasing emphasis on the commercial aspects of its operation.

Announcing a league expansion in 1970, commissioner Phil Woosnam had welcomed "the addition of such great soccer centers as New York and Toronto." By 1974 there was no more talk of soccer centers—NASL franchises were now being awarded to "markets" like Tampa, "the twentieth largest market in the country," said Woosnam, adding that the league was "examining the possibility of expanding into another four of the eight markets that have indicated interest."

It was precisely to avoid this rampant obsession with money that the founders of soccer in England had insisted that the ultimate control of the sport be left in the hands of amateurs. And that, in theory anyway, was still the case in the United States.

The USSFA remained in the picture, too—the same USSFA that had all the trouble sorting out the surplus of pro leagues in 1967. Fifty years of vegetation as the champion of small-time hyphenated-American soccer had left USSFA singularly ill equipped to deal with that situation, and the result was a tangle that ended with everyone in court.

But just as the NASL held on to rise again, USSFA, too, survived, but not as the USSFA of old. As the NASL gained strength, it dragged USSFA forward. The dreadful old office on Fifth Avenue was abandoned for a new one, just a few blocks farther north. But what a difference! The USSFA now had a suite in the Empire State Building. Even the name was altered, the word football was finally dropped, and the United States Soccer Federation (USSF) was born.

---

*The definition included Canadians, naturalized citizens, and resident-alien green-card holders.

The game was exploding, especially at the youth level. All that NASL missionary work, all those clinics, were beginning to bear fruit. In 1979, the USSF's youth (under-19) enrollment hit half a million for the first time. A year later it was 625,000, and increasing at the rate of over 200 kids a day, boys and girls.

Hordes of kids wanted to play, but who was to coach them? Most of them came from middle-class American families with no previous involvement with soccer. Yet it was these parents who were being pressed into service as coaches. The USSF started up its own coaching schools, with a range of licenses for anyone from absolute beginners to professionals.

But the USSF was still an amateur organization that hadn't gotten used to thinking big. The ambitious ideas came from the NASL. In particular, the one about the 1986 World Cup. That had been awarded to Colombia, but by 1982, it was common knowledge that Colombia was going to renege.

Then the USSF should make a bid, said the NASL leaders. They had their own interests very much in mind, of course. Their league was tottering, but they felt that the promise of the World Cup in 1986 could save it.

USSF president Gene Edwards was against the idea because he didn't think there was enough time to prepare, so he was bypassed. The NASL turned to Werner Fricker, a USSF vice president, and conducted all the negotiations with FIFA through him. The bid was made—and brutally rejected by FIFA in 1983, who gave the tournament to Mexico.

The shock was too much for the NASL, which collapsed in 1984. The same year, Fricker became the new President of the USSF. He was backed by former NASL commissioner Phil Woosnam, who masterminded his campaign with electioneering and careful vote-counting, something that had never been seen before at a USSF convention.

A new realism, a modern approach, had arrived for the USSF. Within hours of his election, Fricker ordered the USSF to disband the amateur team that it was preparing for the Los Angeles Olympics, and to use professional players instead. This was something that every other nation was doing, but which Gene Edwards had steadfastly resisted.

Fricker's hardheaded realism also dictated that the USSF would have to get out of New York. The collapse of the NASL put a big dent in the USSF's income, and it fled to Colorado Springs, there to nestle comfortably—and for free—in office space provided by the United States Olympic Committee.

The tranquility and obscurity of Colorado Springs did nothing to dampen Fricker's ambitions. Who would not be optimistic as those numbers continued to increase? Between 1974 and 1984, the number of colleges with men's teams had climbed from 415 to 544. At the beginning of the seventies, some 70,000 boys played high school soccer; by 1984 the figure was 180,000. Figures that kept going up as the number of USSF under-19 youth registrations went on climbing: By 1987 the figure was 1.2 million.

A new phenomenon was on the horizon, too: women's soccer. In 1981 there was no such thing in the colleges. Just three years later, 165 colleges were fielding women's soccer teams.

At the end of the 1970s, when the NASL was at its peak, it had used a slogan "Soccer—the Sport of the 80s." The NASL wasn't around to see it, but soccer was certainly becoming the youth sport of the 1980s.

Fricker's biggest triumph came in 1988 when he secured the 1994 World Cup for the USA. But he soon fell out with FIFA, and in 1990 he lost his position as USSF President, defeated by Alan Rothenberg, who had the backing, even the active intervention, of FIFA to help him.*

FIFA's interest, obviously, was in getting rid of Fricker and moving Rothenberg in as the guy who would ride herd on the World Cup. But it was the USSF members that had done the voting, and as far as they were concerned, they had elected Rothenberg to run their Federation.

So, with the World Cup secured, Rothenberg set about revitalizing the USSF. He brought in Hank Steinbrecher as secretary-general—the first time in nearly 50 years that the USSF had had an American-born secretary, and one with business experience, at that. And it was made known that the USSF offices would soon be moved from their Colorado Springs backwater. In 1992, they would go to Chicago.

Change was long overdue at the USSF, but the most remarkable aspect of the process was that the USSF membership had voted so solidly for Rothenberg. For the USSF is a cumbersome, volunteer organization, not known for imaginative thinking, and with a considerable suspicion of outsiders.

Nominally, it is governed by a national council in which voting strength is divided equally between three groups: the amateurs, the youth, and the professionals. Other members of the council include representatives from the colleges, the high schools, the referees, the coaches, and from affiliated organizations such as the American Youth Soccer Organization (an independent national youth soccer organization with some 460,000 members).

The full council of over 300 delegates meets only once a year. In practice, most of the decisions are taken by the smaller National Board of Directors (twenty-nine members), or the nine-member Executive Committee. This consists of the elected officers: the president, four vice presidents, and the treasurer, plus the immediate past president, and two Olympic representatives. Plus the secretary-general, the only full-time salaried member. All of the officers must be American citizens. There is also the usual collection—over 30 of them—of specialist committees and subcommittees.

For decades the USSF's constitution set out its aim as "supreme control and representation of soccer football in the United States of America." This sweeping claim was an attempt by USSF to invest itself with the same sort of undisputed authority that the national soccer organizations of other

*See chapter 5, page 109.

countries enjoyed. But other countries do not have the strong antitrust laws of the United States.

In the 1960s the USSF was taken to court three times as a result of its attempts to withhold recognition from leagues and teams of which it did not approve. All three cases were settled out of court: The USSF backed down in one by agreeing to recognize the NPSL in 1968, while in the other two it made financial settlements of $25,000 and $30,000.

Since that time, the wording of the USSF constitution has been altered to eliminate all talk of "supreme control"; the aim of USSF is now much more modest, not to say realistic: "to promote soccer in the United States of America."

The ways in which USSF now promotes soccer are as follows:

- It serves as a central registering authority for leagues, teams, and players. For each of these functions, a fee is paid to the USSF. Thus, MLS—the Division I pro league—pays annual dues of $40,000, plus $13,250 for each team. The Division II A-league pays $10,000 a year and $1,875 per team. Amateur players pay annual dues of $1, and youth (under 19) players 50 cents.

- In the event of disputes between clubs over player registration or eligibility it acts as the final arbitrator, as it does on questions of discipline that the state associations cannot, or will not, enforce.

- It attempts to enforce uniformity in the rules throughout the United States (not easy—the colleges and the high schools are only associate members of the USSF, and have always published their own versions of the rules).

- It organizes thirteen national cup competitions: men's open, Amateur, and over-30; women's open and over-30; plus under-19, under-18, under-17 and under-16 for both boys and girls. These are strictly for USSF-registered players.

- It organizes and finances the national teams' programs. It appoints and pays the coaches, and arranges the teams' schedules.

- As the FIFA-affiliated body it grants permission for the playing of international games between American clubs, amateur and pro, and those from foreign countries. From every international club game, USSF takes a cut of the gate, ranging from 5 percent to 10 percent.

- It conducts regular courses, and refresher courses, for the licensing of coaches and referees.

Never a dull moment, then, for the USSF. It is an imposing list of duties, made much more so when you consider the numbers involved. With over 1.8 million youths registered (30 percent of them girls), USSF membership is now approaching 2 million players.

That's the official total, anyway. The Soccer Industry Council of America (SICA, the group that represents the interests of soccer equipment manufacturers) does its own surveys and has revealed that, whatever may be the USSF figure, the number of people who play soccer in the United States is closer to 18.2 million.

Just how the USSF has failed to recruit 16.2 million potential members is something of a mystery. Possibly because the SICA definition of a soccer player includes all those who "played at least once" in 1994, the survey year.

Most of the players are pretty young—the SICA figures have 7.7 million of them under age 12, making soccer the No. 2 sport, behind basketball's 9.7 million, for that age group.

However the numbers are viewed, they add up to something short of ideal for the USSF. They show a bottom-heavy organization, a pyramid with an enormous base of youngsters and amateurs, but that narrows into nothingness without the crowning glory of a pro league.

The idea of soccer as nothing more than a massive recreational sport for tots offends the sport's boosters. Indeed, it offends logic.

How can this be for the world's most popular game, played before huge crowds by highly paid professionals all over world, the game that dominates global television sports coverage, the game that FIFA has described as a $200 billion worldwide industry?

Two hundred billion dollars? Is that mere hype? Hardly. The proof lies in that most widely and closely and passionately followed of all man's sporting activities: the four-yearly extravaganza known as the World Cup.

For one month in the summer of 1994, World Cup soccer dominated the world's television. Fifty-two games were broadcast to 188 countries. The average was 618 million viewers per game. The final was watched by 1.2 billion fans. The cumulative total of viewers for the whole tournament was 32.1 billion.

The figures for viewers within the United States were pretty impressive, too. Over 10 million families watched the final, and the total stadium attendance was 3.5 million, an average of nearly 69,000 for each of the 52 games.

Just what FIFA and Alan Rothenberg and the whole American soccer community had hoped for. With those totals, with that sort of interest . . . everything appeared to be falling into place for the start-up of the new pro league.

–11–
American Soccer:
The Present and the Future

Alan Rothenberg, always optimistic, ever supremely confident, vowed repeatedly that World Cup-94 would be the best ever and that it would make a tidy profit—$20 million was the figure he ventured.

Nothing really remarkable about any of that. Every World Cup has been the best ever, and every one has made a profit. The extent of the profit, perhaps, *was* remarkable: the final figure was around $60 million. Most of that, about $50 million, went into a special USSF Foundation, set up to make sure the money was spent wisely on the development of soccer in the states.

Some of it—quite a lot of it—went into Rothenberg's pocket. On October 18, 1994, three months after the end of the tournament, the World Cup's Board of Directors issued a press release announcing the $60 million surplus. "The results are nothing but stunning," said Peter Ueberroth, chairman of the Board's Compensation Committee. "As little as a year ago the surplus was expected to be approximately $20 million."

On the basis of this incredible trebling of the estimate, it seemed perfectly appropriate that Rothenberg should be rewarded with a $3 million bonus. For three years the man had sustained an incredible work rate of fourteen-hour days and seven-day weeks. During that time, he had turned down a salary on the understanding that he would "eventually be compensated as deemed fair."

The press release was, to put it charitably, deceptive. It soon surfaced that Rothenberg, in addition to the $3 million bonus, was getting another $4 million as salary. This came, said the World Cup Board, from a five-year contract at $800,000 a year.

As Rothenberg took over the World Cup in November 1991, a five-year contract meant that he was being paid until November 1996, over two years beyond the end of the tournament. The tripling of the surplus began to look like a deception, too. After all, it was Rothenberg's office that had come up with the original modest $20 million estimate.

But the biggest objection to Rothenberg's millions was that the profits of World Cup-94 had only been possible because of a huge army of volunteer workers. According to the Organizing Committee's own estimate, there were over 10,000 volunteers at work on World Cup-94, many of them doing highly specialized and responsible work.

Rothenberg, or World Cup-94, did take space in national newspapers to thank "the unselfish dedication of the soccer family and volunteers" in making a success of the World Cup. Thanks was all they got.

None of this did Rothenberg's image much good within the soccer community. In August 1994, when he stood for re-election as USSF President, he ought to have been a shoo-in as the guy who had just bequeathed $50 million to the sport. Anything but. Opposed by USSF treasurer Richard Groff, Rothenberg got only 49 percent of the vote on the first ballot; Groff got 46 percent. Rothenberg took it on the second ballot, but he still got only 53 percent of the votes. And that election was held *before* the USSF members knew about his personal $7 million windfall.

Many had felt that Rothenberg would not run again, that—having done very nicely, thank you, out of the World Cup—he would do the cynical thing and vanish from the soccer scene as suddenly as he had arrived.

They were wrong—Rothenberg had unfinished business to attend to. The matter of the pro league. The one that FIFA was supposed to have mandated when it gave the USA World Cup-94. FIFA's "mandate" had, of course, never been enforceable, never been more than a fervent hope.

There was more than a touch of irony in FIFA's desire to see a pro league in the United States. Only six years earlier it had been FIFA's brusque rejection of the American bid to stage the 1986 World Cup that had helped to kill off the North American Soccer League.

Now, in the wake of the triumphant 1994 World Cup, the possibilities looked good. Some preliminary work had been done during the World Cup. The league had a name, Major League Soccer (MLS), it had a logo, and that was about all. It would be organized and run by Alan Rothenberg.

A conflict of interests, possibly? Rothenberg was also the president of the USSF, the controlling body that had given approval to the MLS as the nation's pro league. Nonsense, said Rothenberg, himself a lawyer, "I recuse myself from any USSF meetings involving league business. I call it a confluence of interests."

Compared to the pro league start-up, running the World Cup had been a breeze. That was a one-month event with a track record of success, something that had been done may times before so that most of the snags could be foreseen, something that fans and sponsors were keen to buy into. A seller's market.

In every important respect, MLS was precisely the opposite. A new league with no track record. Worse, it was saddled with the history of a long line of pro soccer leagues that had flopped in the past. Fans and sponsors, the very same people who had been falling over themselves to be involved in the World Cup, were skeptical. So too were investors. A buyer's market.

Rothenberg's first move, in early 1991, was to form a committee to study the creation of an outdoor pro league. Incredibly, he named as its chairman the high priest of indoor soccer, Earl Foreman—the very same

Earl Foreman who had recently announced to the world that "I don't give two shits about outdoor soccer."

The committee quietly evaporated after one meeting, and Rothenberg began to learn of the barriers that lay in the way of pro soccer. He was quick to realize that the original idea of getting the league going before the World Cup wouldn't work. It would have to wait till the Cup was over. Even so, he remained absurdly gung ho. "I don't see any major hurdles to be overcome," he said in August 1991, and then asked "Do I sound naive?" Oh dear.

The immediate concern was the World Cup. The pro league was shoved on to the back burner, and the power was turned off. By late 1993, FIFA was getting impatient, it wanted to see a business plan for the new league.

Rothenberg duly obliged with details of MLS and its single entity structure. Those were the key words, "single entity." A new type of league, the MLS would own all its clubs. It would not be a confederation of independent franchise owners, like other pro sports leagues. The aim was to prevent war within the league, with clubs going bankrupt as they felt it necessary to outspend each other. The league would run a league-wide marketing program and have a say in team operations. Crucially, it would negotiate all player contracts, in effect imposing a salary cap. MLS lawyers said it was legal. Critics called it socialized soccer. It would kick off in the spring of 1995.

Twenty-nine cities had expressed interest in having an MLS team. They were each asked to sell 10,000 season-ticket deposits as proof that they had the fan base, then twelve cities would be chosen. Only two venues reached the target. There were other problems, particularly in finding suitable stadiums.

The awkward truth was that there was nowhere to play. No soccer stadiums. The NASL had made do with a mishmash of adapted football and baseball facilities. Many of the football fields were too narrow, or had the widely disliked artificial turf; the baseball stadiums were the wrong shape and were likely to cause scheduling conflicts.

What the MLS needed were middle-sized, custom-built soccer stadiums. "It's clear to me that the single biggest impediment to success," said Rothenberg, "is the stadium situation. But if people are going to invest in soccer, they ought to be willing to create first-class, 30,000-seat stadiums. It pencils out at $30 million."

Nice idea, but investors were proving hard to come by, even without the extra expense of building a stadium. Finding investors was made more difficult by the single entity structure. Ten investors were being sought to put up $10 million each. But they would be buying into the league as a whole—the delights and dismays of owning and running his own club were not for the MLS investor.

It didn't fly. A less expensive $5 million unit had to be offered, while those paying $10 million would be a new category of owner-investors, "the local entrepreneurs who want to operate a club." Two examples of the way in which MLS had to draw in its horns.

There were others. The league was supposed to start with twelve clubs; but when the credentials of the twenty-nine cities that wanted teams were examined, only seven were found to be viable. One of those—Long Island, New York—dropped out, and only four more cities came in. The league would go with ten clubs.

The idea of new, soccer-specific stadiums was quietly abandoned. MLS, like the NASL before it, would play in football stadiums, most of which were way too big. No matter, the MLS would downsize them, maybe by using huge tarpaulins to "attractively drape off" the entire upper deck.

Things were not going smoothly for the MLS, and it came as no surprise when, in November 1994, the league announced a year's delay. The new starting date was March 1996.

Through all the setbacks and the delays and the disappointments Rothenberg smiled and played his soccer Dr. Pangloss: everything was for the best. Slowly, the owner-investors were assembled. Seven of them. They included long-time soccer stalwart Lamar Hunt, who had been a key figure in the old NASL, and his son Clark; John Kluge of Metromedia (said to be the third richest man in the USA with a personal fortune of $6.9 billion); and Robert Kraft, owner of the NFL's New England Patriots.

Seven MLS clubs—New York/New Jersey, Boston, Washington, D.C., Columbus, Kansas City, Los Angeles, and Denver—would be run by owner-operators. The other three—Tampa, Dallas, and San Jose—would be run by the league.

The ongoing nonappearance of the MLS did not mean that the country was devoid of soccer leagues. There are plenty of them. The vast majority are regional loops, at best semipro. There are many local leagues in big cities like New York, Los Angeles, and Chicago, direct descendants of the old ethnic leagues. And, for those who like indoor soccer, there is the thirteen-team National Professional Soccer League, and the fifteen-team Continental Indoor Soccer League.

There are two outdoor leagues with some claim to national status. The largest is the United Systems of Independent Soccer Leagues (USISL), a nationwide agglomeration of eighty-four teams. It operates as a three-tier minor league, with twenty-seven amateur clubs, thirty-three semi-pro, and a Select Division of twenty-four clubs. A league of modest ambitions that openly declares that it "has no intention of becoming" major league.

The A-League (formerly the American Professional Soccer League or APSL) had only seven clubs in 1995. It nevertheless claims to be "the benchmark for the continent's ultimate level of professional play."

A claim scornfully dismissed by Rothenberg: "Even to the extent that the APSL is successful, it is not at the level of quality needed. It is not a major league in U.S. terms."

Unfortunately for the A-League's pretensions, when top USISL and A-League clubs played each other in the quarterfinals of the 1995 Open Cup, all three A-League entrants were eliminated by USISL clubs.

Life in the A-League was lived on the edge anyway. With only seven clubs it was barely legitimate by USSF regulations, which stipulated that a pro league must have at least six teams. The USSF clearly intended that those teams should be American—whereas three of the A-League's teams were Canadian.

The A-League staggered through its 1995 season and then bravely announced that it would expand and continue operations in 1996. It was not going to be easy, because the MLS was intent on signing up the best American players, including any that it could lure away from the A-League or the USISL.

The USSF has a master plan for pro soccer, which allows for only one first-division league, and up to four second-division leagues. The APSL has been assigned one of the second-division slots, the other three are vacant, though the USISL's Select Division hopes to claim one of them. The first-division league, of course, is the MLS.

In July 1995 Rothenberg announced: "We now have commitments for some $75 million to fund this league. We have our cities and stadiums selected. Most importantly, we are on our way to bringing in top quality American and international players."

Finally the talk was getting around to the game. It was almost as though the sport had been left to take care of itself, and that it would automatically be of the highest level.

That is a dangerously fanciful assumption. When asked about the caliber of soccer to be presented, Rothenberg had tended to talk of the need for rule changes to produce a more offense-oriented game. Rule changes to Americanize the sport. FIFA, he said, was much more willing to allow such changes than it had been in the NASL days.

In 1994 and 1995 the USISL agreed to serve as a laboratory for the yet-to-be-born MLS. It carried out a bewildering series of rule-change experiments, that included larger goals, kick-ins, corner-kicks as a tie-breaker, an official timer who stopped the clock whenever the ball was not in play, and the counting of team and personal fouls.

Some of these changes, such as the award of a "live shoot-out" against the team that went over the limit on team fouls, were simply fatuous and smacked of gimmickry. Would MLS adopt such changes? "The aim will be to make the game as offense-oriented and entertaining as possible," said spokesman Mark Abbott, "While making sure that we don't fundamentally bury the game."

You can be sure that the rest of the soccer world will be keeping a close eye on that. The Yankees are always under suspicion of wanting to cheapen the sport, to fashion it for television by dividing it into four quarters, by allowing time-outs—even though it has been FIFA that has experimented with time-outs. And Americans are held to want more scoring. Yet when the question of increasing the size of the goals came up, it was not the MLS that was pushing the matter. It was FIFA that was pressuring MLS to make the experiment. FIFA evidently relished the thought of the MLS as an ideal testing ground for rule changes. But the MLS was not too happy to be given the role of a guinea-pig league.

In any case, the rule-change approach has an air of defeatism about it right from the start, a surrender to those who believe that Americans will never take to soccer unless it is dressed up to resemble hockey or football.

Is that the way it has to be? Not at all. There is another approach, the only one that will give long-term success. An approach based on a careful, and knowledgeable, monitoring of the type of soccer, the style of soccer, to be played in the new league.

It is really quite extraordinary that with sponsors and marketing types swarming all over American soccer, so little thought is given to the "product": the sport itself. Most of these people know very little about soccer, so that it is no doubt asking too much of them to make sophisticated distinctions between various styles. But how can they not recognize that there is good soccer, and there is bad soccer?

Astoundingly, the question rarely comes up. Soccer, it seems, is soccer. A homogeneous, inert material that is presumably always acceptable, and therefore always marketable. If only that were so.

The history, the anecdotes, the characters, and the incidents described in this book make it crystal clear: Soccer is a perverse, eccentric, living activity. It comes in many different shapes. It is the best of sports, it is the worst of sports, it is the most exciting of sports, it is the dullest, it is the fastest, it is the slowest, it is the most difficult of sports to play, it is the easiest, it is the most intelligent, it is the most brainless of sports.

It belongs to everyone, and because of that it belongs to no one. It is not a German sport any more than it is Argentine or English or Brazilian. Virtually every country in the world has taken to it, without the necessity for gimmicky rule changes. The Germans have Germanized it a bit, the English have Anglicized it, the Brazilians have Brazilianized it. All done within the sport's rules.

Soccer, no point in denying it, deals in extremes. When it is good, it is a breathtaking sport. But when it is bad, oh dear, what a bore it can be. Soccer people often find it difficult to admit that, but it is a confession that is, or should be, at the heart of American soccer's quest for a pro league.

It must be acknowledged that soccer is not just soccer, and that the game, even at the top professional level, can be of poor quality. Once that admission has been made, a sharply focused aim for the pro league is revealed: To banish, or reduce to a minimum, the bad soccer. Nor is it that difficult to define bad soccer. Bad soccer is boring soccer. Soccer in which not much happens. People who pay money to watch professional sports expect to be entertained. Good soccer is entertaining soccer.

You get entertaining soccer from players who know how to play . . . entertaining soccer. A platitude, but one that gets us to where any discussion of soccer on the field must begin: with the players. It is a given that the MLS must be largely populated by American players. It is the qualities of the American player that will determine its success. We need to know what those qualities are.

Each of the major soccer countries has its own style of playing, one that has developed over many years. So that you can, in broad terms, spell out the characteristics of the German, or the Brazilian, or the Italian player. You cannot do that with American players, for this country has not developed a recognizable soccer style.

Not everyone will agree with that. There are plenty of soccer experts who insist that there is, too, an American style. They point to college soccer where there is, admittedly, a certain uniformity. It is the same sort of game that St. Louis University used to play back in the 1960s and early 1970s when it regularly won the NCAA Division I title, and when the city of St. Louis was thought of as the soccer capital of the United States.

St. Louis was the one city in America that had a long soccer tradition, dating back to before World War I, of well-organized youth programs for American kids. The players produced—most of the top ones went on to St. Louis University—did have a specific St. Louis way of playing. It involved a good deal of movement and off-the-ball running and first-time passing. St. Louis players did not dwell on the ball; they rarely dribbled. They tended to be well built, and gluttons for work. Teamwork was excellent, the pace of the game high, with the accent on offense.

An impressive array of talents, but one that produced a strangely unsatisfactory sort of soccer. Too straightforward, with the emphasis on physical things like running and stamina, and tactically predictable. Soccer without individuality, flair, and inventiveness.

Yet today's college soccer is bursting with teams that play in this way. The style has its proponents, possibly because it contains elements of football. It is inevitable that, in the United States, soccer's merits and demerits will be measured against American sports, that people will try to find suggestions of football or hints of hockey or shades of basketball in the game. But the comparisons can be highly misleading.

Ironically, it is football—soccer's brother in the family of sports—that causes the most problems. At a superficial level the two sports resemble each other: outdoor games played by teams of eleven men on large rectangular fields. But that is about all that remains of their common origin. Beyond that, they diverge so completely that they are comparable only in terms of absolute opposites.

Football is a game of disciplined plays, highly specialized roles, massive substitution, and incessant coaching from the sidelines. Soccer is a fluid game that makes the planning of elaborate plays virtually impossible, that needs players with all-around skills, that permits only limited substitution, and in which the international rules impose limits on coaching from the sidelines.

But the most important difference between the two sports lies in the matter of body contact. Football is a sport that is built around the idea of players colliding with one another, of trying to knock opponents off their feet.

To try to play soccer with that mentality is to destroy the sport. But the trouble is that soccer can be played under a semifootball mentality that seeks to emphasize the physical aspects of the sport. For example: The one form of body contact that soccer does specifically permit is shoulder-charging, with the proviso that it not be "careless, reckless or involving disproportionate force." This is a tactic that can be used within broad limits. It can get as violent as the referee allows, and, particularly at the high school level, many referees have a football background that makes them far too lenient in punishing rough charging and tackling.

Soccer played with a semifootball mentality is high on body contact; running, speed, and that good old coach's panacea, hustle, are pre-eminent. The existence of this type of soccer at the college level depends to a considerable extent on the fact that youth-league and high school soccer permit free substitution, à la football. Substitution is more restricted in college soccer, but not restricted enough. Any number of players can be used in a game, with some minor restrictions on reentry. Nowhere else in the world is anything like that permitted; most countries limit substitution to two or three players, and do not allow a player to be sent back into the game once he has been removed.

Massive substitution strikes at the roots of skillful soccer because it allows, or encourages, a more physical game. Players can be sent into a game to run like mad for ten or fifteen minutes, taken out for a breather, then sent back in. Such players are hardly likely to bother with learning the skills and finesse of the game. Yet, particularly at the youth level, the physical, hustling teams can win. And, naturally enough, if you're going to rely on a power game, then the bigger the players, the better it is.

The ability to substitute repeatedly also greatly expands the importance of the coach *during the game*. He becomes, in effect, a twelfth player, constantly making decisions that affect the flow of the game. Very much like a football coach.

The worldwide trend toward an enhanced role for the coach in soccer has fallen on disturbingly fertile ground in the United States, where coaching is regarded with almost religious awe.

There is no reason to doubt that the aims of the coaching fraternity are constructive and well meaning: to produce better players and better soccer and, of course, to win games. But in practice, much of what they do runs counter to the spirit of soccer, which has traditionally been a players' game.

For soccer to be true to its roots, the game must be controlled by the players on the field. A constant stream of decisions by every player at every moment of the game: whether to stay put or to advance or to retreat, whether to run for a pass or not, or to fake a run, whether to challenge an opponent, whether to tackle or to delay, whether to dribble or to pass or to shoot, and so on, and so on. A game of constant innovation and improvisation, of ever-changing action and reaction.

Can a coach ever hope to control all of that? Of course not, but he can greatly interfere with the process. By imposing carefully worked-out tactics, by assigning specific roles to his players, he can reduce their responsibilities on the field. When that sort of thing happens at the youth level, the resourcefulness of the players is stunted. They grow up accepting that the coach makes a lot of the important decisions. They grow up as unenterprising players who, logically enough, play an unenterprising brand of soccer. But the football-type coach will praise that sort of player, the player who follows instructions, the player who is coachable. More often than not the coachable player is simply the one lacking a soccer personality, the one waiting for the coach to tell him what to do.

The USSF's coaching schools turn out scores of newly licensed coaches each year. No doubt, in technical and theoretical terms, these are knowledgeable people. But the curse of the coaching schools is that they impose orthodoxy. It is like that purported ideal of German military training in which all the cadets, posed a problem, come up with the same answer. In 1987, Walt Chyzowych, who was then in charge of the schools, sent a letter to the teaching staff stating that "it is imperative that the teaching does not deviate from the prepared curriculum . . . it is important that the staff follow the syllabus religiously."

Religiously. No room for original thinking here. The utter stupidity of this rigid approach had been exposed earlier that year when the ex-Peruvian World Cup star Teófilo Cubillas, one of the game's great players, had taken the USSF's "B" license exams. The examiners were three college coaches, theoreticians with little knowledge of the game at its highest level. They failed Cubillas because he did not perform some artificial coaching drill in the way that they wanted. Teófilo Cubillas, who at that time stood in fifth place in the World Cup's all-time scoring table, was adjudged not good enough to coach in the United States.

Former FIFA president Sir Stanley Rous was the man who introduced coaching courses to England in the 1930s. Some forty-five years later, he was asked if he had any regrets about that. He replied: "Yes, it's developed into so much *instruction*. Players who have an instinctive way of playing, or wanting to play, have their mind divided; they're thinking 'Now, what did he tell me to do in this circumstance?,' with the result that their ability is impaired."

Football-influenced soccer is still prevalent in the colleges. Watching it is rather like being given a reading program of endless prose, and monotonous prose at that. One's heart cries out for a little poetry now and then. Surely, it protests, a game like this could never, never in a million years, have captured the imagination of the whole world? Surely there has to be more to soccer than this?

Yes, there is more to soccer, a hell of a lot more. What is missing is the very soul of the sport: ball skill. The off-the-ball side of the game, the running and the hustling, has been developed at the expense of the on-the-ball side. There is a lack of players with individual ball skills, players who have the confidence to hold on to the ball, who can take opponents on and dribble past them, who can change the pace of the game, who can do the unexpected. Players with a soccer personality. When players like that are lacking, soccer becomes a pedestrian game enveloped in an atmosphere of mechanical predictability.

Sadly, it is this incomplete game that is pushed forward as the American style. It is, of course, no such thing. It is not a style at all, merely a sterile copy of how the northern Europeans play, or used to play.

It would be unfair and downright inaccurate to blame this physical, mechanical approach to soccer on football. The ultimate responsibility for it lies with the soccer people themselves. Historically, soccer in the United States has always looked to Europe for its models, especially toward northern Europe: Britain, Germany, Scandinavia—a very important area, soccerwise, one that has produced many great teams and players. But an area noted for a robust, manly approach to the game (though Germany now has a more sophisticated view of the sport).

The United States Soccer Federation, throughout its eighty-year history, has always been a relentlessly Eurocentric organization. British and German ideas and attitudes permeated the sport in this country right from the beginning. They received a further boost in the 1960s from the NASL, which needed English-speaking coaches and players to carry out its missionary and PR work. Thus a new wave of British influence arrived.

The United States is not England or Germany or Denmark, countries that developed their styles in days when they had little ethnic diversity. The American style, when it comes, will be a reflection of what the American player has to offer. It will be a style that allows the full development of all the talent that is available in this huge, ethnically complex nation. At the moment, American soccer—that is to say, the soccer that is controlled by the USSF—is an overwhelmingly middle-class, white sport. There is minimal black involvement, and there has been no great effort on the part of the USSF and other soccer bodies to recruit blacks.

An unsatisfactory state of affairs, but one that might be expected to change as soccer's popularity widens. Then again, maybe not, because the experience of another minority, the Hispanics, is anything but encouraging.

Here we have a rapidly growing ethnic group that is already passionately devoted to soccer. In the New York–New Jersey area, for instance, there are eighteen Hispanic soccer leagues, involving over 200 clubs and some 3,000 players, to say nothing of the youth teams that many clubs run.

Where once the ethnic leagues in the area were German or Italian or Greek, they are now predominantly Hispanic, a reflection of new immigration patterns. Most of the leagues operate outside the jurisdiction of the USSF. Both sides seem to prefer it that way: The Hispanics can get on with running their own affairs in their own language; the soccer authorities do not have to be bothered with troublesome foreigners.

But the split goes much deeper than that. The rise of Hispanic soccer within the United States represents a major challenge to the traditional attitudes of American soccer leaders, because the Hispanics look to Latin America rather than to Europe for their inspiration.

The Latin game, on the field, is very different from the vigorous running game that is so dear to the hearts of the vast majority of American coaches. Greatly simplified, the difference is this: Latin soccer emphasizes technique; European soccer stresses physical power. (For the moment, let us not argue over which is better, we shall come to that shortly.) These are two different approaches to the game, each with its pros and cons. Yet the American soccer leaders have chosen the European style, at the expense of the Latin.

When the USSF appointed Bora Milutinovic as national coach in 1991, there was hope that a change of attitudes might follow. But the Serbian-born Milutinovic, who lived and coached for many years in Mexico, had little effect. His job was carefully limited to producing a team for World Cup-94. The overall philosophy of the national team program—usually a key part of a national team coach's work—was left with the same tired old admirers of size, strength, and stamina.

The Eurocentric approach permeates the USSF's coaching schools. One candidate for a coaching license, having listened to a long analysis of World Cup tactics at the USSF's national licensing course, pointed out that it was very European-oriented, and asked if they could discuss some of the Latin teams. He was told by the instructor that if he was so interested he should "fly your carcass down to South America and find out for yourself."

The prejudice against the Latin players comes close to racism. It will be argued that it is not the players, but the style that is rejected. Which adds up to a distinction without a difference.

And clearly there is economic racism at work. The USSF's Olympic Development Program (ODP) is supposed to identify and train young talent throughout the nation. But for boys to travel to the various district, state, and regional tryouts that may lead to national team selection is an expensive business, it can cost several thousand dollars a year.

The USSF professes to be aware of the problem. In 1991 its secretary-general, Hank Steinbrecher, said: "The Hispanics are a phenomenal resource, but we're not using them. We must have a system that can identify the Hispanic player."

Four years later there was no such system, nor did the USSF have a system of providing financial aid for players whose families could not afford to send them to tryouts.

There had been some halfhearted attempts to increase Hispanic representation within the USSF. In January 1994 Carlos Juarez was appointed a "coaching coordinator," his job supposedly to serve as USSF liaison with Hispanic communities. He resigned after a year, during which time one of the tasks he had been given included coaching the national U-17 girls' team. Teófilo Cubillas, the man the USSF had refused to license in 1987, was recruited as a technical advisor . . . and given nothing to do.

It is an ironic U-turn for the federation, once so ethnic and anti-American, now so pro-American that its definition of the "American player" virtually excludes Latins.

In purely soccer terms, does this matter? That depends on your viewpoint. If you are satisfied with soccer as a massive recreational sport, if you can live with the suggestion of bias, then things can roll merrily along as they are. But if you feel that the pro league is a must—and both FIFA and the USSF have made it clear that this is what they feel—and that the USA should develop as a power in international soccer, then the current direction of American soccer is a disaster.

The European domination, plus the football mentality, has saddled American soccer with an unsophisticated, coach-dominated, hard-running athletic game that has a long track record of failure when offered to the American sports fan as a spectator attraction. A version of soccer that features large-sized players indulging in much running and physical contact. Why on earth would it appeal to Americans? They can get all that, and get it better, in football.

If the MLS is based on that style, it will fail. The soccer will be mindlessly tedious. It will not be entertaining. We are back to that. To face the stark realization that the "American player," as defined by the colleges and the USSF, is not capable of producing the attractive soccer that the pro league will need.

A generalization, of course. Over the past ten years, individual American players have risen above the mediocrity and have proved themselves good enough to play professionally in Europe. Players like Tab Ramos in Spain, John Harkes in England, and Eric Wynalda in Germany.

But they are the exceptions. How to change the approach? Indeed, can it be changed? It can, but it won't be easy. There is no logical reason at all why American soccer should be patterned on that of England or Germany, or any European country. If we are looking for a role model, then how about Brazil? An ex-colony like the United States, a huge country with a vast, ethnically mixed population.

Why not? Using Brazilian soccer as the yardstick would immediately solve the entertainment problem. If there is one thing that soccer fans worldwide agree on, it is that Brazil is always worth watching. Brazilian players are recognized as the supreme artists of the sport.

The point about Brazilian soccer—and Latin American soccer in general—is that it is based on ball skills. It does not exclude anyone, whatever their size or shape. It is an equal opportunity style for any player who has taken the trouble to learn and refine the game's skills. Something that cannot be said of the current American "style" that places a premium on size and strength and regularly rejects good players because they don't run enough or are considered too small.

Can Americans play like Brazilians? The standard response from American coaches is to dismiss the idea as a pipe dream that doesn't correspond to the "characteristics of the American player." That is, to *their* definition

Tab Ramos, the premier American player of the 1990s. Born in Uruguay, Ramos came to the United States at age eleven. After high school at St. Benedict's Prep in Newark and college at North Carolina State, Ramos played professionally in Spain and Mexico. One of the key players in the future of the MLS.
© Peter Robinson: The Football Archive

of the American player's characteristics. It is a mean-spirited response. Probably also self-serving, for would these coaches, these products of the European-oriented USSF coaching schools, know how to coach a Brazilian style? Indeed, one of the problems with any style based on ball skills is that so much of the player's development is outside the reach of the coach. The player teaches himself the skills and tricks of the game.

There is no wand to wave that will have Americans playing like Brazilians tomorrow. Maybe they never will. Maybe they will end up playing more like the Argentines, a skill-based South American style without the flamboyance of the Brazilians.

The crucial thing is to shift the emphasis in training to skill rather than strength, to self-learning rather than coach-imposed drills and tactics. That will set off fundamental changes in the identikit of the American player. For a start, it will give the Hispanics the influence that their passion for the game merits. This is not a matter of them dominating; they will become part of the mix that will bring a true American style.

The change in emphasis must result in a more skillful, more intelligent, more attractive, more exciting game—essential qualities for American soccer if the MLS is to be successful.

There is reason for hope. The national team, under coach Steve Sampson, has suddenly turned adventurous. The cautious tactics of Bora

Milutinovic have been abandoned, and Sampson has vowed a policy of attacking soccer. "The players have to have the freedom to experiment," he said, "They now play in leagues around the world where they do this and they understand how and when to do it. That makes it easier for me to allow that freedom. It's a critical step if American soccer is to improve at the international level. Otherwise we're a very predictable and boring side."

The fact that Sampson was coaching the team at all was an accident. The announcement that Bora Milutinovic had resigned came in April 1995. "No," said Bora the following day, "I was fired." The USSF was in pursuit of a top international coach, Carlos Queiroz of Portugal. If it couldn't get him, it wanted Brazil's World Cup–winning Carlos Alberto Parreira.

Both were available, both proved too expensive. Sampson, an American who had been one of Bora's assistants, got the job on an interim basis. But his results—including a fourth-place finish in the 1995 Copa America—were too good to ignore. He was given a contract to coach the team through World Cup-98 in France.

International success for an American coach at the head of an American team. A major reason for that success was that, for the first time, the team was composed of players with plenty of professional experience, with a pro mentality, with pro discipline. To get all that they had to play overseas.

Did that mean that the colleges were still incapable of producing pro-level players—the accusation that had been leveled by the NASL coaches back in the 1970s?

Not necessarily. An exciting glimpse of what the future could hold for college soccer has been given by the University of Virginia under coach Bruce Arena. A team that has won the NCAA Division I championship four consecutive times, 1991–94, with a mixture of white, black, and Hispanic players, and a skillful, entertaining style of soccer.

Well, said the disparagers, Arena gets all the best players. A grain of truth in that. Arena certainly has an eye for the skillful player . . . but it also meant that the skillful players were there to be found.

Not enough of them, clearly. But the success of Virginia was certain to be noted and, hopefully, copied. To ram home the messages about Hispanic soccer and skillful soccer, Virginia's star player in its first three championships was Claudio Reyna. American born, of Argentine parentage, Reyna proved that exceptional Hispanic players could be reared in the United States.

That was good news for the MLS and, at the same time, bad news. For Reyna chose to forego his senior year, and signed a pro contract with the German Bundesliga club Bayer Leverkusen.

The top American prospect had left the country—at the very moment when the MLS was trying to find ways to bring American players back home.

The ideal for the MLS was to have all the United States national team players under contract. That seemed unlikely, if only because many of them could make more money playing abroad. Others were drawn overseas by the challenge of making it in a foreign country. That was still seen as the ultimate proof of a good player.

The ten teams of the MLS will each have a roster of 18 players. Under the single-entity arrangement, each team will have a strictly enforced player salary budget of only $1.3 million. Spread equally among 18 players, that gives an average of $72,000. Good enough to poach the top players from the A-League or the USISL—but pitifully inadequate for star international players, any one of whom would swallow up the entire budget and then some.

Of the 180 pros needed, forty could be foreigners. (USSF regulations actually permitted only three foreign players on a pro team. But the MLS obtained permission to use four—well, why not? After all, MLS Chairman Rothenberg is also the president of the USSF.) The MLS drew up a hit list of about ten foreign stars, lively charismatic players whom it would like to sign. The flamboyant Mexican goalkeeper, Jorge Campos, was the first to sign. Then came another Mexican, the veteran striker Hugo Sanchez. Bolivia's Marco "El Diablo" Etcheverry, Colombia's Carlos Valderrama and Leonel Alvarez, and Italy's Roberto Donadoni followed.

There was no way that such stars would fit into the stingy club salary limits, but that problem was to be solved by sponsors paying all, or most of their salaries.

But the list of sought-after stars is interesting. Evidently, a lesson has been learned from the Japanese, who started their new J-League in 1993. Each team was limited to five foreign players—and most of the players signed were Brazilians.

The marquee players being sought by MLS are almost exclusively Latin, and they are all *entertainers*. The man who singled out these players and traveled the world to sign them is the MLS Deputy Commissioner, Sunil Gulati. A man who, almost alone among the MLS staff, does know something about the sport of soccer.

That lack of soccer knowledge at the center of MLS remains a very worrying feature of the league. It is not clear where the ultimate power is going to reside. The prime mover of the MLS, Alan Rothenberg, was clearly seen to be losing ground at the end of 1995. The owner-investors were not happy with his leadership style, and greatly unhappy with his $1 million-a-year salary requirement for running MLS. There was persistent, and logical, talk of moving the MLS office from Los Angles to New York. Something that would further diminish the role of the California-based Rothenberg.

A Commissioner was hired to run the league, with Rothenberg in an advisory role. Enter Doug Logan, appointed Commissioner on the strength of twenty years of sports and entertainment promotion and marketing. Soccer experience? Zero. Soccer knowledge? Zero. There was no way of hiding the fact that Logan—whatever his positive attributes—represented a weighty addition to the lack of soccer know-how at MLS.

The vacuum continues among the owners where—except for the Hunts—nobody has any intimate knowledge of the sport of soccer. Whether that also means that they will prove to have no lasting love for the sport, should the league's life prove difficult, remains to be seen.

And the life of the MLS is likely to be difficult. That is the way it has always been for pro soccer leagues in the USA. But they keep coming back, and each time there is more, not less, reason for optimism. Each time there are more Americans playing, and playing better, and there are more fans out there. And each time soccer has increased its strength and its wealth in the rest of the world, and the insatiably expansive demands of international television for an American presence get stronger and stronger.

The soccer atmosphere, both domestic and foreign, is more than ever favorable to a pro league in the United States. It is up to the MLS to provide the missing ingredients: high-quality, entertaining soccer, and owners with long-term commitment to the sport.

Appendix A
Glossary

Soccer, like every other sport, has its own language—in fact it has a whole host of languages. Soccer terms come in Spanish and Portuguese and German and French and Italian and Arabic and, of course, in English. British English, that is. Which poses a problem for Americans, for some of the terms are likely to get confused with similar or identical terms that have slightly or totally different meanings in American sports.

For example, "to tackle" in football (and therefore in American-English) conjures up the picture of a player grabbing another player around the waist and bringing him crashing to the ground. That sort of action is strictly prohibited in soccer—where "to tackle" means using the feet to take the ball away from an opponent's feet.

In soccer we have to accept the British definition. But it is not the purpose of this section to extol the British way of saying things. I happen to believe that the British soccer vocabulary is one of the least imaginative in the world. In this it is a fairly accurate reflection of the way the British play soccer. Brazilian soccer terms, as anyone who has seen Brazilian soccer might expect, are playful, colorful, and generally delightful.

What can be said in favor of the British soccer vocabulary is that it is in English, and it is there. It provides the basis of fundamental terms on which Americans, with their gift for lively language, will build an American English soccer vocabulary.

There follows a list of selected soccer terms, with some personal comments on their meaning, their use and their acceptability. This is not meant to be a comprehensive glossary. It is limited to those terms that—often because of confusion with similar terms in other sports—seem to present problems to American fans.

ADVANTAGE RULE: The referee does not have to stop play every time he detects a foul. If the offending team gains an advantage from the offense, he will certainly do so. But sometimes it is penalizing the innocent team to stop play: if, for instance, a defender deliberately handles the ball to bring it under control but only succeeds in deflecting it to an opponent who is well placed for a shot at goal. To stop play at this moment would penalize the attacking team. In such a case, the referee would apply the so-called advantage rule and allow play to go on.

AGGREGATE SCORE: Many of soccer's most important club competitions are played on a knock-out basis. A draw is conducted to decide the pairings. The two clubs drawn as a pair play each other twice, home-and-home. The winner is decided by adding together the scores from the two games—the aggregate score. If the aggregate score is tied, then the winner is the club that scored more goals on its opponent's field (usually referred to as "the away goals rule"). If the score is still tied under the away goals rule, then 30 minutes of extra time (usually it is *not* sudden death) are played. If that doesn't produce a result, then a penalty shoot-out is used to decide the tie. *See also* Scorelines.

ASSIST: An American term that is gaining acceptance throughout the soccer world. The Italians regularly use the word, while the official FIFA World Cup statistics now include a list of assists. The English find every reason not to use the word. The idea of an American contribution to soccer is evidently more than they can bear.

BALL IN AND OUT OF PLAY: For the ball to pass out of play, *all* of it must be outside *all* of the sideline or goal line (the lines can be up to five inches wide). Thus, a ball on the line is in play. Even a ball resting on the ground just outside the line is in play if any part of it is projecting over the line. Similarly, a goal is not scored until all the ball has passed over all the goal line. The position of the player controlling or dribbling the ball does not matter—he can be standing or running with both feet outside the sideline, but as long as the ball is in play the game goes on.

BICYCLE KICK: A volley in which the player kicks the ball over his own head. This is not just a simple overhead kick, which can be accomplished keeping one foot on the ground. In the true bicycle kick, the player has both feet off the ground. With his body "floating" horizontally he uses a rapid pedaling motion of both legs (hence the bicycle reference) to kick the ball backward. The player is, in effect, performing a somersault as he kicks. This allows him to get his feet above the level of his head so that the trajectory of the ball can be kept down, essential for one of the bicycle kick's most spectacular uses as a shot on goal. The bicycle kick should not be confused with the Scissor Kick (q.v.).

BOOTER: Ugh! This, I suspect, is the invention of some deservedly obscure headline writer looking for an easy way of identifying soccer players. The word has an aura of heavy clumsiness about it, and no self-respecting soccer enthusiast should be caught dead using it. In any case, "to boot" has a more specific soccer meaning and should not be used as though it means simply "to kick." To boot the ball in soccer is to kick it hard and long and usually high; an aimless, thoughtless sort of wallop that is the very antithesis of good soccer.

BOX: The box means the penalty area. Sometimes called the 18-yard box, to distinguish it from the goal area, which is the 6-yard box (for those with a metric turn of mind, the corresponding measurements are 16.5 meters and 5.5 meters).

CLEAR: To kick or head the ball away from the goalmouth, thus killing an immediate threat to the goal. In theory, there ought to be two types of clearance: good, in which the ball is passed to a teammate to start an attack, or bad, in which the ball is hoofed anywhere. In practice, the first, good, type of clearance is always referred to as a pass or as starting an attack. The words "clear" and "clearance" almost always describe those panic situations in which a defender is under pressure and is quite happy to boot the ball aimlessly upfield or out of play.

DEAD BALL: When play is stopped and the ball is not moving, it is a dead ball. All free kicks, including penalty kicks, have to be taken from a dead—i.e., stationary—ball.

FIELD: Soccer fields are by no means all the same size. International rules allow substantial variation, but the length (from 100 to 130 yards) must always be greater than the width (50 to 100 yards). Excessively narrow fields are a major problem in this country. Many soccer fields are modified football fields, whose playing width of just over 53 yards can rarely be sufficiently enlarged to give the minimum 70 yards that a satisfactory soccer field needs. In college soccer, the NCAA allows a length of between 110 and 120 yards, and a width from 65 to 80 yards, with a stipulation that newly constructed facilities must be at least 110 x 65. The recommended optimum size is 120 by 75 yards (109.73m x 68.58m). *See also* Pitch.

FIFTY-FIFTY BALL: A loose ball, or a badly placed pass, that is as near to a player of one team as it is to a player of the opposing team, allowing both an equal chance of controlling it. Bad soccer, in which players lack the technique to pass and control the ball properly, is often a succession of ugly little tackling battles for possession of fifty-fifty balls.

GOAL: All goals, under international rules, must be *scored*—they cannot be awarded by the referee. If a defender (other than the goalkeeper) punches the ball out of the goal, the referee cannot award a goal, even though the ball was clearly going into the net, and even though the defender's action was flagrantly illegal. The referee will eject the player who handled the ball, and give the attacking team a penalty kick.

GOALKEEPER: This is the soccer term, sometimes shortened to goalie, or 'keeper. Beware of imitations, especially one labeled "goal tender." The trouble with goal tender is that it is a hockey term and it is likely to bring with it ideas that cannot be applied to soccer. A hockey goal tender is frequently credited with having "registered a shutout," and with a small goal (6 feet by 4 feet) to guard, it is possible for him to single-handedly defy a barrage of shots. It is theoretically possible for a soccer goalkeeper to do the same. Possible, but rare. His goal is *eight* times as large (twenty-four feet by eight feet) and to remain unbeaten for ninety minutes he needs a lot of help from the defenders playing in front of him. In fact, it is probably not an exaggeration to say that in most soccer shutouts, thanks to his teammates' superior defensive play, the goalkeeper has relatively little to do.

GOAL TENDER: *See* Goalkeeper.

GUARD: *See* Mark.

HAND BALL: An offense in soccer, obviously. What is not so obvious is that the term "hand" includes any part of the arm below the armpit.

HEAD: To head the ball is to play it with the forehead, whether the intention is a clearance, a pass, or a shot at goal. The British describe all three under the general term "header," but the American term "head-shot" to describe a header that is intended as a scoring effort is a useful addition to soccer's vocabulary (and, more than likely, another term of American origin that the English will shun).

KICKER: Like the odious "booter" (q.v.), sometimes used to identify a soccer player. It should be shunned. It is not a particularly pleasant word and it already has a specific soccer meaning. A kicker is a player who tends to kick opponents more than he kicks the ball—a dirty player.

LINESMAN: *See* Referee.

MARK: In man-to-man coverage the defender is said to mark (rather than guard) the attacker. The closer he plays to him, the tighter the marking; the farther away, the looser the marking.

NATIONAL TEAM: An all-star team that represents a country in the various international tournaments (e.g. the World Cup, the Olympic Games, the under-20 World Cup, etc.). National teams are supposed to consist of the very best players in the country, regardless of which club they play for. They are not permanent teams; they are assembled only to play in specific games or tournaments, like the Dream Team that represented the United States in basketball in the 1992 Olympic Games. The clubs are expected to cooperate by releasing the players for the required period (it may be just two or three days, or a month or more for the World Cup). All of the top soccer nations in the world now have a full-time national team coach. Playing for the national team (i.e., representing one's country) was once considered such an honor that clubs rarely refused to release their players. Nowadays, release is less certain. For the World Cup, yes, pro clubs will release their players. But for other national team games, especially for exhibition games, clubs are not so keen to release their highly paid players, who run the risk of injury or who may miss vital club games while away on national team duty.

OFFSIDE: The word is singular. Offside. The origin of the term (see chapter 8, page 178) explains why. How or why the plural version "offsides" arose I have no idea, but it is incorrect.

OWN GOAL: It is, obviously, possible for a player to kick, head, or deflect, the ball into his own goal. If he does so, the score counts for his opponents; and if the ball clearly would *not* have gone in without his intervention, then he, unlucky soul, is listed as the scorer with the letters o.g. (for "own goal") after his name.

PENALTY: Beware! The word "penalty" has a very specific (and very dramatic) meaning in soccer. It should be applied *only* to the award of a penalty kick—i.e., the 12-yard direct free kick taken from the penalty spot with only the goalkeeper to beat. It should never be used in connection with any other offense or free kick situation.

PERIOD: Soccer games are (or should be) divided into two halves: a first half and a second half. The term "period" belongs in games like football and hockey that are played in quarters or thirds. *See also* Time.

PITCH: An English word for a sports field. It is *not* specific to soccer—there are cricket and field hockey and rugby pitches as well. It has come into vogue in the United States, mouthed by those who feel they are showing some special inside knowledge when they use it. They are merely being pretentious. The American term *field* is all that is required.

PROMOTION and RELEGATION: Soccer leagues throughout the world usually feature a number of divisions. In England, for instance, there are Premier, First, Second, and Third divisions; in Italy, Serie A, B, and C. The weakest clubs are in the lower divisions, the big pro clubs are in the top division. The composition of the divisions changes each season. The top clubs in each lower division (usually the first three or four) are promoted to the division above, whose bottom three or four clubs are relegated (demoted) to replace them.

Thus each division features two competitions: one at the top to decide the championship and promotion places, the other at the bottom to avoid relegation.

PUNT: A useful way of measuring the sophistication of a soccer crowd is to listen to their reaction to a long punt by the goalkeeper. If they *ooh* and *aah* as the ball arcs downfield for 40 or 50 yards, chances are that they don't know too much about soccer. A long punt, assessed by football criteria, is impressive. By soccer standards it is next to useless. As a pass, the high towering punt has two major drawbacks: The ball is in the air too long, allowing opponents plenty of time to cover the intended receiver, and when the ball finally does come down, the angle and the speed of its descent make it extremely difficult for a forward to control. The defender, of course, doesn't have to control it—he merely heads or hoofs it back whence it came. To the reader who asks why, then, do goalkeepers constantly punt the ball, I can only reply that it is something of a mystery to me, too.

REFEREE: The man in charge. His decisions on the field are final. He starts the game and, because under international rules he is also the official timekeeper, he (and not the scoreboard clock, should there be one) says when it is over. No player can enter or leave the field without his consent. He calls the fouls and has the power to caution players or to eject them from the game. He is also responsible for seeing that the ball and the players' equipment conform to the rules. He is assisted by two linesmen, but their function is strictly advisory. If a linesman, for example, waves his flag to indicate offside, the referee does not have to whistle for the infraction—he is entitled to overrule the linesman and allow play to continue.

RELEGATION: *See* Promotion and Relegation.

SCISSOR KICK: The side volley. The ball is kicked in the direction that the player is facing. The player leans sideways, throws his legs upward, and volleys the ball forward with a scissorlike motion as the kicking leg passes forward over the other leg. Not to be confused with the Bicycle Kick (q.v.).

SCORELINES: The convention used throughout the soccer world is to name the home team first. Thus, a scoreline of AC Milan 3 Lazio 2, tells you not only that Milan won the game, but also that the game was played in Milan. A scoreline of AC Milan 0 Lazio 1 indicates an away win for Lazio at Milan. The American convention of listing the winning team first is an annoying one to soccer fans, as it fails to indicate the home team. This is often vital information. There are certain two-leg cup ties (e.g., in the various European cup competitions, see pages 311–332), in which goals scored on an opponent's field may count double. (Soccer, however, does use the American system for tournaments such as the World Cup that are played at a fixed site, and where there is in effect only one home team, the host nation.) *See also* Aggregate Score.

SHUTOUT: *See* Goalkeeper.

SIDELINES: Also called touchlines. A ball that goes out of play over the sidelines is said to have gone into touch.

SPOT KICK: A penalty kick, so called because the ball is placed on the penalty spot, 12 yards in front of goal.

STATISTICS: Inevitably, Americans have brought statistics to soccer, a sport in which, traditionally, records have not been particularly plentiful. The theory behind most of the statistics—to plot the shape and progress of a game with figures—is excellent. But soccer is a game that is proving stubbornly resistant to having its portrait drawn in columns of numbers. I can only say that soccer statistics, particularly those such as shots on goal, or saves, should be viewed with caution. Many of them will be judgment calls by the scorekeeper, who may or may not be reliable. Also, special soccer considerations must be taken into account when assessing the figures (*See* the discussion of shutouts under Goalkeeper.)

TACKLE: To use the feet in attempting to take the ball from an opponent's feet. A tackle may be accompanied by a legitimate shoulder charge, but there must be no holding, pushing, tripping, elbowing, or hip-checking. Clean tackling—the ability to strip the ball from an opponent without fouling—requires considerable skill. Unfortunately, the leniency shown to defenders during the 1970s and 1980s has meant that many defenders are not good tacklers. They simply clatter into the guy with the ball, often from behind, and—if called for a foul—protest, "But I got the ball, ref!" Possibly, but only by demolishing the opponent as well. FIFA has recently outlawed the more violent tackles from behind.

TIME: Traditionally, soccer games have always been divided into two halves: forty-five minutes per half in professional games, less (thirty or thirty-five minutes) for youth games.

TIME-OUT: The referee alone can stop the clock in soccer. Coaches are not permitted to call time-outs. But . . . FIFA carried out experiments with time-outs during the 1995 U-17 World Cup in Ecuador. Coaches were allowed to call one 90-second time-out in each half.

TRANSFER FEE: In most soccer countries, a player's contract still belongs to his club, even after it has expired. When the player is traded to another club, the new club has to purchase the contract, often paying huge sums of money for it. This is the transfer fee—it goes to the old club, not to the player. Under this system, players obviously do not become free agents when their contract has expired. However, change is certainly on the way as the result of a ruling from the European Court of Justice in 1995 that declared the current system illegal.

WALL-PASS: The give-and-go. So called because in soccer games played by boys in streets, the ball is bounced off a wall rather than passed to a teammate.

Appendix B
The Rules of Soccer

These are the 1995 rules of soccer as authorized by the International Football Association Board and published by the Fédération Internationale de Football Association. Their official title is Laws of the Game. They are the basis for the playing of soccer all over the world.

The Field of Play

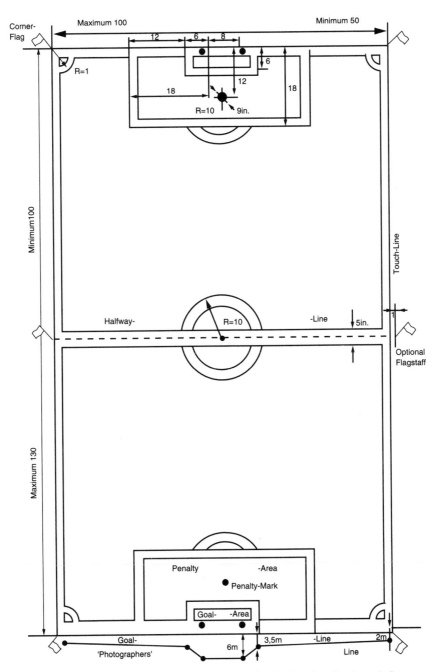

Corner-
Flag

Maximum 100

Minimum 50

R=1

Minimum100

12

6

8

6

12

18

18

R=10   9in.

Touch-Line

Halfway-

R=10

-Line

5in.

Optional
Flagstaff

Maximum 130

Penalty   -Area

Penalty-Mark

Goal-   -Area

Goal-

'Photographers'

6m

3,5m

-Line

Line

2m

(N. B. All measurements are in yards and inches unless otherwise marked)

(1) Dimensions. The field of play shall be rectangular, its length being not more than 130 yards nor less than 100 yards and its breadth not more than 100 yards nor less than 50 yards. (In international matches the length shall be not more than 120 yards nor less than 110 yards and the breadth not more than 80 yards nor less than 70 yards.) The length shall in all cases exceed the breadth.

(2) Marking. The field of play shall be marked with distinctive lines, not more than 5 inches in width (not by a V-shaped rut) in accordance with the plan, the longer boundary lines being called the touch-lines and the shorter the goal-lines. A flag on a post not less than 5 ft. high and having a non-pointed top, shall be placed at each corner; a similar flag-post may be placed opposite the half-way line on each side of the field of play, not less than 1 yard outside the touch-line. A halfway-line shall be marked out across the field of play. The centre of the field of play shall be indicated by a suitable mark and a circle with a 10 yards radius shall be marked round it.

(3) The Goal-Area. At each end of the field of play two lines shall be drawn at right-angles to the goal-line, 6 yards from each goal-post. These shall extend into the field of play for a distance of 6 yards and shall be joined by a line drawn parallel with the goal-line. Each of the spaces enclosed by these lines and the goal-line shall be called a goal-area.

(4) The Penalty-Area. At each end of the field of play two lines shall be drawn at right-angles to the goal-line, 18 yards from each goal-post. These shall extend into the field of play for a distance of 18 yards and shall be joined by a line drawn parallel with the goal-line. Each of the spaces enclosed by these lines and the goal-line shall be called a penalty-area. A suitable mark shall be made within each penalty-area, 12 yard from the mid-point of the goal-line, measured along an undrawn line at right-angles thereto. These shall be the penalty-kick marks. From each penalty-kick mark an arc of a circle, having a radius of 10 yards, shall be drawn outside the penalty-area.

(5) The Corner-Area. From each corner-flag post a quarter circle, having a radius of 1 yard, shall be drawn inside the field of play.

(6) The Goals. The goals shall be placed on the centre of each goal-line and shall consist of two upright posts, equidistant from the corner-flags and 8 yards apart (inside measurement), joined by a horizontal cross-bar the lower edge of which shall be 8 ft. from the ground.

For safety reasons, the goals, including those which are portable, must be anchored securely to the ground.

The width and depth of the cross-bars shall not exceed 5 inches (12 cm). The goal-posts and the cross-bars shall have the same width.

Nets may be attached to the posts, cross-bars and ground behind the goals. They should be appropriately supported and be so placed as to allow the goal-keeper ample room.

Footnote:

Goal nets. The use of nets made of hemp, jute or nylon is permitted. The nylon strings may, however, not be thinner than those made of hemp or jute.

LAW I

DECISIONS OF THE INTERNATIONAL F.A. BOARD

(1) In international matches the dimensions of the field of play shall be: maximum 110 x 75 metres; minimum 100 x 64 metres.

(2) National associations must adhere strictly to these dimensions. Each national association organising an international match must advise the visiting association, before the match, of the place and the dimensions of the field of play.

(3) The Board has approved this table of measurements for the Laws of the Game:

130 yards	....	120 metres
120 yards	....	110
110 yards	....	100
100 yards	....	90
80 yards	....	75
70 yards	....	64
50 yards	....	45
18 yards	....	16,50
12 yards	....	11
10 yards	....	9 ,15
8 yards	....	7,32
6 yards	....	5,50
1 yard	....	1
8 feet	....	2,44
5 feet	....	1,50
28 inches	....	0,71
27 inches	....	0,68
9 inches	....	0,22
5 inches	....	0,12
3/4 inch	....	0,019
1/2 inch	....	0,0127
3/8 inch	....	0,010
14 ounces	....	396 grams
16 ounces	....	453 grams
8 .5 lb./sq.in.	....	600 gr/cm²
15 .6 lb./sq.in.	....	1100 gr/cm²

(4) The goal-line shall be marked the same width as the depth of the goal-posts and the cross-bar, so that the goal-line and goal-posts will conform to the same interior and exterior edges.

(5) The 6 yards (for the outline of the goal-area) and the 18 yards (for the outline of the penalty-area) which have to be measured along the goal-line, must start from the inner sides of the goal-posts.

(6) The space within the inside areas of the field of play includes the width of the lines marking these areas.

(7) All associations shall provide standard equipment, particularly in international matches, when the Laws of the Game must be complied with in every respect and especially with regard to the size of the ball and other equipment which must conform to the regulations. All cases of failure to provide standard equipment must be reported to FIFA.

(8) In a match played under the rules of a competition if the cross-bar becomes displaced or broken, play shall be stopped and the match abandoned unless the cross-bar has been repaired and replaced in position or a new one provided without such being a danger to the players. A rope is not considered to be a satisfactory substitute for a cross-bar.

In a friendly match, by mutual consent, play may be resumed without the cross-bar provided it has been removed and no longer constitutes a danger to the players. In these circumstances, a rope may be used as a substitute for a cross-bar. If a rope is not used and the ball crosses the goal-line at a point which, in the opinion of the referee is below where the cross-bar should have been, he shall award a goal.

The game shall be restarted by the referee dropping the ball at the place where it was when play was stopped, unless it was within the goal-area at that time, in which case it shall be dropped on that part of the goal-area line which runs parallel to the goal-line, at the point nearest to where the ball was when play was stopped.

(9) National associations may specify such maximum and minimum dimensions for the cross-bars and goal-posts, within the limits laid down in Law I, as they consider appropriate.

(10) Goal-posts and cross-bars must be made of wood, metal or other approved material as decided from time to time by the International F.A. Board. They may be square, rectangular, round, half-round or elliptical in shape.

Goal-posts and cross-bars made of other materials and in other shapes are not permitted. The goal-posts must be of white colour.

(11) Any kind of publicity is forbidden in connection with, or on, the field of play. In particular, no advertising material may be displayed at any level on nets, corner flags or goalposts, nor shall such appurtenances of the game have any extraneous equipment attached to them (cameras, microphones, etc.). The reproduction of a FIFA, Confederation, National Association, League, Club or any other logo on the field of play (turf) is also forbidden.

(12) 'Curtain-raisers' to international matches should only be played following agreement on the day of the match, and taking into account the condition of the field of play, between representatives of the two associations and the referee (of the international match).

(13) National associations, particularly in international matches, should

– restrict the number of photographers around the field of play,
– have a line (photographers' line) marked behind the goal-lines at least two metres from the corner flag going through a point situated at least 3.5 metres behind the intersection of the goal-line with the line marking the goal-area to a point situated at least six metres behind the goal-posts,
– prohibit photographers from passing over these lines,
– forbid the use of artificial lighting in the form of "flashlights".

(14) A mark may be made off the field of play, 11 yards from the corner flag and at right angles to the goal-line, to help the referee ensure that this distance is observed when a corner kick is being taken.

LAW II

The Ball

The ball shall be spherical; the outer casing shall be of leather or other approved materials. No material shall be used in its construction which might prove dangerous to the players.

The circumference of the ball shall not be more than 28 in. and not less than 27 in. The weight of the ball at the start of the game shall not be more than 16 oz. nor less than 14 oz. The pressure shall be equal to 0.6-1.1 atmosphere (=600-1,100 gr/cm 2) at sea level. The ball shall not be changed during the game unless authorised by the referee.

DECISIONS OF THE INTERNATIONAL F.A. BOARD

(1) The ball used in any match shall be considered the property of the association or club on whose ground the match is played, and at the close of play it must be returned to the referee.

(2) The International Board, from time to time, shall decide what constitutes approved materials. Any approved material shall be certified as such by the International Board.

(3) The Board has approved these equivalents of the weights specified in the Law: 14 to 16 ounces = 396 to 453 grams.

(4) For FIFA competition matches and competition matches under the auspices of the Confederations, only footballs which have been tested and which have been shown to meet the minimum technical requirements set forth in Law II, shall be permitted for use. Acceptance of a football for use in the above-mentioned competitions will be conditional upon the football bearing one of the following designations to indicate that it has met the minimal technical requirements:

– The official "FIFA APPROVED" logo
– The official "FIFA INSPECTED" logo
– The reference "International Matchball Standards" (together with other such indications of technical conformity, as requested by FIFA).

In all other matches the ball used must satisfy the requirements of Law II. National Associations or Competitions may require the use only of balls bearing one of the aforementioned designations.

(5) If the ball bursts or becomes deflated during the course of a match, the game shall be stopped and restarted by dropping the new ball at the place where the first ball became defective, unless it was within the goal-area at that time, in which case it shall be dropped on that part of the goal-area line which runs parallel to the goal-line, at the point nearest to where the ball was when play was stopped.

(6) If this happens during a stoppage of the game (place-kick, goal-kick, corner-kick, free-kick, penalty-kick or throw-in), the game shall be restarted accordingly.

Number of Players

(1) A match shall be played by two teams, each consisting of not more than eleven players, one of whom shall be the goalkeeper.

(2) Up to a maximum of three substitutes may be used in any match played in an official competition under the auspices of FIFA, the Confederations or the National Associations.

The rules of the competition shall state how many substitutes may be nominated, up to a maximum of five.

The names of the substitutes must be given to the referee prior to the commencement of the match.

Substitutes not so named may not take part in the match.

(3) In other matches, up to five substitutes may also be used provided that the teams concerned reach an agreement on a maximum number, and that the referee is informed before the match. If the referee is not informed, or no agreement is reached before the commencement of the match, no more than three substitutes shall be permitted.

The names of the substitutes must be given to the referee prior to the commencement of the match.

(4) Any of the other players may change places with the goalkeeper, provided that the referee is informed before the change is made, and provided also that the change is made during a stoppage of the game.

(5) When a goalkeeper or any other player is to be replaced by a substitute, the following conditions shall be observed:

(a) The referee shall be informed of the proposed substitution, before it is made.

(b) The substitute shall not enter the field of play until the player he is replacing has left, and then only after having received a signal from the referee.

(c) He shall enter the field during a stoppage in the game, and at the halfway line.

(d) A player who has been replaced shall not take any further part in the game.

(e) A substitute shall be subject to the authority and jurisdiction of the referee whether called upon to play or not.

(f) The substitution is completed when the substitute enters the field of play, from which moment he becomes a player and the player whom he is replacing ceases to be a player.

Punishment:

(a) Play shall not be stopped for an infringement of paragraph 4. The players concerned shall be cautioned immediately the ball goes out of play.

(b) If a substitute enters the field of play without the authority of the referee, play shall be stopped. The substitute shall be cautioned and removed from the field or sent off according to the circumstances. The game shall be restarted by the referee dropping the ball at the place where it was when play was stopped, unless it was within the goalarea at that time, in which case it shall be dropped on that part of the goal-area line which runs parallel to the goal-line, at the point nearest to where the ball was when play was stopped.

(c) For any other infringement of this Law, the player concerned shall be cautioned, and if the game is stopped by the referee to administer the caution, it

LAW III

shall be restarted by an indirect free-kick, to be taken by a player of the opposing team from the place where the ball was when play was stopped, subject to the overriding conditions imposed in Law XIII.

DECISIONS OF THE INTERNATIONAL F.A. BOARD

(1) The minimum number of players in a team is left to the discretion of national associations.

(2) The Board is of the opinion that a match should not be considered valid if there are fewer than seven players in either of the teams.

(3) A player who has been ordered off before play begins may only be replaced by one of the named substitutes. The kick-off must not be delayed to allow the substitute to join his team.

A player who has been ordered off after play has started may not be replaced.

A named substitute who has been ordered off, either before or after play has started, may not be replaced.

(This decision only relates to players who are ordered off under Law XII. It does not apply to players who have infringed Law IV.)

Players' Equipment

(1) (a) The basic compulsory equipment of a player shall consist of a jersey or shirt, shorts, stockings, shinguards and footwear.

(b) A player shall not wear anything which is dangerous to another player.

(2) Shinguards, which must be covered entirely by the stockings, shall be made of a suitable material (rubber, plastic, polyurethane or similar substance) and shall afford a reasonable degree of protection.

(3) The goalkeeper shall wear colours which distinguish him from the other players and from the referee.

Punishment:

For any infringement of this Law, the player at fault shall be instructed to leave the field of play by the referee, to adjust his equipment or obtain any missing equipment, when the ball next ceases to be in play, unless by then the player has already corrected his equipment. Play shall not be stopped immediately for an infringement of this Law. A player who is instructed to leave the field to adjust his equipment or obtain missing equipment shall not return without first reporting to the referee, who shall satisfy himself that the player's equipment is in order. The player shall only re-enter the game at a moment when the ball has ceased to be in play.

DECISIONS OF THE INTERNATIONAL F.A. BOARD

(1) In international matches, international competitions, international club competitions and friendly matches between clubs of different national associations, the referee, prior to the start of the game, shall inspect the players' equipment and prevent any player whose equipment does not conform to the requirements of this Law from playing until such time as it does comply. The rules of any competition may include a similar provision.

(2) If the referee finds that a player is wearing articles not permitted by the Laws and which may constitute a danger to other players, he shall order him to take them off. If he fails to carry out the referee's instruction, the player shall not take part in the match.

(3) A player who has been prevented from taking part in the game or a player who has

been sent off the field for infringing Law IV must report to the referee during a stoppage of the game and may not enter or re-enter the field of play unless and until the referee has satisfied himself that the player is no longer infringing Law IV.

(4) A player who has been prevented from taking part in a game or who has been sent off because of an infringement of Law IV, and who enters or re-enters the field of play to join or re-join his team, in breach of the conditions of Law XII (j), shall be cautioned.

If the referee stops the game to administer the caution, the game shall be restarted by an indirect free-kick, taken by a player of the opposing side, from the place where the ball was when the referee stopped the game, subject to the overriding conditions imposed in Law XIII.

LAW V

Referees

A referee shall be appointed to officiate in each game. His authority and the exercise of the powers granted to him by the Laws of the Game commence as soon as he enters the field of play.

His power of penalising shall extend to offences committed when play has been temporarily suspended, or when the ball is out of play. His decision on points of fact connected with the play shall be final, so far as the result of the game is concerned. He shall:

(a) enforce the Laws.

(b) refrain from penalising in cases where he is satisfied that, by doing so, he would be giving an advantage to the offending team.

(c) keep a record of the game; act as timekeeper and allow the full or agreed time, adding thereto all time lost through accident or other cause.

(d) have discretionary power to stop the game for any infringement of the Laws and to suspend or terminate the game whenever, by reason of the elements, interference by spectators, or other cause, he deems such stoppage necessary. In such a case he shall submit a detailed report to the competent authority, within the stipulated time, and in accordance with the provisions set up by the National Association under whose jurisdiction the match was played. Reports will be deemed to be made when received in the ordinary course of post.

(e) from the time he enters the field of play, caution and show a yellow card to any player guilty of misconduct or ungentlemanly behaviour. In such cases the referee shall send the name of the offender to the competent authority, within the stipulated time, and in accordance with the provisions set up by the national association under whose jurisdiction the match was played.

(f) allow no person other than the players and linesmen to enter the field of play without his permission.

(g) stop the game if, in his opinion, a player has been seriously injured; have the player removed as soon as possible from the field of play, and immediately resume the game. If a player is slightly injured, the game shall not be stopped until the ball has ceased to be in play. A player who is able to go to the touch- or goal-line for attention of any kind, shall not be treated on the field of play.

(h) send off the field of play and show a red card to any player who, in his opinion, is guilty of violent conduct, serious foul play, the use of foul or abusive language or who persists in misconduct after having received a caution.

(i) signal for recommencement of the game after all stoppages.

(j) decide that the ball provided for a match meets with the requirements of Law II.

DECISIONS OF THE INTERNATIONAL F.A. BOARD

(1) Referees in international matches shall wear a blazer or blouse the colour of which is distinct from the colours worn by the contesting teams.

(2) Referees for international matches will be selected from a neutral country unless the countries concerned agree to appoint their own officials.

(3) The referee must be chosen from the official List of International Referees. This need not apply to amateur and youth international matches.

(4) The referee shall report to the appropriate authority misconduct or any misdemeanour on the part of spectators, officials, players, named substitutes or other persons which take place either on the field of play or in its vicinity at any time prior to, during, or after the match in question so that appropriate action can be taken by the authority concerned.

(5) Linesmen are assistants of the referee. In no case shall the referee consider the intervention of a linesman if he himself has seen the incident and from his position on the field, is better able to judge. With this reserve, and the linesman neutral, the referee can consider the intervent'on, and if the information of the linesman applies to that phase of the game immediately before the scoring of a goal, the referee may act thereon and cancel the goal.

(6) The referee, however, can only reverse his first decision so long as the game has not been restarted.

(7) If the referee has decided to apply the advantage clause and to let the game proceed, he cannot revoke his decision if the presumed advantage has not been realised, even though he has not, by any gesture, indicated his decision. This does not exempt the offending player from being dealt with by the referee.

(8) The Laws of the Game are intended to provide that games should be played with as little interference as possible, and in this view it is the duty of referees to penalise only deliberate breaches of the Law. Constant whistling for trifling and doubtful breaches produces bad feeling and loss of temper on the part of the players and spoils the pleasure of spectators.

(9) By par. (d) of Law V the referee is empowered to terminate a match in the event of grave disorder, but he has no power or right to decide, in such event, that either team is disqualified and thereby the loser of the match.

He must send a detailed report to the proper authority who alone has power to deal further with this matter.

(10) If a player commits two infringements of a different nature at the same time, the referee shall punish the more serious offence.

(11) It is the duty of the referee to act upon the information of neutral linesmen with regard to incidents that do not come under the personal notice of the referee.

(12) The referee shall not allow any person to enter the field until play has stopped, and only then if he has given him a signal to do so.

(13) A referee (or where applicable a linesman or fourth official) shall not be held liable for (1) any kind of injury suffered by a player, official or spectator, (2) any damage to property of any kind, or (3) any other loss suffered by any individual, club, company, association or similar body, due or which may be due to any decision which he may take in terms of the Laws of the Game or in respect of the normal procedures required to hold, play and control a match.

Such a decision may be

(a) a decision that the condition of the field of play or its surrounds or that the weather conditions are such as to allow or not to allow a match to take place,

(b) a decision to abandon a match for whatever reason,

(c) a decision as to the condition of the fixtures or equipment used during a match including the goal-posts, cross-bar, corner-posts and the ball,

(d) a decision to stop or not to stop a match due to spectator interference or any problem in the spectator area,

(e) a decision to stop or not to stop play to allow an injured player to be treated,

(f) a decision to request or insist that an injured player be removed from the field of play for treatment,

(g) a decision to allow or not to allow a player to wear certain apparel or equipment,

(h) a decision (in so far as this may be his responsibility) to allow or not to allow any persons (including team or stadium officials, security officers, photographers or other media representatives) to be present in the vicinity of the field of play,

LAW V

(i) any other decision which he may take in accordance with the Laws of the Game or in conformity with his duties in terms of the Federation, Association or League Rules or Regulations under which the match is played.

(14) The coach may convey tactical instructions to players during the match.

The coach and other officials, however, must remain within the confines of the technical area , where such an area is provided and they must conduct themselves, at all times, in a responsible manner.

(15) In tournaments or competitions where a fourth official is appointed, his role and duties shall be in accordance with the guide-lines approved by the International Football Association Board.

Linesmen

Two linesmen shall be appointed, whose duty (subject to the decision of the referee) shall be to indicate:

(a) when the ball is out of play,

(b) which side is entitled to a corner-kick, goal-kick or throw-in,

(c) when a substitution is desired.

They shall also assist the referee to control the game in accordance with the Laws. In the event of undue interference or improper conduct by a linesman, the referee shall dispense with his services and arrange for a substitute to be appointed. (The matter shall be reported by the referee to the competent authority.)

The linesmen should be equipped with flags by the club on whose ground the match is played.

DECISIONS OF THE INTERNATIONAL F.A. BOARD

(1) Linesmen, where neutral, shall draw the referee's attention to any breach of the Laws of the Game of which they become aware if they consider that the referee may not have seen it, but the referee shall always be the judge of the decision to be taken.

(2) In international "A" matches, national associations should appoint neutral linesmen from the International List.

(3) In international matches linesmen's flags shall be of a vivid colour, bright reds and yellows. Such flags are recommended for use in all other matches.

(4) A linesman may be subject to disciplinary action only upon a report of the referee for unjustified interference or insufficient assistance.

Duration of the Game

The duration of the game shall be two equal periods of 45 minutes, unless otherwise mutually agreed upon, subject to the following:

(a) Allowance shall be made in either period for all time lost through substitution, the transport from the field of injured players, time-wasting or other cause, the amount of which shall be a matter for the discretion of the referee.

(b) Time shall be extended to permit a penalty-kick being taken at or after the expiration of the normal period in either half.

The half-time interval shall not exceed fifteen minutes.

Competition rules shall clearly stipulate the duration of the half-time interval.

The duration of the half-time interval may be altered only with the consent of the referee.

DECISIONS OF THE INTERNATIONAL F.A. BOARD

(1) If a match has been stopped by the referee, before the completion of the time specified in the rules, for any reason stated in Law V, it must be replayed in full unless the rules of the competition concerned provide for the result of the match at the time of such stoppage to stand.

(2) Players have a right to an interval at half-time.

The Start of Play

(a) **At the beginning of the game,** choice of ends and the kick-off shall be decided by the toss of a coin. The team winning the toss shall have the option of choice of ends or the kick-off. The referee having given a signal, the game shall be started by a player taking a place-kick (i.e. a kick at the ball while it is stationary on the ground in the centre of the field of play) into his opponents' half of the field of play. Every player shall be in his own half of the field and every player of the team opposing that of the kicker shall remain not less than 10 yards from the ball until it is kicked-off; it shall not be deemed in play until it has travelled the distance of its own circumference. The kicker shall not play the ball a second time until it has been touched or played by another player.

(b) **After a goal has been scored,** the game shall be restarted in like manner by a player of the team losing the goal.

(c) **After half-time;** when restarting after half-time, ends shall be changed and the kick-off shall be taken by a player of the opposite team to that of the player who started the game.

Punishment

For any infringement of this Law, the kick-off shall be retaken, except in the case of the kicker playing the ball again before it has been touched or played by another player; for this offence an indirect free-kick shall be taken by a player of the opposing team from the place where the infringement occurred, subject to the overriding conditions imposed in Law XIII.

A goal shall not be scored direct from a kick-off.

(d) **After any other temporary suspension;** when restarting the game after a temporary suspension of play from any cause not mentioned elsewhere in these Laws, provided that immediately prior to the suspension the ball has not passed over the touch-or goal-lines, the referee shall drop the ball at the place where it was when play was suspended, unless it was within the goal-area at that time, in which case it shall be dropped on that part of the goal-area line which runs parallel to the goal-line, at the point nearest to where the ball was when play was stopped. It shall be deemed in play when it has touched the ground; if, however, it goes over the touch- or goal-lines after it has been dropped by the referee, but before it is touched by a player, the referee shall again drop it. A player shall not play the ball until it has touched the ground.

If this section of the Laws is not complied with, the referee shall again drop the ball.

LAW VIII

DECISIONS OF THE INTERNATIONAL F.A. BOARD

(1) If, when the referee drops the ball, a player infringes any of the Laws before the ball has touched the ground, the player concerned shall be cautioned or sent off the field according to the seriousness of the offence, but a free-kick cannot be awarded to the opposing team because the ball was not in play at the time of the offence.

The ball shall therefore be again dropped by the referee.

(2) Kicking-off by persons other than the players competing in a match is prohibited.

Ball in and out of Play

The ball is out of play:

(a) when it has wholly crossed the goal-line or touch-line, whether on the ground or in the air.

(b) when the game has been stopped by the referee.

The ball is in play at all other times from the start of the match to the finish including:

(a) if it rebounds from a goal-post, cross-bar or corner-flag post into the field of play.

(b) if it rebounds off either the referee or linesmen when they are in the field of play.

(c) in the event of a supposed infringement of the Laws, until a decision is given.

DECISIONS OF THE INTERNATIONAL F.A. BOARD

(1) The lines belong to the areas of which they are the boundaries. In consequence, the touch-lines and the goal-lines belong to the field of play.

LAW X

Method of Scoring

Except as otherwise provided by these Laws, a goal is scored when the whole of the ball has passed over the goal-line, between the goal-posts and under the cross-bar, provided it has not been thrown, carried or intentionally propelled by hand or arm, by a player of the attacking side, except in the case of a goalkeeper, who is within his own penalty-area.

The team scoring the greater number of goals during a game shall be the winner; if no goals or an equal number of goals are scored, the game shall be termed a "draw".

DECISIONS OF THE INTERNATIONAL F.A. BOARD

(1) Law X defines the only method according to which a match is won or drawn; no variation whatsoever can be authorised.

(2) A goal cannot in any case be allowed if the ball has been prevented by some outside agent from passing over the goal-line. If this happens in the normal course of play, other than at the taking of a penalty-kick: the game must be stopped and restarted by the referee dropping the ball at the place where the ball came into contact with the interference, unless it was within the goal-area at that time, in which case it shall be dropped on that part of the goal-area line which runs parallel to the goal-line, at the point nearest to where the ball was when play was stopped.

(3) If, when the ball is going into goal, a spectator enters the field before it passes wholly over the goal-line and tries to prevent a score, a goal shall be allowed if the ball goes into goal unless the spectator has made contact with the ball or has interfered with play, in which case the referee shall stop the game and restart it by dropping the ball at the place where the contact or interference occurred, unless it was within the goal-area at that time, in which case it shall be dropped on that part of the goal-area line which runs parallel to the goal-line, at the point nearest to where the ball was when play was stopped.

Off-side

1. A player is in an off-side position if he is nearer to his opponents' goal-line than the ball, unless:

(a) he is in his own half of the field of play, or

(b) he is not nearer to his opponents' goal-line than at least two of his opponents.

2. It is not an offence in itself to be in an off-side position

A player shall only be penalised for being in an off-side position if, at the moment the ball touches, or is played by one of his team, he is, in the opinion of the referee, involved in active play by:

(a) interfering with play, or

(b) interfering with an opponent, or

(c) gaining an advantage by being in that position.

3. A player shall not be declared off-side by the referee

(a) merely because of his being in an off-side position, or

(b) if he receives the ball direct from a goal-kick, a corner-kick or a throw-in.

4. If a player is declared off-side, the referee shall award an indirect free-kick, which shall be taken by a player of the opposing team from the place where the infringement occurred, unless the offence is committed by a player in his opponents' goal area, in which case the free-kick shall be taken from any point within the goal area.

DECISIONS OF THE INTERNATIONAL F.A. BOARD

---

(1) Off-side shall not be judged at the moment the player in question receives the ball, but at the moment when the ball is passed to him by one of his own side. A player who is not in an off-side position when one of his colleagues passes the ball to him or takes a free-kick, does not therefore become off-side if he goes forward during the flight of the ball.

2. A player who is level with the second last opponent or with the last two opponents is not in an off-side position.

LAW XII

Fouls and Misconduct

A player who commits any of the following six offences in a manner considered by the referee to be careless, reckless or involving disproportionate force:

(a) kicks or attempts to kick an opponent; or

(b) trips an opponent; or

(c) jumps at an opponent; or

(d) charges an opponent; or

(e) strikes or attempts to strike an opponent; or

(f) pushes an opponent;

or who commits any of the following four offences:

(g) when tackling an opponent makes contact with the opponent before contact is made with the ball; or

(h) − holds an opponent or
− spits at an opponent; or

(i) handles the ball deliberately, i.e., carries, strikes or propels the ball with his hand or arm (this does not apply to the goalkeeper within his own penalty-area);

shall be penalised by the award of a **direct free-kick** to be taken by the opposing team from the place where the offence occurred, unless the offence is committed by a player in his opponents' goal-area, in which case the free-kick shall be taken from any point within the goal-area.

Should a player of the defending team intentionally commit one of the above ten offences within the penalty-area, he shall be penalised by a **penalty-kick.**

A penalty-kick can be awarded irrespective of the position of the ball, if in play, at the time an offence within the penalty-area is committed.

A player committing any of the five following offences:

1. playing in a manner considered by the referee to be dangerous, e.g. attempting to kick the ball while held by the goalkeeper;

2. charging fairly, i.e. with the shoulder, when the ball is not within playing distance of the players concerned and they are definitely not trying to play it;

3. when not playing the ball, impeding the progress of an opponent, i.e. running between the opponent and the ball, or interposing the body so as to form an obstacle to an opponent;

4. charging the goalkeeper except when he

(a) is holding the ball;

(b) is obstructing an opponent;

(c) has passed outside his goal-area.

5. when playing as a goalkeeper and within his own penalty-area:

(a) from the moment he takes control of the ball with his hands, he takes more than 4 steps in any direction whilst holding, bouncing or throwing the ball in the air and catching it again, without releasing it into play, or

(b) having released the ball into play before, during or after the 4 steps, he touches it again with his hands, before it has been touched or played by a player of the opposing team either inside or outside of the penalty area, or by a player of the same team outside the penalty area, subject to the over-riding conditions of 5(c), or

(c) touches the ball with his hands after it has been deliberately kicked to him by a team-mate, or

(d) indulges in tactics, which in the opinion of the referee, are designed to hold up the game and thus waste time and so give an unfair advantage to his own team,

shall be penalised by the award of an **indirect free-kick** to be taken by the opposing side from the place where the infringement occurred, subject to the overriding conditions imposed in Law XIII.

A player shall be **cautioned and shown the yellow card** if:

(j) he enters or re-enters the field of play to join or rejoin his team after the game has commenced, or leaves the field of play during the progress of the game (except through accident) without, in either case, first having received a signal from the referee showing him that he may do so. If the referee stops the game to administer the caution, the game shall be restarted by an indirect free-kick taken by a player of the opposing team from the place where the ball was when the referee stopped the game, subject to the overriding conditions imposed in Law XIII.

If, however, the offending player has committed a more serious offence he shall be penalised according to that section of the law he infringed.

(k) he persistently infringes the Laws of the Game;

(l) he shows, by word or action, dissent from any decision given by the referee;

(m) he is guilty of ungentlemanly conduct.

For any of these last three offences, in addition to the caution, an indirect free-kick shall also be awarded to the opposing side from the place where the offence occurred, subject to the overriding conditions imposed in Law XIII, unless a more serious infringement of the Laws of the Game was committed.

A player shall be **sent off the field of play and shown the red card,** if, in the opinion of the referee, he:

(n) is guilty of violent conduct;

(o) is guilty of serious foul play;

(p) uses foul or abusive language;

(q) is guilty of a second cautionable offence after having received a caution.

If play is stopped by reason of a player being ordered from the field for an offence without a separate breach of the Law having been committed, the game shall be resumed by an **indirect free-kick** awarded to the opposing side from the place where the infringement occurred, subject to the overriding conditions imposed in Law XIII.

DECISIONS OF THE INTERNATIONAL F.A. BOARD

(1) If the goalkeeper either strikes an opponent by throwing the ball at him or pushes him with the ball while still holding it, the referee shall award a penalty-kick, if the offence took place within the penalty-area.

(2) If a player leans on the shoulders of another player of his own team in order to head the ball, the referee shall stop the game, caution the player for ungentlemanly conduct and award an indirect free-kick to the opposing side.

(3) A player's obligation when joining or rejoining his team after the start of the match to 'report to the referee' must be interpreted as meaning 'to draw the attention of the referee from the touch-line'. The signal from the referee shall be made by a definite gesture which makes the player understand that he may come into the field of play; it is not necessary for the referee to wait until the game is stopped (this does not apply in respect of an infringement of Law IV), but the referee is the sole

LAW XII

judge of the moment in which he gives his signal of acknowledgement.

(4) The letter and spirit of Law XII do not oblige the referee to stop a game to administer a caution. He may, if he chooses, apply the advantage. If he does apply the advantage, he shall caution the player when play stops.

(5) If a player covers up the ball without touching it in an endeavour not to have it played by an opponent, he obstructs but does not infringe Law XII par. 3 because he is already in possession of the ball and covers it for tactical reasons whilst the ball remains within playing distance. In fact, he is actually playing the ball and does not commit an infringement; in this case, the player may be charged because he is in fact playing the ball.

(6) If a player positions his arms to impede an opponent and steps from one side to the other, moving his arms up and down to delay his opponent, forcing him to change course, but does not make "bodily contact" the referee shall caution the player for ungentlemanly conduct and award an indirect free-kick.

(7) If a player impedes the progress of the opposing goalkeeper, in an attempt to prevent him from putting the ball into play in accordance with Law XII, 5 (a), the referee shall award an indirect free-kick.

(8) If, after a referee has awarded a free-kick, a player protests violently by using abusive or foul language and is sent off the field, the free-kick should not be taken until the player has left the field.

(9) Any player, whether he is within or outside the field of play, whose conduct is ungentlemanly or violent, whether or not it is directed towards an opponent, a colleague, the referee, a linesman or other person, or who uses foul or abusive language, is guilty of an offence, and shall be dealt with according to the nature of the offence committed.

(10) If, in the opinion of the referee, a goalkeeper lies on the ball longer than is necessary, he shall be penalised for ungentlemanly conduct and

(a) be cautioned and an indirect free-kick awarded to the opposing team;

(b) in case of repetition of the offence, be sent off the field.

(11) The offence of spitting at officials and other persons, or similar unseemly behaviour shall be considered as violent conduct within the meaning of section (n) of Law XII.

(12) If, when a referee is about to caution a player, and before he has done so, the player commits another offence which merits a caution, the player shall be sent off the field of play.

(13) If, in the opinion of the referee, a player who is moving toward his opponent's goal with an obvious opportunity to score a goal is impeded by an opponent, through unlawful means, i.e. an offence punishable by a free-kick (or a penalty-kick), thus denying the attacking player's team the aforesaid goal-scoring opportunity, the offending player shall be sent off the field of play for serious foul play in accordance with Law XII (o).

(14) If, in the opinion of the referee, a player, other than the goalkeeper within his own penalty area, denies his opponents a goal, or an obvious goal-scoring opportunity, by intentionally handling the ball, he shall be sent off the field of play for serious foul play in accordance with Law XII (o).

(15) The International F.A. Board is of the opinion that a goalkeeper, in the circumstances described in Law XII 5 (a), will be considered to be in control of the ball by touching it with any part of his hands or arms. Possession of the ball would include the goalkeeper intentionally parrying the ball, but would not include the circumstances where, in the opinion of the referee, the ball rebounds accidentally from the goalkeeper, for example after he has made a save.

(16) Subject to the terms of Law XII, a player may pass the ball to his own goalkeeper using his head or chest or knee, etc. If, however, in the opinion of the referee, a player uses a deliberate trick in order to circumvent article 5(c) of Law XII, the player will be guilty of ungentlemanly conduct and will be punished accordingly under the terms of Law XII; that is to say, the player will be cautioned and shown the yellow card and an indirect free-kick will be awarded to the opposing team from the place where the player committed the offence.

In such circumstances, it is irrelevant whether the goalkeeper subsequently touches the ball with his hands or not. The offence is committed by the player in attempting to circumvent both the text and the spirit of Law XII.

Free-kick

Free-kicks shall be classified under two headings: "direct" (from which a goal can be scored direct against the offending side), and "indirect" (from which a goal cannot be scored unless the ball has been played or touched by a player other than the kicker before passing through the goal).

When a player is taking a direct or an indirect free-kick inside his own penalty-area, all of the opposing players shall be at least ten yards (9.15 m) from the ball and shall remain outside the penalty-area until the ball has been kicked out of the area. The ball shall be in play immediately it has travelled the distance of its own circumference and is beyond the penalty-area. The goal-keeper shall not receive the ball into his hands, in order that he may thereafter kick it into play. If the ball is not kicked direct into play, beyond the penalty-area, the kick shall be retaken.

When a player is taking a direct or an indirect free-kick outside his own penalty-area, all of the opposing players shall be at least ten yards from the ball, until it is in play, unless they are standing on their own goal-line, between the goal-posts. The ball shall be in play when it has travelled the distance of its own circumference.

If a player of the opposing side encroaches into the penalty-area, or within ten yards of the ball, as the case may be, before a free-kick is taken, the referee shall delay the taking of the kick, until the Law is complied with.

The ball must be stationary when a free-kick is taken, and the kicker shall not play the ball a second time, until it has been touched or played by another player.

Notwithstanding any other reference in these Laws to the point from which a free-kick is to be taken:

1. Any free-kick awarded to the defending team, within its own goal-area, may be taken from any point within the goal-area.

2. Any indirect free-kick awarded to the attacking team within its opponent's goal-area shall be taken from the part of the goal-area line which runs parallel to the goal-line, at the point nearest to where the offence was committed.

Punishment:

If the kicker, after taking the free-kick, plays the ball a second time before it has been touched or played by another player, an indirect free-kick shall be taken by a player of the opposing team from the spot where the infringement occurred, unless the offence is committed by a player in his opponent's goal-area, in which case the free-kick shall be taken from any point within the goal-area.

LAW XIII

DECISIONS OF THE INTERNATIONAL F.A. BOARD

(1) In order to distinguish between a direct and an indirect free-kick, the referee, when he awards an indirect free-kick, shall indicate accordingly by raising an arm above his head. He shall keep his arm in that position until the kick has been taken and retain the signal until the ball has been played or touched by another player or goes out of play.

(2) Players who do not retire to the proper distance when a free-kick is taken must be cautioned and on any repetition be ordered off. It is particularly requested of referees that attempts to delay the taking of a free-kick by encroaching should be treated as serious misconduct.

(3) If, when a free-kick is being taken, any of the players dance about or gesticulate in a way calculated to distract their opponents, it shall be deemed ungentlemanly conduct for which the offender(s) shall be cautioned.

Penalty-kick

A penalty-kick shall be taken from the penalty-mark and, when it is being taken, all players with the exception of the player taking the kick, properly identified, and the opposing goalkeeper, shall be within the field of play but outside the penalty-area, at least 10 yards from the penalty mark and must stand behind the penalty mark.

The opposing goalkeeper must stand (without moving his feet) on his own goal-line, between the goal-posts, until the ball is kicked. The player taking the kick must kick the ball forward; he shall not play the ball a second time until it has been touched or played by another player. The ball shall be deemed in play directly it is kicked, i.e. when it has travelled the distance of its circumference. A goal may be scored directly from a penalty-kick. When a penalty-kick is being taken during the normal course of play, or when time has been extended at half-time or full-time to allow a penalty-kick to be taken or retaken, a goal shall not be nullified if, before passing between the posts and under the cross-bar, the ball touches either or both of the goal-posts, or the cross-bar, or the goal-keeper, or any combination of these agencies, providing that no other infringement has occurred.

Punishment:

For any infringement of this Law:

(a) by the defending team, the kick shall be retaken if a goal has not resulted.

(b) by the attacking team other than by the player taking the kick, if a goal is scored it shall be disallowed and the kick retaken.

(c) by the player taking the penalty-kick, committed after the ball is in play, a player of the opposing team shall take an indirect free-kick from the spot where the infringement occurred, subject to the overriding conditions imposed in Law XIII.

DECISIONS OF THE INTERNATIONAL F.A. BOARD

---

(1) When the referee has awarded a penalty-kick, he shall not signal for it to be taken, until the players have taken up position in accordance with the Law.

(2) (a) If, after the kick has been taken, the ball is stopped in its course towards goal, by an outside agent, the kick shall be retaken.

(b) If, after the kick has been taken, the ball rebounds into play, from the goalkeeper, the cross-bar or a goal-post, and is then stopped in its course by an outside agent, the referee shall stop play and restart it by dropping the ball at the place where it came into contact with the outside agent, unless it was within the goal-area at that time, in which case it shall be dropped on that part of the goal-area line which runs parallel to the goal-line, at the point nearest to where the ball was when play was stopped.

(3) (a) If, after having given the signal for a penalty-kick to be taken, the referee sees that the goalkeeper is not in his right place on the

LAW XIV

goal-line, he shall, nevertheless, allow the kick to proceed. It shall be retaken, if a goal is not scored.

(b) If, after the referee has given the signal for a penalty-kick to be taken, and before the ball has been kicked, the goal-keeper moves his feet, the referee shall, nevertheless, allow the kick to proceed. It shall be retaken, if a goal is not scored.

(c) If, after the referee has given the signal for a penalty-kick to be taken, and before the ball is in play, a player of the defending team encroaches into the penalty-area, or within ten yards of the penalty-mark, the referee shall, nevertheless, allow the kick to proceed. It shall be retaken, if a goal is not scored.

The player concerned shall be cautioned.

(4) (a) If, when a penalty-kick is being taken, the player taking the kick is guilty of ungentlemanly conduct, the kick, if already taken, shall be retaken, if a goal is scored.

The player concerned shall be cautioned.

(b) If, after the referee has given the signal for a penalty-kick to be taken, and before the ball is in play, a colleague of the player taking the kick encroaches into the penalty-area or within ten yards of the penalty-mark, the referee shall, nevertheless, allow the kick to proceed. If a goal is scored, it shall be disallowed, and the kick retaken.

The players concerned shall be cautioned.

(c) If, in the circumstances described in the foregoing paragraph, the ball rebounds into play from the goalkeeper, the cross-bar or a goal-post, and a goal has not been scored, the referee shall stop the game, caution the player and award an indirect free-kick to the opposing team from the place where the infringement occurred, subject to the overriding conditions imposed in Law XIII.

(5) (a) If, after the referee has given the signal for a penalty-kick to be taken, and before the ball is in play, the goalkeeper moves from his position on the goal-line, or moves his feet, and a colleague of the kicker encroaches into the penalty-area or within 10 yards of the penalty-mark, the kick, if taken, shall be retaken.

The colleague of the kicker shall be cautioned.

(b) If, after the referee has given the signal for a penalty-kick to be taken, and before the ball is in play, a player of each team encroaches into the penalty-area, or within 10 yards of the penalty-mark, the kick, if taken, shall be retaken.

The players concerned shall be cautioned.

(6) When a match is extended, at half-time or full-time, to allow a penalty-kick to be taken or retaken, the extension shall last until the moment that the penalty-kick has been completed, i.e. until the referee has decided whether or not a goal is scored, and the game shall terminate immediately the referee has made his decision.

After the player taking the penalty-kick has put the ball into play, no player other than the defending goalkeeper may play or touch the ball before the kick is completed.

(7) When a penalty-kick is being taken in extended time:

(a) the provisions of all of the foregoing paragraphs, except paragraphs (2) (b) and (4) (c) shall apply in the usual way, and

(b) in the circumstances described in paragraphs (2) (b) and (4) (c) the game shall terminate immediately the ball rebounds from the goalkeeper, the cross-bar or the goal-post.

Throw-in

When the whole of the ball passes over a touch-line, either on the ground or in the air, it shall be thrown in from the point where it crossed the line, in any direction, by a player of the team opposite to that of the player who last touched it. The thrower at the moment of delivering the ball must face the field of play and part of each foot shall be either on the touch-line or on the ground outside the touch-line. The thrower shall use both hands and shall deliver the ball from behind and over his head. The ball shall be in play immediately it enters the field of play, but the thrower shall not again play the ball until it has been touched or played by another player. A goal shall not be scored direct from a throw-in.

Punishment:

(a) If the ball is improperly thrown in the throw-in shall be taken by a player of the opposing team.

(b) If the thrower plays the ball a second time before it has been touched or played by another player, an indirect free-kick shall be taken by a player of the opposing team from the place where the infringement occurred, subject to the overriding conditions imposed in Law XIII.

DECISIONS OF THE INTERNATIONAL F.A. BOARD

(1) If a player taking a throw-in plays the ball a second time by handling it within the field of play before it has been touched or played by another player, the referee shall award a direct free-kick.

(2) A player taking a throw-in must face the field of play with some part of his body.

(3) If, when a throw-in is being taken, any of the opposing players dance about or gesticu- late in a way calculated to distract or impede the thrower, it shall be deemed ungentlemanly conduct, for which the offender(s) shall be cautioned.

(4) A throw-in taken from any position other than the point where the ball passed over the touch-line shall be considered to have been improperly thrown in.

LAW XVI

Goal-kick

When the whole of the ball passes over the goal-line excluding that portion between the goal-posts, either in the air or on the ground, having last been played by one of the attacking team, it shall be kicked direct into play beyond the penalty-area from any point within the goal-area by a player of the defending team. A goalkeeper shall not receive the ball into his hands from a goal-kick in order that he may thereafter kick it into play. If the ball is not kicked beyond the penalty-area, i.e. direct into play, the kick shall be retaken. The kicker shall not play the ball a second time until it has touched or been played by another player. A goal shall not be scored direct from such a kick. Players of the team opposing that of the player taking the goal-kick shall remain outside the penalty-area until the ball has been kicked out of the penalty-area.

Punishment:

If a player taking a goal-kick plays the ball a second time after it has passed beyond the penalty-area, but before it has touched or been played by another player, an indirect free-kick shall be awarded to the opposing team, to be taken from the place where the infringement occurred, subject to the overriding conditions imposed in Law XIII.

DECISIONS OF THE INTERNATIONAL F.A. BOARD

(1) When a goal-kick has been taken and the player who has kicked the ball touches it again before it has left the penalty-area, the kick has not been taken in accordance with the Law and must be retaken

Corner-kick

When the whole of the ball passes over the goal-line, excluding that portion between the goal-posts, either in the air or on the ground, having last been played by one of the defending team, a member of the attacking team shall take a corner-kick, i.e. the whole of the ball shall be placed within the quarter circle at the nearest corner-flagpost, which must not be moved, and it shall be kicked from that position. A goal may be scored direct from such a kick. Players of the team opposing that of the player taking the corner-kick shall not approach within 10 yards of the ball until it is in play, i.e. it has travelled the distance of its own circumference, nor shall the kicker play the ball a second time until it has been touched or played by another player.

Punishment:

(a) If the player who takes the kick plays the ball a second time before it has been touched or played by another player, the referee shall award an indirect free-kick to the opposing team, to be taken from the place where the infringement occurred, subject to the overriding conditions imposed in Law XIII.

(b) For any other infringement the kick shall be retaken.

Appendix C
The Members of FIFA

The controlling body for soccer worldwide is:

Fédération Internationale de Football Association
Hitzigweg 11
8030 Zurich,
Switzerland

In 1995 the membership of the Fédération Internationale de Football Association stood at 191 countries.

For ease of administration, the member nations are grouped into six regional confederations.

Africa

Confédération Africaine de
*   Football (CAF)*
5 Gabalaya Street
11567 El Borg
Cairo
AR Egypt

Algeria
Angola
Benin
Botswana
Burkina Faso
Burundi
Cameroon
Cape Verde Islands
Central African Republic
Chad
Congo
Djibouti

Egypt
Equatorial Guinea
Ethiopia
Gabon
Gambia
Ghana
Guinea
Guinea-Bissau
Ivory Coast
Kenya
Lesotho
Liberia
Libya
Madagascar
Malawi
Mali
Mauritania
Mauritius
Morocco
Mozambique
Namibia

Niger
Nigeria
Rwanda
São Tome e Principe
Senegal
Seychelles
Sierra Leone
Somalia
South Africa
Sudan
Swaziland
Tanzania
Togo
Tunisia
Uganda
Zaire
Zambia
Zimbabwe

Associate member:
Réunion

America–North, Central, and Caribbean

*Confederación Norte/
   Centroamericana y del
   Caribe de Fútbol
   (Concacaf)
725 Fifth Avenue,
   17th floor
New York, NY 10022*

Antigua and Barbuda
Aruba
Bahamas
Barbados
Belize
Bermuda
Canada
Cayman Islands
Costa Rica
Cuba
Dominica
Dominican Republic
El Salvador
Grenada
Guatemala
Guyana
Haiti
Honduras
Jamaica
Mexico
Netherlands Antilles
Nicaragua
Panama
Puerto Rico
St.Kitts and Nevis
Saint Lucia
St.Vincent and the
   Grenadines
Surinam
Trinidad and Tobago
United States

Associate member:
Virgin Islands

America–South

*Confederación
   Sudamericana de
   Fútbol (CSF, or
   Conmebol)
Ed. Banco do Brasil
   Piso 4
Nuestra Señora de la
   Asunción 540
Asunción
Paraguay*

Argentina
Bolivia
Brazil
Chile
Colombia
Ecuador
Paraguay
Peru
Uruguay
Venezuela

Asia

*Asian Football
   Confederation (AFC)
Wisma Olympic Council
   of Malaysia
1st floor, Jalan Hang Jebat
50150 Kuala Lumpur
Malaysia*

Afghanistan
Bahrain
Bangladesh
Brunei Darussalam
Cambodia
China PR
Chinese Taipei (Taiwan)
Hong Kong
India
Indonesia
Iran
Iraq
Japan
Jordan

Kazakhstan
Korea DPR (North)
Korea Republic (South)
Kuwait
Kyrgyzstan
Laos
Lebanon
Macao
Malaysia
Maldives Republic
Myanmar
Nepal
Oman
Pakistan
Philippines
Qatar
Saudi Arabia
Singapore
Sri Lanka
Syria
Tadjikistan
Thailand
Turkmenistan
United Arab Emirates
Uzbekistan
Vietnam
Yemen

Associate members:
Bhutan
Guam

Provisional member:
Palestine

Europe

*Union of European
   Football Associations
   (UEFA)
Chemin de la Redoute 54
P.O.Box 303
CH-1260 Nyon,
Switzerland*

Albania
Armenia
Austria
Azerbaijan

Belarus
Belgium
Bulgaria
Croatia
Cyprus
Czech Republic
Denmark
England
Estonia
Faroe Islands
Finland
France
Georgia
Germany
Greece
Hungary
Iceland
Ireland, Northern
Ireland, Republic
Israel*
Italy
Latvia
Liechtenstein
Lithuania

Luxembourg
Macedonia
Malta
Moldova
Netherlands
Norway
Poland
Portugal
Romania
Russia
San Marino
Scotland
Slovakia
Slovenia
Spain
Sweden
Switzerland
Turkey
Ukraine
Wales
Yugoslavia

Provisional member:
Bosnia-Herzegovina

Oceania

Oceania Football
*   Confederation (OFC)*
P.O.Box 62-586
Central Park
Auckland 6
New Zealand

Australia
Cook Islands
Fiji
New Zealand
Papua New Guinea
Solomon Islands
Tahiti
Tonga
Vanuatu
Western Samoa

Associate members:
American Samoa
New Caledonia
Niue Island
Northern Marianas

* Geographically, Israel belongs to the Asian region, but for political reasons it plays its games, both national team and club, within the European region.

Appendix D
Worldwide Winners

NATIONAL TEAM COMPETITIONS

I. Global

The World Cup
Official Title: The FIFA World Cup.
Eligible: National teams from all member nations of FIFA (see pages 311–313).
Frequency: Every four years, between the Olympic Games cycle, in a pre-determined host nation. The 1998 World Cup will be staged in France.
Format: Thirty-two teams take part in the final tournament. They are made up as follows: 15 teams from Europe, 5 teams from South America, 5 teams from Africa, 3 teams from Asia, 3 teams from North and Central America. The 32nd berth is decided by a play-off between the winner of the Oceania qualifying group and a team from Asia.

A series of regional elimination games is played, starting about two years before the finals, to reduce the huge number of entries. For the 1998 World Cup, over 150 nations entered. When the elimination rounds are over, 30 nations have survived. These join the host nation and the defending champions, which qualify automatically, to make up the final 32.

At the World Cup draw, which is staged about six months before the final tournament, the 32 nations are drawn into eight groups of four. Within each group, each team plays the other three once. First and second place in each group advance to a knock-out stage, the pairings having been decided in advance.

**FIRST WORLD CUP,
URUGUAY, 1930**
13 finalists, 13 nations entered

Group 1
France 4 Mexico 1
Argentina 1 France 0
Chile 3 Mexico 0
Chile 1 France 0
Argentina 6 Mexico 3
Argentina 3 Chile 1
   Qualifier: Argentina

Group 2
Yugoslavia 2 Brazil 1
Yugoslavia 4 Bolivia 0
Brazil 4 Bolivia 0
   Qualifier: Yugoslavia

Group 3
Romania 3 Peru 1
Uruguay 1 Peru 0
Uruguay 4 Romania 0
   Qualifier: Uruguay

Group 4
USA 3 Belgium 0
USA 3 Paraguay 0
Paraguay 1 Belgium 0
   Qualifier: USA

Semifinals
Argentina 6 USA 1
Uruguay 6 Yugoslavia 1

Final
Uruguay 4 Argentina 2
   Champion: URUGUAY

**SECOND WORLD CUP,
ITALY, 1934**
16 finalists, 32 nations entered

First round
Italy 7 USA 1
Czechoslovakia 2 Romania 1
Germany 5 Belgium 2
Austria 3 France 2
Switzerland 3 Netherlands 2
Sweden 3 Argentina 2
Hungary 4 Egypt 2

Second round
Germany 2 Sweden 1
Austria 2 Hungary 1
Italy 1 Spain 1
(Italy 1 Spain 0, replay)
Czechoslovakia 3 Switzerland 2

Semifinals
Czechoslovakia 3 Germany 1
Italy 1 Austria 0

3rd-place Game
Germany 3 Austria 2

Final
Italy 2 Czechoslovakia 1 (o/t)
   Champion: ITALY

**THIRD WORLD CUP,
FRANCE, 1938**
16 finalists, 25 nations entered

First round
Switzerland 1 Germany 1
(Switzerland 4 Germany 2, replay)
Cuba 3 Romania 3
(Cuba 2 Romania 1, replay)
Hungary 6 Dutch East Indies 0
France 3 Belgium 1
Czechoslovakia 3 Netherlands 0
Brazil 6 Poland 5
Italy 2 Norway 1

Second round
Sweden 8 Cuba 0
Hungary 2 Switzerland 0
Brazil 1 Czechoslovakia 1
(Brazil 2 Czechoslovakia 1, replay)

Semifinals
Italy 2 Brazil 1
Hungary 5 Sweden 1

3rd-place Game
Brazil 4 Sweden 2

Final
Italy 4 Hungary 2
   Champion: ITALY

**FOURTH WORLD CUP,
BRAZIL, 1950**
13 finalists, 24 nations entered

Pool 1

Brazil 4 Mexico 0
Yugoslavia 3 Switzerland 0
Yugoslavia 4 Mexico 1
Brazil 2 Switzerland 2
Brazil 2 Yugoslavia 0
Switzerland 2 Mexico 1
   Qualifier: Brazil

Pool 2

Spain 3 USA 1
England 2 Chile 0
USA 1 England 0
Spain 2 Chile 0
Spain 1 England 0
Chile 5 USA 2
   Qualifier: Spain

Pool 3

Sweden 3 Italy 2
Sweden 2 Paraguay 2
Italy 2 Paraguay 0
   Qualifier: Sweden

Pool 4

Uruguay 8 Bolivia 0
   Qualifier: Uruguay

Final pool

Uruguay 2 Spain 2
Brazil 7 Sweden 1
Uruguay 3 Sweden 2
Brazil 6 Spain 1
Sweden 3 Spain 1
Uruguay 2 Brazil 1
   Champion: URUGUAY

**FIFTH WORLD CUP,
SWITZERLAND, 1954**
16 finalists, 41 nations entered

Group 1

Yugoslavia 1 France 0
Brazil 5 Mexico 0
France 3 Mexico 2
Brazil 1 Yugoslavia 1
   Qualifiers: Brazil, Yugoslavia

Group 2

Hungary 9 Korea 0
West Germany 4 Turkey 1
Hungary 8 West Germany 3
Turkey 7 Korea 0
West Germany 7 Turkey 2 (play-off)
   Qualifiers: Hungary, West Germany

Group 3

Austria 1 Scotland 0
Uruguay 2 Czechoslovakia 0
Austria 5 Czechoslovakia 0
Uruguay 7 Scotland 0
   Qualifiers: Uruguay, Austria

Group 4

England 4 Belgium 4
England 2 Switzerland 0
Switzerland 2 Italy 1
Italy 4 Belgium 1
Switzerland 4 Italy 1 (play-off)
   Qualifiers: England, Switzerland

Quarterfinals

West Germany 2 Yugoslavia 0
Hungary 4 Brazil 2
Austria 7 Switzerland 5
Uruguay 4 England 2

Semifinals

West Germany 6 Austria 1
Hungary 4 Uruguay 2

3rd-place Game

Austria 3 Uruguay 1

Final

West Germany 3 Hungary 2
   Champion: WEST GERMANY

**SIXTH WORLD CUP,
SWEDEN, 1958**
16 finalists, 52 nations entered

Group 1

West Germany 3 Argentina 1
Northern Ireland 1 Czechoslovakia 0
West Germany 2 Czechoslovakia 2
Argentina 3 Northern Ireland 1
West Germany 2 Northern Ireland 2

Czechoslovakia 6 Argentina 1
Northern Ireland 2 Czechoslovakia 1
   (play-off)
   Qualifiers: West Germany, Northern
   Ireland

Group 2

France 7 Paraguay 3
Yugoslavia 1 Scotland 1
Yugoslavia 3 France 2
Paraguay 3 Scotland 2
France 2 Scotland 1
Yugoslavia 3 Paraguay 3
   Qualifiers: France, Yugoslavia

Group 3

Sweden 3 Mexico 0
Hungary 1 Wales 1
Wales 1 Mexico 1
Sweden 2 Hungary 1
Sweden 0 Wales 0
Hungary 4 Mexico 0
Wales 2 Hungary 1 (play-off)
   Qualifiers: Sweden, Wales

Group 4

England 2 USSR 2
Brazil 3 Austria 0
England 0 Brazil 0
USSR 2 Austria 0
Brazil 2 USSR 0
England 2 Austria 2
USSR 1 England 0 (play-off)
   Qualifiers: Brazil, USSR

Quarterfinals

France 4 Northern Ireland 0
West Germany 1 Yugoslavia 0
Sweden 2 USSR 0
Brazil 1 Wales 0

Semifinals

Brazil 5 France 2
Sweden 3 West Germany 1

3rd-place Game

France 6 West Germany 3

Final

Brazil 5 Sweden 2
   Champion: BRAZIL

SEVENTH WORLD CUP, CHILE, 1962
16 finalists, 49 nations entered

Group 1

Uruguay 2 Colombia 1
USSR 2 Yugoslavia 0
Yugoslavia 3 Uruguay 1
USSR 4 Colombia 4
USSR 2 Uruguay 1
Yugoslavia 5 Colombia 0
   Qualifiers: USSR, Yugoslavia

Group 2

Chile 3 Switzerland 1
West Germany 0 Italy 0
Chile 2 Italy 0
West Germany 2 Switzerland 1
West Germany 2 Chile 0
Italy 3 Switzerland 0
   Qualifiers: West Germany, Chile

Group 3

Brazil 2 Mexico 0
Czechoslovakia 1 Spain 0
Brazil 0 Czechoslovakia 0
Spain 1 Mexico 0
Brazil 2 Spain 1
Mexico 3 Czechoslovakia 1
   Qualifiers: Brazil, Czechoslovakia

Group 4

Argentina 1 Bulgaria 0
Hungary 2 England 1
England 3 Argentina 1
Hungary 6 Bulgaria 1
Argentina 0 Hungary 0
England 0 Bulgaria 0
   Qualifiers: Hungary, England

Quarterfinals

Yugoslavia 1 West Germany 0
Brazil 3 England 1
Chile 2 USSR 1
Czechoslovakia 1 Hungary 0

Semifinals

Brazil 4 Chile 2
Czechoslovakia 3 Yugoslavia 1

3rd-place Game
Chile 1 Yugoslavia 0

Final
Brazil 3 Czechoslovakia 1
   Champion: BRAZIL

EIGHTH WORLD CUP, ENGLAND, 1966
16 finalists, 70 nations entered, 51 played

Group 1
England 0 Uruguay 0
France 1 Mexico 1
Uruguay 2 France 1
England 2 Mexico 0
Uruguay 0 Mexico 0
England 2 France 0
   Qualifiers: England, Uruguay

Group 2
West Germany 5 Switzerland 0
Argentina 2 Spain 1
Spain 2 Switzerland 1
Argentina 0 West Germany 0
Argentina 2 Switzerland 0
West Germany 2 Spain 1
   Qualifiers: West Germany, Argentina

Group 3
Brazil 2 Bulgaria 0
Portugal 3 Hungary 1
Hungary 3 Brazil 1
Portugal 3 Bulgaria 0
Portugal 3 Brazil 1
Hungary 3 Bulgaria 1
   Qualifiers: Portugal, Hungary

Group 4
USSR 3 North Korea 0
Italy 2 Chile 0
Chile 1 North Korea 1
USSR 1 Italy 0
North Korea 1 Italy 0
USSR 2 Chile 1
   Qualifiers: USSR, North Korea

Quarterfinals
England 1 Argentina 0
West Germany 4 Uruguay 0
Portugal 5 North Korea 3
USSR 2 Hungary 1

Semifinals
West Germany 2 USSR 1
England 2 Portugal 1

3rd-place Game
Portugal 2 USSR 1

Final
England 4 West Germany 2 (o/t)
   Champion: ENGLAND

NINTH WORLD CUP, MEXICO, 1970
16 finalists, 71 nations entered

Group 1
Mexico 0 USSR 0
Belgium 3 El Salvador 0
USSR 4 Belgium 1
Mexico 4 El Salvador 0
USSR 2 El Salvador 0
Mexico 1 Belgium 0
   Qualifiers: USSR, Mexico

Group 2
Uruguay 2 Israel 0
Italy 1 Sweden 0
Uruguay 0 Italy 0
Israel 1 Sweden 1
Sweden 1 Uruguay 0
Israel 0 Italy 0
   Qualifiers: Italy, Uruguay

Group 3
England 1 Romania 0
Brazil 4 Czechoslovakia 1
Romania 2 Czechoslovakia 1
Brazil 1 England 0
Brazil 3 Romania 2
England 1 Czechoslovakia 0
   Qualifiers: Brazil, England

Group 4
Peru 3 Bulgaria 2
West Germany 2 Morocco 1
Peru 3 Morocco 0
West Germany 5 Bulgaria 2
West Germany 3 Peru 1
Bulgaria 1 Morocco 1
   Qualifiers: West Germany, Peru

Quarterfinals
Uruguay 1 USSR 0
Italy 4 Mexico 1
Brazil 4 Peru 2
West Germany 3 England 2 (o/t)

Semifinals
Italy 4 West Germany 3 (o/t)
Brazil 3 Uruguay 1

3rd-place Game
West Germany 1 Uruguay 0

Final
Brazil 4 Italy 1
  Champion: BRAZIL

**TENTH WORLD CUP,
WEST GERMANY, 1974**
*16 finalists, 95 nations entered,
89 played*

Group 1
West Germany 1 Chile 0
East Germany 2 Australia 0
West Germany 3 Australia 0
East Germany 1 Chile 1
East Germany 1 West Germany 0
Australia 0 Chile 0
  Qualifiers: East Germany,
  West Germany

Group 2
Brazil 0 Yugoslavia 0
Scotland 2 Zaire 0
Brazil 0 Scotland 0
Yugoslavia 9 Zaire 0
Scotland 1 Yugoslavia 1
Brazil 3 Zaire 0
  Qualifiers: Yugoslavia, Brazil

Group 3
Netherlands 2 Uruguay 0
Sweden 0 Bulgaria 0
Netherlands 0 Sweden 0
Bulgaria 1 Uruguay 1
Netherlands 4 Bulgaria 1
Sweden 3 Uruguay 0
  Qualifiers: Netherlands, Sweden

Group 4
Italy 3 Haiti 1
Poland 3 Argentina 2
Argentina 1 Italy 1
Poland 7 Haiti 0
Argentina 4 Haiti 1
Poland 2 Italy 1
  Qualifiers: Poland, Argentina

Semifinal Group A
Brazil 1 East Germany 0
Netherlands 4 Argentina 0
Netherlands 2 East Germany 0
Brazil 2 Argentina 1
Netherlands 2 Brazil 0
Argentina 1 East Germany 1
  Winner: Netherlands
  Runner-up: Brazil

Semifinal Group B
Poland 1 Sweden 0
West Germany 2 Yugoslavia 0
Poland 2 Yugoslavia 1
West Germany 4 Sweden 2
Sweden 2 Yugoslavia 1
West Germany 1 Poland 0
  Winner: West Germany
  Runner-up: Poland

3rd-place Game
Poland 1 Brazil 0

Final
West Germany 2 Netherlands 1
  Champion: WEST GERMANY

**ELEVENTH WORLD CUP,
ARGENTINA, 1978**
16 finalists, 101 nations entered

Group 1
Italy 2 France 1
Argentina 2 Hungary 1
Italy 3 Hungary 1
Argentina 2 France 1
Italy 1 Argentina 0
France 3 Hungary 1
  Qualifiers: Italy, Argentina

Group 2

Poland 0 West Germany 0
Tunisia 3 Mexico 1
Poland 1 Tunisia 0
West Germany 6 Mexico 0
Tunisia 0 West Germany 0
Poland 3 Mexico 1
Qualifiers: Poland, West Germany

Group 3

Brazil 1 Sweden 1
Austria 2 Spain 1
Austria 1 Sweden 0
Brazil 0 Spain 0
Brazil 1 Austria 0
Spain 1 Sweden 0
Qualifiers: Austria, Brazil

Group 4

Netherlands 3 Iran 0
Peru 3 Scotland 1
Netherlands 0 Peru 0
Iran 1 Scotland 1
Scotland 3 Netherlands 2
Peru 4 Iran 1
Qualifiers: Peru, Netherlands

Semifinal Group A

Italy 0 West Germany 0
Netherlands 5 Austria 1
Netherlands 2 West Germany 2
Italy 1 Austria 0
Netherlands 2 Italy 1
Austria 3 West Germany 2
Winner: Netherlands
Runner-up: Italy

Semifinal Group B

Brazil 3 Peru 0
Argentina 2 Poland 0
Poland 1 Peru 0
Argentina 0 Brazil 0
Brazil 3 Poland 1
Argentina 6 Peru 0
Winner: Argentina
Runner-up: Brazil

3rd-place Game

Brazil 2 Italy 1

Final

Argentina 3 Netherlands 1 (o/t)
Champion: ARGENTINA

TWELFTH WORLD CUP, SPAIN, 1982
24 finalists, 109 nations entered

Group 1

Italy 0 Poland 0
Cameroon 0 Peru 0
Italy 1 Peru 1
Cameroon 0 Poland 0
Poland 5 Peru 1
Cameroon 1 Italy 1
Qualifiers: Poland, Italy

Group 2

Algeria 2 West Germany 1
Austria 1 Chile 0
West Germany 4 Chile 1
Austria 2 Algeria 0
Algeria 3 Chile 2
West Germany 1 Austria 0
Qualifiers: West Germany, Austria

Group 3

Belgium 1 Argentina 0
Hungary 10 El Salvador 1
Argentina 4 Hungary 1
Belgium 1 El Salvador 0
Belgium 1 Hungary 1
Argentina 2 El Salvador 0
Qualifiers: Belgium, Argentina

Group 4

England 3 France 1
Czechoslovakia 1 Kuwait 1
England 2 Czechoslovakia 0
France 4 Kuwait 1
Czechoslovakia 1 France 1
England 1 Kuwait 0
Qualifiers: England, France

Group 5

Honduras 1 Spain 1
Northern Ireland 0 Yugoslavia 0
Spain 2 Yugoslavia 1
Honduras 1 Northern Ireland 1

Yugoslavia 1 Honduras 0
Northern Ireland 1 Spain 0
  Qualifiers: Northern Ireland, Spain

Group 6
Brazil 2 USSR 1
Scotland 5 New Zealand 2
Brazil 4 Scotland 1
USSR 3 New Zealand 0
Scotland 2 USSR 2
Brazil 4 New Zealand 0
  Qualifiers: Brazil, USSR

Semifinal Group A
Poland 3 Belgium 0
USSR 1 Belgium 0
Poland 0 USSR 0
  Winner: Poland

Semifinal Group B
England 0 West Germany 0
West Germany 2 Spain 1
England 0 Spain 0
  Winner: West Germany

Semifinal Group C
Italy 2 Argentina 1
Brazil 3 Argentina 1
Italy 3 Brazil 2
  Winner: Italy

Semifinal Group D
France 1 Austria 0
Austria 2 Northern Ireland 2
France 4 Northern Ireland 1
  Winner: France

Semifinals
Italy 2 Poland 0
West Germany 3 France 3 (o/t)
(West Germany win 5–4 on PKs)

3rd-place Game
Poland 3 France 2

Final
Italy 3 West Germany 1
  Champion: ITALY

THIRTEENTH WORLD CUP, MEXICO, 1986
24 finalists, 121 nations entered

Group A
Bulgaria 1 Italy 1
Argentina 3 South Korea 1
Argentina 1 Italy 1
Bulgaria 1 South Korea 1
Argentina 2 Bulgaria 0
Italy 3 South Korea 2
  Qualifiers: Argentina, Italy, Bulgaria

Group B
Mexico 2 Belgium 1
Paraguay 1 Iraq 0
Mexico 1 Paraguay 1
Belgium 2 Iraq 1
Belgium 2 Paraguay 2
Mexico 1 Iraq 0
  Qualifiers: Mexico, Paraguay, Belgium

Group C
France 1 Canada 0
USSR 6 Hungary 0
France 1 USSR 1
Hungary 2 Canada 0
France 3 Hungary 0
USSR 2 Canada 0
  Qualifiers: USSR, France

Group D
Brazil 1 Spain 0
Algeria 1 Northern Ireland 1
Brazil 1 Algeria 0
Spain 2 Northern Ireland 1
Brazil 3 Northern Ireland 0
Spain 3 Algeria 0
  Qualifiers: Brazil, Spain

Group E
West Germany 1 Uruguay 1
Denmark 1 Scotland 0
West Germany 2 Scotland 1
Denmark 6 Uruguay 1
Denmark 2 West Germany 0
Scotland 0 Uruguay 0
  Qualifiers: Denmark, West Germany, Uruguay

Group F

Morocco 0 Poland 0
Portugal 1 England 0
England 0 Morocco 0
Poland 1 Portugal 0
England 3 Poland 0
Morocco 3 Portugal 1
   Qualifiers: Morocco, England,
   Poland

Second Round

Mexico 2 Bulgaria 0
Belgium 4 USSR 3 (o/t)
Brazil 4 Poland 0
Argentina 1 Uruguay 0
France 2 Italy 0
West Germany 1 Morocco 0
England 3 Paraguay 0
Spain 5 Denmark 1

Quarterfinals

France 1 Brazil 1 (o/t)
(France won 4–3 on PKs)
West Germany 0 Mexico 0 (o/t)
(West Germany won 4–1 on PKs)
Argentina 2 England 1
Belgium 1 Spain 1 (o/t)
(Belgium won 5–4 on PKs)

Semifinals

West Germany 2 France 0
Argentina 2 Belgium 0

3rd-place Game

France 4 Belgium 2 (o/t)

Final

Argentina 3 West Germany 2
   Champion: ARGENTINA

FOURTEENTH WORLD CUP, ITALY, 1990
24 finalists, 109 nations entered

Group A

Italy 1 Austria 0
Czechoslovakia 5 USA 1
Italy 1 USA 0
Czechoslovakia 1 Austria 0

Italy 2 Czechoslovakia 0
Austria 2 USA 1
   Qualifiers: Italy, Czechoslovakia

Group B

Cameroon 1 Argentina 0
Romania 2 USSR 0
Argentina 2 USSR 0
Cameroon 2 Romania 1
USSR 4 Cameroon 0
Argentina 1 Romania 1
   Qualifiers: Cameroon, Romania,
   Argentina

Group C

Brazil 2 Sweden 1
Costa Rica 1 Scotland 0
Brazil 1 Costa Rica 0
Scotland 2 Sweden 1
Costa Rica 2 Sweden 1
Brazil 1 Scotland 0
   Qualifiers: Brazil, Costa Rica

Group D

Colombia 2 UAE 0
West Germany 4 Yugoslavia 1
Yugoslavia 1 Colombia 0
West Germany 5 UAE 1
Colombia 1 West Germany 1
Yugoslavia 4 UAE 1
   Qualifiers: West Germany,
   Yugoslavia, Colombia

Group E

Belgium 2 South Korea 0
Spain 0 Uruguay 0
Spain 3 South Korea 1
Belgium 3 Uruguay 1
Spain 2 Belgium 1
Uruguay 1 South Korea 0
   Qualifiers: Spain, Belgium, Uruguay

Group F

England 1 Ireland 1
Egypt 1 Netherlands 1
England 0 Netherlands 0
Egypt 0 Ireland 0
England 1 Egypt 0
Netherlands 1 Ireland 1
   Qualifiers: England, Ireland,
   Netherlands

Second Round

Cameroon 2 Colombia 1
Czechoslovakia 4 Costa Rica 1
Argentina 1 Brazil 0
West Germany 2 Netherlands 1
Ireland 0 Romania 0 (o/t)
(Ireland won 5–4 on PKs)
Italy 2 Uruguay 0
Yugoslavia 2 Spain 1 (o/t)
England 1 Belgium 0 (o/t)

Quarterfinals

Argentina 0 Yugoslavia 0 (o/t)
(Argentina won 3–2 on PKs)
Italy 1 Ireland 0
West Germany 1 Czechoslovakia 0
England 3 Cameroon 2 (o/t)

Semifinals

Argentina 1 Italy 1 (o/t)
(Argentina won 4–3 on PKs)
West Germany 1 England 1 (o/t)
(West Germany won 4–3 on PKs)

3rd-place Game

Italy 2 England 1

Final

West Germany 1 Argentina 0
Champion: WEST GERMANY

FIFTEENTH WORLD CUP, USA, 1994
24 finalists, 144 nations entered

Group A

USA 1 Switzerland 1
Romania 3 Colombia 1
Switzerland 4 Romania 1
USA 2 Colombia 1
USA 0 Romania 1
Colombia 2 Switzerland 0
Qualifiers: Romania, Switzerland, USA

Group B

Cameroon 2 Sweden 2
Brazil 2 Russia 0
Brazil 3 Cameroon 0
Sweden 3 Russia 1

Brazil 1 Sweden 1
Russia 6 Cameroon 1
Qualifiers: Brazil, Sweden

Group C

Germany 1 Bolivia 0
Spain 2 South Korea 2
Germany 1 Spain 1
South Korea 0 Bolivia 0
Germany 3 South Korea 2
Spain 3 Bolivia 1
Qualifiers: Germany, Spain

Group D

Argentina 4 Greece 0
Nigeria 3 Bulgaria 0
Argentina 2 Nigeria 1
Bulgaria 4 Greece 0
Bulgaria 2 Argentina 0
Nigeria 2 Greece 0
Qualifiers: Nigeria, Bulgaria, Argentina

Group E

Ireland 1 Italy 0
Norway 1 Mexico 0
Italy 1 Norway 0
Mexico 2 Ireland 1
Italy 1 Mexico 1
Ireland 0 Norway 0
Qualifiers: Mexico, Ireland, Italy

Group F

Belgium 1 Morocco 0
Netherlands 2 Saudi Arabia 1
Belgium 1 Netherlands 0
Saudi Arabia 2 Morocco 1
Saudi Arabia 1 Belgium 0
Netherlands 2 Morocco 1
Qualifiers: Netherlands, Saudi Arabia, Belgium

Second Round

Germany 3 Belgium 2
Spain 3 Switzerland 0
Sweden 3 Saudi Arabia 1
Romania 3 Argentina 2
Netherlands 2 Ireland 0
Brazil 1 USA 0
Italy 2 Nigeria 1 (o/t)

Bulgaria 1 Mexico 1 (o/t)
(Bulgaria won 3–1 on PKs)

Quarterfinals
Italy 2 Spain 1
Brazil 3 Netherlands 2
Bulgaria 2 Germany 1
Sweden 2 Romania 2 (o/t)
(Sweden won 5–4 on PKs)

Semifinals
Italy 2 Bulgaria 1
Brazil 1 Sweden 0

3rd place Game
Sweden 4 Bulgaria 0

Final
Brazil 0 Italy 0 (o/t)
(Brazil won 3–2 on PKs)
Champion: BRAZIL

Men's Olympic Soccer Tournament

Eligible: All member nations of FIFA. Originally for amateurs, the Olympic Game qualifications have been much changed in recent years. The tournament is now for players under the age of 23, both amateur and professional, but each team is allowed to field up to three overage players.

Frequency: Every four years, between the World Cup Cycle.

Format: Host nation qualifies automatically. There is no automatic qualification for the defending champion. Regional qualifying rounds establish the other 15 finalists. Places allocated as follows: Europe 5, South America 2, Africa 3, Asia 3, Concacaf 2. The remaining place is decided by a play-off between the winner of the Oceania group and a team from Concacaf.

Winners:

1908	Great Britain	1956	USSR
1912	Great Britain	1960	Yugoslavia
1916	No competition	1964	Hungary
1920	Belgium	1968	Hungary
1924	Uruguay	1972	Poland
1928	Uruguay	1976	East Germany
1932	No competition	1980	Czechoslovakia
1936	Italy	1984	France
1948	Sweden	1988	USSR
1952	Hungary	1992	Spain

Women's Olympic Soccer Tournament

Eligible: All member nations of FIFA. No age restriction. The 1996 tournament, the first ever, will feature eight teams. The qualifiers are: the USA (automatic qualification as host nation) plus the quarterfinalists from the 1995 Women's World Cup: China, Denmark, Japan, Germany, Norway, and Sweden. England, the other quarterfinalist, is ineligible (Olympic regulations recognize only Great Britain), and is replaced by Brazil, which had the best record of the teams eliminated in the first round.

Format: Two groups of four. Winners and second-place teams play semifinals, winners of those games play in the final.

The Under-20 World Cup

Official Title: The World Youth Championship for the FIFA/Coca-Cola Cup.

Eligible: All member nations of FIFA. Players must be 19 years old or younger.

Frequency: Every two years, in predetermined host nation. The 1997 tournament will be played in Malaysia.

Format: Host nation qualifies automatically. There is no automatic qualification for the defending champion. Regional qualifying games establish the other 15 finalists. Places are allocated as follows: Europe 6, South America 3, Asia 2, Concacaf 2, Africa 2, Oceania 1.

Winners:

1977	USSR	1987	Yugoslavia
1979	Argentina	1989	Portugal
1981	West Germany	1991	Portugal
1983	Brazil	1993	Brazil
1985	Brazil	1995	Argentina

The Under-17 World Cup

Official Title: U-17 World Championship for the FIFA/JVC Cup.

Eligible: All member nations of FIFA. Players must be 16 years old or younger.

Frequency: Every two years, in predetermined host nation. The 1997 tournament will be played in Egypt.

Format: Host nation qualifies automatically. There is no automatic qualification for the defending champion. Regional qualifying games establish the other 15 finalists. Places are allocated as follows: Europe 3, South America 3, Africa 3, Asia 3, Concacaf 3, Oceania 1.

Winners:

1985	Nigeria	1991	Ghana
1987	USSR	1993	Nigeria
1989	Saudi Arabia	1995	Ghana

Women's World Cup

Official Title: FIFA World Championship for Women's Football.

Eligible: All member nations of FIFA.

Frequency: Every four years.

Format: Qualifying games are played in each continent. Twelve teams participate in the final tournament, with berths allocated as follows: Europe 5, South America 1, Asia 3, Concacaf 1, Africa 1, Oceania 1.

Winners:

1991	United States	1995	Norway

Indoor World Cup

Official Title: FIFA Indoor (Five-a-side) Football World Championship. Also called the Futsal World Championship.

Eligible: All member nations of FIFA.

Frequency: Every four years. The 1996 tournament will be played in Spain.

Format: Berths allocated as follows: Europe 7, South America 3, Concacaf 2, Asia 2, Africa 1, Oceania 1.

Winners:

1989 Brazil	1992 Brazil

2. Europe

European Championship

Formerly the European Nations Cup. The trophy itself is officially known as the Henri Delaunay Cup.

Eligible: National teams from all the member nations of UEFA (see pages 312–313).

Frequency: Every four years, between the World Cup cycle. England is the host nation for the 1996 tournament.

Format: Since 1980, the final tournament has been played in a predetermined host nation. The host nation qualifies automatically; there is no automatic qualification for the defending champion. Qualifying games, starting some two years before the tournament, establish the other 15 finalists. Final tournament: the 16 finalists are drawn into four groups of four. Top two teams from each group go through to the quarterfinals. Semifinal winners play in the final. There is no third-place game.

Winners:

1960	USSR	1976	Czechoslovakia
1964	Spain	1980	West Germany
1968	Italy	1984	France
1972	West Germany	1988	Netherlands
		1992	Denmark

3. South America

Copa America

Eligible: National teams from all the member nations of the South American Football Confederation (see page 312).

Frequency: Every two years.

Format: Has been changed repeatedly over the years. Most recently, Mexico and the United States have played in the tournament as invited teams. The tournament is staged in a predetermined host nation. Teams are divided into three four-team groups, within which each team plays the other three once. The top two teams from each group plus the two best third-place teams advance to the knockout stage of quarterfinals, semifinals, and final.

Winners:

1917	Uruguay	1947	Argentina
1919	Brazil	1949	Brazil
1920	Uruguay	1953	Paraguay
1921	Argentina	1955	Argentina
1922	Brazil	1956	Uruguay
1923	Uruguay	1957	Argentina
1924	Uruguay	1959	Argentina
1925	Argentina	1963	Bolivia
1926	Uruguay	1967	Uruguay
1927	Argentina	1975	Peru
1929	Argentina	1979	Paraguay
1935	Uruguay	1983	Uruguay
1937	Argentina	1987	Uruguay
1939	Peru	1989	Brazil
1941	Argentina	1991	Argentina
1942	Uruguay	1993	Argentina
1945	Argentina	1995	Uruguay
1946	Argentina		

4. Other Continental Championships

Africa

1957	Egypt
1959	Egypt
1961	Ethiopia
1963	Ghana
1965	Ghana
1968	Zaire
1970	Sudan
1972	Congo
1974	Zaire
1976	Morocco
1978	Ghana
1980	Nigeria
1982	Ghana
1984	Cameroon
1986	Egypt
1988	Cameroon
1990	Algeria
1992	Ivory Coast
1994	Nigeria
1996	South Africa

Asia

1956	South Korea
1960	South Korea
1964	Israel
1968	Iran
1972	Iran
1976	Iran
1980	Kuwait
1984	Saudi Arabia
1988	Saudi Arabia
1992	Japan

Concacaf

1963	Costa Rica
1965	Mexico
1967	Guatemala
1969	Costa Rica
1971	Mexico
1973	Haiti
1977	Mexico
1981	Honduras
1991	United States
1993	Mexico
1996	Mexico

CLUB COMPETITIONS

1. Global

World Club Championship (Toyota Cup)
Eligible: Winners of previous year's European Cup and Libertadores Cup (see below for details of both Cups).
Frequency: Yearly.
Format: Single game. Since 1980, it has been played in December, in Tokyo.

1960 Real Madrid (Spain)	1977 Boca Juniors (Argentina)
1961 Peñarol (Uruguay)	1978 Not played
1962 Santos (Brazil)	1979 Olimpia (Paraguay)
1963 Santos (Brazil)	1980 Nacional (Uruguay)
1964 Inter-Milan (Italy)	1981 Flamengo (Brazil)
1965 Inter-Milan (Italy)	1982 Peñarol (Uruguay)
1966 Peñarol (Uruguay)	1983 Gremio (Brazil)
1967 Racing Club (Argentina)	1984 Independiente (Argentina)
1968 Estudiantes de la Plata (Argentina)	1985 Juventus (Italy)
	1986 River Plate (Argentina)
1969 AC Milan (Italy)	1987 FC Porto (Portugal)
1970 Feyenoord (Netherlands)	1988 Nacional (Uruguay)
1971 Nacional (Uruguay)	1989 AC Milan (Italy)
1972 Ajax (Netherlands)	1990 AC Milan (Italy)
1973 Independiente (Argentina)	1991 Red Star (Yugoslavia)
1974 Atletico Madrid (Spain)	1992 São Paulo (Brazil)
1975 Not played	1993 São Paulo (Brazil)
1976 Bayern Munich (West Germany)	1994 Velez Sarsfield (Argentina)
	1995 Ajax (Netherlands)

2. Intercontinental

Copa Interamericana
Eligible: Winners of the Concacaf Champions Cup and the Liber-tadore Cup (see below for details of both Cups). The winner is the champion club of the Americas.
Frequency: Intended as an annual event, there have been many years when the fixture has not been played.
Format: Two-game home-and-home series.

1969 Estudiantes de la Plata (Argentina)	1980 Olimpia (Paraguay)
	1981 UNAM (Mexico)
1972 Nacional (Uruguay)	1986 Argentinos Juniors (Argentina)
1973 Independiente (Argentina)	
1974 Independiente (Argentina)	1987 River Plate (Argentina)
1976 Independiente (Argentina)	1989 Nacional (Uruguay)
1978 Club America (Mexico)	1990 Nacional (Colombia)

1991 Club América (Mexico)
1992 Colo Colo (Chile)

1993 Not played
1994 Saprissa (Costa Rica)

3. Europe

European Cup

Eligible: The defending champion, plus the champion clubs from 23 of the top UEFA nations (see page 312–313).

Frequency: Yearly.

Dates: Played during the regular European season, starting in August, with the final in May of the following year. Games are played midweek, under floodlights.

Format: Eight of the teams are seeded. The other 16 play a preliminary round, in pairs, home-and-home games. The eight survivors and the eight seeded teams then play a mini-league format, in four groups of four. (At this stage, the competition is called the Champions League.) The winners and second place team from each group advance. Quarterfinals and semifinals are played on a home-and-home, knockout basis. The one-game final is played at a predetermined site.

In the knockout stages, the scores from the two home games are added together to produce a winner. If, after full-time in the second game the aggregate scores are level, the winner is the club that scored the greater number of away goals (i.e., goals scored on the opponent's field). If the score is also level on away goals, 30 minutes of overtime (not sudden death) are played. If the score is still tied after overtime, the winner is decided by a penalty-kick shoot-out.

1956 Real Madrid (Spain)
1957 Real Madrid (Spain)
1958 Real Madrid (Spain)
1959 Real Madrid (Spain)
1960 Real Madrid (Spain)
1961 Benfica (Portugal)
1962 Benfica (Portugal)
1963 AC Milan (Italy)
1964 Inter-Milan (Italy)
1965 Inter-Milan (Italy)
1966 Real Madrid (Spain)
1967 Celtic (Scotland)
1968 Manchester United (England)
1969 AC Milan (Italy)
1970 Feyenoord (Netherlands)
1971 Ajax (Netherlands)
1972 Ajax (Netherlands)
1973 Ajax (Netherlands)
1974 Bayern Munich (West Germany)
1975 Bayern Munich (West Germany)
1976 Bayern Munich (West Germany)
1977 Liverpool (England)
1978 Liverpool (England)
1979 Nottingham Forest (England)
1980 Nottingham Forest (England)
1981 Liverpool (England)
1982 Aston Villa (England)
1983 SV Hamburg (West Germany)
1984 Liverpool (England)
1985 Juventus (Italy)
1986 Steaua Bucharest (Romania)
1987 FC Porto (Portugal)
1988 PSV Eindhoven (Netherlands)
1989 AC Milan (Italy)
1990 C Milan (Italy)
1991 Red Star Belgrade (Yugoslavia)

| 1992 Barcelona (Spain) | 1994 AC Milan (Italy) |
| 1993 Marseille (France) | 1995 Ajax (Netherlands) |

European Cup Winners' Cup

Eligible: The defending champion, plus the cup winners from all the member nations of UEFA (see pages 312–313). The 1995–1996 edition featured 46 teams.

Frequency: Yearly.

Dates: Played during the regular European season—preliminary round starts in late August, with the final in May of the following year. Games are played midweek, under floodlights.

Format: Knockout competition. Teams are drawn in pairs, and play home-and-home ties, as in the early rounds of the European Cup (q.v.), until only two teams remain. These then meet in the one-game final, at a predetermined site.

1961 Fiorentina (Italy)	1977 SV Hamburg (West Germany)
1962 Atlético Madrid (Spain)	1978 RSC Anderlecht (Belgium)
1963 Tottenham Hotspur (England)	1979 Barcelona (Spain)
1964 Sporting Lisboa (Portugal)	1980 Valencia (Spain)
1965 West Ham United (England)	1981 Dynamo Tbilisi (USSR)
1966 Borussia Dortmund (West Germany)	1982 Barcelona (Spain)
	1983 Aberdeen (Scotland)
1967 Bayern Munich (West Germany)	1984 Juventus (Italy)
	1985 Everton (England)
1968 AC Milan (Italy)	1986 Dynamo Kiev (USSR)
1969 Slovan Bratislava (Czechoslovakia)	1987 Ajax (Netherlands)
	1988 Mechelen (Belgium)
1970 Manchester City (England)	1989 Barcelona (Spain)
1971 Chelsea (England)	1990 Sampdoria (Italy)
1972 Rangers (Scotland)	1991 Manchester United (England)
1973 AC Milan (Italy)	1992 Werder Bremen (Germany)
1974 FC Magdeburg (East Germany)	1993 Parma (Italy)
	1994 Arsenal (England)
1975 Dynamo Kiev (USSR)	1995 Real Zaragoza (Spain)
1976 RSC Anderlecht (Belgium)	

UEFA Cup

(From its beginning in 1958 until 1971, this was known as the Fairs Cup.)

Eligible: 64 top clubs from all member nations of UEFA (see pages 312–313), other than the champions or Cup winners. Places are allocated to each country according to the country's previous showing in the tournament. Thus, strong countries like Germany and Italy have more places than Norway or Switzerland.

Frequency: Yearly.

Dates: During the regular European season, from August through May of the following year. Games are played midweek under floodlights.

Format: As for the Cup Winners Cup (q.v.), except that the final is played as a two-leg home-and-home series.

1958 Barcelona (Spain)	1978 PSV Eindhoven (Netherlands)
1959 Not played	1979 Borussia Mönchengladbach
1960 Barcelona (Spain)	(West Germany)
1961 Roma (Italy)	1980 Eintracht Frankfurt (West
1962 Valencia (Spain)	Germany)
1963 Valencia (Spain)	1981 Ipswich Town (England)
1964 Real Zaragoza (Spain)	1982 IFK Göteborg (Sweden)
1965 Ferencvaros (Hungary)	1983 RSC Anderlecht (Belgium)
1966 Barcelona (Spain)	1984 Tottenham Hotspur (England)
1967 Dynamo Zagreb (Yugoslavia)	1985 Real Madrid (Spain)
1968 Leeds United (England)	1986 Real Madrid (Spain)
1969 Newcastle United (England)	1987 IFK Göteborg (Sweden)
1970 Arsenal (England)	1988 Bayer Leverkusen (West
1971 Leeds United (England)	Germany)
1972 Tottenham Hotspur (England)	1989 Napoli (Italy)
1973 Liverpool (England)	1990 Juventus (Italy)
1974 Feyenoord (Netherlands)	1991 Inter-Milan (Italy)
1975 Borussia Mönchengladbach	1992 Ajax (Netherlands)
(West Germany)	1993 Juventus (Italy)
1976 Liverpool (England)	1994 Inter-Milan (Italy)
1977 Juventus (Italy)	1995 Parma (Italy)

European Super Cup

Eligible: Winners of previous season's European Cup and Cup Winners' Cup.

Frequency: Yearly.

Format: Two-game home-and-home series.

1972 Ajax (Netherlands)	1984 Juventus (Italy)
1973 Ajax (Netherlands)	1985 Not played
1974 Not played	1986 Steaua Bucharest (Romania)
1975 Dynamo Kiev (USSR)	1987 FC Porto (Portugal)
1976 RSC Anderlecht (Belgium)	1988 Mechelen (Belgium)
1977 Liverpool (England)	1989 AC Milan (Italy)
1978 RSC Anderlecht (Belgium)	1990 AC Milan (Italy)
1979 Nottingham Forest (England)	1991 Manchester United (England)
1980 Valencia (Spain)	1992 Barcelona (Spain)
1981 Not played	1993 Parma (Italy)
1982 Aston Villa (England)	1994 AC Milan (Italy)
1983 Aberdeen (Scotland)	1995 Ajax (Netherlands)

4. Concacaf

Concacaf Champions Cup

Eligible: The top two clubs from all member nations of Concacaf (see page 312).

Frequency: Yearly, though the competition suffered from an erratic schedule in its early years.

Format: Knockout competition. Clubs, drawn in pairs, play each other home-and-home.

1962	Guadalajara (Mexico)	1982	UNAM (Mexico)
1963	Racing (Haiti)	1983	Atlante (Mexico)
1967	Alianza (El Salvador)	1984	Violette (Haiti)
1968	Toluca (Mexico)	1985	Defence Force (Trinidad &
1969	Cruz Azul (Mexico)		Tobago)
1971	Cruz Azul (Mexico)	1986	Liga Deportiva Alajuelense
1972	Olimpia (Honduras)		(Costa Rica)
1973	Transvaal (Surinam)	1987	Club América (Mexico)
1974	Municipal (Guatemala)	1988	Olimpia (Honduras)
1975	Atlético Español (Mexico)	1989	UNAM (Mexico)
1976	Aguila (El Salvador)	1990	Club América (Mexico)
1977	Club América (Mexico)	1991	Puebla (Mexico)
1979	FAS (El Salvador)	1992	Club América (Mexico)
1980	UNAM (Mexico)	1993	Saprissa (Costa Rica)
1981	Transvaal (Surinam)	1994	Cartagines (Costa Rica)

5. South America

Copa Libertadores

Eligible: The reigning champion, plus the top two teams from each member nation of the South American Football Confederation (see page 312).
Frequency: Yearly.
Format: First round of minileague play (four groups of 4 teams, one of 5 teams) eliminates 5 teams. Remaining 16 then play knockout competition; teams are drawn in pairs, which play home-and-home series.

1960	Peñarol (Uruguay)	1977	Boca Juniors (Argentina)
1961	Peñarol (Uruguay)	1978	Boca Juniors (Argentina)
1962	Santos (Brazil)	1979	Olimpia (Paraguay)
1963	Santos (Brazil)	1980	Nacional (Uruguay)
1964	Independiente (Argentina)	1981	Flamengo (Brazil)
1965	Independiente (Argentina)	1982	Peñarol (Uruguay)
1966	Peñarol (Uruguay)	1983	Gremio (Brazil)
1967	Racing Club (Argentina)	1984	Independiente (Argentina)
1968	Estudiantes de la Plata	1985	Argentinos Juniors
	(Argentina)		(Argentina)
1969	Estudiantes de la Plate	1986	River Plate (Argentina)
	(Argentina)	1987	Peñarol (Uruguay)
1970	Estudiantes de la Plata	1988	Nacional (Uruguay)
	(Argentina)	1989	Nacional Medellin (Colombia)
1971	Nacional (Uruguay)	1990	Olimpia (Paraguay)
1972	Independiente (Argentina)	1991	Colo Colo (Chile)
1973	Independiente (Argentina)	1992	São Paulo (Brazil)
1974	Independiente (Argentina)	1993	São Paulo (Brazil)
1975	Independiente (Argentina)	1994	Vélez Sarsfield (Argentina)
1976	Cruzeiro (Brazil)	1995	Gremio (Brazil)

Supercopa

Winners are awarded the João Havelange trophy.
Eligible: Previous winners of the Copa Libertadores.
Frequency: Yearly.
Format: Knockout competition. Clubs are drawn in pairs and play each other in a home-and-home series. There were 17 entries for the 1995 edition: 7 clubs from Argentina, 5 from Brazil, 2 from Uruguay, one each from Chile, Paraguay, and Colombia.

1988	Racing Club (Argentina)	1992	Cruzeiro (Brazil)
1989	Boca Juniors (Argentina)	1993	São Paulo (Brazil)
1990	Olimpia (Paraguay)	1994	Independiente (Argentina)
1991	Cruzeiro (Brazil)	1995	Independiente (Argentina)

INDIVIDUAL AWARDS

1. Global

FIFA World Player of the Year

	Winner	*Club*	*National Team*
1991	Lothar Matthäus	Inter-Milan	West Germany
1992	Marco Van Basten	AC Milan	Netherlands
1993	Roberto Baggio	Juventus	Italy
1994	Romário	Barcelona	Brazil
1995	George Weah	AC Milan	Liberia

2. Europe

European Player of the Year

	Winner	*Club*	*National Team*
1956	Stanley Matthews	Blackpool	England
1957	Alfredo Di Stéfano	Real Madrid	Argentina/Spain
1958	Raymond Kopa	Real Madrid	France
1959	Alfredo Di Stéfano	Real Madrid	Argentina/Spain
1960	Luis Suarez	Barcelona	Spain
1961	Enrique Sivori	Juventus	Argentina/Italy
1962	Josef Masopust	Dukla-Prague	Czechoslovakia
1963	Lev Yashin	Dynamo Moscow	USSR
1964	Denis Law	Manchester United	Scotland
1965	Eusebio	Benfica	Portugal
1966	Bobby Charlton	Manchester United	England
1967	Florian Albert	Ferencvaros	Hungary
1968	George Best	Manchester United	Northern Ireland
1969	Gianni Rivera	AC Milan	Italy
1970	Gerd Müller	Bayern Munich	West Germany
1971	Johan Cruyff	Ajax	Netherlands

continues

European Player of the Year Continued

	Winner	Club	National Team
1972	Franz Beckenbauer	Bayern Munich	West Germany
1973	Johan Cruyff	Barcelona	Netherlands
1974	Johan Cruyff	Barcelona	Netherlands
1975	Oleg Blokhin	Dynamo Kiev	USSR
1976	Franz Beckenbauer	Bayern Munich	West Germany
1977	Allan Simonsen	B.Mönchengladbach	Denmark
1978	Kevin Keegan	SV Hamburg	England
1979	Kevin Keegan	SV Hamburg	England
1980	Karl-Heinz Rummenigge	Bayern Munich	West Germany
1981	Karl-Heinz Rummenigge	Bayern Munich	West Germany
1982	Paolo Rossi	Juventus	Italy
1983	Michel Platini	Juventus	France
1984	Michel Platini	Juventus	France
1985	Michel Platini	Juventus	France
1986	Igor Belanov	Dynamo Kiev	USSR
1987	Ruud Gullit	AC Milan	Netherlands
1988	Marco Van Basten	AC Milan	Netherlands
1989	Marco Van Basten	AC Milan	Netherlands
1990	Lothar Matthäus	Inter-Milan	West Germany
1991	Jean-Pierre Papin	Marseille	France
1992	Marco Van Basten	AC Milan	Netherlands
1993	Roberto Baggio	Juventus	Italy
1994	Hristo Stoichkov	Barcelona	Bulgaria
1995	George Weah	AC Milan	Liberia

3. South America

South American Player of the Year

	Winner	Club	National Team
1971	Tostão	Cruzeiro	Brazil
1972	Teófilo Cubillas	Alianza Lima	Peru
1973	Pelé	Santos	Brazil
1974	Elias Figueroa	Internacional	Chile
1975	Elias Figueroa	Internacional	Chile
1976	Elias Figueroa	Internacional	Chile
1977	Zico	Flamengo	Brazil
1978	Mario Kempes	Valencia	Argentina
1979	Diego Maradona	Argentinos Juniors	Argentina
1980	Diego Maradona	Boca Juniors	Argentina
1981	Zico	Flamengo	Brazil
1982	Zico	Flamengo	Brazil
1983	Sócrates	Corinthians	Brazil
1984	Enzo Francescoli	River Plate	Uruguay
1985	Julio César Romero	Fluminense	Paraguay
1986	Antonio Alzamendi	River Plate	Uruguay
1987	Carlos Valderrama	Deportivo Cali	Colombia

	Winner	*Club*	*National Team*
1988	Ruben Paz	Racing Buenos Aires	Uruguay
1989	Bebeto	Vasco Da Gama	Brazil
1990	Raul Amarilla	Olimpia	Paraguay
1991	Oscar Ruggeri	Vélez Sarsfield	Argentina
1992	Rai	São Paulo	Brazil
1993	Carlos Valderrama	Atlético Junior	Colombia
1994	Cafu	São Paulo	Brazil
1995	Enzo Francescoli	River Plate	Uruguay

4. Africa

African Player of the Year

	Winner	*National Team*
1970	Salif Keita	Mali
1971	Ibrahim Sunday	Ghana
1972	Cherif Souleymane	Guinea
1973	Tshimimu Bwanga	Zaire
1974	Paul Moukila	Congo
1975	Ahmed Faras	Morocco
1976	Roger Milla	Cameroon
1977	Dhiab Tarak	Tunisia
1978	Abdul Razak	Ghana
1979	Thomas N'Kono	Cameroon
1980	Jean Manga Onguene	Cameroon
1981	Lakhdar Belloumi	Algeria
1982	Thomas N'Kono	Cameroon
1983	Mahmoud Al-Khatib	Egypt
1984	Theophile Abega	Cameroon
1985	Mohamed Timoumi	Morocco
1986	Badou Zaki	Morocco
1987	Rabah Madjer	Algeria
1988	Kalusha Bwalya	Zambia
1989	George Weah	Liberia
1990	Roger Milla	Cameroon
1991	Abedi Pele	Ghana
1992	Abedi Pele	Ghana
1993	Abedi Pele	Ghana
1994	George Weah	Liberia
1995	George Weah	Liberia

Appendix E

The United States

The controlling body for soccer in the United States is:

United States Soccer Federation
U.S. Soccer House
1801–1811 S. Prairie Avenue
Chicago, IL 60616

UNITED STATES OLYMPIC TEAM

1924 Final Tournament in Paris:
USA 1	Estonia 0
USA 0	Uruguay 3

1928 Final Tournament in Amsterdam:
USA 2	Argentina 11

1936 Final Tournament in Berlin:
USA 0	Italy 1

1948 Final Tournament in London:
USA 0	Italy 9

1952 Final Tournament in Helsinki:
USA 0	Italy 8

1956 Final Tournament in Melbourne:
USA 1	Yugoslavia 9

1960 Qualifying round
Mexico 2	USA 1
USA 1	Mexico 1

USA failed to qualify for final tournament in Rome.

1964 Qualifying round
USA 0	Suriname 1
USA 4	Panama 2
USA 1	Mexico 2

USA failed to qualify for final tournament in Tokyo.

1968 Qualifying round
USA 1	Bermuda 1
Bermuda 1	USA 0

USA failed to qualify for final tournament in Mexico City.

1972 Qualifying round,
1st Preliminary
USA 1	El Salvador 1
USA 3	Barbados 0
El Salvador 1	USA 1
Barbados 1	USA 3

2nd Preliminary
Jamaica 1	USA 1
Mexico 1	USA 1

Guatemala 3	USA 2
USA 2	Guatemala 1
USA 2	Mexico 2
USA 2	Jamaica 1

USA qualified for the final tournament in Munich:

USA 0	Morocco 0
USA 0	Malaysia 3
USA 0	West Germany 7

1976 Qualifying round

Bermuda 3	USA 2
USA 2	Bermuda 0
Mexico 8	USA 0
USA 2	Mexico 4

USA failed to qualify for final tournament in Montreal.

1980 Qualifying round

USA 5	Bermuda 0
Bermuda 0	USA 3
USA 1	Costa Rica 1
Costa Rica 0	USA 1
USA 2	Suriname 1
Suriname 4	USA 2

USA qualified for
Final Tournament in Moscow, *but did not compete because of U.S. boycott.*

1984 Los Angeles
As host nation, USA qualified automatically for
Final Tournament:

USA 3	Costa Rica 0
USA 0	Italy 1
USA 1	Egypt 1

1988 Qualifying round

Canada 2	USA 0
USA 3	Canada 0
USA 4	Trinidad and Tobago 1
Trinidad and Tobago 0	USA 1
El Salvador 2	USA 4
USA 4	El Salvador 1

USA qualified for Final Tournament in Seoul:

USA 1	Argentina 1
USA 0	South Korea 0
USA 2	USSR 4

1992 Qualifying round

USA 8	Haiti 0
Panama 1	USA 1
USA 7	Panama 1
Haiti 0	USA 2
Mexico 1	USA 2
USA 4	Honduras 3
Honduras 3	USA 4
USA 3	Mexico 0
USA 3	Canada 1
USA 1	Canada 2

USA qualified for
Final Tournament in Barcelona:

USA 1	Italy 2
USA 3	Kuwait 1
USA 2	Poland 2

1996: Atlanta
As host nation, USA qualified automatically for
Final Tournament.

UNITED STATES NATIONAL TEAM: WORLD CUP RECORD

1930: Final Tournament in Uruguay:

USA 3	Belgium 0
USA 3	Paraguay 0

Semifinal

USA 1	Argentina 6

1934 Qualifying round:

USA 4	Mexico 2

USA qualified for
Final Tournament in Italy:

USA 1	Italy 7

1938 *USA did not enter tournament*

1950 Qualifying round:

USA 0	Mexico 6
USA 1	Cuba 1
USA 2	Mexico 6
USA 5	Cuba 2

USA qualified for
Final Tournament in Brazil:

USA 1	Spain 3
USA 1	England 0
USA 2	Chile 5

1954 Qualifying round:

Mexico 4	USA 0
Mexico 3	USA 1
Haiti 2	USA 3
Haiti 0	USA 3

USA failed to qualify for final tournament in Switzerland.

1958 Qualifying round:

Mexico 6	USA 0
USA 2	Mexico 7
Canada 5	USA 1
USA 2	Canada 3

USA failed to qualify for final tournament in Sweden.

1962 Qualifying round:

USA 3	Mexico 3
Mexico 3	USA 0

USA failed to qualify for final tournament in Chile.

1966 Qualifying round:

USA 2	Mexico 2
Mexico 2	USA 0
Honduras 0	USA 1
Honduras 1	USA 1

USA failed to qualify for final tournament in England.

1970 Qualifying round:

Canada 4	USA 2
USA 1	Canada 0
USA 6	Bermuda 2
Bermuda 0	USA 2
Haiti 2	USA 0
USA 0	Haiti 1

USA failed to qualify for final tournament in Mexico.

1974 Qualifying round:

Canada 3	USA 2
USA 2	Canada 2
Mexico 3	USA 1
USA 1	Mexico 2

USA failed to qualify for final tournament in West Germany.

1978 Qualifying round:

Canada 1	USA 1
USA 0	Mexico 0
Mexico 3	USA 0
USA 2	Canada 0
Canada 3	USA 0

USA failed to qualify for final tournament in Argentina.

1982 Qualifying round:

USA 0	Canada 0
Canada 2	USA 1
Mexico 5	USA 1
USA 2	Mexico 1

USA failed to qualify for final tournament in Spain.

1986 Qualifying round:

Netherlands Antilles 0	USA 0
USA 4	Netherlands Antilles 0
Trinidad and Tobago 1	USA 2
USA 1	Trinidad and Tobago 0
Costa Rica 1	USA 1
USA 0	Costa Rica 1

USA failed to qualify for final tournament in Mexico.

1990 Qualifying round:

Jamaica 0	USA 0
USA 5	Jamaica 1
Costa Rica 1	USA 0
USA 1	Costa Rica 0
USA 1	Trinidad and Tobago 1
USA 2	Guatemala 1
El Salvador 0	USA 1
Guatemala 0	USA 0
USA 0	El Salvador 0
Trinidad and Tobago 0	USA 1

USA qualified for
Final Tournament in Italy:

USA 1	Czechoslovakia 5
USA 0	Italy 1
USA 1	Austria 2

1994: As host nation, USA qualified automatically for
Final Tournament:

USA 1	Switzerland 1
USA 2	Colombia 1
USA 0	Romania 1

Second round:

USA 0	Brazil 1

UNITED STATES NATIONAL TEAM ALL-TIME APPEARANCE RECORDS*

		Games Played	Years Active
1	Marcelo Balboa	109	1988–
2	Paul Caligiuri	108	1984–
3	Bruce Murray	95	1985–
4	Tony Meola	89	1988–
5	Desmond Armstrong	84	1987–
6	Hugo Perez	79	1984–
7	Chris Henderson	73	1990–
8	Cobi Jones	72	1992–
9	Peter Vermes	70	1988–
10	Eric Wynalda	69	1990–
11	Alexi Lalas	67	1989–
12	Tab Ramos	66	1988–
13	John Harkes	63	1987–
14	Fernando Clavijo	61	1990–
15	Michael Windischmann	58	1984–1990
	John Doyle	58	1987–
17	Dominic Kinnear	56	1990–
18	Thomas Dooley	55	1992–
	Mike Sorber	55	1992–
20	Jeff Agoos	53	1988–

As of February 20, 1996

UNITED STATES NATIONAL TEAM ALL-TIME LEADING GOAL SCORERS*

		Goals	Games	Years
1	Eric Wynalda	22	69	1990–
2	Bruce Murray	21	93	1985–
3	Hugo Perez	16	79	1984–
4	Frank Klopas	13	44	1987–
5	Marcelo Balboa	12	109	1977–1988
	Rick Davis	12	49	1988–
	Joe-Max Moore	12	46	1992–

As of February 20, 1996

COLLEGE SOCCER

NCAA DIVISION I: MEN

1959	St. Louis		1968	Michigan State and
1960	St. Louis			Maryland
1961	West Chester			(co-champions)
1962	St. Louis		1969	St. Louis
1963	St. Louis		1970	St. Louis
1964	Navy		1971	Howard
1965	St. Louis		1972	St. Louis
1966	San Francisco		1973	St. Louis
1967	St. Louis and Michigan		1974	Howard
	State (co-champions)		1975	San Francisco

continues

NCAA DIVISION I: MEN CONTINUED

1976	San Francisco	1987	Clemson
1977	Hartwick	1988	Indiana
1978	San Francisco	1989	Virginia and Santa Clara (co-champions)
1979	Southern Illinois		
1980	San Francisco	1990	UCLA
1981	Connecticut	1991	Virginia
1982	Indiana	1992	Virginia
1983	Indiana	1993	Virginia
1984	Clemson	1994	Virginia
1985	UCLA	1995	Wisconsin
1986	Duke		

NCAA DIVISION I: WOMEN

1982	North Carolina	1989	North Carolina
1983	North Carolina	1990	North Carolina
1984	North Carolina	1991	North Carolina
1985	George Mason	1992	North Carolina
1986	North Carolina	1993	North Carolina
1987	North Carolina	1994	North Carolina
1988	North Carolina	1995	Notre Dame

INDIVIDUAL AWARDS

HERMANN TROPHY

Awarded to the best player of the year. Voted on by Division I college coaches and journalists.

1967	Dov Markus	Long Island University
1968	Manuel Hernandez	San Jose State
1969	Al Trost	St. Louis
1970	Al Trost	St. Louis
1971	Mike Seerey	St. Louis
1972	Mike Seerey	St. Louis
1973	Dan Counce	St. Louis
1974	Farrukh Quraishi	Oneonta State
1975	Steve Ralbovsky	Brown
1976	Glenn Myernick	Hartwick
1977	Billy Gazonas	Hartwick
1978	Angelo Di Bernardo	Indiana
1979	Jim Stamatis	Penn State
1980	Joe Morrone Jr	Connecticut
1981	Armando Betancourt	Indiana
1982	Joe Ulrich	Duke
1983	Mike Jeffries	Duke
1984	Amr Aly	Columbia
1985	Tom Kain	Duke
1986	John Kerr	Duke
1987	Bruce Murray	Clemson
1988	Ken Snow	Indiana

HERMANN TROPHY CONTINUED

1989	Tony Meola	Virginia
1990	Ken Snow	Indiana
1991	Alexi Lalas	Rutgers
1992	Brad Friedel	UCLA
1993	Claudio Reyna	Virginia
1994	Brian Maisonneuve	Indiana
1995	Mike Fisher	Virginia

WOMEN'S HERMANN TROPHY
Awarded to the best player of the year. Voted on by Division I coaches and journalists.

1988	Michelle Akers	Central Florida
1989	Shannon Higgins	North Carolina
1990	April Kater	Massachusetts
1991	Kristine Lilly	North Carolina
1992	Mia Hamm	North Carolina
1993	Mia Hamm	North Carolina
1994	Tisha Venturini	North Carolina
1995	Shannon MacMillan	Portland

MISSOURI ATHLETIC CLUB (MAC) MEN'S AWARD
Awarded to best college player of the year. The recipient must be an American citizen, either by birth or naturalization. Voted on by 1,100 college and junior college coaches.

1986	John Kerr	Duke
1987	John Harkes	Virginia
1988	Ken Snow	Indiana
1989	Tony Meola	Virginia
1990	Ken Snow	Indiana
1991	Alexi Lalas	Rutgers
1992	Claudio Reyna	Virginia
1993	Claudio Reyna	Virginia
1994	Todd Yeagley	Indiana
1995	Matt McKeon	St. Louis

MISSOURI ATHLETIC CLUB (MAC) WOMEN'S AWARD
Awarded to best college player of the year. The recipient must be an American citizen, either by birth or naturalization. Voted on by 1,100 college and junior college coaches.

1991	Kristine Lilly	North Carolina
1992	Mia Hamm	North Carolina
1993	Mia Hamm	North Carolina
1994	Tisha Venturini	North Carolina
1995	Shannon MacMillan	Portland

⚽ Index

A

Abbes, Claude, 43
Abelardo, 145
AC Milan (Italy), 22, 115, 151, 154–56, 167, 171
Ademir, 32
Advocaat, Dick, 114
AFC, *see* Asian Football Confederation
African Football Confederation (CAF)
   member nations, 311
   nations championship, 327
African Player of the Year, 335
Agents, 152, 163
Aggregate scores, 277
Ajax (Netherlands), 63, 209
Albert, Florian, 52, 54
Alberto, Carlos, 61, 208, 209
Albertosi, Enrico, 53, 60, 61
Aldair, 133
Aldridge, John, 99, 125
A-League, 263
Algeria
   and 1982 World Cup, 80–81
Allende, Salvador, 62
Allofs, Klaus, 92
Altafini, Jose, (Mazzola) 43, 46
Altobelli, Alessandro, 83, 84
Alvarez, Leonel, 274
Alvez, Fernando, 103
Amaral, 72
Amarildo, 47, 49
Amateurs
   control of sport by, 10, 11, 166, 227, 244, 245, 255, 256

   numbers of, 176, 177
   in Olympics, 18, 139–40, 324
   referees as, 177
American Amateur Football Association (AAFA), 244
American Football Association (AFA), 244
Americanization of soccer, 244, 253, 254–55, 264–65
American Professional Soccer League (APSL), *see* A-League
American Soccer League (ASL), 245
American Youth Soccer Organization (AYSO), x, 257
Andersson, Kennet, 130
Andrade, José, 33n, 138
Andrade, Victor, 33, 34, 37, 193
Andreolo, Michele, 27
Angellilo, Antonio, 41–2
Antognoni, Giancarlo, 77, 83
Apolloni, Luigi, 236
Aravena, Orlando, 96–97
Arconada, Luis, 77
Arday, Samuel, 238
Ardiles, Osvaldo, 74, 212
Arena, Bruce, 146, 273
Argentina
   origins of soccer in, 14–15
   player development in, 159–161, 162
   training schedule, 164–65
   and 1928 Olympics, 18, 138
   and 1964 Olympics, 141
   and 1930 World Cup, 21–22, 187
   and 1934 World Cup, 25
   and 1958 World Cup, 41–42
   and 1966 World Cup, 54

and 1974 World Cup, 64, 65
and 1978 World Cup, 68–70, 72–75, 212–213
and 1982 World Cup, 78, 79, 81–82
and 1986 World Cup, 86–87, 89, 90, 91–95
and 1990 World Cup, 97–98, 101, 103, 104–106
and 1994 World Cup, 116, 124–25, 127
Arsenal (England), 156–59, 184–87
Asian Football Confederation (AFC) member nations, 312
Aston, Ken, 47
Australia
    and 1974 World Cup, 61, 64
    and 1994 World Cup, 116
Austria
    professionals in, 14
    Wunderteam, 17, 23–24, 25, 188
    and Olympics, 137, 139
    and 1934 World Cup, 23–24, 25
    and 1938 World Cup, 26–27
    and 1950 World Cup, 29
    and 1954 World Cup, 36, 38
    and 1982 World Cup, 80–81
Azcarraga, Emilio, 85
Azkargorta, Xavier, 116

B

Babington, Carlos, 64
Baggio, Dino, 126, 129
Baggio, Roberto, 104, 125, 127, 129, 131, 132, 134, 151, 236
Bahr, Walter, 31
Balbo, Abel, 98, 122
Balboa, Marcelo, 121, 129
Baldivieso, Julio, 119
Ball, Alan, 55, 56, 206, 207
Banks, Gordon, 51, 54, *55*, 58
Barbosa, 33
Barcelona (Spain), 78, 117, 224–5
Baresi, Franco, 126, 132, 134, 236
Barriskill, Joe, 248
Basile, Alfio, 116, 117
Batista, João, 82

Batista, José, 90
Batista, Sergio, 105, 219
Batistuta, Gabriel, 124
Bats, Joël, 92, 93
Battiston, Patrick, 83, 232
Bauer, 34, 193
Bayer Leverkusen (Germany), 273
Bearzot, Enzo, 72, 77, 82, 88, 214
Bebeto, 129, 130, 134, 135, 144
Beckenbauer, Franz, x, 51, 59, 62, *63*, 66, 70, 71, 87, 106, 108, 110, 210–12, 214, 251
Belanov, Igor, 91
Belgium 172
    and 1920 Olympics, 138
    and 1982 World Cup, 79, 81
    and 1986 World Cup, 91, 92–93
    and 1994 World Cup, 126–27
Bellini, Luiz, 51
Bellone, Bruno, 92
Bene, Ferenc, 52, 54
Benfica (Portugal), 51
Bergkamp, Dennis, 130
Berlusconi, Silvio, 115, 167, 170
Berthold, Thomas, 104, 218
Bertoni, Daniel, 74, 76, 212
Best, Ed, 111, 112–13
Best, George, x, 228, 251
Betancourt, Armando, 79n
Betancur, Belisario, 108
betting on soccer, 170–71
bicycle kick, 277
Bilardo, Carlos, 86–87, 93, 94, 98, 218, 220
Biyik, Omam, 98
Blackburn Olympic (England), 10, 180
Blackburn Rovers (England), 10, 167
Blanchflower, Danny, xix
Blatter, Sepp, 107–08, 109, 135, 226, 232, 233–4, 240
Boca Juniors (Argentina), 159–61, 171
Bolivia
    and 1950 World Cup, 30
    and 1994 World Cup, 116–17, 119–120
Bonhof, Rainer, 66, 67
Boniek, Zbigniew, 70, 83
Boninsegna, Roberto, 60

Bonner, Pat, 103, 127
Borras, Omar, 90, 91
Bosio, Edoardo, 14
Bosman, Jean Marc, 172
Boy, Thomas, 92
Bozsik, Jozsef, 37n, 38, 195, 197–8
Branco, 92, 130, 133, 134, 221
Brandts, Erny, 73
Brazil
    origins of soccer in, 15
    as role model for USA, 271–72
    and 1976 Olympics, 142
    and 1984 Olympics, 143
    and 1988 Olympics, 143–44
    and 1930 World Cup, 20
    and 1934 World Cup, 25
    and 1938 World Cup, 27–29
    and 1950 World Cup, 29–33, 192–93,
      117, 194
    and 1954 World Cup, 34, 37
    and 1958 World Cup, 42–43, 44–45,
      198–201
    and 1962 World Cup, 46–49, 201
    and 1966 World Cup, 51, 52–53
    and 1970 World Cup, xxi, 57–61,
      208–209
    and 1974 World Cup, 62, 64, 65
    and 1978 World Cup, 71–72, 73–74
    and 1982 World Cup, 78, 79, 81–82
    and 1986 World Cup, 86, 89, 92
    and 1990 World Cup, 96–97,
      100–101, 220
    and 1994 World Cup, 115–17, 119,
      122–23, 128–30, 132–35, 221–22,
      236
Bregy, Georges, 121
Brehme, Andreas, 92, 93, 103, 104, 106
Breitner, Paul, 66, 77, 84
Briegel, Hans-Peter, 77, 83, 94
Britain, 12, 41; *see also* England;
    Ireland, Northern; Scotland;
    Wales
Brito, 208
Brizio Carter, Arturo, 119–20, 127, 240
Brolin, Tomas, 130, 132
Brown, José, 93
Buchan, Charlie, 184, 187

Budai, Lazslo, 205
Bukovi, Marton, 195
Bulgarelli, Giacomo, 53
Bulgaria
    and 1968 Olympics, 141
    and 1966 World Cup, 52
    and 1986 World Cup, 88–89
    and 1994 World Cup, 115, 124, 125,
      127–28, 130–32
Burgnich, Tarcisio, 59, *60*
Burns, Mike, 144
Burruchaga, Jorge, 94, 219
Butcher, Terry, 92
Butragueño, Emilio, 91

C

Cabrini, Antonio, 77, 83
Caçador, Rui, 239
CAF, *see* African Football Confederation
Cafu, 134
Cale, Chuck, 110
Caligiuri, Paul, 97, 121, 144
Camacho, José, 77
Cameroon
    and 1982 World Cup, 80
    and 1990 World Cup, 97, 98, 102–03,
      104
    and 1994 World Cup, 117–118,
      122, *123*
Caminero, José, 129
Campos, Jorge, 274
Canada
    and 1986 World Cup, 90, 95
Cañedo, Guillermo, 85
Caniggia, Claudio, 98, 101, 105, 124,
    127, 171
Cardenosa, Julio, 71–72
Card system for referees, 57
Careca, 82, 86, 92
Carlos, 89, 92
Carter, Raich, 153n
Casiraghi, Pierluigi, 126
Castillo, Augusto Lamo, 79
Catennacio, see formations
Cecchi Gori, Mario, 166

Cecchi Gori, Vittorio, 166
Cerezo, Toninho, 78
Chapman, Herbert, 184–87, 188, 194
Charlton, Bobby, xxiv, 51, 54, 206
Charlton, Jack, xx, *55*, 99, 101, 103, 113, 115, 125, 127
Chelsea (England), 148
Chile
    and 1962 World Cup, 45–49
    and 1974 World Cup, 62, 64
    and 1990 World Cup, 96–97
    and 1994 World Cup, 115
China, 241
Chinaglia, Giorgio, 133, 251, 252
Christian Brothers College (USA), 137
Christov, Vojtech, 79, 214
Chyzowych, Walt, 268
Clark, Frank, 221
Clarke, Adrian, 156–59
Clemente, Javier, 128
Clinton, President, 119, 128
Clodoaldo, 59, 209
Club teams
    international competitions, 147–50
    structure of, 166–68
    training routines, 163–65
    youth development by, 153–63
Coaches
    attitudes of, 225, 227, 229–30, 237, 267–8
    background of, 230
    licensing of, 165, 207, 229, 256, 268
    salaries of, 165–66
Codesal, Edgar, 106
Cohen, George, *55*
Colaussi, Gino, 29
college soccer, xi, 100, 153, 161, 242–45, 253–55, 258, 266–68, 273, 339–41
Collovati, Fulvio, 77
Collymore, Stan, 171
Colombia
    pirate league in, 173
    and 1986 World Cup, 85, 108
    and 1990 World Cup, 99, 102–103
    and 1994 World Cup, 116, 121–122
Coluna, Mario, 51

Combi, Gianpiero, 26
Commercialism, 35, 95–96, 108, 131, 166–67, 255, 259, 260
Concacaf (Football Confederation of North and Central America and the Caribbean), 76, 312, 327, 328–329, 331
Conejo, Gabelo, 100, 101
Conmebol, *see* South American Confederation
Conti, Bruno, 83
Continental Confederations, 174–75, 176, 311–13
Continental Indoor Soccer League, 263
Cooke, Jack Kent, 248, 249
Copa America, 174, 273, 326–27
Copa Interamericana, 228–29
Copa Libertadores, 150, 174, 332
Cordoba, Oscar, 122
Corinthians (Brazil), 15, 168
Corinthians (England), 15
Corner kicks as tie-breaker, 237
Corver, Charles, 83
Costa, Flavio, 193
Costa Rica
    and 1990 World Cup, 100, 101
Costacurta, Allessandro, 132
Coutinho, Claudio, 71–72, 73, 74
Cox, Bill, 247
Cristaldo, Luis, 119
Cromwell, Oliver, 4
Cruyff, Johan, x, 63, 65, 66, 67, 71, 114, 171, 210, *211*, 224, 230, 251
CSF, *see* South American Confederation
CSKA Moscow (Russia), 152
Cubillas, Teófilo, 268, 270
Cuciuffo, Jose, 92
Cup tournaments, 147–150, 314–333
    origins of, 9–10
    popularity of, 10, 13
Czechoslovakia
    and 1920 Olympics, 138
    and 1964 Olympics, 141
    and 1980 Olympics, 142
    and 1934 World Cup, 25–26, 189
    and 1962 World Cup, 46, 47, 49,
    and 1990 World Cup, 100, 101

Czeizler, Lajos, 34
Czibor, Zoltan, 37, 40

D

Da Guia, Domingos, 28–29, 31
Dahlin, Martin, 144, 237
Dallas Tornado (U.S.), 250, 252
Danubian school of soccer, 188–90
Davis, Rick, 253, 255
Defensive tactics, 183–87, 189, 198,
    201–204, 208, 213–14, 227–29, 233
    and FIFA technical reports, 216,
        220–21
    and low scores, 202–02, 234–35
Delaunay, Henri, 19
Denmark
    and 1908 Olympics, 137
    and 1988 Olympics, 143
    and 1912 Olympics, 138
    and 1948 Olympics, 139
    and 1986 World Cup, 87–88, 89–90,
        91
Derwall, Jupp, 77, 83
Deyna, Kazimierz, 64
D'Hooge, Dr Michel, 124
Diaz, Ramón, 98
Didi, 42, 43, 45, 57
Dienst, Gottfried, 56
Di Stéfano, Alfredo, 46, 47, 148, *149*,
    171, 173, 198, 220
Donadoni, Roberto, 103, 105, 274
Dooley, Thomas, 121
Drake, Ted, 187, 194
Dremmler, Wolfgang, 83
Drug testing, 50n, 64, 70, 90, 106n, 117,
    123, 124–25,
Dunga, 101, 133, 134–35, 221

E

East Germany
    and 1964 Olympics, 141
    and 1972 Olympics, 142
    and 1976 Olympics, 142
    and 1980 Olympics, 142
    and 1974 World Cup, 62, 65
Eder, 79
Edinho, 91
Edwards, Gene, 108, 256
Effenberg, Stefan, 120
Egypt
    and 1964 Olympics, 141
    and 1990 World Cup, 99
Elkjaer, Preben, 88, 90
Ellis, William Webb, 6n
El Grafico, 116
El Salvador
    and 1982 World Cup, 76, 80
England
    coaches' income, 165
    FIFA boycotted by, 16–17, 27n
    Football Association, 7–13
    Football League, 11, 13, 148, 151,
        169–70
    origins of soccer in, 2–13
    players' income, 150–51
    Premiership, 150–151, 169–70
    training schedule, 163–64
    violent fans, 87, 96, 99, 231–32
    youth development in, 156–59,
        162–63
    and 1950 World Cup, 30–31
    and 1954 World Cup, 36
    and 1958 World Cup, 41, 42
    and 1966 World Cup, xx–xxi,
        50–52, 54–56, 205–07
    and 1970 World Cup, 57–59
    and 1982 World Cup, 78, 81
    and 1986 World Cup, 87, 90, 91–92
    and 1990 World Cup, 96, 99, 102,
        104, 105
English Schools Football Association,
    162
Enrique, Hector, 94, 219
Ercolani, Alessandro, 154–56, 161–62
Ertegun, Ahmet, 251
Ertegun, Nesuhi, 251, 253
Escobar, Andres, 122, 125
Eskandarian, Andranik, 71
Etcheverry, Marco, 116, 120, 274
Etherington, Gary, 254

Ettori, Jean-Luc, 82
Europe
    members of FIFA, 312–13
    spread of soccer in, 13–14
European Championship, 326
European Cup, 147–49, 204, 231–32, 329–330
European Cup Winners' Cup, 148–50, 330
European Player of the Year, 333–34
European Super Cup, 331
Eusebio, 51, 52, 53, 54, 206, 207
Evani, Alberigo, 144
Everaldo, 58

F

Fabbri, Edmondo, 51
Facchetti, Giacinto, 51, 141, 204, 210
Fahed, Sheik, 80
Fair Play Campaign, 232
Falcão, 78, 79, 86
Farkas, Janos, 52
Fédération Internationale de Football Association, *see* FIFA
Felix, xxi, 58, 208
Fenwick, Terry, 92
Feola, Vicente, 42, 43, 44, 46, 51, 198–99, 201n
Fernandez, Luis, 87
Ferrari, Giovanni, 27, 29, 188
Ferreira, Manuel, *20*
Ferri, Ricardo, 100
Feyenoord (Netherlands), 62, 209
FIFA
    British boycott of, 16–17, 27n
    Congress, *174*
    Fair Play Campaign, 232
    Football 2000 Task Force, 232–33, 236, 240
    formation of, 16
    functions of, 16, 173–75
    member nations, 174, 311–13
    and players' agents, 152
    playing rules standardized by, 16, 222–240, 254
    rule changes, 118, 119–20, 226, 264
    structure of, 173–75
    technical reports, 207, 214–221
    and U.S. soccer, 107–11, 244, 249, 257, 258, 261–62
    and World Cup, *see* World Cup
    World Player of the Year, 171n, 333
Fillol, Ubaldo, 75
Finney, Tom, 30
Fiorentina (Italy), 166
Fischer, Klaus, 83
Fluminense (Brazil), 168
Fontaine, Just, 43, 44
Football, American
    influence on U.S. soccer, 244, 246, 266–67, 268
Foreman, Earl, 253, 261
Formations, 180–226
    Argentina 1986, 212–13
    Brazilian diagonal, 192–94
    catenaccio, 203–05, 210, 214, 222, 227–28
    England 1966, 205–07
    4-4-2, 205–08
    4-3-3, 201–02
    4-2-4, 198–201
    Hungary 1954, 194–98
    metodo, 188–90
    pyramid, 181–83
    Swiss bolt, 190–91
    3-4-3, *see* W-M
    total soccer, 209–12, 215, 218, 219
    verrou, *see* Swiss bolt
    whirl, 210
    W-M, 184–87, 190
Förster, Bernd, 82
Förster, Karl-Heinz, 94
France
    and 1908 Olympics, 137
    and 1924 Olympics, 138
    and 1968 Olympics, 141
    and 1976 Olympics, 142
    and 1984 Olympics, 143
    and 1930 World Cup, 19, 20
    and 1938 World Cup, 26–27
    and 1958 World Cup, 43–44
    and 1978 World Cup, 72

France (*cont.*)
    and 1982 World Cup, 77, 80, 82–83,
        214–15
    and 1986 World Cup, 87, 90, 91,
        92, 93
    and 1994 World Cup, 115
Franklin, Neil, 30
Fredricksson, Erik, 98
Friaça, 33
Fricker, Werner, 108–109, 256–57
Friedel, Brad, 129, 144

G

Gadocha, Robert, 64, 65
Gaetjens, Joe, 31
Gallego, Americo, 81
Galván, Luis, 75
Galt FC (Canada), 137
Gambetta, Schubert, 193
Gambling, 170–71
Gansler, Bob, 97, 100, 110
Garrincha, 42, 43, 45, 47, *48*, 49, 51,
    200–01, 205
Gascoigne, Paul, 102, 104
Gazzanigga, Silvio, 61
Gelei, Jozsef, 54
Gemmill, Archie, 71
Genoa Cricket and Football Club
    (Italy), 14
Gentile, Claudio, 81–84, 217,
    229, 232
Gento, Francisco, 46
Geovani, 144
Germany *see also* West Germany, and
    East Germany
    coaches' income, 165
    players' income, 151
    violent fans, 99
    and 1936 Olympics, 139
    and 1938 World Cup, 27
    and 1950 World Cup, 29
    and 1994 World Cup, 119–20,
        127, 130
Gerson, 58, 60, 61, 208–09
Ghana
    and 1995 u-17 World Cup, 238

Ghiggia, Alcide, 33, 41, 193
Gilmar, 51
Giresse, Alain, 77, 80, 87
Giusti, Ricardo, 219
Goal-scoring rate, 34, 106, 201–202, 118,
    133, 136, 221
Goikoetxea, Andoni, 129
Gomes, Ricardo, 132
Gomez, Gabriel, 122
Gonella, Sergio, 74
Gonzalez, Matias, 193
Goycochea, Sergio, 98, 103, 104,
    105, 106
Graziani, Francesco, 83
Great Britain, in Olympics, 137–39
Greaves, Jimmy, 51, 230
Greece
    and 1994 World Cup, 115, 124, 125
Gren, Gunnar, 43
Grillon, André, 141
Groff, Richard, 261
Grondona, Julio, 124
Grosics, Gyula, 38, 198
Guaita, Enrico, 25, 26
Gulati, Sunil, 274
Gullit, Ruud, 97, 114

H

Haan, Arie, 73, 74
Hacking, 7, 9, 229
Haiti
    and 1974 World Cup, 61, 64
Haller, Helmut, 54, *55*
Hamrin, Kurt, 43
Hanot, Gabriel, 147
Happel, Ernst, 71, 211, 212
Harkes, John, 121, 122, 144, 271
Hässler, Thomas, 99, 119, 120, 130, 144
Havelange, João, 68, 69, 76, 95, 106,
    108, 109, 110, 111, 118, 125, 135,
    232–33, 240–41
Helmer, Thomas, 127
Herberger, Sepp, 27, 34, 35–6, 38, 40,
    46, 51
Hermann Trophy, 79n, 340–41
Herrera, Helenio, 204

Heysel Stadium disaster 1985, 231–32
Hidegkuti, Nandor, 37, 38, 39, 40, 52, 195–97
Hiden, Rudi, 23
Hierro, 128
Higuita, Rene, 102–03
Hispanic players in U.S., 269–71, 272
Hitler, Adolf, 139
Hodge, Steve, 91
Hofheinz, Roy, 248
Hogan, Jimmy, 23, 188
Hohberg, Juan, 37–38, 59
Holland, *see* Netherlands
Holzenbein, Bernd, 66
Honduras
    and 1982 World Cup, 76, 79
Hooliganism, *see* violence
Hopcraft, Arthur, 177n
Horvath, Johann, 25
Houghton, Ray, 125
Houseman, René, 72, 213
Hungary
    Magic Magyars, 34, 37–39, 40, 140, 194–99
    and 1908 Olympics, 137
    and 1952 Olympics, 140
    and 1960 Olympics, 140
    and 1964 Olympics, 141
    and 1968 Olympics, 141
    and 1972 Olympics, 142
    and 1938 World Cup, 29, 190
    and 1954 World Cup, 34, 37–39, 194–99
    and 1966 World Cup, 52, 53, 54
Hunt, Lamar, 248, 250, 251, 252, 263, 275
Hunt, Roger, 206–07
Hurst, Geoff, 55, 56, 206–07, *247*

I

Illgner, Bodo, 104, 120, 130
India
    and 1948 Olympics, 139
Indonesia
    and 1956 Olympics, 140

Indoor soccer, 176, 241, 252–53, 263, 326
Indoor World Cup, 326
Intercollegiate Soccer Association (U.S.), 253
Inter-Milan (Italy), 14, 47, 141, 155, 204
International Football Association Board, 12, 13, 175
International Olympic Committee (IOC), 137, 138, 139, 144
International Soccer League (ISL), 247
Iran
    and 1978 World Cup, 71
Ireland, Northern
    and 1958 World Cup, 41, 42, 43
    and 1982 World Cup, 80
    and 1986 World Cup, 89
Ireland, Republic of
    and 1990 World Cup, 99, 101, 103,
    and 1994 World Cup, 113, 115, 125, 126, 127
Italy
    and *catenaccio*, 72, 202–05, 214, 227–28
    foreign players in, 24, 35, 41–42, 46
    origins of soccer in, 14
    players' income in, 151
    referees in, 177, 234,
    use of *oriundi*, 24, 27, 42, 46
    youth development in, 154–56
    and 1936 Olympics, 139
    and 1960 Olympics, 140–41
    and 1988 Olympics, 143–44
    and 1992 Olympics, 144
    and 1934 World Cup, 22–26, 188–90
    and 1938 World Cup, 27–29, 190
    and 1954 World Cup, 35
    and 1958 World Cup, 41
    and 1962 World Cup, 46–47
    and 1966 World Cup, 51, 53
    and 1970 World Cup, 59–61
    and 1974 World Cup, 64
    and 1978 World Cup, 72–74, 214
    and 1982 World Cup, 77–78, 81–84, 215
    and 1986 World Cup, 88–89, 91
    and 1990 World Cup, 95–96, 100, 103, 104–05

Italy (*cont.*)
  and 1994 World Cup, 115, 119,
    125–26, 129, 131, 132–34, 236
Iustrich, 57

J

Jair da Costa, 204
Jair Rosa Pinto, 32
Jairzinho, xxi, 58, 59, 61, 65, 208, 209
James, Alex, 187, 219–220
Jansen, Wim, 66
Japan
  formation of pro league, 274
  and 1968 Olympics, 141
  and 1994 World Cup, 118
Jean-Joseph, Ernst, 64
Jennings, Pat, 89
Johnston, Harry, 196
Johnston, Willy, 70
Jones, Cobi, 144
Jongbloed, Jan, 66, 67, 71, 73, 75
Jonquet, Robert, 43
Jorginho, 132, 133, 144
Josimar, 89, 91
Juarez, Carlos, 270
Junior, 78, 86, 142
Juskowiak, Erich, 43
Juventus (Italy), 14, 151, 167, 171, 231

K

Kempes, Mario, 74–76, 212
Keough, Harry, 31
Kissinger, Henry, 66, 108
Klein, Abraham, 82
Klinsmann, Jürgen, 99, 103, 120, 144
Kluge, John, 263
Kocsis, Sandor, 37, 38, 39, 40, 195
Koeman, Ron, 103
Kohler, Jürgen, 119
Kooiman, Cle, 121
Kopa, Raymond, 43
Korea, North
  and 1966 World Cup, 51–52, 53

Korea, South (Republic of)
  and 1988 Olympics, 143
  and 1994 World Cup, 118, 120
Kostadinov, Emil, 115
Kowalczyk, Wojtech, 144
Kraft, Robert, 263
Krol, Rudi, 75
Kucera, Rudi, 46
Kuwait
  and 1982 World Cup, 80
Kuznetsov, Oleg, 98

L

Lacoste, Carlos Alberto, 69
Lalas, Alexi, 121, 122, 144
Langenus, John, *20*, 21
Lato, Grzegorz, *63*, 64, 65
Laudrup, Michael, 88
Laws of soccer, *see* rules
Lazaroni, Sebastião, 96, 100–101,
  220
Lazio (Italy), 14, 27
Leão, 72
Lebrun, Albert, 29
Lee, Francis, 58
Lentini, Gianluigi, 171
Leonardo, 128, 130, 132
Leonhardsen, Oyvind, 125
Leônidas, 27–28, 32
L'Equipe, 147–48
Letchkov, Iordan, 130
LeTellier, Scott, 112
Liebrich, Werner, *36*, 38
Liedholm, Nils, 41, 45
Liekoski, Timo, 146
Limpar, Anders, 144
Lineker, Gary, 90, 92, 104
Linesmen, 12, 233, 234
Littbarski, Pierre, 77, 82, 92, 99
Liverpool (England), 171, 231
Logan, Doug, 274
Lopez, Juan, 193–94
Luis Enrique, 129, 133
Luque, Leopoldo, 72, 74, 75, 78,
  212

M

McCabe, Jack, 233
McGregor, William, 11
Mackay, Dave, 238–39
MacLeod, Ally, 70
Madrid, Miguel de la, 88
Magyars, Magic, *see* Hungary
Maier, Sepp, 65–67
Major Indoor Soccer League (MISL), 252–53
Major League Soccer (MLS), ix–xi, 261–64, 271, 272, 273–75
    single entity structure of, 262
Makanaky, Cyrille, *102*
Maldini, Paolo, 126
Manchester United (England), 41, 148, 168
Manning, Randolph, 245
Maradona, Diego, 24n, 78, 106, 160
    skill of, 87, 89, 92–93, 101, 220
    fouls against, 79, 81, 214, 217
    in World Cup, 78, 79, 81, 87, 89, 91–92, *93*, 98, 101, 104–6, 116, 124–25, 127, 214, 217, 219–20
Marchegiani, Luca, 125
Marcio Santos, 133, 134
Marinho, Francisco, 65
Marzolini, Silvio, 160
Mascheroni, Ernesto, 187
Maschio, Humberto, 41, 46, 47
Masopust, Josef, 49
Maspoli, Roque, 33, 37, 193
Massaro, Daniel, 126, 134
Matthäus, Lothar, 87, 92, 94, 98, 103, 120, 130
Matthews, Stanley, xv–xix, 30, 153n, 205
Maturana, Francisco, 122
Mauro Silva, 133, 134
Mazinho, 133, 134
Mazzola, Sandro, 51, 141, 204
Meazza, Giuseppe, 24, 25, 27, 29, 188
Meisl, Hugo, 23, 25, 147, 188
Meisl, Willy, 17, 23, 210

Mejia Baron, Miguel, 127
Menotti, Cesar Luis, 70, 74, 76, 78, 81, 212–13
Meola, Tony, 114, 121, 122, 129
Meszoly, Kalman, 52
metodo, *see* formations
Mexico
    and 1968 Olympics, 141
    and 1980 Olympics, 142
    and 1934 World Cup, 24
    and 1970 World Cup, 56, 58, 59
    and 1986 World Cup, 85–86, 89, 91, 92
    and 1990 World Cup, 97
    and 1994 World Cup, 115, 126, 127–28
Michel, 89
Michel, Henri, 118
Michels, Rinus, 63, 71, 210, 221
Miguez, Omar, 33
Milan *see* AC Milan
Milanello, 154–56
Milla, Roger, 98, 102–03, 118, 123
Miller, Charles, 15
Milutinovic, Bora, 86, 100, 110, 114, 121, 128, 129, 270, 272–73
Miró, Joan, 79
Missouri Athletic club (MAC) Award, 341
Mitic, Rajko, 32
Mitropa Cup, 147
Möller, Andy, 130
money
    bonuses, 61, 150–51
    coaches' salaries, 165–66
    negative effect on game, 227
    players' salaries, 150–52, 274
    sponsors, 95–96, 151, 168
    television, 168–70
    ticket prices, 168
    transfer fees, 171–72
    World Cup income, 22, 25n, 61–62, 95–96, 112, 135–36, 260
Monti, Luisito, 24, 188–89
Monzon, Pedro, 105
Moore, Bobby, xx, 51, *55*, 205

Moore, Joe-Max, 144, *145*,
Moreira, Aimoré, 46, 201
Moreira, Zezé, 46
Morlock, Max, 38
Morocco
    and 1986 World Cup, 90
    and 1994 World Cup, 117, 126
Müller, Gerd, 59, 62, 66, 67, 70
Murray, Bruce, 100
Mussolini, Benito, 22, 26

N

Nanninga, Dirk, 75, 212
Nasazzi, José, *20*, 21
National Collegiate Athletic Association
    (NCAA), xi, 254
National Professional Soccer League
    (NPSL), 249
National Professional Soccer League
    (indoor), 263
National teams
    selection of, 11–12, 279
Neeskens, Johan, 66, 71
Negrete, Manuel, 91, 92
Nelinho, 73–4
Nervi, Pier Luigi, 22n, 96
Netherlands
    and 1974 World Cup, 61, 62–63,
        65–67, 209–10
    and 1978 World Cup, 71, 73, 74–76,
        211–12
    and 1990 World Cup, 97, 99, 103
    and 1994 World Cup, 114, 126, 129–30
Netto, Igor, 41
Netzer, Günter, 62
Neves, Tancredo, 49
New York Cosmos (U.S.), 70, 133,
    251–252
New York Times, 113
Nigeria
    and 1987 u-17 World Cup, 236
    and 1994 World Cup, 117, 118, 124,
        125, 127
North American Soccer League
    (NASL), x, xi, 153, 249–57, 261

Norway
    and 1920 Olympics, 138
    and 1936 Olympics, 139
    and 1938 World Cup, 27
    and 1994 World Cup, 114, 126
Nottingham Forest (England), 171
numbering of players, 181, 195–96, 224

O

Oceania Football Confederation
    member nations, 313
Ocwirk, Ernst, 194
OFC, *see* Oceania Football
    Confederation
Olarticoechea, Julio, 98, 105, 218
Olguin, Jorge, 74
Olivieri, Aldo, 27
Olsen, Egil, 126
Olsen, Jesper, 91
Olympic Development Program (ODP),
    270
Olympic soccer tournament
    amateur players in, 19, 139–40
    eligibility rules, 17, 19, 138, 143, 144,
        145 324
    U.S. in, 336–337
    winners 324
    women's tournament, 145, 324
    1896 (Athens), 137
    1900 (Paris), 137
    1904 (St Louis),137
    1908 (London), 137
    1912 (Stockholm), 138
    1920 (Antwerp), 138
    1924 (Paris), 18, 138
    1928 (Amsterdam), 18, 138–39
    1932 (Los Angeles), 139
    1936 (Berlin), 139
    1948 (London), 139
    1952 (Helsinki), 140
    1956 (Melbourne), 140
    1960 (Rome), 140–41
    1964 (Tokyo), 141
    1968 (Mexico City), 141
    1972 (Munich), 141–42

1976 (Montreal), 142
1980 (Moscow), 142
1984 (Los Angeles), 108, 143
1988 (Seoul), 143–44
1992 (Barcelona), 144–45
Olympique-Marseille (France), 235
Orlando, 51
Orsi, Raimondo, 24, 26
Ortiz, Oscar, 74, 78, 212, 213
Oscar, 79
Overath, Wolfgang, 51, 55, *63*
Owairan, Saeed, 126

P

Pagliuca, Gianluca, 125, 129, 134, 14426
Pak Doo Ik, 53
Palermo Football and Cricket Club (Italy), 14
Palotas, Peter, 195
Panagoulias, Alkis, 124, 143
Paraguay
  and 1930 World Cup, 20
  and 1986 World Cup, 91
  and 1994 World Cup, 116
Parker, Paul, 104
Parreira, Carlos Alberto, 80, 117, 132–33, 135, 221, 223, 236, 273
Pasculli, Pablo, 218
Passarella, Daniel, 72, 74, 87, 160
Pavarotti, Luciano, 125
Pearce, Stuart, 104
Pelé, x, *44*, 56–57, *60*, 101, 108, 110, 121, 171–72, 230
  fouls against, 52–53, 54, 56
  in World Cup, 42–45, 46, 47, 49, 51, 52, 53, 58, *60*, 61
  skill of, xxi, 43, 200, 209
  with New York Cosmos, 250–51
penalty kick shoot-out, *see* tiebreakers
Peñarol (Uruguay), 15
Penev, Dimitar, 128, 131
Pereira, José, 53
Pereira, Luis, 63n
Pérez, Julio, 193

Peru
  in 1936 Olympics, 139
  in 1964 Olympics, 141
  in 1970 World Cup, 57, 59
  in 1978 World Cup, 69, 70, 72, 73
Peters, Martin, 55
Petrescu, Dan, 122
Petrovic, Ljupko, 235–36
Peucelle, Carlos, 187, 227
Pimenta, Ademar, 28
Pinheiro, 37
Piola, Silvio, 27, 28–29
Piontek, Sepp, 88
pirate leagues, 30, 173, 245, 249
Planicka, Frantisek, 26
Platini, Michel, 72, 77, 82, 87, 92, 142, 228
Platt, David, 102, 104
Poland
  and 1936 Olympics, 139
  and 1972 Olympics, 142
  and 1976 Olympics, 142
  and 1992 Olympics, 144–45
  and 1974 World Cup, 62, 64, 65–66
  and 1978 World Cup, 70,
  and 1982 World Cup, 81, 83
Poortvliet, Jan, 74
Portugal
  and 1966 World Cup, 51, 52–53
Pozzo, Vittorio, 23, 24, 27, *28*, 29, 30, 139, 188
Princeton University, 242, 243
professionalism, rise of, 10–11, 14, 15
Puc, Antonin, 26
Puhl, Sandor, 129, 133
Pumpido, Nery, 98
Puskas, Ferenc, *36*, 37, 38–39, 40, 46, 140, 151, 195, 196
Pyramid, *see* formations

Q

Queiroz, Carlos, 273
Quico, 145
Quiniou, Joel, 90, 132
Quirarte, Fernando, 89
Quiroga, Ramon, 73

R

Radice, Gigi, 166
Raducioiu, Florin, 130
Rahn, Helmut, 39, 41, 43
Rai, 133
Rainea, Nicolae, 81–82
Ramos, Tab, 121, 122, 128, 133, 144,
  271, *272*
Ramsey, Sir Alf, 51, 54, 56, 57, 62,
  206, 207
Rappan, Karl, 190
Rattin, Antonio, 54
Ravelli, Thomas, 131, 132
Raynor, George, 41, 44, 207
Real Madrid (Spain), 46, 86, 148,
  149, 167
Red Star (Yugoslavia), 235–36
referees, 12, 21–22, 233–34, 280
  age of, 234
  as amateurs, 177
  fees paid to, 177
  pressures on, 177
  professional, 234
  and the World Cup, 78, 234
Referees' Committee, FIFA, 233, 240
Reinaldo, 82
Rensenbrink, Robby, 75
Rep, Johnny, 66–67, 75
Reyna, Claudio, 144, 273
Rijkaard, Frank, 103
Rimba, Miguel, 117
Rimet, Jules, 19, 20, 21, 26, 33, 39
Rincon, Freddy, 102
Riva, Gigi, 59
Rivelino, 58, 60, 71, 208, 209
Rivera, Gianni, 51, 59
Roberto Dinamite, 82
Roberts, Herbie, 186–87
Robson, Bobby, 99, 102
Robson, Brian, 157
Rocco, Nereo, 204
Rocha, Ricardo, 132
Rocheteau, Dominique, 82
Rojas, Roberto, 96–97, 115
Romania
  and 1930 World Cup, 20

and 1994 World Cup, 121, 122, 125,
  127, 130–131
Roma (Italy), 171
Romário, 117, *123*, 130, 132, 134–35,
  144, 221, *228*
Rossi, Paolo, 72, 77–78, 82, 83, *84*,
  90, 154
Rothenberg, Alan, ix, 109–113, 131, 135,
  257, 259, 260–64, 274
Rothlisberger, Kurt, 127
Rotor–Volgograd (Russia), 152
Rous, Sir Stanley, 49, 68, 268
Rugby
  origins of, 6n, 7, 9
Rules of soccer
  advantage rule, 276–77
  changes in, 118, 119–20, 178–79,
    183–84, 226, 233, 237–40, 264
  first formulated, 7–9
  offside, 178, 279
  text of official FIFA rules, 282–310
Rummenigge, Karl-Heinz, 70, 77, 82, 83,
  84, 87, 94
Russia *see* also USSR
  player salaries, 152
  and 1994 World Cup, 115–16, 122
Rutgers University, 243

S

Sacchi, Arrigo, 125, 132, 134, 223
Sadyrin, Pavel, 115
St. Louis University, 254, 266
St. Rose Kickers (USA), 137
Saldanha, João, 57
Salenko, Oleg, 123
Salinas, Julio, 129
Sampdoria (Italy), 171
Sampson, Steve, 272–73
Samuels, Howard, 252
Sanchez, Erwin, 116, 120
Sanchez, Hugo, 86, 274
Sanchez, Leonel, 47
Sanchez, Rafael, 159–62
Sanon, Emmanuel, 64
Santamaria, José, 37, 46, 77
Santana, Telê, 78, 86, 216

Santos, Djalma, 45, 46, 49, 51

Santos, Nilton, 42, 46, 198

São Paulo (Brazil), 15

Saudi Arabia
    and 1994 World Cup, 118, 126–27

Saura, Enrique, 79

Schiaffino, Juan, 33, 37, 38, 41, 193, 194

Schiavio, Angelo, 26

Schillaci, Salvatore, 100, 103, 104, 105

Schnellinger, Karl-Heinz, 55, 59

Schön, Helmut, 51, 70, 73

Schrijvers, Peter, 73

Schroiff, Wilhelm, 49

Schumacher, Toni, 82–83, *84*, 87,
    94, 232

Schuster, Bernd, 77

Schwarz, Stefan, 130

Scirea, Gaetano, 77, 83–84, 214, 215

Scotland
    and 1954 World Cup, 34, 36
    and 1974 World Cup, 62, 64
    and 1978 World Cup, 70–71
    and 1982 World Cup, 79
    and 1986 World Cup, 89, 90
    and 1990 World Cup, 100

Sebes, Gustav, 37, 38, 195

Security at stadiums, 21, 62, 87, 91, 96,
    99, 111–12, 113, 119

Seeler, Uwe, 41, 51, *55*, 59

Sekularac, Dragan, 46

Serena, Aldo, 103, 105

Sergi, 128

Serginho, 79, 82, 216

Shilton, Peter, 91–92, 104

shoot-out, *see* tiebreakers

Sicily, xxiii–xiv, 100

Signori, Giuseppe, 134

Silverdome, Detroit, 110–11, 121, 122

Simonsson, Agne, 45

Sindelar, Matthias, 23

Sirakov, Nasko, 130

Sivori, Omar, 41, 46

skill, vs power, 9, 86, 228–29, 266–67,
    268–69, 270, 271, 272

Skoglund, Lennart, 43

soccer
    derivation of name, 9
    early history of, 1–7

first rules, 7–9

terminology, 180–81, 184, 198, 205,
    224, 276–81

Soccer Industry Council of America
    (SICA), x–xi, 259

Sócrates, 78, 86, 89

Song, Rigobert, *123*

Sorber, Mike, 121, 121

Sormani, Angelo, 46

South America
    spread of soccer in, 14–16

South American Football Confederation
    (CSF or CONMEBOL), 146
    member nations, 312

South American Player of the Year,
    334–35

Spain
    and 1920 Olympics, 138
    and 1992 Olympics, 144–45
    and 1934 World Cup, 25
    and 1938 World Cup, 26
    and 1950 World Cup, 31
    and 1954 World Cup, 35
    and 1962 World Cup, 46, 47
    and 1978 World Cup, 71–72
    and 1982 World Cup, 77, 79–80, 81
    and 1986 World Cup, 89, 91, 92
    and 1990 World Cup, 100
    and 1994 World Cup, 115, 120,
        128, 129

Spinosi, Luciano, 64

sponsors, 95–96, 151, 168

stadiums, in U.S., 262–63

Stafford Rangers (England), xxii

Staniek, Ryszard, 145

statistics and soccer, 280–81

Steinbrecher, Hank, 146, 257, 270

Stewart, Ernie, 121, 122

Stiehl, Paul, 109

Stiles, Nobby, xx, 205, 206

Stoichkov, Hristo, 125, 128, 130, 131–32

street soccer, 2–5, *6*, 222, *223*,

Stupar, Miroslav, 80

Suarez, Luis, 46, 204

substitutions, 37n, 57, 212, 213, 266–67

Supercopa (South America), 333

Svensson, Karl, *44*, 45

Svensson, Tommy, 132

Svoboda, Frantisek, 26
Sweden
   and 1948 Olympics, 139
   and 1952 Olympics, 140
   and 1950 World Cup, 30, 32
   and 1954 World Cup, 35
   and 1958 World Cup, 41–45
   and 1974 World Cup, 65
   and 1978 World Cup, 71
   and 1994 World Cup, 115, 122, 127,
      130–32
Swiss bolt, *see* formations
Switzerland
   and 1924 Olympics, 138
   and 1938 World Cup, 27
   and 1950 World Cup, 31, 193
   and 1954 World Cup, 35, 36
   and 1994 World Cup, 115, 121,
      122, 128

T

Tactics, 178–226, 227–28. *See also*
   formations
Taffarel, Claudio, 101, 128, 132,
   134, 144
Tahuichi (Bolivia), 116
Tarantini, Alberto, 74
Tardelli, Marco, 84
Tassotti, Mauro, 129, 132, 133, 144
Televisa (Mexico), 85, 90
   effects on attendance, 168
   income from, 169–70
   influence on game, 238, 114, 238
   television xiii, 168–70, 249–52, 252
   and World Cup, 35, 56, 85, 90, 95,
      109, 112, 114, 135, 170, 259
Terminology, soccer, 180–81, 184, 198,
   205, 224, 276–81
Thomas, Clive, 71
Thring, J.C., 7, 229
tiebreakers, 78, 234–37
Tigana, Jean, 77, 87
Tilkowski, Hans, 55–56
time-outs, 238–39, 281
time-wasting, 239

Tognoni, Guido, 109, 111, 113
Tomaszewski, Jan, 66
Torino, (Italy), 30n, 171
Toro, Jorge, 48
Tostão, xxv, 52, 57–58, 60, 65, 208, 209
total soccer, *see* formations
Toth, Jozsef, 205
Tottenham Hotspur (England), 138
Toye, Clive, 250–51
Toyota Cup, 328
tragedies
   Heysel stadium deaths, 231–323
   Lima, Peru, crowd disaster, 141
   Manchester United plane crash, 41
   Torino plane crash, 30n
training schedules
   England, 164
   Argentina, 164–65
transfer fees, 171–73, 204, 281
Trésor, Marius, 72, 77
Tschenscher, Kurt, 58
Turek, Anton, 39
Turkey
   and 1954 World Cup, 35–36

U

UEFA, 148–49, 174
   member nations, 312–13
UEFA Cup, 149, 330–31
Ufarte, Roberto Lopez, 79
Under-17 World Cup, *see* World Cup,
   under-17
Under-20 World Cup, *see* World Cup,
   under-20
Union of European Football Associa-
   tions, *see* UEFA
United Soccer Association (USA), 249
United States *see also* USSF
   antitrust laws and soccer, 258
   college soccer, xi, 100, 153, 242–45,
      253–55, 258, 266–68, 273,339–41
   European influence in, 269–71
   Hispanic players in, 269–73
   immigrant influence, 244–45, 269
   negative attitudes to soccer, x, 246

Olympic team record, 336–37
pro soccer in, ix–xi, 107–108,
    244–45, 248–53, 254–55, 259,
    261–64, 271, 273–75
soccer history, 242–59
style of play, 266–73
television and soccer, ix, 249–52
World Cup record, 337–38
youth soccer in, xiii–xiv, 257, 259,
    259, 267, 268
and 1924 Olympics, 138
and 1936 Olympics, 139
and 1956 Olympics, 140
and 1972 Olympics, 141
and 1980 Olympics, 142
and 1984 Olympics, 143
and 1988 Olympics, 143
and 1992 Olympics, 144
and 1996 Olympics, 146
and 1930 World Cup, 20–21
and 1934 World Cup, 24
and 1950 World Cup, 30–31
and 1990 World Cup, 97, 100
and 1994 World Cup, 114, 121–22,
    128–29, 130
United States Football Association
    (USFA), 244–46
United States Olympic Committee, 256
    United States Soccer Federation
        (USSF), 255–59, 261, 268, 270,
        272, 274, 336
    United States Soccer Football
        Association (USSFA), 246–50,
        253, 255–56
United States Youth Soccer Association
    (USYSA), x, 222
United Systems of Independent Soccer
    Leagues (USISL), 263–64, 274
Uruguay
    and 1924 Olympics, 18–19, 138
    and 1928 Olympics, 18, 138
    and 1930 World Cup, 19–21, 187
    and 1950 World Cup, 30, 32–33, 117,
        193–94, 198
    and 1954 World Cup, 34, 37–38
    and 1966 World Cup, 52, 54
    and 1970 World Cup, 59–60

and 1974 World Cup, 65
and 1986 World Cup, 89–90, 91
and 1990 World Cup, 103
and 1994 World Cup, 115, 117
USA Today, 113, 119
USSF, *see* United States Soccer
    Federation
USSR, *see also* Russia
    and 1956 Olympics, 140
    and 1972 Olympics, 142
    and 1980 Olympics, 142–43
    and 1988 Olympics, 143–44
    and 1987 u–17 World Cup, 236
    and 1950 World Cup, 29
    and 1958 World Cup, 41, 42
    and 1962 World Cup, 46, 47
    and 1970 World Cup, 58, 59
    and 1974 World Cup, 62
    and 1982 World Cup, 79, 81
    and 1986 World Cup, 90, 91
    and 1990 World Cup, 98

V

Valdano, Jorge, 93, 219
Valderrama, Carlos, 102, 121, 274
Van Basten, Marco, 114, 151, 171n
Van der Ende, Mario, 128
Van der Kerkhof, Rene, 74
Varela, Obdulio, 32, 34, 37, 193
Vautrot, Michel, 105
Vavá, 42, 43, 45, 48, 49, 200
Vermes, Peter, 100
verrou, see formations
Vialli, Gianlucca, 100, 104, 171
Vicini, Azeglio, 97, 100, 103, 104, 220
Videla, Jorge, 76
violence
    by fans, 87, 91, 96, 99, 111–12, 231
    rough play, 52–53, 79, 81, 83, 98, 118,
        208, 214, 217, 228–29, 232, 233,
        239–240
Virginia, University of, 146, 273
Völler, Rudi, 93, 94, 99, 103
Vogts, Berti, 66, 120
Vutzov, Yvan, 89

W

Waddle, Chris, 104
Wales
  and 1958 World Cup, 41, 42, 43
Walker, Jack, 167
Wall Street Journal, 112
Walter, Fritz, 39, 41
Wanderers (England), 10
Warner Communications, 251, 252
Weah, George, 171
Weber, Josip, 127
Weber, Wolfgang, 55
West Germany, *see also* Germany
  and 1972 Olympics, 141
  and 1988 Olympics, 143–44
  and 1954 World Cup, 34, 35–37,
    38–39
  and 1958 World Cup, 40–41, 43
  and 1966 World Cup, 54–56
  and 1970 World Cup, 59
  and 1974 World Cup, 62, *63*–67, 210
  and 1978 World Cup, 69, 70, 72,
    73, 211
  and 1982 World Cup, 77, 78, 80–81,
    82–84
  and 1986 World Cup, 87, 88, 89–90,
    92, 93–94
  and 1990 World Cup, 98–99, 103–106
Westerhof, Clemens, 118, 127
whirl, *see* formations
Whiteside, Norman, 80
Will, David, 240
Williams, Bert, 31
Wilson, Ray, *55*
Winter, Aron, 130
W-M, *see* formations
Women's Hermann Trophy, 341
Women's Olympic Soccer Tournament,
  145–46, 324
women's soccer, 176, 241, 257, 324, 325,
  340–41
Women's World Cup, 241, 325
Woodward, Vivian, 137–38

Woosnam, Phil, 153, 250, 252, 254,
  255, 256
World Cup, *see also* individual countries
  in Argentina (1978), 68–76, 319–320
  in Brazil (1950), 29–33, 316
  in Chile (1962), 45–49, 317–18
  and commercialism, 35, 50, 61–62,
    95–96, 108, 131
  in England (1966), 50–56, 318
  expansion of, 68, 69, 76, 85, 314
  in France (1938), 26–29, 315
  in Germany (1974), 61–67, 319
  goal-scoring in, 34, 106, 136,
    201–202, 118, 133, 221
  income from, 22, 25n, 61–62, 95–96,
    112, 135–36, 260
  in Italy (1934), 22–26, 315
  in Italy (1990), 95–106, 322–23
  mascots, 50, 56, 61, 78–79, 96,
    111, 119
  in Mexico (1970), 56–61, 318–19
  in Mexico (1986), 85–95, 321–22
  origins of, 18–19
  qualifying system, 76, 64, 314
  in Spain (1982), 76–84, 320–21
  sponsors of, 95
  statistics, 314–24
  in Sweden (1958), 40–45, 316–17
  in Switzerland (1954), 34–39, 316
  and television, 35, 56, 85, 90,
    95, 109, 112, 114, 129, 135,
    170, 259
  tiebreakers in, 78, 83, 92, 101, 103,
    104, 105, 128, 130–31, 134–35,
    234–37
  trophy, 50, 61
  in Uruguay (1930), 19–22, 315
  in USA (1994), ix–x, 107–136,
    323–24
  in 2002, 118
World Cup, under-17, 236, 238–39,
  241, 325
World Cup, under-20, 239, 240, 325
Wright, Mark, 99
Wright, Tommy, 58

Wunderteam, 17, 23, 24, 25, 188
Wynalda, Eric, 121, 271

Y

Yashin, Lev, 41, 43, 46, 47, 140
Yekini, Rashidi, 144
youth players
    in Argentina, 159–621
    and education, 153, 155, 158–59, 161
    in England, 156–59, 161–63
    in Italy, 154–56, 161–62
    numbers of, 176, 241, 256, 257, 259
    in U.S., ix–x, 257, 259, 259, 267, 268
Yugoslavia
    and 1948 Olympics, 139–40
    and 1952 Olympics, 140
    and 1956 Olympics, 140
    and 1960 Olympics, 140
    and 1980 Olympics, 143
    and 1984 Olympics, 143
    and 1950 World Cup, 29, 31–32
    and 1962 World Cup, 45, 49

    and 1982 World Cup, 79
    and 1990 World Cup, 98, 103

Z

Zagalo, Mario, 45, 57, 106, 201
Zaire
    and 1974 World Cup, 61, 64
Zakarias, Jozsef, 195, 198
Zambia
    and 1988 Olympics, 143
Zamora, Jesús, 77
Zamora, Ricardo, 25, 138, 145
Zeman, Walter, 38
Zenga, Walter, 105
Zetti, 117
Zhechev, Dobromir, 52
Zico, 71, 78, 79, 82, 86, 92, 217
Zizinho, 32
Zoff, Dino, 63, 64, 73, 74, 77, 81, 83
Zola, Gianfranco, 127
Zózimo, 48
Zubizarreta, Andoni, 129

Paul Gardner is one of the world's top soccer writers. His controversial column "SoccerTalk" appears each week in *Soccer America*. His work has also appeared in *The New York Times, Sports Illustrated, The Sporting News, USA Today, The Village Voice, The New York Daily News,* as well as in the English newspapers *The Times, The Observer, The Independent, The Guardian,* and *The European*. He is the author of three books on soccer, and *Nice Guys Finish Last*, a study of sport and American culture. He wrote the award-winning instructional film *Pelé: The Master and His Method*.

On television, he was ABC's color commentator for its regular weekly telecasts of NASL games (1979–80), and for the first-ever live telecast of a World Cup final in the USA, from Madrid in 1982. In 1986 he was the color commentator on NBC's month-long coverage of the World Cup from Mexico.

Born in England in 1930, Paul Gardner studied pharmacy at the University of Nottingham and is a Fellow of the Royal Pharmaceutical Society of Great Britain. He has lived in New York City since coming to the United States in 1959.